OUR HISTORY

As Told in Diaries,

OF THE 20TH

Journals and Letters

CENTURY

Also by Travis Elborough:

The Bus We Loved: London's Affair with the Routemaster

*The Long-Player Goodbye: The Album from
Vinyl to iPod and Back Again*

Wish You Were Here: England on Sea

London Bridge in America: The Tall Story of a Transatlantic Crossing

A Walk in the Park: The Life and Times of a People's Institution

As co-editor with Nick Rennison:

*A London Year: 365 Days of City Life in
Diaries, Journals and Letters*

*A Traveller's Year: 365 Days of Travel Writing
in Diaries, Journals and Letters*

With the cartographer Alan Horsfield:

Atlas of Improbable Places

OUR HISTORY

As Told in Diaries,

OF THE 20TH

Journals and Letters

CENTURY

Compiled by Travis Elborough

Michael O'Mara Books Limited

First published in Great Britain in 2017 by
Michael O'Mara Books Limited
9 Lion Yard
Tremadoc Road
London SW4 7NQ

A CIP catalogue record for this book is available from the British Library.

Papers used by Michael O'Mara Books Limited are natural, recyclable
products made from wood grown in sustainable forests. The manufacturing
processes conform to the environmental regulations of the country of origin.

ISBN: 978-1-78243-735-2 in hardback print format
ISBN: 978-1-78243-736-9 in ebook format

1 2 3 4 5 6 7 8 9 10

www.mombooks.com

Cover and interior design by Jade Wheaton
Typeset by Claire Cater
Printed and bound by CPI Group (UK) Ltd, Croydon, CR0 4YY

CONTENTS

INTRODUCTION

The 20th Century is a stranger to me – I wish it well …

Mark Twain, Notebooks, December 1900

*What is a diary as a rule? A document useful to
the person who keeps it, dull to the contemporary
who reads it, invaluable to the student,
centuries afterwards, who treasures it!*

Ellen Terry, *The Story of My Life*, 1908

*Advice to Young Journal Keeper. Be Lenient with
yourself. Conceal your worst faults, leave out your
most shameful thoughts, actions and temptations. Give
yourself all the good and interesting qualities you want
and haven't got. If you should die young, what comfort
would it be to your relatives to read the truth and have
to say: It is not a pearl we have lost but a swine?*

Rosamond Lehmann, *Invitation to the Waltz*, 1932

It is now nearly two decades since the millennial celebrations served as the send-off to the twentieth century in the collective popular imagination. The preceding one hundred years had seen the world's bloodiest ever wars and most horrific acts of violence – alongside some of the greatest advances in science, technology, global communication, navigation, documentation, medicine, and civil and legal rights. The Britain of 1900 was a place mostly powered by steam and horse; its maps were tinged pink with the territories of the Empire. The Britain of 1999, however, was at one (just about) with the hyperlink and the information superhighway; its economy was grateful for the pink pound.

The journey from the Britain ruled by Queen Victoria to the one guided by a (then) still immensely popular Tony Blair is what this anthology sets out to chart. It presents a chronological survey of the country from 1900 to 1999, constructed not from official documents or press reports but from accounts left in diaries, journals or the odd letter, the voices of people speaking about the turns in their fate – and their country's – as they occurred.

For me, the appeal of reading diaries has always been their immediacy and intimacy. That unique sense of being addressed directly, and sometimes extremely candidly, by someone from an age other than our own is intensely seductive.

There are moments when what they say might be strange, revolting, or even alienating. But, in my experience, more frequently the distances melt away, common humanity is reaffirmed and empathy with our forebears enhanced.

The aim of this book is simply to try to supply a flavour of those years in the words of those who were born, lived and died during that time, who suffered its lows, relished its highs and enjoyed its possibilities, as well as resented its limitations.

Some of the contributors to these pages are figures of state or men and women of some importance in the world of art, literature or politics. The advantage of drawing on material from the great and the good is that they often offer a front-row seat at some of the most momentous incidents of the recent past, providing pen portraits of the most significant figures in their orbit.

Ordinary people, though, are no less likely to be affected by national and international events, or to meet people of note as they go about their days. And, at times, the very fact that they experienced big events through the prism of their daily lives, or at the remove of conversations and news reports, makes their accounts all the more compelling. The diaries, journals and letters left by the obscure, the unsung and the entirely unknown provide a vital and fascinating portrait of how life was *actually* lived, offering, as they do, a window on to what the man or woman on the street really made of the stuff of history at the time.

By assembling a range of differing voices, and by shifting between the epoch-making and the personal or domestic, this book hopes to offer a richly impressionistic picture of the last century – an experience for the reader that is perhaps closer to eavesdropping than anything else.

The twentieth century offers millions of things worthy of inclusion here. Inevitably, some notable events are absent and some obscure ones present. Likewise, while as wide a range of writers and views as possible were sought, some points of view are missing. Diaries are often kept for brief and intense periods, and in response to particular circumstances. For this reason, there are occasions when the voices of one or two diarists come to dominate particular years, while more of a polyphony is sustained elsewhere.

With over a hundred diarists spread over a hundred years, here is twentieth-century Britain first-hand and in all its idiosyncrasies. It is another country, where they certainly did things differently, and one that is well worth a visit.

CHAPTER ONE

EVERYTHING WAS DIFFERENT THEN: 1900-1913

In his memoir *Diary of a Black Sheep*, published in 1964, Richard Meinertzhagen – soldier, spy, ornithologist, self-aggrandizing diarist and quite possibly murderer – looked back wistfully on the final years of the nineteenth century:

> What a wonderful world it was when I joined the Army. Queen Victoria seemed everlasting as supreme head of the British Empire. Britain had no allies except Japan and she gave no trouble; and yet we controlled about a quarter of the human race. We paid little or no attention to the views of neutrals; the United States was not yet adult; the Royal Navy made it unnecessary to pay attention to unfriendly Powers; there were no international organisations to which we had to pay attention. Everybody seemed happy. Wages were low and so was the cost of living. Trade unions had not yet assumed dictatorship; crime, especially murder, was rare; raids on banks were unknown. China was asleep, Russia a slave state (and still is), the United States was growing up, and the African not yet aware of a civilised future.

Not everyone shared Meinertzhagen's rosy view of these times. Millions had spent the years toiling in Britain and across the Empire for pitifully low wages, living and working in conditions of appalling squalor with only parish relief or the workhouse to see them through the worst of times. However happy they may have seemed, life for many Britons and those under British colonial rule remained 'nasty, brutish and short'. The average life expectancy of a man in 1900 was forty-seven; for women, fifty; and the under-fives accounted for one-third of deaths annually. Each year about 1,200 miners perished in pit accidents, 1,000 people were killed in workshops and 400 railway employees died on their lines.

And yet the extraordinarily long reign of Queen Victoria – who had at the turn of the century been on the throne for sixty-three years and counting – and the extent of her empire (covering a quarter of the globe) meant that many opening their eyes on 1 January 1900 did feel, as Meinertzhagen said, that Britain was a stable and almost unassailably superior power. This was the wave-ruling, never-shall-be-slaves Britain of 'Rule, Britannia!', a nation whose cast-iron self-confidence was reasserted in Sir Edward Elgar's 'Land of Hope and Glory', with lyrics by A. C. Benson, whose line 'Wider still and wider shall thy bounds be set' implied that further colonial expansion was both desirable and inevitable.

'Land of Hope and Glory' was composed in the wake of a hard-fought British victory in the Boer War in 1902, a victory that Queen Victoria herself did not live to see. The campaign's success was secured with the support of large numbers of volunteers, not just from the UK but also from Canada, Australia and New Zealand. Described as 'the last of the gentlemen's wars', this conflict was between the British, who controlled the Cape and Natal regions in southern Africa, and the Boers or Afrikaners of Dutch, French Huguenot and German stock who had established the independent republics of the Orange Free State and the Transvaal further to the north. War broke out in the summer of 1899 when the Boers feared that the British were planning to take the gold-rich regions around Johannesburg and the Witwatersrand.

For those at home it was a war, like dozens since the defeat of Napoleon, waged in some far-off land, in a style Wellington himself could just about have recognized, with a cavalry, pith helmets, buglers and scouts. There were no aeroplanes, mustard gas nor tanks, but it did include a dry run for barbed-wire-ringed 'concentration camps'. Here was where khaki uniforms, much better for blending in with the scorched veldt, finally supplanted the robin redbreast tunics of old. It made a household name of Colonel Baden-Powell, whose triumphant defence of the besieged town of Mafeking became a rallying point of the war in the popular press.

Not everyone was as taken with these celebrations, nor was everyone equally moved by the passing of Queen Victoria in 1901. But the monarch's death, coming in the opening months of the twentieth century, was a tidy enough end to the age that since 1851 had been named in her honour.

At Victoria's funeral, Kaiser Wilhelm II, her grandson, rode beside the new king, Edward VII, and an escort of men from the German army brought up the rear of the procession. London's streets reportedly fell silent for the duration of the ceremony. Today's perpetual background engine noise of buses and cars had not yet arrived; the first electric tram would not make its way on to the capital's streets until April of that year.

Within a decade, the horse cab was all but extinct. New, 'modern conveniences', from powered flight to transatlantic radio transmissions, seemed to be invented every day. Self-consciously modern art and literature were humdrum. The perimeters of reality itself were being bent by the theories of Albert Einstein and Sigmund Freud, and its geographical limits tested by the voyages of Scott, Shackleton and Amundsen.

Politically, Britain would come to be rocked by constitutional crises, demands for Irish independence, strikes and the emergence of the parliamentary Labour Party. But perhaps the most dominant single issue in the years leading up to the First World War was the campaign for women's suffrage – a campaign that, thanks to Emmeline, Christabel and Sylvia Pankhurst, was fought with great resolve, courage and militancy.

AN OLD QUEEN ON THE NEW CENTURY

I begin today a new year & a new century, full of anxiety & fear of what may be before us! May all near & dear ones be protected, above all darling Vicky, who is so far from well. I cannot help feeling thankful that, after all, dear Arthur has not gone out to this terrible war. I hope & pray dear Christie may be spared & many a tried & devoted friend. I pray God may spare me yet a short while to my children, friends & dear country, leaving me all my faculties & to a certain extent my eyesight! May He bless our arms & give our men strength to fulfil their arduous task. — Dull & damp. Did not go out in morning, as I had a little cold, but in the afternoon took a short drive in a closed carriage with Harriet P. — Letters & telegrams pouring in, many kind ones from everyone. — Large dinner in the Durbar Room. Everyone in the house, & all the children, excepting little Maurice. The marine band played during & after dinner quite beautifully.

Queen Victoria, Journal, 1 January 1900

PENETRATING FOG

After the clear, starry sky which we admired last night as we walked the terrace while the church bells of Penshurst were ringing out the old year, and the new one in, it was a disappointment to find on awaking a fog which seemed to penetrate through everything. Here is a good motto for the new, or any other, year by Sidney Smith: 'Take short views, hope for the best, and trust in God.'

Lord Ronald Sutherland Gower, *Old Diaries*, 1 January 1900

HORSE WHIPPED BY ELECTRICITY

Oh! my dear, the WAR. Are they insane? The poor Martyrs – mown down for the stupidity of those who should have used their intelligence.

I saw in the papers the other day some brute has invented a Fiend's idea in the way of a whip for horses – an Electric whip! What next! Great God, what next! It is time for motors – I always go in one now.

Ellen Terry, Letter to Stephen Coleridge, 8 January 1900

BOERS ROUTED

We 8 drove the usual way to Buckingham Palace, & I received a perfect ovation from thousands & thousands of people assembled along the whole route. There were deafening cheers, & waving of handkerchiefs & small flags, quite indescribably enthusiastic. It was most touching. I drove in through the principal gate, like for a triumphal entry, & inside the Quadrangle were assembled Members of the Hse of Lords & Hse of Commons, who cheered very much & sang 'God save the Queen' ... Got some good news from Ld Roberts, who had completely routed the Boers, having turned their flank.* They had a very strong position, which would have caused as much loss had we been obliged to make a frontal attack. — After luncheon, Lenchen [her daughter] introduced Mrs Dick Conyngham, whose brave husband was killed on Jan 6th at the defence of Ladysmith. She is very pleasing & pretty ...

It was getting a little cold by the time we came home, but not unpleasantly so. There were many flags hung out & across the streets. ... During dinner there was a great deal of cheering & singing outside, & I went to the window, a light being held behind me. The cheering was tremendous. There were several thousand people assembled. — Tosti & Mme Tosti came & sang charmingly. George C. was in high spirits & talked a great deal.

Queen Victoria, Journal, 8 March 1900

* *The Boers struck first on 12 October 1899 at Kraaipan, in a surprise attack. They drove quickly towards the major British garrison at Ladysmith, as well as smaller ones at Mafeking and Kimberley. The speed of the Boer mobilization resulted in many early victories against*

scattered British forces and allowed the Boers to occupy the Cape Colony and Colony of
Natal. By March, the British troops were beginning to recover ground.

⁓

PRICE OF THE BOER WAR

This week has passed in much the same way as usual. Last Saturday evening
Mother met me at Woodgrange Park Station. Dad did not get home till gone
twelve p.m. Some of the clerks were to work all night and part of Sunday. It is
all to do with the taxes which are to be raised on everything to pay for this war.

Ruth Slate, Diaries, 10 March 1900

⁓

BIRDING WITH FRIENDLY NATIVES

Made my first acquaintance with Essex. I went to Beadwell Quarry, a quaint
little place at the mouth of the Blackwater in country very much like the fens
but no sedge. Glorious day, blazing sun. Sat on many gates and enjoyed myself
hugely. Gossiped with many natives – nice people all.

Walked round the sea wall to near Southminster and saw good salt marshes
which should be full of birds in the winter. A pair of birds got up out of a pond
and I am pretty sure they were greenshanks.

A. F. R. Wollaston, *Letters and Diaries*, 21 April 1900

⁓

REMEMBERING THE GREAT EXHIBITION

Dear Arthur's birthday. May God bless & protect him. How well I remember the
Opening of the Great Exhibition on this day. — Went down to the Mausoleum
with Beatrice & placed fresh wreaths there. A beautiful day. — Before going
out I invested Sir George White with the Grand Cross of my own Victorian

order, saying that I gave it him as a personal mark of my high appreciation of his services. He answered that nothing could gratify him more than being the possessor of my own order. He hopes to go to the North of Ireland, whence he comes from, & in July to take up his command in Gibraltar, which had been given him before he went to the Cape ...

Queen Victoria, Journal, 1 May 1900

LAND FOR LONDONERS

A wet morning, so remained in doors. – Satisfactory news from S. Africa. & Victoria B. came to luncheon, & we took tea with her at Frogmore, going afterwards to the Mausoleum & driving round by Datchet. It was damp & rainy. – Saw Mr Balfour before dinner. Spoke about the war, &c. In the Hse of Commons, the most important thing was a Bill for the working classes, enabling them to buy land a little way out of London, to relieve the congested state of the town, & prevent its too rapid increase.

Queen Victoria, Journal, 9 May 1900

VICTORY IN MAFEKING

Great things have been happening since I made my latest notes. Last Sunday evening, we all went to the Forest Gate Chapel, to hear Joseph Hocking preach. How shall I describe the beautiful sermon we heard? I have never listened to anyone to compare with him. You feel you cannot lose one word he utters. He quoted Lord Byron, Robert Burns and Ruskin. He also spoke of Cecil Rhodes.* How after the relief of Kimberley he made a speech about the wealth and grandeur of England, not even mentioning the orphans, widows and bereaved parents. The people stamped and shouted 'Hear! Hear!', even though it was a Sunday. We were all sorry when he had finished.

This morning I had quite a task to get up White Post Lane. They are laying down lines for the electric tramway. The Boer report that Mafeking is relieved has been confirmed today. In London, the excitement was dreadful, we heard.

Ruth Slate, Diaries, 21 May 1900

* Rhodes had served as prime minister of the Cape Colony in South Africa from 1890 to 1896. He was a financier, statesman and imperialist known for founding the De Beers diamond company and establishing the Rhodes scholarship at Oxford University.

AIMING TO IMPROVE

I have been thinking how nice it would be, if I could go to some evening classes this winter. I have been up and about with Jessie each morning this week and the weather has been splendid. Jessie went to Earl's Court Women's Exhibition yesterday. I stayed in and scrubbed the office floor this morning. I am still far from well, my teeth are so bad. Ewart has also has been ill, with inflammation of the lungs. I am going to try to be better-tempered. I think that, and a habit of dwelling on the past, is a great deal the cause of my indispositions, such are they rare. I am getting quite a skilled hairdresser.

Ruth Slate, Diaries, 15 September 1900

SUMMER HAZE

Another pleasant week has passed; the weather perfect, a real Indian summer, hazy in the mornings, but clearing up later, with brilliant sunshine till the gloaming; this had made expeditions on the loch in the steam-launch enjoyable.

Lord Ronald Sutherland Gower, *Old Diaries*, 16 September 1900

NEW ROAD HOGS

Lord Carnavon is becoming a public nuisance as a motor scorcher. He was summoned again to-day. Clouds of dust as high as the neighbouring trees, said the police witnesses, rose up as his car whizzed along the road. By careful timing and measurements the superintendent calculated the rate of speed at a mile in two and a half minutes, or twenty-four miles an hour!

Frank Butler, the hon. secretary of the Auto-mobile Club in Piccadilly, is very angry with the police. They hauled him before the New Romney magistrates yesterday for scorching in his new Panhard at eighteen miles per hour; but he got off.

Ladies who persist in riding bicycles in long skirts must expect to get hurt. I saw a handsome Junoesque figure to-day [Mrs Sands], dressed in laces and flounces, riding on a bicycle in Sloane Street. Her skirt became entangled and she came down with a crash. My tailor tells me that women flatly refuse to wear short skirts for fear of exposing their legs.

R. D. Blumenfeld, Diaries, 2 October 1900

YOUNG WINSTON

I went yesterday to Bermondsey to hear young Winston Churchill speak after his Tory victory at Oldham. He spoke in support of Harry Cust, late editor of the *Pall Mall*. Churchill is tall and slight, with brown curly hair, and a boyish face. He simply radiates self-confidence. He began in the true Randolphian style, and at once started to lecture his audience, which was inclined to be enthusiastic. He likened the Liberal Party to the hornet, with the head biting the tail, and the tail stinging the head. The brains of the Liberal Party were all in the tail. He was getting on quite nicely in a speech, half his father and half debating society, when a woman interrupted him, and he lost his temper. Then he said he never was in favour of women's suffrage, and the woman's questions proved that women should not be entrusted with the vote. Someone booed him, and he again lost his temper, talked about 'Yahoos', and said it was more dangerous to face pro-Boers than Boers. Mr Churchill will, in time, acquire the habit of disarming interrupters with a smile. He is still new at the game, but from what I saw of him I think he will never be content to be a back-bencher.

These Post Office people are very conservative. I heard Sir William Preece, the chief engineer of the Post Office, deliver himself to-day of an unequivocal statement that 'wireless telegraphy is not, and cannot be, a commercial success'. In spite of the delicate and interesting experiments of young Marconi, who is half Italian and half Irish, Preece held that wireless telegraphy cannot supersede the present wire system. 'It may be used under exceptional circumstances by the Army and Navy, but commercially it is impossible.'

Lord Iveagh, the great Irish brewer, is an authority for the statement that women clerks in offices are a great success. He recently tried the experiment of employing lady clerks on the staff of the Guinness Brewery, mostly daughters of employees, and there has been not a single failure.

R. D. Blumenfeld, Diaries, 5 October 1900

⌒*⌒

BELLS OFFICIALLY END CENTURY

We began the New Year and the New Century – the twentieth – by an early celebration at our church here. Last night was a clear and starry one, and we waited out on the terrace of the garden listening to Penshurst Church bells ringing out the old year.

Lord Ronald Sutherland Gower, Old Diaries, 1 January 1901

⌒*⌒

FINAL DIARY

At 5.30 went down to the Drawing room, where a short service was held by Mr Clement Smith, who performed it so well, & it was a great comfort to me. — Rested again afterwards, then did some signing & dictated to Lenchen.

Queen Victoria, Journal, 13 January 1901

QUEEN'S HEALTH IN DOUBT

Very alarming reports of the Queen's health have appeared in the papers in the last two days; we hear the Prince of Wales and Princess Louise have gone to Osborne … I much fear it is the beginning of the end. One cannot realise what a loss her death would be to everyone.

Lord Ronald Sutherland Gower, *Old Diaries*, 20 January 1901

DEATH OF THE QUEEN

This evening, at half past seven, we heard that the dear Queen had passed away an hour before. She is now at peace and at rest, after life's 'pilgrimage' as she called it in a letter written to me in the summer of '84. A better, or nobler, woman never lived, and her memory and her example will go down to the ages as that of the best, and one of the greatest, sovereigns …

Lord Ronald Sutherland Gower, *Old Diaries*, 22 January 1901

Our Mem. Service at 12, crowded, all in deep black. H. read the lesson, by far the most impressive bit of the service, except perhaps the beautiful singing of 'Then shall the righteous'.

Mary Gladstone, Diaries, 2 February 1901

This morning I saw what I could, over the heads of a vast crowd, of the funeral procession of the Queen. The people were not, on the whole, deeply moved, whatever journalists may say, but rather serene and cheerful.

Afterwards, Legge, Fred Terry and Hooley lunched with me at the Golden Cross Hotel, and all was very agreeable and merry.

Arnold Bennett, Journals, 2 February 1901

OUT WITH THE OLD

Leslie Stephen says: 'The old ideals have become obsolete, and the new are not yet constructed … We cannot write living poetry on the ancient model. The gods and heroes are too dead, and we cannot seriously sympathize with the idealized prize-fighter.'

Thomas Hardy, Diaries, 11 May 1901

PLAGUES OF PLENTY

We stopped on our way south at the Byles at Bradford. There at dinner we met a certain Dr Rabagliati, author of various books on the subject of diet. By chance, the conversation drifted on to public health. Suddenly, the little man fired up and gave us a discourse on the one cause of disease – eating too much and at too frequent intervals. He was an enthusiast and described in convincing detail how cancer, influenza, pneumonia and all modern diseases arose from the one incontrovertible tendency to eat more than was necessary! Even the working class and slum-dwellers were going to perdition by overfeeding! Bar air, drink, dissipation were nothing to this terrible and accused habit of overfeeding. But apart from the rhetoric, he gave so many instances of recovery from chronic complaints by systemic abstemiousness that I was persuaded.

Beatrice Webb, Diaries, 1 October 1901

FIT FOR THE NEW KING

Workmen are still busy at Buckingham Palace preparing it as a residence for the King and Queen in the coming summer. His Majesty, abandoning Marlborough House to the Prince and Princess of Wales, means to make Buckingham Palace his regular town residence.

Sir Henry Lucy, The Diaries of a Journalist, 2 November 1901

SPEED LIMITS

The Automobile Club are going to propose that they will no longer oppose the compulsory fixing of identification numbers or letters on autocars provided that the absurd twelve-mile limit is abolished and the speed limit is left open, so that people may only be prosecuted when they drive dangerously. They are much cheered by Mr Henry Chaplin's [Viscount Chaplin] public statement that in his opinion twenty-five miles per hour is not an excessive speed, and it is not dangerous provided brakes are sound and drivers are safe. The principal danger, to my mind, is still the difficulty of controlling restive horses, particularly on country roads, when swift-moving autocars approach.

R. D. Blumenfeld, Diaries, 7 December 1901

NEW HABITS, NEW FACES

After dinner last night at the Carlton, I saw four women in the lounge smoking cigarettes quite unconcernedly. One of them had a golden case, and she was what is called a chain smoker. Dr Gunton, who was with me, told me that most women now smoke at home. 'That's what makes them so nervy,' he said, 'but when I tax them with over-smoking they nearly always deny it.' ...

'BP' [General Baden-Powell] is tired of the adulation which he gets wherever he goes. He says he still cannot go to a theatre or public place without being cheered at and mobbed. The hero of Mafeking is going back to Africa this month to take charge of a new force of Colonial police.

There will be 20,000 men and 30,000 horses to cover a territory of 200,000 square miles in the Transvaal and Orange River Colony. The late Queen Victoria never forgave him for having sketched his own portrait on the emergency stamps which he devised for Mafeking during the siege.

The revival of *Iolanthe*, after nineteen years, has brought Mr W. S. Gilbert from his retirement at Harrow, to superintend the rehearsals. He is very sad about it all, for both Sir Arthur Sullivan and D'Oyly Carte have died in the past year or so, and he misses all the old faces ...

R. D. Blumenfeld, Diaries, 10 December 1901

VICTORIOUS

I came down by train from Harrow this morning with Sir Ernest Cassel, who has a house at Stanmore.

Sir Ernest told me he had just received word that Cecil Rhodes is ill in South Africa, and that he is not likely to live. Rhodes has chosen some place in the hills, somewhere in Rhodesia, where he intends to be buried.

Cassel also showed me a letter from Lord Kitchener, in which he stated that the Boers are beginning to surrender, and are giving up arms willingly and asking for peace. It looks now as if the war in South Africa is at last actually over.*

R. D. Blumenfeld, Diaries, 18 January 1902

* Lord Horatio Kitchener was the Governor of Sudan. In 1900 he was appointed chief of staff to Lord Roberts, British commander in the Boer War. The unconditional surrender of the Boers and the absorption of their republics into the Union of South Africa would not be agreed until May.

⌒✺⌒

HIGH-SOCIETY BRIDGE

With the incoming of bridge, poker has ceased to be an after-dinner study in London society. The Duke of Devonshire, who, with his consort, was a few years ago a devotee of that interesting game, is now a slave to bridge.

Sir Henry Lucy, The Diaries of a Journalist, 28 February 1903

⌒✺⌒

A LITTLE ENGLANDER

Went to dinner with Winston Churchill. First impression: restless, almost intolerably so, without capacity for sustained and unexcited labour, egotistical, bumptious, shallow-minded and reactionary, but with a certain personal magnetism, great pluck and some originality, not of intellect but of character. More of an American speculator than the English aristocrat. Talked exclusively about himself and his electioneering plans, wanted me to tell him of someone who would get statistics for him.

But I dare say he has a better side, which the ordinary cheap cynicism of his position and career covers up to a casual dinner acquaintance.

Bound to be unpopular, too unpleasant a flavour with his restless, self-regarding personality and lack of moral and intellectual refinement ... he is, at heart, a little Englander. But his pluck, courage, resourcefulness and great tradition may carry him far, unless he knocks himself to pieces like his father.

Beatrice Webb, Diaries, 8 July 1903

* Churchill entered Parliament as a Tory in 1900. He would break with them over tariff reform in 1904 and join the Liberals, only to rejoin the Conservative Party in 1925.

CATERING BY MOTOR CAR

A company called the 'Motor Dinner Company' has been started for supplying people not only with meals at fixed hours, but glass, china, knives and forks, napkins, etc. If a person has friends coming to dinner, he has merely to telephone the company the number of guests expected and the hour; at that time arranged a car arrives with all that is needed – even waiters. After dinner, the room is cleared and everything removed. These people also supply wine.

Bhawani Singh, *Travel Pictures*, 20 May 1904

THE FIRST RUSSIAN REVOLUTION

I am greatly moved by the news from Russia. Certainly, a year ago I never hoped to see all that. It's just ½ century since the Crimean War, forty-two since the liberation of the peasants – a great civic work in which even we Poles were allowed to participate … this great event opened the way to a general reform of the state.

Joseph Conrad, Letter to Mrs Ada Galsworthy, 2 November 1905

BLAKE BONKERS

I drove off to [the] Athenaeum [Hotel]. Wrote letters, and went to see the Blake exhibition. Surely people must be cracked who make such a fuss about Blake's little funny drawings. There is some imagination in them and much quaintness. But the absurd old men with beards like ferns or carrots – the strange glooms and flames and tornadoes of vapour, the odd, conventional faces, the muscular backs, the attenuated thighs! Blake was a childish spirit who loved his art, and had a curious, naive use of both word and line and colour; and some fine, simple thoughts about art and life. But he was certainly not 'all there' – and to make him out as a kind of supreme painter and poet is simply ridiculous.

A. C. Benson, Diaries, 23 June 1906

FEMALE CONFIDENCES

Eva came in the evening, but it was bitterly cold, and the ground snow-covered; we could not have our usual walk. Eva told of the pain she feels over the frequent conflict between her emotions and intellect. Sometimes she fancies intellectual occupations could fill her life, she said; at others, there comes a strong longing for love, and the touch of baby fingers. Is it wrong to feel this last longing, she wondered? Surely this must be evidence of the true woman-nature growing, as I think it is meant to grow, in all of us and it means pain when it has to go unsatisfied. We spoke of Charlotte Brontë who, with her passionate nature, married an 'ordinary' man, and we wondered if this longing had been hers, proving itself stronger than the love of intellectual pursuits after all. I could wish Eva a good man's love above all things else – but love seems half pain too.

Ruth Slate, Diaries, 26 January 1907

BECOMING A SUFFRAGETTE

On Tuesday I spent a very pleasant evening with May at a Women's Suffrage meeting, held in the hall at the back of St Ethelburga's. The speaker was an elderly lady, Mrs Stope, but she put forward the splendid arguments or reasons why women should have the vote, clearly and skilfully. Dr Cobb, whom I am beginning to admire very much, also spoke for the cause – the only opposition came from a young and self-satisfied youth, and an elderly gentleman whose ideas I should imagine to be very conservative. Dr Cobb was for limiting the Franchise. This was a new idea to me, and I saw some sense in it. He thinks voters should be put through an examination or test before being allowed to exercise their privilege. I really believe May, in her inmost heart, became a 'Suffragette' that night.

Ruth Slate, Diaries, 11 February 1907

HOLIDAY JAUNT

Rather an indistinct day. Fine and hot, though storms predicted (Bank Holiday) …

Went off at 1.00. The swallows at Erith were sitting on the telegraph wires in hundreds, the wires quite bent with the weight.

I rode to Somersham and Chatteris, lunching by the wayside close to a huge plant of dead-nettle with purple flowers, covered with peacock-butterfly caterpillars – black, pointed, writhing things. At Chatteris I drank and explored the hot, dull, yellow town. There is one huge house in it, like a suburban mansion, the kind of place I remember in Richmond, yellow brick, with a pediment – but the drive is grass-grown and the garden all weeds; the

Rectory, I think. Then out towards Stonea, and finally got to the Ireton Way.

A good many Bank Holiday people about. Just beyond Mepal there was a party lunching by the roadside, a respectable tradesman, I should guess, and his family. Two of the girls shouted impudent, rude things to me – incredible manners. The English middle class expresses its joy of heart by being rude. That is our idea of geniality and humour. Home to tea – in mildly good spirits, after a feeble, melancholy morning, making plans and devising how I should live in every home I passed.

A. C. Benson, Diaries, 5 August 1907

THE FIRST (AND LAST) PM TO DIE AT NUMBER 10

Campbell-Bannerman died this morning in Downing Street. To the last he was tranquil and thoughtful.

His breakdown dates from November last, when the German Emperor was paying a visit to this country. With the cares of State on his shoulders, the Premier felt himself compelled to attend all the State Functions arranged in honour of the visit. He was present at the reception at Windsor, and, on returning to his room, said to his secretary, 'I have been standing for two hours, and I must have rest.' The custom that compels personages invited to be present at such receptions to remain standing throughout their course, however prolonged it may be, is, in the case of those advanced in years, sheer cruelty.

These things are all very well in Germany. But they are among customs whose import into this country the staunchest Free Trader would gladly see prohibited.

Sir Henry Lucy, The Diary of a Journalist, 22 April 1908

OBSESSED WITH SEX

Last Monday I delivered an address to the Fabians* here. The central idea was Socialism as the creator of liberty – but I talked at some length of the family and idea of sexual morality. My friends say I am obsessed with sex nowadays; perhaps this is true.

The family is going to be the crux of the whole social question, and someone has got to open the eyes of these virgins.

If we ever are to break the family or – which is a better way of putting it – secure liberty for other forms of social organization, it will be not primarily through the dissemination of those theories, but because of the growth of personal dislike for the institution, which I find a very large proportion of my friends have in common with me.

Frederic 'Ben' Keeling, Letter to Mrs Townsend, 1 June 1908

* *The left-leaning Fabian Society, founded in 1884, is today Britain's oldest political think tank.*

AT THE MERCY OF GERMANY

Last night I met at dinner Sir George White, whose tenacious hold on what was not more than a fortified camp saved South Africa to the Empire. He takes the gloomiest view of the military position in this country, more especially with respect to artillery.

The country is at the mercy of Germany. When the hour strikes, he says, Germany will pick a quarrel with France, in five days be at the gates of Paris, will demand the French Navy as the price of peace, and with its own fleet will be more than a match for England.

This seems fantastic, but it is the view of a man whose level-headedness has been proved on many momentous occasions. His panacea is conscription.

Sir Henry Lucy, *The Diary of a Journalist*, 1 June 1908

MISS PANKHURST'S STAND

Up to City [for] 12 o'clock. Met Wal at Charing Cross. Hyde Park Demonstration by Women's Social and Political Union. Most marvellous sight, outreaching the procession of the previous week in numbers – I should think by thousands – but my sympathies are more with the others. We joined the throng around Miss Pankhurst's stand for a time, but the crush was becoming very dangerous, so we fought our way out. Miss Pankhurst was wearing robes and [a] college cap, and made an inspiring figure in an inspiring spectacle. I should very much like a picture of her as she stood, a smile on her almost beautiful face, a slender arm outstretched, appealing for an audience, which a gang of roughs, stationed right in the front, refused for some time to give her. It was all very wonderful, but I could not help thinking their object would not be half-attained – the crowd seemed to be more intent on amusement than anything else.

Ruth Slate, Diaries, 21 June 1908

ISADORA DUNCAN'S MODERN DANCE

Left as arranged, but saw nothing of Wal at Charing Cross so proceeded alone to the theatre. I could not write in cold words an account of that evening – or what it meant to me. I do not think I have ever seen anything more exquisite than Miss Duncan's dancing, and my heart went out to the woman herself and loved her … The whole thing was a revelation to me. I had felt that somewhere must be the dancing that expresses the emotions – and here at last it was found! No tawdry drop scene disturbed the effect – nothing jarred – just neutral tinted curtains, carpeted stage, soft, light, lovely music – and this exquisite figure and face crowned with warm chestnut hair.

The lady I sat next to and myself soon got into conversation and this added to my enjoyment. She was alone and had come much in the same way as I had. Both of us had read the articles in the *Daily News* and *New Age*, and both felt we were to go …

The lady had a good pair of opera glasses with her, which she would insist on my using frequently, thereby enabling me to see the face of this woman I really loved because she had shown me something so wondrously beautiful. When it was over, no one stirred, so she came back and danced again. Still people only rose, and cries of 'Bravo' rent the air and deafening clapping – so she danced yet again. My new-found friend and I walked out together, and were turning in the direction of Charing Cross, when I suddenly espied Wal a little way in front. A hasty adieu, and this kind lady and I had parted. I would like to have known her name, and to have parted a little less hurriedly.

Wal and I walked on and I soon became aware of a great coolness in his manner. My note had upset him. I then learned he had left the garden party early and had been at the theatre all the while. How he could still be angry after such beauty passed my comprehension, but he did not share my enthusiasm – or would not. I was taken to Ealing like a naughty child and felt too tired to rebel.

Ruth Slate, Diaries, 11 July 1908

TEETOTALLERS TACKLE ROUGHS

Breakfasted again with L. G. [Lloyd George], and played golf with him all day.

We discussed the reasons why lawyers are not more successful as politicians. He said they fail to impress the public mind because their training robs them of that mental distinction necessary for public success. He spoke in high terms of Asquith, saying he had a remarkable clear, forcible mind, and that his defects were due to a legal training, which had curbed his imagination and vivacity.

We discussed the forthcoming Suffragist meeting at the Albert Hall, at which L. G. was to be the principal speaker. He said that interrupters should be dealt with in the most drastic manner, as if they were men. He related his experiences at pro-Boer meetings, and said that the best checkers-out were the young teetotallers, who made short work of roughs.

Lord Riddell, *More Pages from My Diary*, 27 November 1908

INFLEXIBLE GRACE

W. G. Grace [the cricketer] and I went to Chatham to visit the *Inflexible*, the new warship which his son is Commander. It was wonderful to see the boyish manner in which W. G. (now 60) climbed about.

Lord Riddell, *More Pages from My Diary*, 11 December 1908

~

ECONOMISING ON THE RAILWAYS

The new economical arrangements of the railway companies limiting the number of trains running per day, reduced the opportunity of first-class passengers to obtain a whole carriage for themselves or their limited party.

George Grossman tells me that, accustomed as he is in the pursuit of his profession to make frequent railway journeys in the course of the year, he never fails to obtain a compartment to himself. The means are simple. He is at the station early, seats himself in a lavatory compartment by preference, and keeps a bright look-out from the window on the platform side. When he sees anyone approaching with evident intent of entering, he turns up his collar, with swift movement, pulls his hair down over his forehead, and assumes an absolutely idiotic expression. As the intruder approaches closer he breaks into a childish smile, and with a crooked forefinger beckons him or her to enter. 'Come along, my dear,' he says, if the person happens to be a lady. 'Plenty of room, sir,' is his encouraging address to a gentleman.

Of course, both flee, and he has the carriage to himself all the way.

Sir Henry Lucy, *The Diary of a Journalist*, 26 December 1908

~

'RED-LETTER EVENING'

Spent a 'red-letter evening'! Wal came up and together we attended a meeting organised by the Women's Labour League on behalf of unemployed women. The meeting was held at the Memorial Hall, Farringdon. However, we found room at the back of the gallery, and stood for preference, as that was the only way to see the speakers. There were so many speakers – Mr and Mrs Ramsay MacDonald, George Lansbury (Labour MP), Esther Dicks, Margaret Bondfield and Mrs Despard had spoken before we left and others were to follow. Esther Dicks spoke as a working girl.

She had toiled in Ammunition Works for 1s ½d [1 shilling, ½ pence] a thousand bullets, seen fingers cut off and similar accidents, frequently; also, women carried out if factory 'black' through the effects of gunpowder – all for 1½d a thousand. She had tasted the miseries of tramping the streets in search of employment; the bitterness of seeing 'want' written on the home faces, without bringing in the means to alleviate it. She made a fine and telling speech.

Needless to say, I was ready to fall down and worship Margaret Bondfield and Mrs Despard, especially Mrs Despard, whose face and gestures have been in my mind ever since.

Wal, of course, was not so enthusiastic as myself, and spoke of Socialism as stirring up class and sex strike. Again, I could not agree with him and said so, and this time I seemed able to let myself go and spoke with a fluency and fervour which surprised myself.

Ruth Slate, Diaries, 21 January 1909

YOUTHFUL-LOOKING POLAR EXPLORERS

Last night [I went] … to meet Lieutenant Shackleton on his return from the Antarctic regions, where he planted a flag a considerable way nearer the pole than was reached by his predecessor [Captain Scott].

No one is prepared to find in the hero of this latest expedition … an almost boyish-looking man. I do not know his exact age, but as he told me that the ideal age for an Antarctic voyager is thirty, I suppose that is about the number of his years. Three of his companions who were present at the dinner are equally youthful in appearance. Remembering their privations, which finally reached a stage at which starvation actually gripped them, the men look in the perfection of health, and are already beginning to yearn for the sight of the frozen seas and wastes of snow. Shackleton certainly means to go South again, this time to cover the last hundred miles which hunger blockaded last January.

Sir Henry Lucy, *The Diary of a Journalist*, 16 June 1909

⌒*μ*⌒

WOMEN'S INDEPENDENCE

Jenny in bed. I was talking about S's speech (on Woman Suffrage) and, arguing laughingly, said that women had best do first what their fathers and then what their husbands advise them. 'No,' said Jenny. 'They ought to be independent, like the United States of America!'

John Bailey, Diaries, 28 June 1909

⌒*μ*⌒

FOLLY OF FLIGHT

Had a visit this evening from Lieutenant Ernest Shackleton, the explorer, who has just returned from the Antarctic. He is anxious that the Government or some private person should give him money enough to go on another expedition, and thinks that [£]20,000 would be sufficient. Shackleton thinks there is much more to be got out of an expedition of this sort than can be had from financing, say, these spectacular attempts at flying the Channel by flying machine. Only to-day, for instance, Monsieur Paulhan flew eighty-two miles continuously, which shows that the flying machine is no longer a toy in the hands of an expert; but what is the use of expending large sums of these trans-Channel flights which always come to grief, except in proper hands?

Thus, last week M. Blériot flew the Channel in half an hour thirty-three minutes to be exact.

Mr H. Latham has tried it twice and failed. The first time, he fell into the sea and was rescued by following vessels. I agree with Shackleton that these things represent a foolish waste of money. Besides, flying across the Channel means nothing after you have done it. You can't carry goods or passengers.

R. D. Blumenfeld, Diaries, 25 August 1909

◆

A DIVIDED NATION

After the election. The Coalition [is] back with something over a hundred majority – a clear anti-Lord majority and, abstracting the Irish, a majority for the budget.

What is remarkable is the dividing of England into two distinct halves, each having its own large majority for is own cause: the South Country – the suburban, agricultural, residential England – going Tory and tariff reform, and the North Country and dense industrial populations (excluding [the] Birmingham area) going radical socialist, a self-conscious radical socialist.

Beatrice Webb, Diaries, 27 January 1910

◆

LOSING KING EDWARD VII – AND A TOOTH

The day quite lovely. The papers are now absolutely unreadable, one idiotic gush of false sentiment and fatuous panegyric. One hunts through for a few words of sense or fact, and reads an obituary notice of someone else with relief.

What a proof it all is that we don't any of us really believe in personal immortality. If we did, all this ghastly humbug, which must be as distasteful to the poor man, if he is conscious, as it is to me, would be impossible. With what face should we meet the dear ones about whom we had lied so effusively and gushed so hypocritically? It is all very disgusting.

The place is quiet; half the college has gone to the funeral. The garden is delicious, especially the great burst of speedwell, just where the path under the bastion turns up to the arbour.

In the afternoon we motored out to Harlton, through fragrant air, the fields golden with buttercups. Everything has come out with a wild rush of leaf and bloom. Here we left the car and struck up from Eversden by the old clunch-pit into the Mareway. The landscape deliciously hazy …

We got back late, and I had a note from Cooke to say he would bring a dentist at 6.00. A young, shy, pleasant man appeared, and produced probes and horrid forceps. Five useless attempts, and each attempt was more painful – but wholesome pain, not sickening, nasty pain like dressing a wound. At last the vile claw got hold.

A. C. Benson, Diaries, 20 May 1910

~

RE-FORMING MARRIAGE

Much bothered by callers. Found Inge, and walked with him down the river to Waterbeach. He was rather lively; much interested in the Divorce Commission.

It does really seem to me ridiculous to base legislation on a chance saying of Christ in the Gospel – not a dictum, but an answer to a question – and on another saying of St Paul, which admits religious differences as a reason for divorce! What a hopeless nation we are for precedents!*

A. C. Benson, Diaries, 28 June 1910

* Between 1909 and 1910, in response to campaigners' calls following a series of legislative failures in Parliament, a Royal Commission was convened to examine ways of reforming the country's divorce laws, which had been established in the Victorian period and only allowed remarriage after divorce in a proved case of a wife's adultery or a husband's cruelty.

~

CREMATION CATCHING ON

It is interesting to note how slowly the process of cremation is assimilated with British customs. There are throughout the country thirteen crematoria, the principal being situated at Woking. This was opened in 1885, and I am told that in the intervening quarter of a century the number of cremations does not far exceed 3,000, an infinitesimal proportion of the daily burials in the metropolitan area, which is the chief contributory.

The late Sir Henry Thompson was the earliest apostle of cremation in this country. He set people thinking by an article published thirty-six years ago in one of the monthly magazines. The seed thus sown resulted in the formation of a cremation society, and the building of the crematorium at Woking. The enterprise promptly received what seemed a death-blow by issue of an order from the Home Office forbidding the practice of cremation.

After an interval of five years, during which the crematorium was closed, the edict of the sapient Home Secretary was annulled by a judgment delivered in court by Mr Justice Stephen.

The cost of cremation at Woking, or its off-shoot at Golders Green, is five guineas. There are accessory charges, but the aggregate expense does not exceed that of the average earth burial.

Sir Henry Lucy, *The Diary of a Journalist*, 18 September 1910

BERNARD SHAW BY THE BEACH

To-day I am resting more enjoyably. I caught the 9 a.m. from Leeds to Scarborough and walked here in glorious sunshine and wind along the coast. I gave myself a good luncheon (to the frugal a half-crown luncheon and half a bottle of wine once a month is Ambrosia and Nectar – why don't the rich find that out?) and have spent the afternoon reading *Getting Married* [by Bernard Shaw], and watching the sunlight and the sea and the cliffs of Flamborough Head. By God! life is good. It might be good for nearly, very nearly, all men.

Getting Married is wonderful.

There is Truth and Life in this thing.

Frederic 'Ben' Keeling, Letter to Mrs Townsend, 26 February 1911

NOT-SO-AMAZING ARNOLD BENNETT

Finished reading *The Card* by Arnold Bennett. I am amazed at his reputation. The book is great rubbish; clever rubbish, of course; but no joy, no sorrow in it; no passion, no emotion; no human – not any other sort of – nature, and least of all, any poetry. The man is a clever, cold, shallow journalist.

John Bailey, Diaries, 30 April 1911

CORONATION OF GEORGE V

This was Coronation Day. I reached the Abbey at seven o'clock this morning and found my place high up in the Triforium, from which there was a splendid view. I sat entranced throughout the morning until two o'clock. It was the most wonderful sight of my life. Pageant after pageant, picture after picture, unrolling before our eyes. I do not think it is possible to put one's emotions into words. The vast area covered with gorgeous costumes, colours, flowers, blazoned on all sides, procession on procession all culminating in the wonderful coronation scenes. I think the thing which impressed me most was when the young Prince of Wales appeared before his royal father to do obeisance as those before him had done. The young prince stepped forward and bowed low before his father. Sweeping his robes of the Garter to each side as he advanced up the steps of the throne, he knelt down and said: 'I, Edward Prince of Wales, do become your liege, man of life and limb and of earthly worship; and faith and truth I will bear unto you, to live and die against all manner of folks. So help me God.'

The boy touched the royal crown with his forefinger and then kissed the King on the left cheek.

Custom prescribes this. But as he got up, the parent reached out his hand and drew his son to him and kissed him.

R. D. Blumenfeld, Diaries, 22 June 1911

NATIONAL RAILWAY STRIKE

The strike is magnificent. Nothing else really matters. It is strange to see things in Leeds, crowds of railway men in the streets, most of them extraordinarily solemn and sober men in their Sunday clothes, just as you see them in an Adult School of PSA meeting, very English. By God! there is good stuff there, for all the dumbness and slowness. Of course, they are an extraordinary contrast with the dockers. They are never unemployed, and the dockers are chronically under-employed. At dinner-time I saw detachments of Lancers come out of one of the stations through a large crowd. Hundreds of soldiers have been sent into Leeds. There has been hardly any disorder, or even horse-play, but a lot of successful picketing.

In one of the Liberal Christian epochs of my youth, I used to offer up prayers to God with a mental qualification, 'if he exists', for the sake of honesty. I feel as if I could almost pray now in the same way for the strikers. It will be an awful thing if they are in any way defeated. God help the strikes, if there be a god. In any case, they must help themselves.

Frederic 'Ben' Keeling, Letter to Mrs Townsend, 18 August 1911

~

LLOYD GEORGE ATTACKED

On Saturday L. G. was violently assaulted by a male suffragette. I called to see him this morning. He had a little cut on his eye and told me that he had been stunned by a leather case bound with metal which had been thrown through the window of his car. He said he thought the act had been committed in a moment of excitement. The case contained papers which enabled the police to trace a man, now in custody. L. G. left me to see the detectives.

We subsequently had another chat. He referred in bitter terms to the fact that those responsible for financing the suffragette movement were engaging bravoes to inflict personal injury upon members of the Government. He said that the people who should be prosecuted were the people who found the money and employed these men. I asked him why the Suffragettes were attacking him, as he had declared himself strongly in favour of votes for women. His explanation was peculiar. He said they were attacking him 'because they thought he was a little devil who had a knack of getting things through, and that if stimulated he would secure the vote'.

Lord Riddell, *More Pages from My Diary*, 17 December 1911

~

TITANIC REMEMBRANCE

A great service for the victims of the *Titanic*. We were told that thousands were unable to get in.*

Rev. W. R. Inge, *Diary of a Dean*, 19 April 1912

* *Launched from Belfast in May 1911, the* Titanic *was touted by its owners, the White Star Line, as the last word in luxury travel, and an 'unsinkable' vessel. En route from Southampton to New York City, it struck an iceberg and floundered, with the loss of over 1,500 lives.*

POLITICAL MANOEUVRES

Saw L. G. [Lloyd George] at the requests of certain employers concerned in the dock strike, and put before him proposals for a settlement. He saw the Prime Minister, and it was arranged that Wedgwood Benn, one of the Junior Whips, should see Gosling, the men's leader. But I am doubtful if anything will come of it ...

I asked why Mrs Pankhurst had been released. L. G. said, 'They could not make her retain any food. She was dying, so they had to release her.'

Lord Riddell, *More Pages from My Diary*, 28 June 1912

FLOODED BY FOREIGN CARS

When I came down from Cumberland recently on the Great North Road, I appeared to encounter an enormous number of cheap foreign cars, so I determined to see if we could not establish the popularity of British-made cars over the machines produced by foreign countries. I gave a luncheon at the Ritz Hotel to representatives of seventeen British automobile manufacturing companies, with Lord Montague in the chair ...

A letter was read from the Duke of Westminster, in which he said that the invasion of the American cars 'threaten[s] to deprive thousands of English workers of employment, and the way out is to start a vigorous campaign throughout the country to advance the cause of British Imperial preference'.

R. D. Blumenfeld, *Diaries*, 16 September 1912

MODERN ART EXHIBITS

Post-Impression Exhibition. Self-satisfied smiles of most people as they entered. One large woman of ruling classes with a large voice and a *face-à-mains* [lorgnette], in front of a mediocre picture: 'Now no one will ever persuade me that the man who painted that was serious. He was just pulling our legs.' Self-satisfied smiles all over the place all the time. One reason of the popularity of these shows is that they give the grossly inartistic leisured class an opportunity to feel artistically superior. A slight undercurrent of appreciation here and there. A woman to whom a young man pointed out a pencil drawing by Matisse said: 'That's what I call beautiful.' (It was.)

I met Frank Harris. He was prepared on principle to admire everything, though there was a large proportion of absolutely uninteresting work. When I said I had seen much better Picassos than there were there, he hardened at once. 'I find it all interesting,' he said grimly.

Arnold Bennett, Journals, 8 October 1912

ANGLO-GERMAN RELATIONS

I lunched at the Goldsmiths' Hall to meet the German delegates who have come over to promote better relations between the two countries. I sat next to Dr Spiecker, whom I liked greatly when I was in Germany in 1911, on a similar mission.

Rev. W. R. Inge, *Diary of a Dean*, 30 October 1912

SERIOUS OUTLOOK IN THE BALKANS

Spent the day with L. G. [Lloyd George], Masterman and Illingworth at Walton Heath. L. G. very worried and nervous regarding the Balkan crisis. He said he had slept badly. Also that outlook was serious, and that the war between Austria and Russia, which would involve France and Germany, seemed probable.

Great Britain might even be involved. Pointing to a bank of dark and lowering clouds, he exclaimed, 'That is emblematic of the situation. It may be a regular Armageddon.'

We drove back to Downing Street to tea. L. G. sent for the Foreign Office box, which was awaiting him, and read the dispatches while we were at tea. When he finished he seemed somewhat relieved and said the situation was a little more hopeful.

Lord Riddell, *More Pages from My Diary*, 9 November 1912

REPELLING SUFFRAGETTES

Interesting discussion by L. G. [Lloyd George] and Winston [Churchill] on the proper method of repelling assaults by Suffragettes. They agreed it was difficult not to retaliate. W. said that in the case of a violent assault he thought it would be permissible to beat the assailant off, although it was most repugnant to treat a woman with violence. A violent woman must take her chance. A man could not stand still and allow himself to be injured, perhaps for life.

Lord Riddell, *More Pages from My Diary*, 5 December 1912

DEATH OF THE POLAR EXPLORERS

How terrible this news is about Captain Scott & four of his party having been dead twelve months – dying from starvation & a terrible blizzard eleven miles from food, shortly after having found the South Pole. And how grand the way they died – especially Captain Oates, who went out into the blizzard to die that his weakness might not delay his four companions, who refused to leave him. 'Greater love hath no man than this.'

Vera Brittain, *Chronicle of Youth*, 12 February 1913

* Captain Robert Falcon Scott embarked on his second expedition to the Antarctic in 1910 determined to be the first explorer to reach the South Pole. When he and his four-man party reached the South Pole on 17–18 January 1912, however, they were disappointed to discover they'd been pipped to the post by the Norwegian explorer Roald Amundsen. All of Scott's party died from cold and hunger on the 800-mile journey back to their base camp. The bodies of Scott, Dr Edward A. Wilson and Henry 'Birdie' Bowers were discovered by a search party in November 1912.

SERVICE FOR A HERO

Memorial service for Captain Scott of the Antarctic and his four companions. The mob broke through the cordon of police into the reserved part of the cathedral.

Rev. W. R. Inge, *Diary of a Dean*, 14 February 1913

LLOYD GEORGE'S HOUSE BOMBED

Early this morning my bedside telephone rang, and a message came through to say that part of the house I am building for L. G. at Walton Heath had been blown to smithereens by the Suffragettes.

Lord Riddell, *More Pages from My Diary*, 19 February 1913

THE GERMAN POSITION

Had a long talk with General French.*

He spoke highly of Seely, and said he had acted with great judgement and coolness in trying situations. He described him as the right man in the right place – a man with sufficient knowledge of military affairs to enable him to form a sound judgement, but one who did not place too much reliance on his own military experience. The General said that the Germans and Austrians were not ready for war, but that in twelve months' time their position would be much improved. He seemed to regard war as certain in the future.

Lord Riddell, *More Pages from My Diary*, 23 February 1913

Field Marshal John Denton Pinkstone French, 1st Earl of Ypres, was an acclaimed hero of the Boer War, during which he led the British to victory at the Battle of Elandslaagte. In 1912 he became Chief of the Imperial General Staff of the British Army. J. E. B. Seely, 1st Baron Mottistone, was the Secretary of State for War from 1912 until 1914.

⁓

SAD TO BE A WOMAN

On the way to golf I induced Mother to disclose a few points on sexual matters which I thought I ought to know, though the information is always intensely distasteful to me & most depressing – in fact, it quite put me off my game! I suppose it is the spiritual-&-intellectual-development part of me that feels repugnance at being brought too closely into contact with physical 'open secrets'. Alas! Sometimes it feels sad to be a woman! Men seem to have so much more choice as to what they are intended for. Still, I suppose our position improves with the years, & I must be thankful not to have lived in Homeric Greece instead of 20th-century England.

Vera Brittain, *Chronicle of Youth*, 4 March 1913

⁓

PICTURING THE DIVINE

I went to the Hippodrome to-night to see that extraordinary cinematograph *From [the] Manger to [the] Cross, or Jesus of Nazareth*. Somehow the fact of seeing it in pictures – & the pictures really were beautiful – made the reality of it all seem so much nearer. What a strange combination of mythology, travesty & history that great story seems to be – & yet it is all so wonderful, & the Spirit, which is what really matters, is so living & so embodied in all, that we can despise none of the forms in which it is pictured, however exaggerated or imperfect.

Vera Brittain, *Chronicle of Youth*, 8 March 1913

HATEFUL SOCIETY

A splendid, fine morning but as I know I have to go out and change the cheque and pay the bills, I can do nothing and I feel wretched. Life is a hateful business, there's no denying it.

When G. and J. were talking in the park of physical well-being and of how they could still look forward to 'parties', I nearly groaned. And I am sure J. could get a great deal of pleasure out of pleasant society. I couldn't. I've done with it and can't combat it at all now. I had so much rather lean idly over the bridge and watch the boats and the free, unfamiliar people and feel the wind blow. No, I hate society.

Katherine Mansfield, Journals, 31 March 1913

NO TO 'FLESH FOODS'

Am reading the essay of 'Fruitarianism' lent me by Cecil – it is very convincing. I should like to try again to do without flesh food, but think it hardly wise unless I first gain a proper understanding of vegetarianism.

Eva Slawson, Diaries, 16 April 1913

POST BY AIRSHIP

Lunching to-day at the club, Sir J. Henniker Heaton, the postal reformer, said: 'Within three years there will leave daily from the GPO [Government Printing Office] airships for Bombay, Cairo, Paris, Berlin and so on.'

He prefers penny postage to a Channel tunnel; more useful.

R. D. Blumenfeld, Diaries, 24 April 1913

DERBY DEATH

Aunt Edie met me at the Bank – she told me a suffragette had thrown herself before the King's horse at the Derby, receiving terrible injuries.* I cannot express what a shock this news was to me – can such martyrdom and sacrifice really be necessary? Will it hasten the longed-for result?

Eva Slawson, Diaries, 4 June 1913

* *The suffragette in question was Emily Wilding Davison, who four days later died of her injuries in Epsom Cottage Hospital.*

FALTERING TRUST IN POLITICIANS

This has been an amazing week. On Thursday came the bombshell that Alec Murray (now in Bogota, South America) had been investing in [the] American Marconi [company], both on his own account and on account of 'a trust' – no doubt with party funds, but we shall hear more later. The disclosure was made owing to the failure and absconding of a stockbroker. No one in the Cabinet knew of these dealings, which have caused dire dismay in the Liberal Party. L. G. [Lloyd George] and Rufus astounded.

On Saturday and Sunday I spent several hours with L. G., who was evidently very depressed.

Lord Riddell, *More Pages from My Diary*, 8 June 1913

* The Marconi affair centred on allegations that members of the Liberal Party had attempted to profit from insider knowledge that the government intended to issue a contract to the British Marconi telecommunications company by buying up shares in its American operation.

MYSTICAL RECITAL

We went to tea with Mrs Stuart Moore, who writes on the mystics under the name of Evelyn Underhill, and met Rabindranath Tagore, the Indian poet and mystic, with his son and daughter-in-law. He is a very remarkable-looking man, like an Old Testament prophet. He recited some of his own poetry in Bengali, in a curious musical recitative.

Rev. W. R. Inge, *Diary of a Dean*, 9 June 1913

ALWAYS THE VOTE

Some pleasant music at Miss Leith's this evening, and a quiet reading. Miss Leith is an ardent suffragette. I am afraid I felt rather weary of it all – not because I have not the cause of women at heart, but because I notice the militant suffragettes so seldom discuss the fundamentals of progress amongst women – it is always 'the Vote'.

Eva Slawson, Diaries, 18 June 1913

A SEX SCANDAL

The feeling between the two parties is very bitter.

The Marconi affair has left great bitterness on both sides. Now a fresh cause of friction has arisen in relation to a brothel in Piccadilly recently raided by the police. Papers found on the premises contained the names of some patrons of the establishment. Malicious rumours have been set on foot that some of these names were those of prominent men on both sides. The rumours are a pack of lies but they have engendered much resentment and bad feeling.

Lord Riddell, *More Pages from My Diary*, 9 July 1913

* *Following a sensational trial in which it was impugned that many members of the establishment visited her high-class brothel above Piccadilly tube station, Queenie Gerald was convicted of keeping an immoral house and living off the earnings of prostitution and sentenced to three months in prison – a sentence that Christabel Pankhurst, for one, noted was far more lenient than the three years handed down to some suffragettes.*

✍

SENSATIONAL WOMEN

Sons and Lovers has been well received, hasn't it? I don't know whether it has sold so well. The damned prigs in the libraries and bookshops daren't handle me because they pretend they are delicate-skinned and I am hot. May they fry in Hell.

I don't like England very much, but the English *do* seem rather lovable people. They have such a lot of gentleness. There seems to be a big change in England, even in a year: such a dissolving down of old barriers and prejudices. But I look at the young women, and they all seem such sensationalists, with half a desire to expose themselves. Good God, where is there a woman for a really decent earnest man to marry? They don't want husbands and marriages any more – only sensation.

D. H. Lawrence, Letter to Ernest Collings, 22 July 1913

ZEST FOR FLYING

At tea were joined by Winston [Churchill] and his wife and Lady Ridley.

Talked afterwards with Winston, who spoke of flying, which he said had done him much good and given [him] a new zest to life. The aeroplane, contrary to his expectation, now gave greater promise than the waterplane.

Lord Riddell, *More Pages from My Diary*, 16 November 1913

MRS PANKHURST ARRESTED

It was so cosy at home this evening – the shop closed, we sat and worked. Gertie came home with the news that Mrs Pankhurst has again been arrested – militancy will thus receive a fresh impulse. I admire Mrs Pankhurst, and feel she has fought a good and brave fight. I know how terribly hard it is for the human spirit not to retaliate – yet I think if even one retaliates oneself it does not seem right to incite others to violence.

Eva Slawson, Diaries, 4 December 1913

STUPID MEN

We went to a little dance at the Briggs'. Although I danced every dance hard & had what I suppose everyone would call a good time, it leaves me with a very unsatisfied feeling to have met so many stupid & superficial men, with whom all the girls are obviously so pleased. How I wish I could meet a good, strong, splendid man, full of force & enthusiasm, & earnest about his life! There must *be* such!

Vera Brittain, *Chronicle of Youth*, 20 December 1913

CHAPTER TWO

BRITAIN DURING THE GREAT WAR: 1914-1918

On 1 January 1914, David Lloyd George, Chancellor of the Exchequer in Asquith's Liberal government, gave a speech in which he stated: 'Never have the prospects for world peace been so bright.' He was, of course, to be proved spectacularly wrong in his prognostication. Whole books have been devoted to the events that led to the outbreak of the First World War; here, diarists give their reactions to the news as it unfolded, and to developments on the home front as the war progressed over the seemingly endless months and years. It was in this 'Great War' – thanks to the aerial bombardment of the Zeppelin airships and, later, Gotha aeroplanes – that Britain's streets joined the battlefields as conflict zones for perhaps the first time since the Civil War.

But a few preliminaries are perhaps necessary to set the scene.

A world war was not inevitable. The incident on 28 June 1914 that propelled the major European military powers towards war was, at its simplest, the nearly bungled, almost chance assassination of Franz Ferdinand, the heir presumptive to the Austro-Hungarian throne, and his morganatic wife. The perpetrator was a nineteen-year-old Serbian nationalist called Gavrilo Princip.

In 1908, Austria-Hungary had annexed Bosnia and Herzegovina – territory coveted by Serbia – from the Ottoman Turks. This was a significant event, but a major war had been avoided. In addition, the 'great powers' of Great Britain, France, Russia and Germany had then avoided being drawn into the Balkan crises of 1912 and 1913, when Serbia, Greece, Bulgaria and Romania decided to take on the Ottomans, whose empire was in decline, leaving a power vacuum.

Similar moderation could easily have prevailed in 1914. And Britain, in particular under Asquith's premiership, was perhaps the most anxious of all for peace. But Austria-Hungary was in no mood for compromise and promptly declared war on Serbia on 28 July 1914.

Neither Germany, Austria's blood brother, nor Russia, Serbia's obvious Slavic champion, looked especially favourably on the prospect of war either. But faced with the fear of being caught off guard, Russia – itself an autocratic state with insurgent elements – pushed aside its qualms against supporting a politic that had actively abetted the murder of an archduke, and tooled up to counter Austrian mobilization. Germany, in turn, mobilized to counter Russia. France, in an alliance with Russia and eager to regain the provinces of Alsace and Lorraine lost to Germany in 1871, duly entered the fray. It was only when Germany invaded neutral Belgian territory with the aim of advancing on France that the British government was stirred into action.

Asquith had a note demanding withdrawal from Belgium issued to Berlin on 4 August 1914. When no reply was received, hostilities immediately commenced between the two nations.

✣

ART ACTION

Surely there was seldom such barbarity as that of the Suffragette who in the National Gallery this morning slashed & cut with a hatchet Velázquez's famous [*Rokeby*] *Venus*! They say the damage is serious but not, they hope, irreparable. Poor artist & genius! ...

Vera Brittain, Chronicle of Youth, 10 March 1914

THE INTERMEDIATE SEX

A quiet evening – Ruth read a little aloud from Edward Carpenter* … His poem on the Urnings led us to talk of the 'intermediate sex'; we wondered whether the great teachers Christ and Buddha belonged to this category, having in themselves the experiences and nature of either sex – then we talked of the procreation of children by the intermediate sex either naturally or by thought and ended in a confusion of ideas, having lost the thread of our discussion.

Eva Slawson, Diaries, 13 April 1914

* *Edward Carpenter was an openly gay nudist, socialist, proto-environmentalist poet, writer and political pamphleteer and campaigner. An apostle for sandal-wearing, he derided shoes as 'leather coffins'.*

✱

MORE BRAINS THAN BROTHERS

I had a violent argument with Mr Risigari this morning as I was playing the piano badly, & he complained that my 'being so mad on studying' had upset my music. I said I was sorry but much as I liked music it would have to take second place as I could not earn my living by it. He gave me an exclamation of horror at me wanting to earn my living. He said that independence was all very well up to a point but what were fathers for? I replied very heatedly that I did not intend to be kept by mine, that I had more brains than my brothers & why shouldn't I use them! …

Vera Brittain, *Chronicle of Youth*, 27 May 1914

✱

ASSASSINATION OF ARCHDUKE FERDINAND

H. G. Wells came over to tea. While we were talking, news came that Austria's Crown Prince and his wife have been assassinated by a Serbian. That will mean war. Wells says it will mean more than that. It will set the world alight. I don't see why the world should fight over the act of a lunatic.

R. D. Blumenfeld, Diaries, 28 June 1914

WELL-BEING RESTORED BY BEETHOVEN

Went with R. to the Albert Hall to the *Empress of Ireland* Memorial Concert* with massed bands. We heard the *Symphonic Pathetique*, Chopin's *Funeral March*, *Trauermarsch* from *Götterdämmerung*, the *Ride of the Valkyries* and a solemn melody from Bach.

This afternoon I regard as a mountain peak in my existence. For two solid hours I sat like an Eagle on a rock gazing into infinity – a very fine sensation for a London Sparrow …

I have an idea that if it were possible to assemble the sick and suffering day by day in the Albert Hall and keep the Orchestra going all the time, then the constant exposure of sick parts to such heavenly air vibrations would ultimately restore to them the lost rhythm of health …

The concert restored my moral health. I came away in love with people I was hating before and full of compassion for others I usually condemn …

W. N. P. Barbellion, *The Journal of a Disappointed Man*, 29 June 1914

* *RMS* Empress of Ireland *was an ocean liner that sank in the Saint Lawrence River following a collision with the Norwegian collier SS* Storstad *in the early hours of 29 May 1914. Of the 1,477 people on board, 1,012 died.*

CHANGED MAN

Frieda and I were married this morning at the Kensington registrar's office. I thought it was a very decent and dignified performance. I don't feel a changed man, but I suppose I am one.

D. H. Lawrence, Letter to Mrs S. A. Hopkins, 13 July 1914

TEMPERANCE IN DANGER

At 10.45 to Mablethorpe, where Proudfoot met me. To Vicar for luncheon. At 3 addressed a rally of the Lincolnshire Labourers' Temperance Union.

This League, begun at Heckington in 1906, has a large nominal membership in various parts of the county, but is in imminent danger of collapse and disappearance.

Edward Lee Hicks, *The Life and Letters Of*, 23 July 1914

TENSIONS AT HOME AND ABROAD

This evening I telephoned L. G. [Lloyd George] informing him of the Dublin Riots and that several people had been killed. He was much distressed, and said the incident would cause fresh and serious complications. He spoke at length of the foreign situation. He said that Austria had made demands on Serbia which no self-respecting nation could comply with, and that such demands, when addressed by a great nation to a small one, were in the nature of bullying threats. He said the situation was serious, but he thought there would be peace – in fact, he thought so very strongly.

Lord Riddell, *More Pages from My Diary*, 26 July 1914

NATIONAL FEELING

How horrible this threatened war is! Where is the sense of the human race? The only thing is, that I don't think [it] can be argued that capitalism, even the armament firms, are the main force behind it. The big national and racial feelings are there. One may not share them; my renewal of patriotism doesn't really involve any war cult, but one has to recognise them. The Southern Slav movement is the most important of all the national movements in Europe now. I have thought for some time that it would probably prove to be the storm-centre of Europe, but I had no idea anything like this was coming so soon. I can't help thinking we and Germany will settle it somehow. I can't believe in the Russians and French politically or strategically.

Frederic 'Ben' Keeling, Letter to Miss C. Townsend, 30 July 1914

WAR AFTER THE FINAL WICKET

Went down home to Easton with our *Daily Express* cricket eleven to play Easton Lodge. We were beaten. After [the] match we learned that Germany had declared war on Russia and had marched into Luxembourg, thus violating her treaty engagements. If this country does not stand up for Right and Honour she will be for ever damned.

R. D. Blumenfeld, Diaries, 1 August 1914

A DEPARTING GERMAN

Had a visit this morning from Herr Kurt Buetow, the German tutor to Mr H. G. Wells's two boys. He came to bid us good-bye, since he has been called home to Germany to take his place in the Army. He was very stiff and formal and polite, but evidently sorry to leave England.

Came up to town early. In St James's Park, just below the German Embassy, I met Prince Lichnowski, the German Ambassador, looking terribly sad. 'I am afraid we can do no more,' he said. 'I have just seen Sir Edward Grey,* and you are likely to take sides with the French.'

Moratorium to be declared to-morrow. No debt settlements. So there'll be no money panics.

R. D. Blumenfeld, Diaries, 2 August 1914

Edward Grey, 1st Viscount Grey of Fallodon, was Foreign Secretary.

THE FIRST CALL-UP

Taylor called away from our office this morning. Afternoon order arrived for all Territorials to immediately join their respective corps. Gray and Crocker called away later – three total from our firm. Bank holiday extended to Tuesday and Wednesday. Mr Asquith informed the House this afternoon that Sir E. Grey had given the German Government notice for a satisfactory reply as to the neutrality of Belgium by 12 o'clock tonight.

Albert Best, Diaries, 4 August 1914

WAR DECLARED

War was declared at midnight. It was really a relief to hear this definitely announced. Every day seemed like weeks, everything was unsettled, and we were wishing one minute for peace at any price, and the next were furious at the idea that we might back out of our treaty obligations … I don't suppose many of us ever thought it would become a reality in our time, and that we were destined to live in the most stirring days of our history. But now it was on us, and so suddenly that it seemed like a bad dream that we should soon wake from to find our world unchanged.

Winifred Tower, Diaries, 4 August 1014

∾

BANK HOLIDAY

It was a strange London on Sunday: crowded with excursionists to London and balked would-be travellers to the Continent, all in a state of suppressed uneasiness and excitement. We sauntered through the crowd to Trafalgar Square, where Labour, socialist and pacifist demonstrators, with a few trade union flags, were gesticulating from the steps of the Monument to a mixed crowd of admirers, hooligan warmongers and merely curious holiday-makers …

The closing of the Bank for four days and the paralysis of business (no one seems to know whether the closing is limited to banks and many businesses have stopped because there is no money to pay wages) gives the business quarters of London a dispirited air. Every train that steams out of London, every cart in the street, is assumed to be commandeered by the Government for the purposes of war …

Beatrice Webb, Diaries, 5 August 1914

∾

LAYING IN FOR WAR

On arriving at Brightlingsea on Monday afternoon, I was told that petrol could not be got in the district; that it was fetching up to 10s. a tin at Clacton; and that Baggaley, the regular hirer of motor cars at B'sea, had gone forth in an attempt to get petrol. At Clacton yesterday the price was 2s. 3d. or 2s. 4d. a gallon. I have 60 gallons in stock …

At the fish shop, slight increases of price in poultry and eggs. The man said there was no chance for him to make money (in response to a friendly jibe of

Marguerite's). He said he expected to get no more fish after that day …

Sir Edward Grey's outstanding mistake, in his big speech, was the assertion that the making of war would not much increase our suffering. It will enormously increase it.

The hope for us is in the honesty and efficiency of our administration. The fear for France springs from the fact that the majority of French politicians are notoriously rascals, out for plunder … The seriousness of the average French private will atone for a lot, but it will not – for instance – create boots for him. The hope for France is that the German army, arrogant in its traditions etc., may be lower than its reputation …

I am told, convincingly, that a firm at Clacton is making an extra £50 a week out of bread, through increased charges for which there is no justification. It appears that the farmers all round have raised the price of butter 3d. a pound …

Edith Johnston recounts how her father is laying in ammunition against the time when the populace will raid the countryside demanding provisions; he, being a farmer, is to be called on early in the proceedings, and he is determined to give out his stores evenly and not to the strongest. Each morning he summons all his men and explains to them the course of the war, so that they shall not be misled by rumours. Edith thinks that a war is necessary and advisable, as the population is too thick.

Arnold Bennett, Journals, 6 August 1914

YOUR KING AND COUNTRY NEED YOU

The first appeal for recruits pasted on the walls to-day. It is printed in national colours. Within a deep red border, in vivid blue letters on a white background, are the words, 'Your King and Country need You' – 'YOU' being heavily underscored. Lord Kitchener, who has been appointed Secretary of State for War, is confident 'that this appeal will be at once responded to by all those who have the safety of our Empire at heart'. The recruiting headquarters is in Old Scotland Yard, off Whitehall. As I passed there this evening I saw a big throng of young men still in straw hats, waiting their turn to get [in] and, in the old phrase, 'take the King's shilling'.

Michael MacDonagh, *The Diary of a Journalist*, 6 August 1914

WOMEN'S WAR WORK

To-day I started the only work it seems possible as yet for women to do – the making of garments for the soldiers. I started knitting sleeping-helmets, and as I have forgotten how to knit, & was never very brilliant when I knew, I seemed to be an object of some amusement. But even when one is not skilled it is better to proceed slowly than to do nothing to help.

Vera Brittain, *Chronicle of Youth*, 6 August 1914

GETTING SHIP-SHAPED

Back to my rooms where I found a telegram from the Admiralty ordering me to join the SS *Mantua* at Tilbury Docks, 'forthwith'. The last word sounded rather urgent so I packed up, wrote letters until 3 a.m., and at 5 a.m. caught a train to Tilbury where I arrived before breakfast. I had forgotten that the Navy is either shaven clean or bearded, so I clipped off my moustaches with a pair of scissors in the train from Fenchurch Street. The other occupant of the carriage probably thought I was a German trying to disguise myself. After all it appeared that 'forthwith' was not such an urgent word as it sounded, and I might have waited a few days as the ship is nowhere near ready for sea. SS *Mantua* is one of the modern P. and O. liners, and the day war was declared she had just returned from a cruise in the Baltic with a shipload of tourists. The ship is 11,000 tons and is now being converted from a floating hotel into an armed merchant cruiser – presumably to patrol trade routes or something of that kind …

A. F. R. Wollaston, *Letters and Diaries*, 7 August 1914

CO-OPERATING FOR THE WAR

The Edmonton Co-op. has just opened a branch near here, and I have joined. I am rather glad to be a co-operator again. It was one of my earliest enthusiasms; I made my mother buy everything from the local Co-op. when I was fifteen, and in some ways it is the finest of the British working-class achievements. The Co-ops are, of course, of enormous value now in keeping down prices. Bread was still at the normal price at my Co-op. on Wednesday, whereas it had gone up a penny everywhere else.

Frederic 'Ben' Keeling, Letter to Mrs Townsend, 7 August 1914

THE SPIRIT OF PEACE

Ruth met me at the office this afternoon and we made our way to Finsbury Gardens, intending to talk and rest there, but found it packed with horses and gun carriages – it all looked very warlike! After inspecting it all we made our way to the Relief Committee meeting at Devonshire House ... a gentleman spoke of the great calamity of the war ...

Then Miss Fox Howard spoke of the need of helping in our towns ... We could best help the world often by remaining at our posts, by spreading the spirit of peace, and checking panic.

The suggestion made as to the relief work was that Friends should band themselves together to assist the alien Germans in this country – they were in danger of rough usage and want, and we might hold out a friendly hand at this time ...

Eva Slawson, Diaries, 14 August 1914

ADJUSTING TO THE UNIFORM

I got my uniform yesterday for the first time, and felt very conscious of eight flaming brass buttons and two stripes of gold braid with a strip of red (for blood presumably) between them, which are the recognition of my rank and quality. The peaked cap is an abominable thing.

This evening I walked over to the railway station to buy papers, and was mistaken by a lady for a railway official. She was much more embarrassed than I was when she found out her mistake, and it showed me that I am not nearly so conspicuous as I seemed to myself to be.

A. F. R. Wollaston, *Letters and Diaries*, 14 August 1914

PREPARING FOR THE WORST

Haldane dined with us last night; serious with the first bad news of the war – the fall of Namur. He was full of his past participation in diplomacy and military organisation. He was greatly admiring of Kitchener,* and anxious to tell us that it was he who insisted on 'K' going to the War Office. 'K' says we must prepare for a three years' war and is expecting initial disasters. The Germans expect to walk through the French Army 'like butter', and our own Expeditionary Force they consider a mere 'demonstration' …

Beatrice Webb, Diaries, 24 August 1914

*Born in County Kerry, Ireland, in 1850, Kitchener, who had previously fought with General Gordon at Khartoum and served as Governor of Sudan, Commander in Chief of India and Proconsul of Egypt, was appointed Secretary of State for War at the outbreak of the First World War.

⚓

DRILLING WITH THE ARTISTS' RIFLES

Most people are cursing me for enlisting, but I think the argument about being wanted at home can be pushed too far …

Rupert Brooke has dropped out. He wants a commission after all, and thinks he can get one through pushing in various quarters.

God it's good to feel one's muscles stiff after four hours' drilling. I don't think I shall ever stoop again. I have thought of going into the Kitchener Army. But our battalion is really a very fine corps, one of the crack Territorial Corps; and although there are stories that Kitchener … won't use them for foreign service, it seems impossible …

I get more and more furious at the attacks on Germans here. It is so damnably mean dismissing wretched governesses and servants and so on. Even this 'smash German trade' movement has a touch of the mean about it, but I suppose that is inevitable. It looks as if this might be a particularly brutal war.

Frederic 'Ben' Keeling, Letter to Mrs Townsend, 24 August 1914

END OF THE WEEK-END

We have given up the week-end habit. That I believed at one time could never be brought about. But there it is, the week-end habit has gone by the board. There are no country-house parties. Country houses are turned into Red Cross hospitals, and one or two male members of each country-house family is at the front fighting the Germans or, perhaps already, lying stark on the field …

R. D. Blumenfeld, Diaries, 29 August 1914

ARRIVALS FROM BELGIUM

There is to be seen almost every day at Victoria railway station the arrival of parties of Belgians who are pouring into England in tens of thousands, torn from their homes and flying before the devastating advance of the Germans: a spectacle unparalleled, perhaps, since the flight to this country of the French Huguenots.

Michael MacDonagh, *The Diary of a Journalist*, 31 August 1914

WELCOME TO ARMY LIFE

On arriving at Paddington we were allowed to scatter for lunch, and rallied again for the train to Bodmin at 1.30. We decided unanimously that the transport arrangements were not creditable to the Committee of Railway Managers. The train was an ordinary one and the amount of space reserved quite insufficiently, many having standing room only. Notwithstanding, the journey down was a hilarious one – beer and singing ad lib – it was many days before we were so cheerful again. We had two changes, and did not reach Bodmin till after dark. There we were met by a sergeant and marched up without delay to the Barracks.

Our reception there was not encouraging; at the gate we were each presented with one blanket, and told that the sleeping accommodation was over-full, and that we must do as best we could in the open. Some 20 of us accordingly stationed ourselves under a small group of trees.

Food was the next question; although we had been given no opportunity for a meal since Paddington, nothing was provided for us. Luckily, the canteen was still open, and by dint of much pushing we managed to secure a tin of corned beef and bottled beer …

It so happened that we shared our 'pitch' with a rabble from Handsworth, Birmingham – a district which is, I believe, notorious. These worthies kept us supplied with a constant stream of lewdness, mostly of a very monotonous kind; there was one real humorist who made some excellent jokes, but they are scarcely repeatable. At about 2 a.m. we were joined by several unfortunates who had found their tents already occupied (by lice), and preferred the open air and the wet grass …

George Butterworth, Diaries, 2 September 1914

⚬⚬⚬

COUNTING THE COST OF WAR

Had luncheon at 10 Downing St. Poor Margot [Asquith] had just seen a fresh casualty list full of intimates killed or wounded, and was altogether utterly upset and despairing.

Mary Gladstone, Diaries, 8 September 1914

⚬⚬⚬

CRUDE HEROISM

I feel angry with the *Daily Mirror* – I consider it to be full of cheap patriotism! What a hero it makes of any stripling who shoots a German however treacherously. It has a crude notion of heroism.

Eva Slawson, Diaries, 17 September 1914

COMPULSORY JABS

Our party had its first casualty, Roland Ellis being down with a chill or influenza. After he spent an uncomfortable day in the tent, his brother lodged a respectful but firm protest, and got permission to remove him to a private room at Aldershot.

This, of course, was a special favour; an ordinary private would have been kept in the camp until dangerously ill …

In the afternoon we had our turn in the local swimming bath – an unsavoury business – and later on were inoculated for enteric.* This operation is similar to [a] vaccination, and affects different men in different degrees. Irritation of the arm and occasional sickness may be expected for about two days.

The inoculation was not compulsory, but we were warned that those refusing would almost certainly be sent down to the 7th Battalion, which consists chiefly of undesirables, and will probably never be of very much use …

George Butterworth, Diaries, 18 September 1914

* *This was a vaccination against typhoid or intestinal infections.*

⌖

HALF A YEAR AT THE MOST

Lunched with Ball and Charles Hobhouse at [the] Athenaeum [Hotel]. Ball told me Lord Rothschild says he cannot think the Germans can stand the financial strain more than another six months.

John Bailey, Diaries, 23 September 1914

⌖

CATCHING MINES

We are spending another quiet week-end at W-on-Sea. I am sitting on the front at West Bay in the most glorious sunshine, cloudless sky, and the sea like a lake. One can hardly believe that we are actually facing the wicked North Sea, which is so full of mines. The only thing to remind one of it is the little feel of black, mysterious 'Mine-catchers' that anchor close in shore, and go forth every night to net in the cruel mines …

Mrs Hallie Eustace Miles, *Untold Tales of War-time*, 26 September 1914

LEARNING THE ART OF SOLDIERING

I got my uniform this morning – at least, coat and trousers; caps are still unattainable. The trousers are new, but the coat has had a good deal of wear and all the buttons needed sewing on, in addition to which I had the pleasurable task of sewing on my stripes.

Yesterday we were inspected by the King in the morning, in the afternoon I began to learn semaphore with the regimental sergeant-major, and in the evening bayonet fighting. It is extraordinary what a lot there is to learn about pigsticking one's fellow men. I am bad at it …

Frederic 'Ben' Keeling, Letter to Mrs Townsend, 27 September 1914

MISSING IN ACTION

A friend of mine, whose son is in one of the cavalry regiments, sat with me at lunch the other day, when a general from the War Office came up and condoled him on the loss of his son. The young officer was reported 'missing', and that is, perhaps, the worst feature of any casualty list, because a missing man may be wounded, lying for days in an open field or ditch, without having been found, and finally dying of sheer exhaustion or starvation or thirst or all of them. The father flinched when the news of the boy's disappearance was told him, and that afternoon the boy's name appeared in the casualty list as 'missing'. He seems to have been missing for a week, and my friend got home that afternoon to find a letter from his son's army bankers stating that they had received a letter from him asking them to forward some money to a place in Germany where he was a prisoner. The Germans did not allow the boy to write home to his parents, but had no objection to his getting money from his bankers. It is difficult to understand how the letter got through except through some underground arrangement.

R. D. Blumenfeld, Diaries, 29 September 1914

⁓

WORK CONQUERS WORRY

The most terrible day since the war began. The fall of Antwerp! I managed to pull myself together and do a little more Carducci; reading an Aristo[tle] book for [the] *Times*. It is best to do one's daily work and not sit over newspapers all day.

John Bailey, Diaries, 10 October 1914

⁓

THE GERMAN MENACE

Looked in at Devonshire House to see D. about motors. London agog between German waiters and Zeppelins.* The Admiralty have charge of air guarding. Some apprehension that while Zeppelins may do some damage, Winston shells in pursuit may do more …

All the Germans in Hotel Restaurants having been discharged, there are 2,000 of them unemployed in and about Shaftesbury Avenue.

Viscount Sandhurst, *From Day to Day*, 22 October 1914

Named after their inventor, Count von Zeppelin, a retired German army officer, these cigar-shaped manned, aluminium-framed airships were filled with highly flammable hydrogen, and although they could travel at up to 85 mph and carry up to 2 tonnes of bombs, they were often at the mercy of weather conditions.

BUYING BUTTONHOLE FLAGS

Loitered at a dirty little Fleet Street bookshop where Paul de Kock's *The Lady [The Girl] with the Three Pairs of Stays* was displayed prominently beside a picture of Oscar Wilde.

In Fleet Street, you exchange the Whitechapel sausage restaurants for Taverns with 'snacks at the bar', and the chestnut roasters, with their buckets of red-hot coals, for Grub Street camp followers, selling *L'Independance Beige* or pamphlets entitled, 'Why We Went to War'.

In the Strand you may buy war maps, buttonhole flags, etc., etc. I bought a penny stud ...

W. N. P. Barbellion, *The Journal of a Disappointed Man*, 24 October 1914

OFF, READY OR NOT

Today we have been instructed to hold ourselves in readiness to go abroad on Friday, Oct 30. Not being anywhere near ready the message is rather sarcastic; we have damaged rifles, many men are short of clothing and equipment. Headquarters is in confusion, lots of us are recruits, and the rest are imperfectly trained. I never saw so incompetent a set of officers or such a pathetic waste of good material.

Robert Scott Macfie, Letter to his family, 27 October 1914

WARSHIPS OFF YARMOUTH

The amazing news greeted us this morning that German warships had been within a few miles of Yarmouth, dropping bombs and mines which shook the windows of the homes ...

Eva Slawson, Diaries, 4 November 1914

CHILD'S PLAY

The children got up an amusing charade for us. They came into the drawing-room dressed up, Craufurd as the Kaiser, with formidable moustaches; Edward as 'Gussie', the Empress; Catherine as the Crown Prince with a pickelhaube; Paula looking very pretty in a crimson dressing gown and a red cap. She strutted up and down before the mirror admiring herself. Craufurd began, 'I have come to say that I must make peace; I have been losing too many of my men. I am sorry I plunged into this war.' 'Very well, Kaiser, but you must build again all the houses and churches you have burnt.' 'I can't put back Reims Cathedral; there is too much fine work in it.' Then followed a harlequinade between Willy and Gussie, the little girls dancing about with glee. It was a very pretty sight.

Rev. W. R. Inge, *Diary of a Dean*, 5 November 1914

WAR POEMS

I don't care what you do with my war poem. I don't particularly care if I don't hear of it any more. The war is dreadful. It is the business of the artist to follow it home to the hearts of individual fighters – not to talk in armies and nations and numbers – but to track it home …

D. H. Lawrence, Letter to Harriet Monroe, 17 November 1914

FAR FROM HOME

I have just been to a Belgian 'At Home' in a schoolroom. It was got up by a young wife whose husband is at the front, and her only comfort is trying to cheer the poor refugees. So she has these little 'At Homes' every week for lonely Belgians … I heard the Belgian National Hymn for the first time. There was a sweet refrain which everyone joined in; some of the older Belgians sang it with streaming eyes, and such a far-away look in their eyes. One knew that they were seeing their old homes, and many other things besides. Two little Belgian girls danced so prettily, and their young brother played the accompaniment; the proud (very fat) parents insisted on going on the platform too! It was all most interesting and touching …

Mrs Hallie Eustace Miles, *Untold Tales of War-time*, 5 December 1914

FIRST ZEPPELIN RAID

It is a specially anxious time just now. Last night there was a German raid on the East Coast by Zeppelins and Aeroplanes. They attacked Yarmouth and King's Lynn, and even Sandringham. There have been several killed by the cruel bombs. So we are on the tip-toe of expectancy that they will continue these visits, and try hard to get to London. Such awful things are prophesied; it makes one's heart stand still to hear of all that may be going to happen to our beloved England …

We have to be prepared to fly to our basements, and have candles ready, and 'lamps trimmed', like the wise Virgins; for at the first sign of a raid over London all the gas and electric light will be turned off at the mains, and everything will be in pitch darkness …

Mrs Hallie Eustace Miles, *Untold Tales of War-time*, 26 January 1915

⌐*%*⌐

MAN'S MILITARISM

I have been reading the newspaper today. I feel so indignant at the suggestion that children should be taken from school and put to work on the land. If this is done, I can see many old battles for reform will have to be fought over again, and it is all because of this terrible war – to suit man's militarism! Also, it is suggested women should work upon the land. So we may take a share when the world is at war, but in time of peace we are not considered worthy of political freedom!

Eva Slawson, Diaries, 29 January 1915

⌐*%*⌐

AN AEROPLANE OVER THE SUSSEX DOWNS

On the Downs on Friday I opened my eyes again, and saw it was daytime. And I saw the sea lifted up and shining like a blade with the sun on it. And high up, in the icy wind, an aeroplane flew towards us from the land – and the men ploughing and the boys in the fields on the table-lands, and the shepherds, stood back from their work and lifted their faces. And the aeroplane was small and high, in the thin, ice-cold wind. And the birds became silent and dashed to cover, afraid of the noise. And the aeroplane floated high out of sight. And below, on the level earth away down, were floods and stretches of snow, and I knew I was awake. But as yet my soul is cold and shaky and earthy.

I don't feel so hopeless now I am risen. My heart has been as cold as a lump of dead earth, all this time, because of the War. But now I don't feel so dead. I feel hopeful. I couldn't tell you how fragile and tender this hope is – the new shoot of life. But I feel hopeful now about this War. We should all rise again from this grave – though the killed soldiers will have to wait for the last trump.

D. H. Lawrence, Letter to Lady Cynthia Asquith, 30 January 1915

WRETCHED NIETZSCHE

A slight attack of 'flu' is bowling me over. There is a glimpse of sun. The trees look as though they were hanging out to dry. My cold gained on me all day. I read the lonely Nietzsche; but I felt a bit ashamed of my feelings for this man in the past. He is, if you like, 'human, all too human'. Read until late, I felt wretched simply beyond words. Life was like sawdust and sand. Talked stories to J.

Katherine Mansfield, Journals, 1 February 1915

WOMEN PREACHERS

I heard a woman preach & take the service to-day at Manchester College Chapel – the Unitarian place. It made me wish that women were allowed to do this in other churches instead of having the brainless & callow that are put into the Church because their parents know they will be unfit for everything else.

Vera Brittain, *Chronicle of Youth*, 7 February 1915

SCENES FROM THE FRONT

I went up to the Scala Theatre to see some war pictures really taken at manoeuvres. A long talk with the manager – he showed me all the machinery, very interesting. All the apparatus is close to the entrance and behind the audience in a masonry box – two men to work it.

Viscount Sandhurst, *From Day to Day*, 19 February 1915

ENTERTAINING THE TROOPS

I am taking my dear 'Loyal Choir' to help entertain 200 soldiers and officers who are being given a dinner at the Westminster Palace Hotel before they go out to the Front ...

Our Patriotic Tea was packed on Thursday last. We had beautiful Entertainments, helped by many professionals ... A good many wounded soldiers were there as our guests. One lady bought up all the shirts at the 'Women's Emergency' Stall, and gave the soldiers one each.

Mrs Hallie Eustace Miles, *Untold Tales of War-time*, 28 February 1915

*

WOUNDED ON BOGNOR PIER

Monica has a motor-car every day to drive her out, so we go too. To-day we drove to Bognor ... I saw a soldier on the pier, with only one leg. He was young and handsome and strangely self-conscious, and slightly ostentatious but confused. As yet, he does not realise anything, he is still in shock. And he is strangely roused by the women, who seem to have a craving for him. They look at him with eyes of longing, and they want to talk to him ...

So they are making a Coalition government. I cannot tell you how icy cold my heart is with fear. It is as if we were all going to die ...

D. H. Lawrence, Letter to Lady Ottoline Morrell, March 1915

*

POOR PROSPECTS IN ASHFORD

We are here for an indefinite time – billets very comfortable, other prospects poor. No progress whatsoever to report, except that we are now khaki clad.

These strikes are a nuisance, and I see there is a small one of the NER [North East Railways]. Personally, I should do three things –

1. Hang (or bayonet) all employers whose profits show an increase on previous year.

2. Imprison for duration of the war all those who organize cessation of labour in important industries.

3. Make Lord Robert Cecil* dictator for [the] duration of war, as being the only man in Parliament who has anything useful to say.

George Butterworth, Diaries, 5 March 1915

Lord Robert Cecil was a Conservative politician, diplomat and peace activist who was to serve as Minister of Blockade in the latter part of the war.

⁓

DEATH AT THE FRONT

While talking to Agnes, Dossie came in very pale. 'There is a rumour Will is killed,' and then, almost directly after, she said it was true.

Felt bowled over. Somehow it is absolutely unbelievable; the greatest blow in the whole war, and by far the greatest loss. Darling Will, and think that it is death that has revealed him fully to us. Tragic and piteous beyond all words. Gerty's heart was broken when he went. Now she is still and gentle and striving for resignation to the will of God.*

Mary Gladstone, Diaries, 15 April 1915

William Glynne Charles Gladstone was the last of four generations of Gladstones to serve in the House of Commons. The second Member of Parliament to be killed in action during the First World War, he was killed, aged just twenty-nine, by a German sniper near Laventie, in France, on 13 April 1915. With the special permission of the King and Parliament, Gladstone's body was exhumed and brought back from France for burial at home. But his was the last body to be repatriated during the war, his case prompting Major Fabian Ware to secure an order banning all future repatriations.

MURDEROUS PHASE

The War is entering upon a very serious phase; one knew that with Spring and better weather a terrible struggle would have to take place, and it is taking place. It is too awful to read of the Germans using bombs with asphyxiating gases for our brave men. It isn't fighting, it is murder ...

Mrs Hallie Eustace Miles, *Untold Tales of War-time*, 25 April 1915

SINKING OF THE *LUSITANIA*

I spent a day motoring with an officer on 'sick leave' up through Glen Coe – where snow still lay deep in the gullies – across a howling waste to Tyndrum, Loch Lomond, and Inveraray; back to Loch Awe. We went through a hundred miles of the most beautiful part of the Highlands, and so far as we could see the whole world was at peace. I don't think either of us gave a thought to the war until we got back to our hotel and heard the first rumour that the *Lusitania* had been sunk.

What unspeakable devils they are. But after their diabolical chlorine gas attacks can one really be surprised at anything they do now? When they advertised in New York that they were going to sink the L., I was so convinced that they meant to do it that I offered odds of ten to one on their attempt.*

A. F. R. Wollaston, *Letters and Diaries*, 7 May 1915

---

* *The* Lusitania, *a British liner that the Germans believed was carrying munitions, was torpedoed off the coast of Ireland by a U-boat. Before it sailed from New York, the German government had placed advertisements in American newspapers warning that the ship would be regarded as a legitimate target and that neutral US citizens should avoid sailing on it. Its sinking would serve only to increase anti-German sentiment both in Britain and the US.*

A POET'S PREMATURE DEATH

Rupert Brooke's death seems a peculiarly tragic episode. I have felt it more as we started soldiering together when the war broke out. It has intensified my conviction that I shall not come back – or rather my expectation – for the feeling has no rational basis and I can imagine myself analysing it with interest after the war. Still, it is there. I wonder if most men who think and have not been accustomed to face Death before have it when they go on active service.

Frederic 'Ben' Keeling, Letter to E. S. P. Haynes, 9 May 1915

GERMAN SHOPS ATTACKED

The rioting in E. London continued with great violence today – any German shops being wrecked and in some cases any with a foreign name; Russians and Belgians suffered. Porters and carriers at Smithfield have joined in the boycott, one supposed to have declared he wouldn't move a German meal if a carcass was hung round with diamonds; German butchers', bakers' and tobacconists' shops demolished and looted; troops and 30,000 special constables called out and a great deal of scuffling and many heads broken with batons; one German ducked in a horse trough at Smithfield …

Rumours that the Germans in London are to set up a-light – and indeed after and since the *Lusitania* the public nerve has been very much on the stretch.

Viscount Sandhurst, *From Day to Day*, 12 May 1915

INTERNMENT OF GERMANS

I heard the Prime Minister in the House of Commons this evening announcing the Government's new plan for the treatment of Germans in this country.

Naturalised subjects of enemy origin, numbering about 8,000, are to be left at liberty, unless there is a sufficient reason for internment in individual cases. Male enemy aliens of military age, seventeen to fifty-five, are to be interned. Males over the military age, and women and children, are, in suitable cases, to be repatriated ...

Several Members in all quarters of the House urged more dramatic measures should be taken against naturalised Germans, especially those 'in high places' from whom, they argued, the greater danger was to be apprehended. Asquith, however, refused to treat all naturalised aliens as spies and enemies ... Even the majority of the aliens who were not naturalised were, he believed, decent, honest people. To initiate a vendetta against them would be, he contended, not only disgraceful from the moral point of view, but impolitic from the point of view of the country's best interests.

The prevailing atmosphere of the House was anything but calm. Members of all parties were in so great a rage even against naturalised Germans that they were foaming at the mouth.

There is a scarcity of bread in parts of the East End of London where German bakers have been rooted out by the process of their shops being pillaged and wrecked ... A publican named 'Strachan' – an old Scottish name – was taken to be German and had his windows smashed.

Michael MacDonagh, *The Diary of a Journalist*, 13 May 1915

DISPATCHED TO THE FRONT

It is a queer thing that I should have found the social and emotional environment that suits me best in the Army. I wonder if I could ever find a family an adequate substitute for a regiment. If I do come back from the war I shall want to keep up a bit of soldiering as long as I can. I feel as if I couldn't live for evermore without bugle calls. They have eaten into my soul.

Of course, I have experienced all the advantages of war for nine months. Now I come up against the horrors ...

Frederic 'Ben' Keeling, Letter to Miss Eva Spielmann, 15 May 1915

NEW LITERARY VOICES

'Georgian Poets.'* It is a pity that these promising young writers adopted such a title. The use of it lacks the modesty of true genius, as it confused the poetic chronology, and implies that the hitherto recognised original Georgians – Shelley, Keats, Wordsworth, Byron, etc. – are negligible; or at any rate says that they do not care whether it implies such or no.

Thomas Hardy, Diaries, 27 May 1915

* *Counting Rupert Brooke, Walter de la Mare and Edward Thomas among their number and adopting their name following the coronation of George V in 1911, the Georgians as a literary movement stressed the importance of lyric and took inspiration from nature and the countryside.*

✐

PAGEANT FOR WOMEN IN MUNITIONS

For the first time since the outbreak of the War the streets of London were brightened to-day with colour and beauty. It was a dramatic and very moving procession of women through the West End offering Lloyd George, who has been appointed to the specially created office of Minister of Munitions in the National Government, the help of women in the making of war materials and other forms of national work. The organisers were Mrs Pankhurst and the other ladies who were prominent in the late Suffragette agitation – that militant movement for the franchise in which women displayed such amazing audacity, resourcefulness and exuberance.

As for the procession to-day, it included a 'Pageant of the Allies' … The place of honour was given to Belgium. The soul of that martyred but unconquerable land was vividly typified by a tall, slender lady dressed in mourning, with a purple veil bound around her head and flowing in a long streamer behind … She walked barefoot through the slush of the roadways – heavy rain having fallen earlier – and on her delicately chiselled face there was an expression of pride and sorrow and devotion, all of a high degree ...

Michael MacDonagh, The Diary of a Journalist, 17 July 1915

A NURSE DEPARTS

The day has come at last. After a week of rushing and scrambling feeling certain that I should never be ready, Monday morning has arrived. Boxes are packed, the last strap is buckled and we are really ready ...

Our train leaves Paddington at 10.30 ... We ran down to Plymouth very quickly, there they shunted our bit of the train and it took us about another hour to run round to the docks at Devonport. There were lots of boats there. Transports, battleships in for repairs – oh, such grim-looking things. Coming along through the peaceful country, it seemed impossible to realize that there really was this fiendish war going on but now it was brought home to us ...

We came back on deck & had a very welcome cup of tea, sorted out our luggage & had what we wanted taken down to our cabins. The cabins are very small, there is just room for our holdalls underneath the berths, our cushions, rugs and clothes have to live on the end of our berths when we are asleep and we can only dress two at a time. There are 80 Sisters on board (the greatest number that has ever gone out together), 400 officers (169 of which are RAMC [Royal Army Medical Corps]) & I think about 1,100 men. Nobody knows where they are going to, but there are rumours that we are going to a small island much nearer the Dardanelles than Alexandria. I wonder if it is true. Things seemed to be rather at sixes and sevens ...

Florence Oppenheimer, Diaries, 19 July 1915

THE PAVILION GOES TO WAR

The sailing-crafts which crowd the beach at Brighton look strangely unfamiliar. The names by which they were distinguished, such as *My Pretty Jane, Old Bob Riley, The Prairie Flower* – recalling the popular songs of long ago – have all disappeared, and in their place are figures coldly abstract and unsuggestive. By order of the Authorities, the boats have been registered and numbered. Whatever the reason for the change, it can hardly have been that the names and their associations were thought to be too frivolous in war-time even for Brighton – hitherto so gay and irresponsible. As the official numbers are painted in large and distinctive figures, one surmises that it has been done so that the boats might be identified from a distance out at sea ...

Several base hospitals have been established in the neighbourhood for Indians as well as for British soldiers. There could be no better testimony to the healing and recuperating qualities of its air ... Brighton has willingly given up the one unique building it possesses. That is the Pavilion, with its fantastic domes and minarets, which recall the beginnings of Brighton as a holiday resort in the days of the Regency. The place, with its lawns and gardens, is now shut in by a high wooden fence. It has become a hospital for the Indian soldiers. The Eastern and bizarre aspect of the Pavilion must have afforded a very incongruous contrast with the fine ladies and gentlemen who accompanied the Regent on his visits. Now, at least, by a strange turn of events, the fantasies of the Pavilion and its uses have become harmonised. It is quite a thrilling experience to see in the grounds dusky and turbaned Oriental warriors nursing wounds received in a war of European nations.*

Michael MacDonagh, *The Diary of a Journalist*, 20 July 1915

* *Over 1.3 million Indian soldiers served in the First World War, with some 74,000 losing their lives fighting in the conflict across Europe, Mesopotamia, and North and East Africa.*

LOVE ON LEAVE

I found Roland playing about with his papers in my room.

I looked out of the window to the sea below and asked him to take me down to it … We walked along the beach & sat down on the end of a breakwater a few yards from where the waves were breaking. For a while I said nothing, but looked out across the water and listened to the soothing lullaby of its eternal song. I felt then that I could ask for nothing better of life than to sit there for ever with the sound of the sea in my ears and Roland standing on the beach beside me.

At last we began to talk a little – quite tentatively – about the engagement.

In a minute or two he offered to show me the trenches on the grass plain …

He told me they were just the same as those on the front. The parapet was well above his head, & the ground all boarded. He explained to me various technical details, such as the use of periscopes, ways of taking cover from shells, the difference between fire trenches & reserve & communication trenches etc. He told me the French had a habit of burying a dead man in his dug-out by just putting him inside and blocking up the entrance …

Roland told me that every day in the trenches he was accustomed to pass by the foot of a dead man who had been buried in the parapet. By this time the foot had become quite black, but he saw it every day & thought nothing of it. I asked him if he thought this callousness was a permanent thing & meant the loss of sensitiveness ever after. He said he did not think so; it was an acquired necessity in war …

Vera Brittain, *Chronicle of Youth*, 22 August 1915

OMNIBUSES BLOWN TO BITS

My first experience of a Zeppelin raid. Bombs dropped only a quarter of a mile away and shrapnel from the guns fell on our roof …

A great fire is burning in London, judging by the red glare. At midnight sat and drank sherry and smoked a cigar with Mr – my braces descending from my trousers like a tail and shewing in spite of [my] dressing-gown. Then went home and had some neat brandy to steady my heart. H. arrived soon after midnight. A motor-omnibus in Whitechapel was blown to bits. Great scenes in the city.

W. N. P. Barbellion, *The Journal of a Disappointed Man*, 8 September 1915

◌✿◌

'WAKE UP, LONDON!'

Explosions and counter-explosions of the agitation for and against conscription are being heard daily in London.

Meanwhile, nothing is being left undone to keep voluntary recruiting alive. To-day there was a 'monster recruiting rally', in which five columns of Regulars and Territorials, each twelve hundred strong, started from five different centres, north, south, east, and west led by bands.

I accompanied one of the columns on its entire march through the City, along Holborn and Oxford Street, and up Tottenham Court Road to Camden Town. 'Wake up, London!' was the motto of the rally. It certainly caused a great stir everywhere. In its widespread influence it was the most remarkable recruiting demonstration that London has ever seen.

Michael MacDonagh, *The Diary of a Journalist*, 2 October 1915

◌✿◌

ORDER OF THE WHITE FEATHER

New but unofficial recruiters have appeared on the scene. These are the young women who have formed what they call the 'Order of the White Feather', which they publicly and forcibly confer upon any young man in 'civies' whom they come upon anywhere, and whom they think should be in khaki ...

Going home in a tramcar the other night I was a witness of the presentation of white feathers. The victims were two young men who were rudely disturbed from their reading of the evening paper by the attack of three young women.

'Why don't you fellows enlist? Your King and Country want you. We don't.' One of the girls was a pretty wench. She dishonoured one of the young men, as she thought, by sticking a white feather in his buttonhole, and a look of contempt spoiled for a moment her lovely face.

Those tactics seem to me to be uncomprehending. Those who use them assume that all men are alike; mere machines that can march so many miles an hour and fire so many rounds of ammunition – only some are 'shirkers' evading their duty as citizens. No allowance appears to be made to the infinite variety of constitution, temperament, emotion, disposition, and of idiosyncrasies among men. Fundamentally speaking, Nature makes heroes or cowards from us first, in our mother's womb, without in the least consulting us.

Michael MacDonagh, *The Diary of a Journalist*, 6 October 1915

ON NIGHT WATCH

An emergency call came and the result was that I was standing by a lamp-post in Queen's Gate at 1.15 a.m. It was a lovely night of stars and I read some poetry in the intervals of talking to policemen and others. I saw no Zeppelin and heard nothing after the distant guns at 3.30. I only saw some flashes in the sky, like fireworks without any scattering of sparks, quite silent.

John Bailey, Diaries, 13 October 1915

INDECENT NOVEL SUPPRESSED

More tiresomeness is that a magistrate has suppressed the sale of *The Rainbow*, and Methuen's [an English publishing house] under orders to deliver up all existing copies. This is most irritating. Some interfering person goes to the police magistrate and says, 'This book is indecent, listen here.' Then the police magistrate says, 'By Jove, we'll stop that.' Then the thing is suppressed. But I think it is possible to have the decision reversed.*

D. H. Lawrence, Letter to Lady Cynthia Asquith, 9 November 1915

* *Lawrence's* The Rainbow, *which featured emotionally frank portrayals of sex out of marriage and a lesbian affair, was seized and suppressed under the 1857 Obscene Publications Act. The prosecutor in the trial, Herbert Muskett, declared: 'Although there might not be an obscene word to be found in the book, it was in fact a mass of obscenity of thought, idea, and action.' The judge, Sir John Dickinson, was of the same mind; in his summing-up he said the book had 'no right to exist in the wind of war'. A hangman was then employed to publicly burn 1,011 copies of the book outside the Royal Exchange in London.*

AWAITING A SOLDIER'S RETURN

It does not feel at all like Christmas Eve on which I am writing this, although Mrs Leggatt & I spent nearly all night filling the soldiers' red bags, which we made, with crackers, sweets and nuts. But if I have not the Christmas feeling, there is at least joy in my heart; I can think of nothing else but the probability of seeing him in two days' time. For I cannot, dare not, call it certainly yet – dare not even allow myself to feel thrilled.

Vera Brittain, *Chronicle of Youth*, 24 December 1915

SYMPATHY FROM LORD KITCHENER

I had just finished dressing when a message came to say that there was a telephone message for me; I sprang up joyfully, thinking to hear in a moment the dear dreamed-of tones of the beloved voice.

But the telephone message was not from Roland but from Clare; it was not to say that Roland had arrived, but instead had come this telegram:

'T223. Regret to inform you that Lieut. R. A. Leighton 7th Worcesters died of wounds on December 23rd. Lord Kitchener sends his sympathy.'

Vera Brittain, *Chronicle of Youth*, 27 December 1915

PALACE INTERNMENT CAMP

To-day I visited Alexandra Palace, those extensive buildings and grounds in North London, where close on a thousand civilian prisoners of war, males of military age, are interned. They are German subjects who lived and carried on their avocations in London … Most of those at Alexandra Palace are waiters, barbers, cooks, bakers and tailors. There are also several who held responsible positions as hotel managers and commercial agents …

Wives and children may visit the Palace once a week. British-born wives of the interned are paid sustenance allowance by the State. On the whole, the prisoners seem comfortable and contented – as well they may.

Michael MacDonagh, The Diary of a Journalist, 28 December 1915

∽

WHAT A DIFFERENCE A YEAR MAKES

This time last year he was seeing me off on Charing Cross station after David Copperfield – and I had just begun to realise I loved Him. He is lying in the military cemetery at Louvencourt – because a week ago He was wounded in action and had just 24 hours of consciousness more and then went 'to sleep in France'. And I, who in impatience felt a fortnight ago that I could not wait another minute to see Him, must wait till all Eternity. All has been given me, and all taken away again – in one year.

So I wonder where we shall be – what we shall all be doing – if we all still shall be – this time next year.

Vera Brittain, Chronicle of Youth, 31 December 1915

∽

A WAR-TIME DIET

I am living like a rabbit, or more accurately, like Adam and Eve, on the living herbs and fruits of the earth. I began dropping butcher's meat about 15 December, eating sometimes an apple or a banana, sometimes an egg, for breakfast.

Mary Gladstone, Diaries, 1 January 1916

POEM FROM A PACIFIST

Really I cannot kill the so-called Hun;
My conscience bids me conflict rude to shun
What though he bayonets children, poisons wells
and tramples peaceful cities into hell? –
He is my brother ...

Anonymous, Letter to the *Daily Express*, 12 January 1916

SETTING THE STANDARDS TOO HIGH

The extension of the Military Service Act to unmarried men is causing scarcely a ripple on the surface of public life! What an unexpected and happy outcome of all the predictions of trouble that were indulged in during the progress of the measure through the House of Commons! ... The hordes of 'come-and-fetch me', which the Labour leaders, Thomas and Snowden, spoke of, making the Treasury bench shiver with apprehension, have proved to be phantoms.

What has happened is that the tribunals set up by the Act for the hearing of claims for exemption from service are being encumbered and clogged with work.

At the City Tribunal, Guildhall, I was told that twenty thousand claims for exemption have already been lodged. While I was there a clerk claimed exemption on the grounds that he had offered himself for enlistment in the Territorials three times, and on each occasion was rejected for defective eyesight. Major de Rothschild, the military representative, said it was no longer a disqualification for the Army: 'It does not matter how short-sighted he is; so long as he is physically fit to wield a bayonet he is fit for service abroad.' ... Speaking to Major de Rothschild afterwards I was informed that the standard of physical fitness has been considerably lowered, and that men who were exempted for medical reasons are now being called up for re-examination. The original standard was, in fact, too high ...

Michael MacDonagh, *The Diary of a Journalist*, 15 March 1916

SISTER SPIRITS

A week ago I was beguiled into going to a small Sale of Work, got up by Friends in aid of a Belgian fund, and there met a girl who has come to York as recently as myself to take up professional gardening.

Our hearts went out to each other at once, and last Wednesday I went to tea with her at her lodgings. In my painfully conventional and ugly clothes I felt ashamed, and fearful lest she should fail to recognise a sister spirit, but we did really meet and know one another ...

Yesterday she came to me. It was a perfect day – the scents and sounds of spring were in the air and the sun shone bright and warm, though only a week ago a blizzard swept the country and we were nearly perished with the extreme cold. We went out for a walk in the afternoon and found some delightful meadows, in one of which we seated ourselves on the trunk of a fallen tree. I enjoyed her physical beauty too and loved to watch her boyish gestures. Such a lovely healthy face and figure; the face very delicate and intelligent. She was wearing a pretty, soft green hat, devoid of trimming and independent of hatpins, and ever anon she lifted it and passed her hand through her hair in a delightfully expressive manner ... She came to my lodgings to tea, and in the evening we sat telling each other the story of our lives, and as I felt the beauty of her a wonderful sense of healing and comfort stole through me ...

Ruth Slate, Diaries, 3 April 1916

⌇⌇⌇

SOLDIER SENT TO QUELL THE EASTER RISING

Noon: Marched out from the Royal Hospital en route for Dublin Castle. All along the road, constant sniping was going on but the Royal Irish, by keeping up a constant fire in the direction of the snipers, prevented them from concentrating their fire on the column. We arrived at Dublin Castle without any casualties.

6 p.m.: 'D' Coy were ordered to proceed along Capel Street, Parnell Street to consolidate the position held by the Royal Irish. We moved out and, on crossing

the bridge over the river from Parliament Street, we came under heavy fire from the Sein Feinners. We proceeded up Capel Street and, on entering Parnell Street, at every cross street we were subjected to rifle fire from the enemy. On arrival at Moore Street, I was instructed to make a barricade right across the street.

Sgt. Maj. Samuel Lomas, Diaries, 27 April 1916

IRISH REPUBLICANS EXECUTED

We paraded at the time appointed, marched to Kilmainham Jail. At 3.45 the first rebel MacDonoghue [Thomas MacDonagh] was marched in blindfolded, and the firing party placed 10 paces distant. Death was instantaneous. The second, P. H. Pierce [Pádraig Pearse], whistled as he came out of the cell … The same applied to him. The third, J. H. Clarke [Tom Clarke], an old man, was not quite so fortunate, requiring a bullet from the officer to complete the ghastly business (it was sad to think that these three brave men who met their death so bravely should be fighting for a cause which proved so useless and had been the means of so much bloodshed).*

Sgt Maj. Samuel Lomas, Diaries, 3 May 1916

* *On Easter Monday 1916, a group of Irish nationalists staged a rebellion against the occupying British government in Ireland. Around 1,600 rebels seized strategic buildings in Dublin, most famously taking over the city's General Post Office. It was there that rebel leader Patrick Pearse proclaimed that Ireland was now an independent republic. Within a week, the British, having imposed a state of martial law, succeeded in suppressing the rebellion. The leaders were arrested and summarily executed by firing squads.*

STONE ME, AN EMINENT VICTORIAN

The statue of Florence Nightingale has been enclosed in a structure of laurel and a flat cake of yellow flowers put behind her head – meant for a halo but looking like an odd umbrageous hat. The attempts of the English to honour people are very infantile.

A. C. Benson, Diaries, 12 May 1916

⤳

AN IRISH FREEDOM FIGHTER IMPRISONED

A painful luncheon party: Mrs Green and Bernard Shaw to consult about the tragic plight of Roger Casement.* He has no money and only two relatives in England – cousins who are school teachers. On reaching London, with his Scotland Yard escort, he appealed to the only solicitor he knew, Charles Russell, who has a large Irish Catholic connection. Russell refused to defend him and sent his clerk to the Tower to tell him so.

Beatrice Webb, Diaries, 21 May 1916

---

* Born in Kingstown, County Dublin, Sir Roger Casement was a British consular official in Brazil and the Belgian Congo. He was knighted in 1911 for his report into the abuses suffered by Peruvian employees in the rubber industry. Horrified by the injustices of colonialism he had witnessed, he retired from the diplomatic service in 1913 and dedicated himself to the cause of Irish nationalism. This led him to pursue German support and guns for an Irish rebellion against the British. On his return from a trip to Germany in April 1916, he was arrested and imprisoned in the Tower of London; he was found guilty of high treason on 29 June 1916. A campaign for a reprieve, organized by George Bernard Shaw among others, was scuppered after passages from Casement's so-called Black Diaries *were circulated and his homosexuality was revealed. He was stripped of his title and executed on 3 August 1916.*

THE BATTLE OF JUTLAND

This morning in bed I heard a man with a milkcart say in the road to a villager at about 6.30 a.m., … 'battle … and we lost six cruisers'.

This was the first I knew of the Battle of Jutland. At 8 a.m. I read in the *Daily News* that the British Navy had been defeated, and thought it was the end of all things. The news took away our appetites …*

W. N. P. Barbellion, *The Journal of a Disappointed Man*, 3 June 1916

* *The British Grand Fleet and the German High Seas Fleet fought for over thirty-six hours off Denmark's Jutland peninsula in this battle, which is deemed to be the largest surface battle in naval history due to the number of battleships and battlecruisers engaged.*

DEATH OF KITCHENER

Came to London Tuesday morning for the Wounded Allies 'War Fair' at the Caledonian Market. Heavy shower. Great success. I sold books at M.'s stall.

News of Kitchener's drowning came at noon on first day. His sister Mrs Parker was at M.'s stall, but she left before it came. The rumour in the afternoon that Kitchener was saved roused cheers, again and again.*

Arnold Bennett, Journals, 8 June 1916

* *Kitchener had sailed from Orkney for Russia aboard the HMS* Hampshire, *an armoured cruiser, on a secret mission to bolster support for the tsar in the war. Unfortunately, the* Hampshire *hit a mine and sank on 5 June 1916. Only twelve survived. The Secretary of State for War was not, contrary to early reports, one of them.*

THE BATTLE OF THE SOMME

Not very optimistic about the big push, which began last Saturday.* Was told that [the] Minister's secretary has seen a telegram, and remarked to the effect that troops had once more overrun the points at which they had been ordered to stop. I didn't hear at what point or points this occurred.

Arnold Bennett, Journals, 6 July 1916

Having shelled the German trenches in northern France for seven days, on 1 July 1916 around 100,000 men were sent over the top in the Somme offensive. In total, 19,240 men were killed, mowed down by machine and rifle fire. It was the single bloodiest day in the history of the British army. The Battle of the Somme was to last 141 days, with total casualties numbering over 1 million on both sides.

A GREAT WAR?

This War is so great and terrible that hyperbole is impossible. And yet my gorge rises at those fatuous journalists continually pratting about this 'Greatest War of all time', this 'Great Drama', this 'world catastrophe unparalleled in human history', because it is easy to see that they are really more thrilled than shocked by the immensity of the War. They indulge in a vulgar Yankee admiration for the Big Thing. Why call this shameful Filth by high-sounding phrases – as if it were a tragedy from Euripides? We ought to hush it up, not brag about it, to mention it with a blush instead of spurting it out brazen-faced.

The War is everything; it is noble, filthy, great, petty, degrading, inspiring, ridiculous, glorious, mad, bad, hopeless yet full of hope. I don't know what to think about it.

W. N. P. Barbellion, The Journal of a Disappointed Man, 31 July 1916

FIGHTING FOR ... THIS

Lying in a hospital train on his way to London he looks out at the hot August landscape of Hampshire, the flat green and dun-coloured fields, the advertisements of Lung Tonic and Liver Pills, the cows-neat villas and sluggish waterways – all these came on him in an irritable delight, at the pale gold of the wheat-field and the faded green of the hazy muffled woods on the low hills. People wave to the Red Cross train – grateful stay-at-homes – even a middle-aged man, cycling along a dusty road in straw hat and blue serge clothes, takes one hand off the handlebars to wave feeble and jocular gratitude. And the soul of the officer glows with fiery passion as he thinks, 'All this I've been fighting for, and now I'm safe home again I begin to think it was worth while.' And he wonders how he could avoid being sent out again.

Siegfried Sassoon, Diaries, 2 August 1916

༄

DRABNESS OF CIVILIAN LIFE

The drabness of civilians is very noticeable! What shabbiness in dress! A remarkable change in the point of view regarding clothes has set in. The cause is to be found on the walls and hoardings. Recruiting posters have been replaced by economy posters. 'Spend Less; Save More.' 'Buy only War Savings Certificates.' Accordingly it is the mode to assume a studied air of personal untidiness. The fashion among men of all classes is to wear hat, coat and trousers long – as long as possible, in time. The only short wear is the feminine skirt.

Women are to be seen at work everywhere. 'Men must fight and women must work – and weep.' You see them at the wheel of motor-cars and motor-drays ... The hall-porter at some of the big hotels is an Amazon in blue or mauve coat, gold-braided peaked cap and high top-boots – a gorgeous figure that fascinates me. But my favourite is the young 'conductorette' on trams and buses, in her smart jacket, short skirts to the knees and leather leggings.

Michael MacDonagh, *The Diary of a Journalist*, 7 August 1916

SWAPPING SERVICE FOR SHELLS

A lady tells me that a housemaid who has been in her service for many years and who was apparently comfortable in her well-appointed quarters, yesterday surprised her by giving the statutory 'month's notice'.

On enquiry she found the girl had obtained a situation in one of the shell factories. The weekly wage was attractively liberal, though probably as it did not include living expenses it was not appreciably in advance of what she had been receiving. But, as she explained, she was not thinking about the money. She was one of a considerable number of girls in her own station of life who had met together and talked the matter over. Moved by Lloyd George's impassioned appeals, they made up their minds to help their country and found no difficulty in obtaining engagements at shell factories …

Sir Henry Lucy, *The Diary of a Journalist*, 26 September 1916

✤

WOUNDED FROM YPRES

Clegg brought Capt. B. (of his Battery) to lunch. Had been out at Ypres ten months and then wounded in the head, in front of right ear. He carries a good scar. He talked well, and said he should like to write if he could. I told him he could.

He said the newspaper correspondents' descriptions of men eager to go over the parapet made him laugh. They never were eager. He related how he had seen a whole company of men extremely pale with apprehension and shaking so that [they] could scarcely load their rifles. Then he said that men who nevertheless did go over in that state were really brave. He told us how his battery saw hundreds, thousands of grey figures coming along only 1,000 yards off, and every man thought he would be a prisoner in ten minutes, when suddenly thousands of Canadians appeared from nowhere, and the Boches [Germans] fled. The cheering was delirious. He told me this very dramatically, but without any effort to be effective. He said he really wanted to be back with the battery. For a long time the fellows wrote to him regularly once a fortnight, and every letter ended with: 'When are you coming back?' …

Arnold Bennett, Journals, 9 October 1916

⁓

RESISTANCE TO PEACE

[W]e still hear from Germany: Frieda's mother, being old and feeling the twilight of death in the air, very sad and wanting only comfort and reassurance, but Frieda's sisters still resistant and rather ugly in spirit. I must say judging from these, I can't feel Germany wants peace yet, any more than England does. Their fulfilment is still in this ugly contending. But I think both countries are getting tired, emotionally tired. They won't be able to work up the fine frenzy of war much longer. The whole show is too nasty and contemptible, essentially.

D. H. Lawrence, Letter to Lady Cynthia Asquith, 11 November 1916

⁓

EXPLOSION IN THE EAST END

There has been a ghastly explosion at the Silvertown Munition Factory.* A 'Loyal Choir' practising was going on, when suddenly there was a rending cracking sound, like a bomb or a gun; naturally, we thought it was Zeppelins, and how we all flew downstairs, kitchen staff and all! But nothing more happened; only the whole place was filled with the most awful smell of gunpowder and gasses. We soon heard what it really was; and terrible news it was too.

Mrs Hallie Eustace Miles, Untold Tales of War-time, 11 November 1916

* *The accidental explosion of 50 tonnes of TNT at the Brunner Mond works in the East End's Silvertown district killed 73 people, injured another 500 and destroyed at least 900 houses while damaging thousands of others.*

WARTIME RESTRICTIONS

This morning on arriving at S. Kensington, went straight to a Chemist's shop, but finding someone inside, I drew back, and went on to another.

'Have you any morphia tabloids?' I asked a curly-haired, nice-looking, smiling youth, who leaned with both hands on the counter and looked at me knowingly, as if he had had unlimited experience of would-be morphinomaniacs.

'Yes, plenty of them,' he said, fencing. And then waited.

'Can you supply me?' I asked, feeling very conscious of myself.

He smiled once more, shook his head and said it was contrary to the Defence of the Realm Act.*

I made a sorry effort to appear ingenuous, and he said: 'Of course, it is only a palliative.'

With a solemn countenance intended to indicate pain, I answered: 'Yes, but palliatives are very necessary sometimes,' and I walked out of the hateful shop discomfited.

W. N. P. Barbellion, *The Journal of a Disappointed Man*, 3 February 1917

* *Introduced in August 1914, the Defence of the Realm Act (DORA) gave the government extensive executive powers, including the right to suppress criticism and commandeer economic resources for the war effort. Under its aegis, opening hours of pubs were cut and beer watered down. On 28 July 1916, it went further to criminalize the possession of opiates and other drugs by anyone not connected to the medical or veterinary professions.*

⸺

COMFORT THROUGH GUM

Food prices are leaping up. Woe to the unfit and the old and the poor in these coming days! We shall soon have nothing left in our pantries, and a piece of Wrigley's chewing gum will be our only comfort.

W. N. P. Barbellion, *The Journal of a Disappointed Man*, 10 March 1917

REVOLUTION IN RUSSIA

Can't say I am delighted at the Russian revolution. The fate of Russia is no interest whatever to me; but from the only point of view I am concerned about – the efficacy of the Alliance – I don't think it will be of any advantage to us.*

Joseph Conrad, Letter to Hugh R. Dent, 19 March 1917

* *Following strikes, mass demonstrations and riots in Petrograd over food and fuel shortages, Tsar Nicholas II was forced by the Russian Duma to abdicate. The Duma established a provisional government and among its first acts was to place the tsar and his family under house arrest. At this time, the provisional government, dominated by Minister of Justice Alexander Kerensky, remained committed to the alliance against Germany.*

⚛

COSTLY TEARS

Oh the loneliness, plus disharmony, of this life... I come up here – why write about it? The hideous nothing worthwhile-ism, the constant chill and repression. Oh my God, what is it, this disparity? Then like a fool [I] cried, making myself uglier than ever. You can't afford it at 50! After tea had a really truly real talk with Ernest, confided all my worry and work worries. It cleared the air between us. Met Mrs Moore in the afternoon. She is in the deepest hump. So's everybody. War, I suppose.

Mrs Henry Dudeney, *A Lewes Diary,* 21 March 1917

⚛

STRIKES ON TYNESIDE

Dined with Sir W. Weir (Director of Air Supply), Major Weir (Flying Staff, W.O.) and Richmond at the Savoy, after spending ½ hour in the Angelica Kaufmann room at Weir's flat.

They began to startle me right off. Weir and Richmond said that the labour situation was acutely bad. Tyne strike not better. Men out at Barrow, and men out at 3 or 4 small factories that worked for Weir. The strikes were not officially countenanced by Trades Unions; organisation alien (USA) working through shop stewards, etc. ...

The Government knew all about it, as the Trades Unions had told them everything as fast as they learnt it ...

Arnold Bennett, Journals, 24 March 1917

⟨𝓶⟩

IRELAND REBELS AGAIN?

Strange rumours on Saturday night. As that Ireland had revolted again and reserve Batteries were being sent from Woolwich to Ireland by special reserve trains. (Apparently quite untrue.) Also, that five German cruisers were 'lying off' Harwich. What the British Fleet was doing meanwhile was not explained. Many troops were undoubtedly drafted into this district, and on Sunday morning Liverpool Street was a pandemonium of returning officers summoned by wire, necessitating special trains.

Arnold Bennett, Journals, 26 March 1917

⟨𝓶⟩

ENCOUNTER WITH SASSOON

Siegfried Sassoon lunched with me at the Reform yesterday. He expected some decoration for admittedly fine bombing work. Colonel had applied for it three times, but [was] finally told that as that particular push was a failure it could not be granted. Sassoon was uncertain about accepting a home billet if he got the offer of one. I advised him to accept it. He is evidently one of the reckless ones. He said his pals said he always gave the Germans every chance to pot him. He said he would like to go out once more and give them another chance to get him, and come home unscathed. He seemed jealous for the military reputation of poets … He said most war was a tedious nuisance, but there were great moments and he would like them again.

Arnold Bennett, Journals, 9 June 1917

⌒◌⌒

WEST END REMAINS

This morning I saw remains of a German aeroplane being motored up Piccadilly.

Arnold Bennet, Journals, 14 June 1917

⌒◌⌒

FINISHED WITH WAR

I am making this statement as an act of wilful defiance of military authority, because I believe the war is being deliberately prolonged by those who have the power to end it.

I am a soldier, convinced that I am acting on behalf of soldiers. I believe that this war, upon which I entered as a war of defence and liberation has now become a war of aggression and conquest. I believe that the purposes for which I and my fellow soldiers entered upon this war should have been so clearly stated as to have made it impossible to change them, and that, had this been done, the objects which actuated us would now be attainable by negotiation.

I have seen and endured the suffering of the troops, and I can no longer be a party to prolong these sufferings for ends which I believe to be evil and unjust. I am not protesting against the conduct of the war, but against the political errors and insincerities for which the fighting men are being sacrificed.

On behalf of those who are suffering now I make this protest against the deception which is being practised on them; also, I believe that I may help to destroy the callous complacency with which the majority of those at home regard the continuance of agonies which they do not share, and which they have not sufficient imagination to realise.

Siegfried Sassoon, Letter to his commanding officer, 6 July 1917

Sassoon's letter was published in The Times on 31 July 1917

⸙

NEW HOUSE OF WINDSOR

The talk of the town is the Proclamation of King George published in the newspapers this morning, declaring that the name of House and Family, hitherto 'Hanover', is henceforth to be 'Windsor', and renouncing all German styles and titles for himself and other descendants of Queen Victoria. The Proclamation was signed at a meeting of the Privy Council held yesterday at Buckingham Palace.

This means a complete severance of the Royal Family from all associations with Germany. It is a matter of high national importance and historic interest …

Michael MacDonagh, *The Diary of a Journalist*, 18 July 1917

⸙

YORKSHIRE WEATHERING THE WAR WITH TYPICAL PHLEGM

It is odd how very much Whitby is changed from what I remember when I came here first. Today quite one-third of the houses on the West side are 'To Let' and closed. I fancy that the rest are either residential, or else are well stocked with visitors during the few holiday weeks – such as this is.

We went last night to see the old Abbey; the West Front is badly injured and the fine early-English doorway is partly in ruins (alas!) and the very interesting West window of the South aisle is in ruins. About fifty bombs fell, they say; the one that did this mischief fell near the W. front. Most of them fell on Abbey Farm (that early eighteenth-century Hall) and the grounds, and on the old lady's cottage who keeps the Abbey. She is eighty this year ...

Edward Lee Hicks, *The Life and Letters of*, 8 August 1917

TUBE SHELTERS

Dined with M. at Waldorf. To get there, strange journey in Tube. Very wet. Very poor women and children sitting on stairs (fear of a raid) ...

S. said he had seen dreadful sights of very poor with babies in Tube on Monday. One young woman was in labour. He asked her if she was and she said she was, and that she had got up because she was told to go with the rest. He got her taken on a stretcher to a hospital ...

Arnold Bennett, Journals, 27 September 1917

FRESH AIR ASSAULT

Yarned at the Reform Club with Harold Massingham, H. W. Massingham, Buckmaster etc.

Then to Turkish Baths.

I was wakened out of my after-bath sleep by news of impending air-raid. This news merely made me feel gloomy ... As soon as I got out to Northumberland Avenue I heard guns. Motors and people rushing. Then guns very close. I began to run. I headed for the Reform Club, and abandoned [the] idea of reaching the flat. Everybody ran ...

All clear at about 9.40.*

Arnold Bennett, Journals, 19 December 1917

* *On this night, five aeroplanes bombed London. Ten people were killed and over seventy injured.*

SHOPPING BOTHER

12.30 – Just back from futile shopping, no margarine, butter, tea or cheese. Ernest bland as usual trying to soothe. Mad with him. Told him he'd have to take his share of the bother.

Mrs Henry Dudeney, *A Lewes Diary*, 2 January 1918

PESSIMISTIC ABOUT PROSPECTS FOR PEACE

The new year opens in gloom. Germany is stronger and more successful relatively to the Allies than she has ever been since the first rush to Paris. The governing class of Britain is no longer certain of ultimate victory. The mass population is irritated by the scarcity of food in the shops; the propertied class is getting more and more frightened at the coming taxation in redemption of war debt, and always swelling demands of manual workers for equality of circumstances. Both sides are preparing for class war.

Litvinov, the Bolshevik 'ambassador', lunched with us on Wednesday … He is pessimistic about the Russian revolution … if European militarism does not destroy it, economic pressure will. When we asked him what was the alternative … he replied: 'We shall become a colony of the German empire.'*

Beatrice Webb, Diaries, 10 January 1918

---

* *In October, the Bolsheviks formed and deposed Russia's provisional government. Led by Vladimir Ilyich Ulyanov (Lenin), they had fought under the slogan of 'Peace, bread and land', and once in power they pulled war-weary Russia out of the war against Germany. Peace did not come to Russia, however; the battle between the communist Red Army and the anti-communist White Army raged for the next two years.*

HEAVY PRICE OF A LIGHT

The streets are frequently unswept for days. This is because the municipal authorities are short of labour.

Yet the burnt match-stick once so common in litter has disappeared not only from the streets but even from the floors of railway smoking-carriages. Matches have become scarce and dear. As a substitute, 'spills' made of scraps of paper are being used domestically, and for their utilisation in clubs and offices it is the custom to keep a night-light burning when fires or gas are not available ...

The importation of foreign matches is now prohibited. The home-made supply is about equal to two-thirds of a box a week for every adult. This admits of the use by each adult of six or seven matches a day, which, in the opinion of the Control Board, ought, with economy, to be sufficient ...

Michael MacDonagh, *The Diary of a Journalist*, 12 January 1918

HUNGER GRIPS

The food shortage is becoming very dreadful, especially for the working classes; and for the munition and other War-workers. They get *so* hungry.

Mrs Hallie Eustace Miles, *Untold Tales of War-time*, 27 January 1918

GERMANS ON OFFENCE

The awful offensive continues, and with it the feeling of hour-to-hour anxiety and suspense, which still goes on as I write this on Monday, when the news is rather better after the awful shock of the first German rush as we heard it on Saturday and Sunday. How one longs and hopes and prays.*

John Bailey, Diaries, 22 March 1918

* Buoyed by the withdrawal of the Russian army following the October Revolution, the Germans launched their intensive Kaiserschlacht, or 'Emperor's Battle', offensive in the spring of 1918, with an aim to breach the British front at Arras.

⌒◆⌒

LAND GIRLS

To-day I was brought into contact with the most important of women's War activities next to the munition-workers – the girls of the Land Army. They had a recruiting procession in London and a meeting in Hyde Park. Before the War there were not more than 90,000 women employed on the land; there are now 260,000. The stretch of grass in Hyde Park where the meeting was held was like a farmyard, there were so many pens with lambs, pigs, ducks and hens.

Michael MacDonagh, *The Diary of a Journalist*, 20 April 1918

NO ANSWER TO THE MODERN MIND

I positively feel, in my hideously modern way, that I can't get into touch with my mind. I am standing gasping in one of those disgusting telephone boxes and I can't 'get through'.

'Sorry. There's no reply,' tinkles out the little voice.

'Will you ring them again – Exchange? A good long ring. There must be somebody there.'

'I can't get any answer.'

Katherine Mansfield, Journals, 21 May 1918

~

VICE TRIAL ROCKS THE ESTABLISHMENT

Nothing is talked about these days but the 'Black Book'. So keen is the public interest in the 'Black Book' that the War has almost receded into forgetfulness. We are hilariously asking each other, 'Well, is your name in the "Black Book"?'

The 'Black Book' has made its appearance in one of the most amazing cases ever heard in a Court of Justice in this country – the criminal prosecution at the Old Bailey of Pemberton-Billing, MP, for an alleged false and defamatory libel on Miss Maud Allen, the celebrated dancer. The alleged libel was published in a weekly newspaper called *Vigilante* (formerly known as *The Imperialist*), owned and edited by Pemberton-Billing and issued only to subscribers. It said Miss Allen was a sexual pervert and based the charge on her dance 'The Vision of Salome', in Oscar Wilde's play *Salome*, which – its public production having been banned by the Censor – has been produced privately by the Independent Theatre on Sundays, the admission fee being five guineas. For the defence it is alleged there is a 'Black Book' containing the names of 47,000 English men and women, compiled by German secret service agents in this country during the last twenty years, with records of their moral weaknesses and sexual vices, and that from these English men and women, it is suggested, the German agents extract valuable information by threats of exposure ...

Greatly to the public disappointment, no copy of the 'Black Book' has been produced – if indeed, it has ever existed. The prosecution contend, of course, that it is a phantom of inventive but unhinged minds.*

Michael MacDonagh, *The Diary of a Journalist*, 2 June 1918

* *Noel Pemberton-Billing, a flamboyant early aviator and aircraft designer, as well as a homophobe and anti-Semite, defended himself in the trial. He won – meaning that, as far as the law was concerned, his outrageous accusations were true.*

FOUR YEARS OF WAR AND THE 'FLU

Nearly four years of it now. I think it was four years ago today that my cinema supper took place, a good many of them gone since then. We were bright enough that night. One gets used to all new conditions but we go off on different lines and in four years are out of hailing distance of where we should otherwise have been. Universal destruction probably deprives us of so much life in the same way that death of an individual dear to us does.

Michael and Nicholas have both had slight attacks of influenza but I hope to hear tomorrow that they are out again. Whether it is Spanish or not I don't know, but it is all over the place ...*

J. M. Barrie, Letter to E. V. Lucas, 3 July 1918

* *A highly contagious and deadly strain of the influenza virus, commonly known as 'Spanish flu' appeared in Europe in the spring of 1918. Its association with Spain had perhaps more to do with war-time reporting restrictions limiting coverage of outbreaks elsewhere than its particular virulence there. It soon turned into a global pandemic, carried far and wide by soldiers returning from the war. In 1918 and 1919 it is estimated that between 20 million and 50 million people died – the higher figure being three times as many as those who died in the war. Victims of the virus often died within days, sometimes hours, of the first symptoms, and those aged between twenty and forty (rather than the very young or elderly, as would normally be the case) proved to be the most susceptible to the strain.*

RULE BY DICTATORSHIP

This is Thursday. Since Monday the compulsory rationing of food has been nationalised, in the sense of being applied to the whole country. The rationing-cards hitherto in use are withdrawn, and national ration-books issued, each containing separate coupons of different colours for the rationed foods, which are sugar, butter, margarine, lard, butchers' meat and bacon. Tea and cheese are not rationed, but authority is given to local food communities to ration them in their areas should they fall short. There is no rationing of potatoes or other vegetables. Nor is bread rationed.

Each and every individual must now have a ration book, if he wants to make sure from day to day of getting a good meal …

We are now living under a Government that rules practically by dictatorship. It compels the citizens to join the Army and fight the Germans; it restricts the citizens to the kind and quantity of food they are to eat …

Are we not to be pitied!

Michael MacDonagh, *The Diary of a Journalist*, 15 July 1918

POLICE STRIKE

The London police, Metropolitan and City, are on strike. About 14,000 constables 'came out' last night! Not a single policeman is on beat duty, and only a few on point duty controlling traffic! This is the amazing news of the day.

The incredible, the inconceivable, the fantastic, certainly the unparalleled has happened.

The public realisation of the gravity of the situation is tempered by the situation's comic-opera absurdity. At the same time, there is a feeling that this fine and devoted body of men, responsible for the maintenance of law and order in times so critical as these, must be labouring under a very sharp sense of grievance and dissatisfaction to have taken a step so extreme and reprehensible

– risking their positions and the loss of respect and appreciations in which they are held by all classes …

The strike was so sudden and unexpected that it has taken the authorities, not to speak of the public, unpleasantly by surprise …

The strike lasted just twenty-four hours. A queer business altogether. Lloyd George has given way. On condition that the strikers return immediately to duty, they are to get an increase of thirteen shillings a week to their pay, and pensions are to be provided for widows …

Michael MacDonagh, *The Diary of a Journalist*, 31 August 1918

KING DREADS REVOLUTION

Saw the King. The King was very nice and showed a surprising grasp of the situation; he, however, did most of the talking and during the forty minutes I was with him I didn't really get much in. He sees pretty well the need for reforms everywhere, and has a wholesome dread of Bolshevism.

Robert Bruce Lockhart, Diaries, 23 October 1918

AUSTRIA SURRENDERS

We hear to-day that Austria has actually surrendered. Surely the Germans cannot hold out much longer, for now they are left nearly alone! It seems sad for the fighting to continue so bitterly and for further precious lives to be sacrificed when Peace is almost in sight. We hear that U-boats are going home under the White Flag, and even sailing our merchant ships.

Mrs Hallie Eustace Miles, *Untold Tales of War-time*, 28 October 1918

THE WORLD TO COME

There is little elation among the general body of citizens about the coming peace ... The absence of public rejoicing and sober looks of private persons arises, I think from preoccupation as to the kind of world we shall all live in when peace has come. Burdened with a huge public debt, living under the shadow of swollen government departments, with a working class seething with discontent, and a ruling class with its traditions and standards topsy-turvy, with civil servants suspecting businessmen and businessmen conspiring to protect their profits, and all alike abusing politicians, no citizen knows what is going to happen.

Beatrice Webb, Diaries, 4 November 1918

WOMEN EMANCIPATED

The political emancipation of women has been completed by the passing in the House of Commons tonight of the Bill name then eligible for election to Parliament. It is styled the Parliament (Qualification of Women) Bill.

Women become qualified for election as Members at twenty-one. Yet, strange to say, they are not allowed to vote for a Member until they are thirty.

There was no division on the Bill. On the contrary, there were hearty and general cheers when it was read the third time. It marks Parliament's appreciation of the splendid services of women in the War.

Michael MacDonagh, The Diary of a Journalist, 6 November 1918

PANDEMONIUM FOR PEACE

Peace! London to-day is a pandemonium of noise and revelry, soldiers and flappers being most in evidence. Multitudes are making all the row they can, and in spite of depressing fog and steady rain, discords of sound and struggling, rushing beings and vehicles fill the streets.

Beatrice Webb, Diaries, 11 November 1918

I got to London about 6.30 and found masses of people in [the] streets and congested Tubes, all waving flags and making fools of themselves – an outburst of mob patriotism. It was a wretched wet night, and very mild. It is a loathsome ending to the loathsome tragedy of the last four years.

Siegfried Sassoon, Diaries, 11 November 1918

VOICE OF BIG BEN

It has become more and more difficult to realise that the War is virtually over. Everything seems like a sort of Symbol of Peace; we can hardly believe that it really is Peace. It is so strange and significant to hear the church clocks chime and strike again, and to hear the boom of Big Ben wafted to us after the long silence; we now notice sounds that we used to hardly hear before the war. When I see lights burning brightly from uncurtained windows, I feel as if we ought to ring up the police station, as we used to do in the Zeppelin days.

Mrs Hallie Eustace Miles, *Untold Tales of War-time*, 14 November 1918

COST OF BEREAVEMENT

I met Captain Griffin (from Walsall) at [the] Reform [Club] yesterday, with Shufflebottom. He had been wounded 9 times, I think, prisoner in Germany. Was reported dead. After he returned to life, his solicitor – among other bills – forwarded the following: 'To Memorial Service (fully choral) 3 guineas.'

Arnold Bennett, Journals, 19 December 1918

GENERAL HAIG RETURNS

Welcome to Sir Douglas Haig and four carriages full of Generals yesterday. Vast crowds in front of the Reform Club. Girls at windows opposite covered their shoulders in the cold with national flags. Reform full of women, boys and kids. In ground- floor room, East, grave members standing on table-clothed tables in front of windows (me too) and in front a dame covering the throats of two small boys. All front windows occupied by women … Handkerchiefs waving, cheering, louder and louder. Then the four carriages … Generals wore no overcoats … Such was the welcome to Haig and co.*

Arnold Bennett, Journals, 20 December 1918

From 1915 until the end of the war, Sir Douglas Haig was Commander-in-Chief of the British Expeditionary Force; after the armistice, and until his retirement in 1921, he served as Commander-in-Chief of the British Home Forces. The remainder of his life was dedicated to the Royal British Legion, which he helped to establish, and which continues to this day to raise money for ex-servicemen and women through the sale of memorial poppies.

REVOLUTION IMMINENT

We are in for all sorts of Reaction. There is likely to be Bolshevism in the country.

Edward Lee Hicks, *The Life and Letters Of*, 29 December 1918

CHAPTER THREE

THE ROARING YEARS: 1919-1928

In an introduction to Dostoyevsky's *The Grand Inquisitor*, which he wrote shortly before his death in 1930, D. H. Lawrence said: 'Today, man gets his sense of the miraculous from science and machinery, radio, aeroplanes, vast ships, Zeppelins, poison gas, artificial silk: these things nourish man's sense of the miraculous as magic did in the past.'

While many of these inventions certainly existed before the First World War, the degree to which new technology penetrated deeper into ordinary life, transforming work, the domestic sphere and social customs is far more palpable in the inter-war period. In 1914 Britain was a country with just 132,000 cars; by 1922 there were 314,769, and within four years that figure had more than doubled to 778,056. Over a million were on the road by the end of the decade. Britain also embarked on the long process of rebuilding the nation after the war. Conservative Prime Minister David Lloyd George called for 'homes fit for heroes' and local authorities were, by law, required to replace slums with the short terraces sketched out in the 'Tudor Walters Report'. The 1920s then ushered in an era of new arterial roads, roadhouse pubs and all-mod-cons suburban housing developments.

In 1920 the British Broadcasting Company (later Corporation) aired its first live broadcast from the Marconi factory in Chelmsford. Lyons' tea shops and Woolworths stores brightened up high streets, with their contemporary, electrically illuminated outlets putting affordable dining and cheap off-the-shelf wares within the reach of millions. By the turn of the decade there were 400 Woolworths spread across the country.

Where an advert for a diet in the *Daily Express* in 1911 helpfully advised 'bony women whose clothes never look well, no matter how expensively dressed' that the solution to being 'Thin, Scraggy and Underdeveloped' was at hand, and a similar product from 1914 was sold under the banner 'How to Get Fat and Be Strong', thinness became the desired look of the 'Bright Young Things' of these modern times.

Women, having worked during the war in traditionally male jobs for the first time, signalled their reluctance to give up such independence by casting off their stays, shortening their skirts and cutting their hair. The vote, granted to women over thirty with property in 1918, was put on a parity with men in 1928 when it was extended to women over the age of twenty-one.

Despite greater prosperity in certain quarters, both politically and economically this was a volatile epoch characterized by high levels of unemployment, inflation, wage stagnation and industrial unrest, culminating in the Hunger Marches and the General Strike of 1926. A Labour government would come to power for the first time, southern Ireland would gain its independence and Soviet Russia would stand for some as an emblem of a new kind of society.

AN ILL-FITTING TRIBUTE

There has been a town meeting over some memorial to Lewes soldiers who have fallen. One illuminated idiot suggested an obelisk with a urinal and cloakrooms underneath it.

Mrs Henry Dudeney, *A Lewes Diary*, 22 January 1919

* *The Lewes Memorial was erected, without a urinal, in 1922.*

JAMES JOYCE DELIVERY

At 9 a.m. I heard the garden gate being forced open (it was frozen to the post) and the postman's welcome footsteps up the path. He dropped a parcel on the porch seat, knocked and went away again. I could not get at my parcel, though I was only a few feet away from it. So I lay and reflected on what it might be. Surely not the book ordered at Bumpus's? Too soon. H.'s promised cigarettes? It sounded too heavy. My own book? An early advance copy? Perhaps.

Nanny came in and settled it. It was the book from B. I was so interested I let her go away without cutting the string. I struggled, but could not tear off the cover, and had to sit with the book on my lap, wondering. She came in to light the fire, and I asked for a knife. She picked the parcel up, took it to the kitchen, and brought the book back opened. I did not like this. I like opening my own parcels.

It was James Joyce's *Portrait of the Artist* – a book which the mob will take fifty years to discover, but having once discovered it will again neglect.

It was cold enough to freeze a brass monkey. I had some diary to post up. The diary seemed to lose all interest and attraction. It was a sore temptation, but I decided to be a Stoic, and wrote till eleven-thirty, though my hands were blue and my nose ran.

Than I read Joyce. An amazing book. Just the book I intended to write – had started it, in fact, when the crash came. He gives the flow of the boy's consciousness – rather a trickle of one thing after another ...

W. N. P. Barbellion, *A Last Diary*, 11 February 1919

LEAGUE OF CLASSES

I believe the strikes are owing to the 'classes' not realising that life has really changed for evermore, in its externals at least. It is not higher wages grudgingly given that will settle the unrest. There must be a 'league of classes', rich and poor to work together sympathetically and putting their cards firmly on the table. The workmen must have access to the business they are in, know all that is happening to it, get a fair wage and then be paid once a year in shares in the business. Cooperation of a real kind, leading to emulation and also to faith in each other.*

J. M. Barrie, Letter to E. V. Lucas, 13 February 1919

* *Many returning from the First World War found not 'a land for heroes', but the same grinding poverty and appalling working conditions that existed before. Inspired in part by the Russian Revolution, railway and transport workers, engineers, miners and cotton workers planned to take industrial action in 1919. These disputes began in earnest in late January when a strike broke out in the docks and shipyards of Belfast and Glasgow demanding a forty-hour work week – a huge reduction from the fifty-four hours and more typically worked. It grew into an all-out general strike in response to the plight of munitions workers now facing unemployment.*

POST-WAR BLUES

Dined at The Club. Kipling told us he had been struck with the number of Colonial soldiers who felt that they had for the first time been in a world which was full of life, of incidents, of variety, of memories of art and history – and who felt they would never again be able to stay content in Australia or Canada, with nothing great in them but space.

John Bailey, Diaries, 27 March 1919

༄

BARREL ORGAN DANCE

On Easter Monday we went up to visit the Murrys* & see Hampstead Heath. Our verdict was that the crowd at close quarters is detestable; it smells, it sticks; it has neither vitality nor colours; it is a tepid mass of flesh scarcely organised into human life. How slow they walk! How passively & brutishly they lie on the grass! How little of pleasure or pain is in them! But they looked well dressed & well fed; & at a distance among the canary-coloured swings & roundabouts they had the look of a picture. It was a summer's day – in the sun at least; we could sit on a mound & look at the little distant trickle of human beings eddying round the chief centres of gaiety & filing over the heath & spotted upon its humps. Very little noise they made; the large aeroplane that came flying so steadily over head made more noise than [the] whole crowd of us. Why do I say 'us'? I never for a moment felt myself one of 'them'. Yet the sight had its charm: I liked the bladders, & little penny sticks, & the sight of two slow elaborate dancers performing to a barrel organ in a space the size of hearthrug.

Virginia Woolf, Diaries, 24 April 1919

* *The writer John Middleton Murry and his wife, Katherine Mansfield, the New Zealand-born short-story writer, were also members, along with the Woolfs, D. H. Lawrence and T. S. Eliot, of the much-mythologized literary cabal, the Bloomsbury Group.*

FLAGGED UP FOR PEACE

Peace signed … bells started ringing, guns thudding at Newhaven, squibs went off in the High Street. Nelson much alarmed bolted into his bedroom. After tea I took him down the High Street to buy a flag (my Armistice one got loose and flew out of the window) and a bit of ribbon for his Victory bow.*

Mrs Henry Dudeney, *A Lewes Diary*, 28 June 1919

* The Treaty of Versailles, signed in the Hall of Mirrors on 28 June, was an attempt to juggle the competing demands of the war's victorious allies, who were represented by the forceful Georges Clemenceau of France, who wanted Germany brought to its knees, and Britain's Lloyd George, who, if bellicose in public, feared extreme retribution would drive Germany towards a Russia-style communist revolution; America's ailing president, Woodrow Wilson, felt that humiliating the loser would pave a poor path to post-war reconciliation. Germany itself had no input on the clauses. Among the treaty's terms, Germany had to admit full responsibility for starting the war, pay reparations (the bulk to Belgium and France), was banned from having an Air Force and had to give up several territories, including Alsace-Lorraine, Hultschin and West Prussia, Posen and Upper Silesia.

PUNISHMENT FOR THE KAISER

I went to the Thanksgiving Service at St Paul's today. I think this is the only public function I was ever at. Beautiful and memorable, of course, and full of colours – and what a glorious organ – it nearly made me musical. Few things could make one's mind travel back into history. But the blinded men! No, no, they don't look cheerful as we are told. They are the saddest thing I have ever seen. They seem so far away. If you want to punish the Kaiser you could do it by leaving him alone with his thoughts among these men.*

J. M. Barrie, Letter to Lady Cynthia Asquith, 6 July 1919

* After the war, Kaiser Wilhelm II went into exile in the Netherlands, where, despite requests

for his extradition and trial for war crimes, he remained for the rest of what proved to be a long life. He died, aged eighty-two, in Doorn, in the Dutch countryside, in 1941.

PEACE CELEBRATED

The great Peace Procession. We breakfasted at 8.15, then off to the Morrisons' in Belgrave Square, only just getting through in time, the crowd being enormous. We saw it all very well, no men in mufti, no smoking, as in [the] Guards' procession, which spoiled that. The marching was very good, especially the British and American. Foch had his Marshal's baton and could not or did not salute the cheering crowd, nor did Beatty, but Haig did, and the Belgian general and some of the others.

I cheered all I could, feeling with Lady Kincloch, who was there, that it was horrid that the people in balconies should appear too fine to cheer.

John Bailey, Diaries, 19 July 1919

Marguerite came home yesterday from the Peace Celebrations on Saturday. She said, '*Tu n'as pas idée*. The air was positively warm with the *frénésie* of the reception of the procession.' The only thing that happened at Thorpe was that the village mob threw an adulterer into the mill pond because he'd attacked a woman's husband. They would have lowered him into a well but they couldn't find a rope.

Arnold Bennett, Journals, 22 July 1919

RAILWAYMEN IN REVOLT

The Great Strike – which has been brewing since the close of the war – has happened. Not the engineers as was expected, nor the miners as the public long expected, but of the railwaymen. Never has there been a strike of anything like this in magnitude or social significance which has burst on the world so suddenly.

We are all at sea as to what will happen.

There are rumours that the government are preparing heroic measures – for confiscating the railwaymen's funds, for starving the railwaymen's families, for running the railways with soldiers; there are equally rumours that the trade unions are preparing the Soviets to take over government of the country. We tend to believe that these suppositions are baseless and that in a week or so there will be a compromise arranged.

Beatrice Webb, Diaries, 28 September 1919

BIRTHDAY RUINS

My birthday. Ernest is giving me silk stockings. I am happy today … And yet because he will gobble his food then blunder up and fling open doors, we had a jolly good row, and so my 50-odd birthday ended. But it is too barbarous. One day he started smoking before I was half through and another day he actually changed his shoes while I was dishing up the pudding.

Mrs Henry Dudeney, A Lewes Diary, 21 October 1919

GERMANS SURRENDER ZEPPELIN

I had a visit at tea-time from General Maitland, the man who crossed the Atlantic twice in an air-ship, and has the simple far-seeing eyes of those who have done the big things. All soldiers have it nowadays to some extent. Nansen has it more than anyone I have seen, as if the eyes – holes in his case, rather than eyes – were fixed for ever on scenes dark to me. Maitland is bringing in the surrendered Zeppelin tomorrow and feels rather sorrowful for its officers, who have to hand it over on English soil. They are to be chivalrously treated. (There is also the possibility of their leaving an infernal machine in it.)

J. M. Barrie, Letter to Lady Cynthia Asquith, 4 June 1920

SPEAKING DIRECTLY TO THE PEOPLE

An invention which is going to have far-reaching political effects … called the 'Amplifier'.

You must realise that by means of this instrument the PM could sit in Downing Street and address audiences of unlimited number simultaneously in Birmingham, Manchester, Liverpool, Cardiff, Edinburgh, and Glasgow. It means incredible addition to the power of the political leader who happens to be the man who most people want to hear; it will also make him much more independent of the press. Just think what it means for the PM to be able as often as he likes to address huge audiences in all the principal centres of population. We have heard a great deal of 'broadcasting' but the 'Amplifier' is destined to have more far-reaching effects politically.

Lionel Curtis, Letter to Thomas Jones, 20 August 1920

✧

STRIKING MINERS

Coal strike began to-day, but accepted with a notable calm.

Arnold Bennett, Journals, 18th October 1920

✧

NEW VULGAR TIMES OF OLD

Dined at the Ritz Restaurant with Jemmy Durham, Lady Agnes and Mr Hankey. The old pre-war throng again and a dance afterwards. Lady A. and I looked at the dancing for some time. The ladies had few clothes and none on their backs. We thought the whole proceedings undignified, indecent, and vulgar. We felt sick of this sort of thing, which belongs to a dead past.

The band was quite good and the new world seemed to be amusing itself in much the same way as a hundred years ago after the other great war with France. We felt very old-fashioned and out of date. The modern post-war public dance is the most blatantly vulgar and indecent performance imaginable. The most suggestive stage dancing is prim in comparison. One can bear almost anything except lack of taste. The war seems to have killed off everyone except the vulgarians.

Lieutenant Colonel Charles à Court Repington, Diaries, 6 March 1921

SUBJECT OF ART

Dined at Literary, for first time as president. It was difficult to face such a dinner with any prospect of festivity with this awful coal strike and apparent attempt at revolution going on around us. But we managed to be cheerful somehow and I even forgot my anxieties.

I had to welcome Binyon, and had a lot of talk with him about art. He welcomes signs of revolt among the younger men against the absurd theory now fashionable that art should have no 'subject' and be a mere affair of 'planes', lines and colours.*

John Bailey, Diaries, 4 April 1921

* *Laurence Binyon was a poet, dramatist and art scholar, chiefly remembered for his First World War memorial verse 'For the Fallen'. For many years he was the Keeper of Oriental Prints and Drawings at the British Museum.*

⌘

MEETING THE TRAMP

Nicholas had a great time with Charlie Chaplin, who came and stayed till two in the morning. Immaculately dressed in evening garb, and carries all off with ease, skill and grace. He has a rather charming speaking voice, and a brain withal. A very forceful creature and likeable. The police who are put on to guard him all produce their own autograph books for him to sign. The ordinary stage drama he called the 'Speakies'.*

J. M. Barrie, Letter to Lady Cynthia Asquith, 18 September 1921

* *Chaplin had released* The Kid, *his first feature-length film as both star and director, earlier that year. With fellow actors Mary Pickford and Douglas Fairbanks and the director D. W. Griffith, he was at the helm of the United Artists film company, an outfit established with the aim of putting moviemakers rather than Hollywood studios in charge of their own output.*

⌘

INDEPENDENCE FOR SOUTHERN IRELAND

The Irish Treaty is the big event since the great war and its warlike peace. The amazing skill with which Lloyd George has carried through the negotiations with his own Cabinet and Sinn Fein has revolutionised the political situation … no other leader could have whipped the Tories to heel and compelled them to recognise the inevitability of Irish Independence. Moreover, the peace puts us right with the world, at any rate until Indian troubles bring up the same question of racial self-determination in a far larger and more complicated way.*

Beatrice Webb, Diaries, 1 December 1921

* *The Anglo-Irish Treaty, signed by an Irish delegation headed by Michael Collins and Arthur Griffith, led to the creation of the Irish Free State, a self-governing dominion comprising twenty-six of Ireland's thirty-two counties.*

ᴄⱯⱭ

CYCLING PAST DERELICT WINDMILLS

The weather promised anything but sunshine today as we pushed our way against a stiff breeze up Chorley New Road at 1.30 p.m. We were bound for Blackpool, and consequently it would be a 'rush'. Via Chorley, Bamber Bridge and Preston we sped, gaining the Blackpool Road – Preston New Road it is called. Being on an excellent surface, flat, with little traffic, we set a rare pace towards Kirkham. About two miles from there is an Inn with the unusual sign of a five-barred gate – the Highgate Inn – and on the wall is painted this ditty:

'This gate hangs high and hinders none,
Refresh yourself and travel on.'

Nearby we sat on a gate and 'refreshed ourselves'. We were in Windmill Lane; hardly a mile passed but we saw a windmill and once we counted four at the same time – all derelict. From Kirkham it was only about nine miles, and six of these were covered by 'hanging on' to a lorry …

Charlie Chadwick, Diaries, 22 March 1922

A PERFECT POLITICIAN

We have made the acquaintance of the most brilliant man in the House of Commons – Oswald Mosley.* 'Here is the perfect politician who is also a perfect gentleman,' I said to myself as he entered the room.

Tall and slim, his features not too handsome to be strikingly peculiar to himself, modest yet dignified in manner, with a pleasant voice and unegotistical conversation, this young person would make his way in the world without his adventitious advantages, which are many – birth, wealth and a beautiful aristocratic wife. He is also an accomplished orator in the old grand style, and an assiduous worker in the modern manner – keeps two secretaries at work supplying him with information but realizes that he has to do the thinking! Such perfection argues rottenness somewhere. I shall not easily forget my desolating experience with the fascinating Betty Balfour. Oswald Mosley reminds me of her in this respect – he seems to combine great personal charm with solid qualities of character, aristocratic refinement with democratic opinions. Is there in him, as there was in the charming Betty, some weak spot which will be revealed?

Beatrice Webb, Diaries, 8 June 1922

---

* *Oswald Mosley entered Parliament for the Conservatives in 1918 representing the constituency of Harrow, then served as an independent in 1922 and 1923 before joining the Labour Party in 1924. He won the seat of Smethwick in the West Midlands for Labour in a by-election in 1926.*

UNDERBRED *ULYSSES*

I should be reading [James Joyce's] *Ulysses* and fabricating my case for and against. I have read 200 pages so far – not a third; and have been amused, stimulated, charmed, interested by the first 2 or 3 chapters – to the end of the Cemetery scene; and then puzzled, bored, irritated, and disillusioned as by a queasy undergraduate scratching his pimples. And Tom,* great Tom, thinks this on a par with *War and Peace*. An illiterate, underbred book it seems to me.

Virginia Woolf, Diaries, 16 August 1922

* *'Tom' is T. S. Eliot. The Woolfs published Eliot's second book,* Poems, *in their Hogarth Press imprint in 1919 and would print an edition of* The Wasteland *in book form in 1923.*

✑

BLINDED BY OEDIPUS COMPLEX

At night read Freud's Psycho-analysis book. Very clever and fascinating, but stuffy and one-sided, seems to me. Anyhow, I read myself blind. Very stupid.

Mrs Henry Dudeney, *A Lewes Diary*, 25 April 1923

✑

IMPROPER WOMEN'S FASHION

Home in time for the royal garden party. The disgusting habit of painting the face gets worse and worse; some of the older women were quite revolting. The vagaries of feminine fashion are extraordinary. I remember a time when women distorted their figures into the semblance of a pyramid, a pouter pigeon, a wasp and a camel. Now they seem to try quite unsuccessfully to look improper.

Rev. W. R. Inge, *Diary of a Dean*, 26 July 1923

✑

LOVABLE LAWRENCE

This week's plays in general have had a bit of a slump, all owing to the political situation, they say, – not P. Pan [*Peter Pan*], which draws in £750 a day regularly. I am reading *Kangaroo* by D. H. Lawrence. In chunks I don't follow him, but it is very vivid, and the coarseness – as if those of an ugly youth creeping out of him like ghosts – are really a very small affair. There are power and poetry in him as in few. He quite misrepresents the feeling of this country in wartime, but perhaps no wonder. A very happy man, with such a passionate interest in himself, roaming the world in search of that self and finding it everywhere. But he is big, and I should think in some ways lovable.

J. M. Barrie, Letter to Lady Cynthia Asquith, 11 January 1924

BRIGHTENED UP BY LYONS

Yesterday afternoon I suddenly decided that I couldn't proceed with my story about Elsie until I had been up to Clerkenwell again. So at 4.50 I got a taxi and went up Myddleton Square. Just before turning to the left into the Square I saw a blaze of light with the sacred name of Lyons* at the top in fire, far higher than anything else; also a cinema sign etc. making a glaring centre of pleasure. I said, surely that can't be the Angel, Islington, and I hoped that it might be some centre that I had never heard of ...

Myddleton Sq., with its Norman windows of its 4-storey houses, and church nearly in the middle, with clock damnably striking the quarters, was very romantic. I walked around the Square, gazing and going up to front-doors and examining door plates and making notes under gas lamps (very damp and chilly). Then I drove to the Angel and saw that it had truly been conquered and annexed by the Lyons ideals. Still, it was doing good up in Islington, much good. Compare its brightness and space to the old Angel's dark stuffiness.

Arnold Bennett, Journals, 15 January 1924

* *J. Lyons & Co. began with a single tea shop in Piccadilly, London, in 1894. In 1909 the chain opened the first of its grander Corner House restaurants in Coventry Street in the West End; by the 1920s it was a national chain. The Corner Houses, in particular, were renowned for their chic art deco interiors.*

FIRST LABOUR GOVERNMENT

At 12.15 I held a Council, at which Mr Ramsay MacDonald was sworn in [as] a member. I then asked him to form a government, which he accepted to do. I had an hour's talk with him, he impressed me very much; he wishes to do the right thing.

Today 23 years ago Grandma died. I wonder what she would have thought of a Labour government.

King George V, Diaries, 22 January 1924

⁓

DOCKERS' STRIKE ENDED

A morning of unparalleled thankfulness. At 7.55 a.m. I just glanced at the paper as I went off to Church, and behold the Strike ended! I just had time to tell the baker standing outside (he was over the moon) and then nipped into the vestry and begged the Vicar for a Thanksgiving. On my way home I met another tradesman and told him. He said the news was 'lovely'. It has been like a nightmare haunting one through day as well as night. I am thankful the Dockers won, as I think they bore many reductions with wonderful resignation, and the employers have really been terribly careless and stupid. After all, how can one compare the Employer, who has cut off a few luxuries, with the Employed, whose very existence is threatened?

Mary Gladstone, Diaries, 21 February 1924

⁓

THE WASTELAND A LARK

T. S. Eliot came to see me at the Reform Club last night, between two of my engagements.

Pale, quiet, well assured. He works at Lloyd's Bank in a department of his own, 'digesting' foreign financial and economic journals. Interesting work, he said, but he would prefer to be doing something else. He edits the *Criterion*, and writes in the evenings. I said to him: 'I want to ask you a question. It isn't an insult. Were the notes to "Wastelands" a lark or serious? I thought they were a skit.' He said they were serious and not more of a skit than some of the things in the poem itself. I understood him. I said I couldn't see the point of the poem. He said he didn't mind what I said as he had definitely given up that form of writing and was now centred on dramatic writing. He wanted to write a drama of modern life (furnished flat sort of people) in a rhythmic prose 'perhaps with certain things in it accentuated by drum-beats'. And he wanted my advice.

Arnold Bennett, Journals, 10 September 1924

FAT DOWN DIET

I now have lemon juice in hot water, with no sugar, instead of my first cup of tea, also apples before a *very* small breakfast of dry toast and weak tea – if this doesn't get my fat down I'll give up dieting! Did not go out today.

Ilene Powell, *Diary of a 1920s Bridget Jones*, 14 January 1925

ROOFTOP ROMANCE

Met Vera as usual and had coffee with the lads in the Oakroom. Went to tea dance with Bill, Mollie, Vera, Clarie and Mervyn. I danced with Jack Gough, Ken Hughes etc. Jack pinched the car and took me to the White Ladies. Danced with all the lads as usual. Stopped Bill from going to the 'Old'. Had a good time, six people asked to take me home. There was a fight and Mrs Morgan fainted. Ticked off J. G. for making love to me on the roof garden! Home at 1.30 o'c.

Ilene Powell, *Diary of a 1920s Bridget Jones*, 7 February 1925

TWO TO TANGO

Slept till 1 o'c. Denny called me with a cup of tea and hot water. Went down and had lunch, then got ready to go out. Phoned mother. Then went to the Triangle at 2.30, came back for tea, went to hippo [the Hippodrome] with M. and N. R. – good show. Finished up at Pam's. Merry evening of music, dancing, wines, trying on frocks. Norman and I entertained the company with stiletto dances, tango etc.

Ilene Powell, *Diary of a 1920s Bridget Jones*, 20 March 1925

MARRIED LOVE DISGUSTING

Dinner of 'The Other Club' last night in Pinafore Room, Savoy. Birkenhead got across the subject of Marie Stopes, and said that he called *Married Love* disgusting etc.

Birkenhead kept on about Marie Stopes. He had no reasonable arguments, and everything (nearly) he said on the subject was either specious or silly; but he phrased his matter well. He never gave in.*

Arnold Bennett, Journals, 15 May 1925

---

* *Dr Marie Stopes was an advocate of birth control and sexual education. Her book,* Married Loved or Love in Marriage, *which addressed issues of female sexual fertility, desire and contraception, initially failed to find a publisher. Backed by Humphrey Vernon-Roe, a philanthropic aircraft manufacturer who would become her second husband, she was finally able to publish the book in 1918; it sold through five printings in the first year alone. In 1921, Stopes and Vernon-Roe founded the Mothers' Clinic for Birth Control in Holloway, North London.*

UNDERGROUND DANCE SCENE

I was at the opening of the Kit Kat Club, which is an enormous place. It is said in the prospectus that 400 couples could dance in comfort. 900 people were there, but over ½ the floor space was filled with tables, the dancing was horrible. Packed mass. We didn't try. It is not a select place. But it is very showy and not absurdly dear like the Embassy. It is all underneath the Capitol Cinema.*

Arnold Bennett, Letter to his nephew, 18 May 1925

* *The Kit Kat Club, which opened in Haymarket in the summer of 1925, came to epitomize the 'Roaring Twenties'. It featured the latest word in decor and 'dance floor equipment', swiftly establishing it as one of the most fashionable 'nocturnal haunts' in London.*

⌇⌇⌇

NIGHTS OF EXCESS

Chris returned. Claud, Alastair and I spent several hours at Victoria meeting various boat trains before at last he arrived – quite unchanged except for the accretion of rather more dirt. He was wearing a Mexican ready-made suit and brought with him some books wrapped in a dirty towel and two halves of a suitcase. We went to Golders Green and drank a little beer and then went to meet my brother at the long bar at the Trocadero. We went to the Florence for dinner, where we drank a lot and Chris discovered he had no money so Baldhead and Alastair had to pay for practically everything all evening. We went to the Savile and drank good port and then to the Café Royal and then to Oddenino's. At the Café Royal we found two men, one of whom Chris appeared to have met in America. We took them to drink with us at Oddenino's. Baldhead threw plates on the floor. We went to Baldhead's flat and drank more. One of the Americans turned out to be the man who had played the monster in a film called *Merry-Go-Round*. We left Baldhead and drank at a place called the Engineer's Club and then to the Savoy, where the mummer [actor] was staying. I got into his bed and Claud sat on the lavatory and worked the plug with his foot for hours. The monster carried round packets of tooth-powder which he said was heroin and everyone took. We returned home at about 4 and cooked sausages – all very drunk.

Evelyn Waugh, Diaries, 25 September 1925

◆

THE REMARKABLE BBC

To my mind by far the most significant event of the last two years is the spread of wireless and the admirable way in which the BBC is using this stupendous influence over the lives of people, in some ways greater than the written word because it is so amazingly selective and under deliberate control, and on the whole an eminently right control. This new power must necessarily be a monopoly and cannot be left to Gresham's law of the bad coin driving out the good. Moreover, there is at present no pecuniary self-interest involved; no one is the richer or poorer because one programme is adopted rather than another. And the result is certainly remarkable. Every item in the day's programme is not to one's taste, but the ensemble is admirable. But what a terrible engine of compulsory conformity in opinion and culture wireless *might* become.

Beatrice Webb, Diaries, 25 December 1925

◆

SEEING IN THE NEW YEAR WITH THE WIRELESS

New Year's Eve. F. and I sat up. Heard on the wireless various features of New Year's Eve in London: dancing at the Albert Hall, Big Ben striking twelve, singing 'Auld Lang Syne', 'God Save the King', 'Marseillaise', hurrahing.

Thomas Hardy, Diaries, 31 December 1925

◆

AMERICAN INVASION

As I passed across the end of the hotel lounge to-night, the noise of the American accent everywhere was simply awful. The American tourists will overrun Europe like the Goths soon. It is positively frightening.

Arnold Bennett, Journals, 7 February 1926

SHAKESPEARE IN FLAMES

The Shakespeare Memorial Theatre at Stratford-upon-Avon was today destroyed by fire. This is sad news. The Library and picture gallery were saved after a long fight and the folios and quartos were removed in time. The roof of the Theatre caved in after the fire had been going 2 hrs and then the tower went. It's all a hopeless mess now, so I am told. I expect it will soon be rebuilt – but it's sad.

Fred Bason, Diaries, 7 March 1926

THE GENERAL STRIKE

The Government have woefully mismanaged the whole business. But the [trade unions] have been equally blameworthy: 1. Miners' impossible formula. 2. Allowing themselves to fall into general strike psychology. General strike declared & at the meeting of the TU [Trades Union] General Council yesterday evident no forethought.* No definite idea of what they are to consider as satisfactory to enable them to finish & go back to work.

Strike cannot settle purely economic problem of bankruptcy of industry.

Ramsay MacDonald, Diaries, 2 May 1926

The Trades Union Congress (TUC) called for a general strike in support of the miners in Wales, Scotland and the North of England who were engaged in action against an enforced pay cut. On 3 May some 2 million workers went on strike across Britain; in the capital, dockers, printers, power station workers, railway men and transport workers joined in the industrial action. The government responded by calling out the army. Non-unionized workers, students, and the likes of novelist Evelyn Waugh joined the strike breakers.

The second day of the general strike: a curious silence over all the land and upon everybody; one can't say whether ominous or not. So far there doesn't seem to be any ugly temper in the people; but it is unthinkable what might happen if the general strike hangs on for a fortnight, and supplies begin to fail, while the government defeats the strikers bit by bit. That would lead to an appalling spirit in the strikers who remain. Perhaps the best sign is the solidarity in the ranks of the unions; if they can maintain their cohesion, there is less likelihood of head-on conflicts on both sides.

A. L. Rowse, Diaries, 5 May 1926

RETURN TO NORMALCY

At 1.00 p.m. I got the good news that the TUC had been to the Prime Minister and informed him that the General Strike was forthwith called off unconditionally. It is indeed a great relief to me, as I have been very anxious about the situation. Our old country can well be proud of itself, as during the last nine days there has been a strike in which 4 million men have been affected; not a shot has been fired and no one killed; it shows what a wonderful people we are ... The Government have remained firm and backed up by the people have won a great victory.

King George V, Diaries, 12 May 1926

The Strike was settled at about 1.15 – or it was then broadcast ... They told us to stand by & await important news. Then a piano played a tune. Then the solemn broadcaster assuming incredible pomp & gloom & speaking one word to the minute read out: Message from 10 Downing Street. The TUC leaders have agreed that [the] Strike shall be withdrawn ... I saw this morning 5 or 6 armoured cars slowly going along Oxford Street; on each two soldiers sat in tin helmets, & one stood with his hand at the gun, which was pointed straight ahead ready to fire. But I also noticed one policeman smoking a cigarette. Such sights I dare say I shall never see again; & don't in the least wish to.

Virginia Woolf, Diaries, 12 May 1926

WHOLESOME ENGLAND

The Bishops have come out of it very badly, bleating for a compromise while the nation was fighting for its life. Cardinal Bourne won golden opinions by saying what our Bishops were too cowardly to say: 'This strike is a sin against God. Catholics must support the Government.'

Rev. W. R. Inge, Diary of a Dean, 18 May 1926

COST OF LABOUR

Churchill's announcement in the House today that the General Strike will have cost the government no more than three-quarters of a million – a sum which the death of a couple of million will pay – puts the cap on the ridiculous heroics of the General Strike. The 3 million strikers will have spent some 3 million pounds of trade union money and lost another 4 or 5 in wages.

The General Strike of 1926 is a grotesque tragedy. The Labour leaders and their immediate followers whether political or individual live in the atmosphere of alternating day-dreams and nightmares; day-dreams about social transformation brought about in the twinkling of an eye, and visions of treachery in their own ranks and malignancy on the other side – all equally fantastic and without foundation. We are all of us just good-natured, stupid folk. The worst of it is that the governing class are as good-natured and stupid as the labour movement. I have lost my day-dreams; I have only the nightmare left – the same sort of nightmare I had during the Great War: that European civilisation is in the course of dissolution.

Beatrice Webb, Diaries, 18 May 1926

RETAIL FASCINATION

We stopped in Harbour Street, at Hyland's and at Woolworth's. I had long been in need of a new cigarette-case (second) and I got one here for 6d. Dorothy received from me a pink pearl necklace with earrings to match, and 1 hat pin and 2 [Moroccan] books to hold snap-shots of Virginia – the whole costing 8s. 6d. No wonder that this shop has a great fascination for the majority of human beings.*

Arnold Bennett, Journals, 11 October 1926

* *The American retailer Frank Winfield Woolworth, who had established a series of 'bazaar' stores in the US, opened his first British branch of the chain in Liverpool in 1909. By 1926 Woolworths could be found across Britain, with nineteen stores in the London area alone;*

by the end of the decade, the estate had swelled to 400 branches. The last shops in Britain closed almost exactly a century after their arrival, on 6 January 2009.

⌒✐⌒

SKIRTS MADE EASY

In the afternoon got out the machine and turned up the hem of the red dress and also put tucks in my petticoats. The fashion now is to be short, almost to the knee. Very comfortable and if one has decent legs and ankles (really, they are wonderful for 60) quite easy.

Mrs Henry Dudeney, *A Lewes Diary*, 29 October 1926

⌒✐⌒

MYSTERY OF MYSTERY WRITER SOLVED

The Mrs Christie* mystery solved. The tiresome woman found at Harrogate. If she is mad, she should be sent to Bedlam. If she is sane, she should be spanked. No patience with such people.

Mrs Henry Dudeney, *A Lewes Diary*, 15 December 1926

* The crime writer Agatha Christie, bestselling author of sixty-six novels and creator of Hercule Poirot and Miss Marple, disappeared from her Surrey home on 3 December 1926. She was discovered eleven days later in a spa hotel in Harrogate with seemingly no memory of how or why she'd ended up there.

⌒✐⌒

NEW IDEAS IN PHYSICS

I read the sketch of Einstein's theory in Sullivan's *Aspects of Science*.* It's not clear to me, but it is the least obscure description of the theory that I have yet seen.

Arnold Bennett, Journals, 7 March 1927

* *Albert Einstein first began to formulate his Theory of General Relativity in 1905 and published it in 1916. As deputy editor of the* Athenaeum *literary review, J. W. N. Sullivan wrote several articles on scientific breakthroughs, including one of the first non-technical discussions of Einstein's theories in English. These were collected and published in two volumes entitled* Aspects of Science.

✑

COWARD WITH HIS PICK OF THE LADIES

Today Mr Noël Coward has sent me a signed photograph. I suppose he is the most talked-about man in the theatre world today. I do think he is brilliant. I can do all that he can do only not so good – and I do not expect I shall ever be *quite* so good. The girls rave about him. He isn't handsome. He isn't snobbish. He is amiable, not a bit 'starchy'. I will tell you, diary, I *do* admire him. If I wasn't me, I rather think that I'd like to be him with a world of lovely ladies at his feet and he can have his choice. Do I envy him? Yes, I bloody do! But I am happy. I hope Mr Coward is as happy this lovely day.

Fred Bason, Diaries, 13 May 1927

✑

DYSTOPIAN *METROPOLIS*

Went to see the *Metropolis* film at the Elite Theatre. Sickening sentimentality. Many good effects, spectacular, spoilt by over-insistence. A footling story. No understanding of psychology of either employers or workmen. 'Adapted by Channing Pollock.' Good God! What captions. Enough to make you give up the ghost. The theatre was very nearly empty.*

Arnold Bennett, Journals, 3 August 1927

* *H. G. Wells, regarded by many as the father of modern science fiction, was equally unimpressed by Fritz Lang's cinematically groundbreaking portrait of a dystopian future*

society. In a review for The New York Times *published on 17 April 1927, he wrote: 'I have recently seen the silliest film. I do not believe it would be possible to make one sillier. And as this film sets out to display the way the world is going, I think [my book]* The Way the World is Going *may very well concern itself with this film. It is called* Metropolis, *it comes from the great Ufa studios in Germany, and the public is given to understand that it has been produced at enormous cost. It gives in one eddying concentration almost every possible foolishness, cliché, platitude, and muddlement about mechanical progress and progress in general served up with a sauce of sentimentality that is all its own.'*

⌀

LEST WE FORGET

Armistice Day. T. came downstairs from his study and listened to the broadcasting of the service at Canterbury Cathedral. We stood for the two minutes' silence. He said afterwards that he had been thinking of Frank George, his cousin who was killed at Gallipoli.

Florence Emily Hardy, Diaries, 11 November 1927

⌀

MUSIC HALL TURNS

I long to go to the Alhambra and see the magician De Biere. He is always worth seeing, for he is so very serious over his act. He is also very clever and one of the few magicians whose work really does mystify me. But I haven't got the price of a gallery seat. I notice that at the Coliseum they got Noni, the very funny clown, and Max Wall, who never fails to make me laugh. Will Hay also on the bill but somehow having seen him three times I feel I know what he and his company will do. Still, it's a good bill and as though the above ain't enough there is Gwen Farrer with her cello and Florence Smithson. It's said that Miss Farrer's old man is or was a millionaire. She's the only millionaire's daughter I have yet seen (indeed, I've actually spoken to her) and I must say that she has what is known as presence … Still, I must confess that in my own heart I do not like this great inequality in the state of people. Riches in Buckingham Palace, Rags in Islington and Walworth.

Fred Bason, Diaries, 2 January 1928

LONDON FLOODED

There was an unprecedented flood in London, owing to a high spring tide meeting the swollen river. Fourteen people were drowned, and the basement of the Tate Gallery, containing drawings by Turner and other matters, was submerged. The water swept over the Embankment and invaded the Houses of Parliament.

Rev. W. R. Inge, *Diary of a Dean*, 6 January 1928

KINGS OF ROAD RACING

The car behaved well. On the way home a Sunbeam, very well driven by an owner-driver, passed us. This could not be permitted; but even after passing us he continued to increase his lead when were doing 53 mph. However, we left him in the end. The fellow could drive. As a rule, nothing passes us except motor bikes. Some of these fellows must do 70 something. They have also an enormous advantage in the matter of cutting-in.

Arnold Bennett, Letter to his nephew, 11 April 1928

THE LATEST FASHION IN FICTION

To the Lighthouse by Virginia Woolf represents the latest fashion in the technique of novel-writing. The story, so far as there is a story, is told by a running description of the 'stream of consciousness' in the principal person's mind. When this person dies, then another mind is taken as the medium;

in this book both are women. To me this method is objectionable because it assumes that the author can see into and describe another's mind. What one suspects is that Virginia is telling you of her own stream of consciousness, the only one she knows 'of her own view and knowledge'. And that brings me to the question: could I record my own consciousness? So often it seems too vague and diverse and disconnected; even one's own consciousness defies description.

Beatrice Webb, Diaries, 28 May 1928

ARRIVAL OF THE 'TALKIES'

Tonight I went to the Piccadilly Theatre (just off Piccadilly Circus) and I saw *The Jazz Singer*, which is a talking film. As you see the man singing you *hear* the man singing. If it wasn't that the noise sort of blares forth like 20 gramophones at once or six strong voices singing at once, it would be a *miracle*. I suppose it *is* a miracle. I had front row and I got a bad headache through looking up at the screen. If this had been a real live show my seat would have been 'best in the house'. As it was talking cinema, it was *worst* in the *cinema*. Still, I ought not to say nothing [*sic*], because Edgar Wallace (of all people) gave me this ticket. He said, 'Perhaps you can use this?' Ever so calm he said it. When I saw what this was I was flabagasted* with joy. All stars was there. I got eleven autographs – plus an ache in my neck and a real sickening headache. A. Jolson is the Jazz Singer. I dont like him: Sings Awfull.

Fred Bason, Diaries, 27 September 1928

* *The spelling throughout is peculiar to Bason.*

WOMEN MAKE ROOM FOR WINE

I am back from speaking at Girton, in floods of rain. Starved but valiant young women – that's my impression. Intelligent, eager, poor; and destined to become school mistresses in shoals. I blandly told them to drink wine and have a room of their own. Why should all the splendour, all the luxury of life, be lavished on the Julians and Francises, and none on the Phares and Thomases?*

Virginia Woolf, Diaries, 27 October 1928

* *These lectures would give rise to Woolf's famous feminist essay 'A Room of One's Own', published the following year.*

CHAPTER FOUR

OF LOVE AND HUNGER: 1929-1938

The collapse of the stock market in New York on 29 October 1929 was to have a devastating effect on the whole global economy.

America itself was plunged into the Great Depression and more than 15 million Americans, a quarter of all wage-earning workers, were unemployed in the opening years of the 1930s. Germany, too, suffered, with rampant inflation and an unemployed population of 7 million. These economic conditions opened the way for the emergence of its new leader, who offered vile and simplistic solutions to the nation's deep problems, which were sadly accepted by an all-too-willing citizenry.

In Britain the picture was more mixed. In 1931 the nation was forced off the gold standard, where the value of the pound was tied to the amount of gold in the economy. This had only been put back in place six years earlier by Chancellor Winston Churchill, and helped to cushion many of the aftershocks in Britain of the Wall Street Crash. The decision to abandon this standard split the still-young first Labour government, however, and a national government was formed to address the potential crisis.

There was degradation and appalling unemployment, which doubled from 1 million to 2 million without work between 1929 and 1931. The northern industrial towns and mining villages of Wales were particularly badly hit, and even those in work in these regions saw their wages fall. The National

Unemployed Workers' Movement continued to demand concessions from both their employers and government in the years following the 1926 General Strike, culminating in the Jarrow March of 1936. One group of workers even instigated a 'Mass Trespass' on Kinder Scout, in the High Peaks, protesting against parts of the open countryside not being accessible to the public.

More than a thousand on the Left were inspired to join the Spanish Civil War when it broke out in 1936. The fighting between the Republicans and the nationalists also gave the Luftwaffe an opportunity to test their bombers.

Still, despite the global economic crisis and political uncertainties, living standards, particularly in the south of England, were improving. Building on the developments of the previous decade, this was the heyday of semi-detached houses, Odeon cinemas and roadhouse pubs in the style Betjeman dubbed 'Brewer's Tudor'.

It was also in the 1930s that poet Charles Madge, film-maker Humphrey Jennings and anthropologist Tom Harrisson hit on the idea of documenting the lives of ordinary people. The Mass Observation Project, begun in 1937, would soon begin asking those ordinary people to keep records of their own lives, and entries from their invaluable diaries feature from this chapter forward. Some, like Nella Last, have belatedly become household names; but in subsequent sections we will meet no less able chroniclers such as Gladys Langford and Kathleen Tipper.

THE COCKTAIL CRAZE

I resolved not to drink cocktails any more. So in the late afternoon I went to a cocktail party. It was convened in the sacred cause of dramatic art. The party had to be serious, but also it had to be smart; it was both. Half the highbrows in London were there. I tried conscientiously to be serious about dramatic art (British variety), and succeeded fairly well at intervals. Very many cocktails were consumed. Up to a few years ago you could not advance the cause of anything without a banquet more or less expensive. Nowadays you do it to cocktails. The change is for the better. The new method takes a shorter time, and less alcohol is swallowed. I am not in favour of cocktails; but the harm of them is exaggerated by the godly. The amount of spirituous liquid in a cocktail is trifling.

The mischief is that people – especially the young – do not confine themselves to one cocktail. At this very party I was talking to a famous man. He said, while drinking a cocktail: 'Cocktails are a great evil. My second daughter is nineteen to-morrow. She went out to dinner the other evening and when she came home she confessed that she had had five cocktails before dinner.' I said: 'But you ought to forbid it.' He said: 'But how can I forbid it? I do forbid it. And they come home and cheerfully announce that they have had five cocktails! You can't put your girls in prison. There it is. That's where we are to-day.'

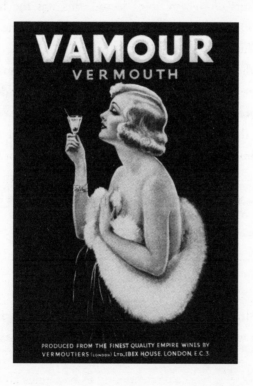

The cocktail craze will pass. And perhaps by the time it has passed we shall know the origin of the word. A cocktailed horse is, I believe, a horse which has had its tail docked. Hence its tail flounces out gaily. Hence it has an air (quite spurious) of vivacity. Hence a cocktail ought to be so called because it gives you the jolly feeling of a horse with its tail up. But actually is it so called for that reason? Nobody can say. All I know with certainty about the cocktail is that it is a source of considerable income to caterers and bar-keepers. Even in a respectable club a cocktail costs a shilling. In a first-rate fashionable hotel it costs half-a-crown (ten francs in France). The material of a cocktail surely cannot cost more than sixpence: a liberal estimate. Add another sixpence for overhead charges – again a liberal estimate – and the hotel is left with eighteen-pence clear: a net profit of 150 per cent. By how many inches per cocktail consumed the sacred cause of dramatic art was pushed forward at the cocktail party I cannot say. My own personal consumption of nourishment was as follows: Olives, one. Cocktails, none.

Arnold Bennett, Journals, 1 January 1929

A CHEERING THRILLER IN THE COLD

This night at the Strand Theatre I saw a great play called *Rope* by Patrick Hamilton.* It's a thriller and everyone cheered it. Will soon sell and be seen by the public and how they will like it. Got the author's autograph and by the way he signed I could guess no one had ever before asked him for his signature. Nice sort of bloke … quiet and almost shy. But knows his onions.

It's bitterly cold weather. I don't often put the weather, but it's what even brass monkeys would suffer from.

Fred Bason, Diaries, 3 March 1929

---

* *In 1948 Hamilton's play was adapted into a successful Hollywood movie by Alfred Hitchcock starring James Stewart, John Dall and Farley Granger. It was Hitchcock's first feature film in colour.*

VIEWING A CONTROVERSIAL STATUE

Examined the new St James's Underground buildings. The Epstein *Night* is superb, *Morning* I am not so sure of. The projection of the lower part of the belly and the receding thighs gives one an uneasy feeling that the foreskin has been stuck onto a sketch elevation of a behind by accident. I like the building extremely. There was a crowd looking at *Morning*; it had only just gone up today (been unveiled, rather) and I was pleased to hear several of the critics were men on the job, and taking a craftsman's interest in it.*

Sylvia Townsend Warner, Diaries, 1 July 1929

When they were unveiled, the sculptor Jacob Epstein's additions to the London Underground Head Offices above St James's Park Tube station (sculptures actually entitled 'Day' and 'Night') were considered obscene by many. Outraged members of the public even tarred and feathered them. To appease angry shareholders of the Underground Railway Company, Epstein was forced to cut 'about an inch and half from the penis of the small boy' represented in the work.

⌁

ENCOUNTERING A SATANIST

I had rather a collapse last night. We went to dinner at the Tour, where I got very drunk on hock, in spite of all intentions to keep a clean palate for Burgundy … We also had Aleister Crowley at the end of the dinner, a most impossible charlatan, looks like a north-country pork manufacturer and speaks with a cockney-American accent … After dinner, we went (*without* the High Priest) to a Russian restaurant in Piccadilly, a dreadful place with sham cossacks, where I regret to say, to my shame, I passed away insensible after drinking some glasses of vodka, and had to be removed home by Dodo, a sad ending to a charming evening.

Dora Carrington, Letter to Lytton Strachey, 18 September 1929

⌁

WALL STREET CRASHES

There's been a complete disaster on the New York Stock Market, everybody is losing millions … but it really serves them right for gambling. Thanks God, Jack has invested my money in gilt-edged securities and never speculated, so I'm perfectly safe, but it really is horrible, people hurling themselves off buildings like confetti.

Noël Coward, Letter to his mother Violet, 6 November 1929

༨

HECTORED BY WAR MEMOIR

I read Graves' *Goodbye to All That*. It is written in a hectoring tone of voice that makes it rouse all the hairs on the spine of one's prejudices, but the war-part is good, and it has a lot of jokes with a tang.

Sylvia Townsend Warner, Diaries, 18 December 1929

༨

A ROOM OF ONE'S OWN CONSIDERED

Sex in literature, *pace* Virginia's new book. The moment you say how women are to write well, you've given away your case, as a feminist. It should be, how people are to write well. And, personally, I mistrust this ambivalence of sex idea. The best male authors are undoubtedly the most male; great writing seems to establish itself in periods of marked sexual distinction, periods of sexual fusion produces only good writing. So why aren't the best female authors to be the most female? However, I haven't yet read V. W.'s book.

Sylvia Townsend Warner, Diaries, 27 December 1929

༨

ARISTOCRATS IMPRESSED BY FASCIST

Lunched with Lady Vera Herbert, where were Sir and Lady Isabella Howard, Lord and Lady Ernle, and Lady Burghclere.

Lady Isabella spoke of the wonderful administrative achievements of Mussolini: land that was bog or desert now growing wheat, total disappearance of beggars from Naples etc.

John Bailey, Diaries, 30 March 1930

⌒◯⌒

INDIAN INDEPENDENCE LEADER ARRESTED

Gandhi arrested;* and now we shall see how deep-rooted is the following of the Indian saint, whether faith will move mountains of Indian disunity and inexperience and upset the British Raj!

Beatrice Webb, Diaries, 4 May 1930

* *In the spring of 1930, Mohandas Karamchand Gandhi (more commonly known as Mahatma Gandhi), the former lawyer turned campaigner for India's independence from British colonial rule, was arrested while leading the so-called Salt March. The march was a protest against the Salt Act, which prohibited Indians from collecting or selling salt and forced them to buy the mineral at an inflated price from British government contractors, who had been given a monopoly on the supply.*

⌒◯⌒

CHEAP EATS AT WOOLWORTHS

I visited every counter of the domestic Woolworth, even to buy boot-polish, and refreshed myself with a sixpenny fish tea – plaice, of course. Cheap, low-class meals are such a pleasure, I wonder I don't take to chewing gum.

Sylvia Townsend Warner, Diaries, 17 September 1930

STARCHED HAIR

Stayed in again. Getting quite a home-bird. Darned some stockings and then washed my hair. Had to wash it twice as I still had some starch in it.

Doris Emily Worpole, Diaries, 20 January 1931

⌀

ALL QUIET AT THE HIPPODROME

Bob called for me about 6.45. Went to Hippodrome and saw *All Quiet on the Western Front*. Thought it was jolly good. Lewis Ayres so nice, fell quite in love with him. Got home about 11 o'clock.

Doris Emily Worpole, Diaries, 13 February 1931

⌀

AN 'ENGLISH HITLER'

An amazing act of arrogance, Oswald Mosley's melodramatic defection from the Labour Party, slamming the door with a bang to resound throughout the political world. A foreign journalist at the Labour Party conference nicknamed him 'the English Hitler'. But the British would not stand a Hitler. I doubt whether he has the tenacity of a Hitler. He also lacks genuine fanaticism. Deep down in his heart he is a cynic.*

Beatrice Webb, Diaries, 25 February 1931

---

* *Ramsay MacDonald's Labour government came to power – only the second Labour administration since the party's founding in 1900 – with a majority of seats in 1929. Mosley was widely viewed as a rising star and a potential future leader; he was given the post of Chancellor of the Duchy of Lancaster. But after disputes over economic policy in the wake of rising unemployment, Mosley left Labour to found his own party, the New Party. In the following year he visited Italy, where he met Benito Mussolini. Inspired by the Fascist* *leader, he returned home, disbanded the New Party and established the right-wing British Union of Fascists.*

✐

CONVERTS TO MOSLEY

Leonard and Virginia Woolf here for the week-end ... Among their intimate friends are the Harold Nicolsons. He is a convert to Mosley and one of his prospective candidates. Reith of the BBC is another disciple. Apparently, Mosley is convinced that he will sweep the constituencies and become Prime Minister in the near future and is already choosing his Cabinet!

Beatrice Webb, Diaries, 1 April 1931

✐

DOWN AND OUT IN LECHEROUS MOOD

When we had gone a mile or two we came to an orchard, and the others at once went in and began stealing apples. I had not been prepared for this when we started out, but I saw that I must either do as the others did or leave them, so I shared the apples; I did not, however, take any part in the thefts for the first day, except to keep guard. We were going more or less in the direction of Sevenoaks, and by dinner time we had stolen about a dozen apples and plums and fifteen pounds of potatoes. The others also went in and tapped whenever we passed a baker's or a teashop, and we got quite a quantity of broken bread and meat. When we stopped to light a fire for dinner we fell in with two Scotch tramps who had been stealing apples from an orchard nearby, and stayed talking with them for a long time. The others all talked about sexual subjects, in a revolting manner. Tramps are disgusting when on this subject, because their poverty cuts them off entirely from women, and their minds consequently fester with obscenity. Merely lecherous people are all right, but people who would like to be lecherous, but don't get the chance, are horribly degraded by it. They remind me of the dogs that hang enviously round while two other dogs are copulating. During the conversation, Young Ginger related how he and some others on Trafalgar Square had discovered one of their number to be a 'Poof', or Nancy Boy. Whereupon they had instantly fallen upon him, robbed him of 12/6d, which was all he had, and spent it on themselves. Evidently, they thought it was quite fair to rob him, as he was a Nancy Boy.

George Orwell, Diaries, 29 August 1931

ARCH COMMENTARY ON MODERN LIFE

What a crew these Bright Young Things are! Overheard at Boulestin's the other day. Young highbrow male: 'The reason Czecho-Slovakians have no body-urge is that their insteps are insufficiently arched!' Young highbrow female: 'Oh, my dear, don't you think arches are terribly unimportant?'

Cannot understand why motoring depresses me. I think it is the open face of Nature and the dread of being left alone with a ploughed field and the naked sky. Is it that I don't like being left alone with my conscience? Or is it just the natural reaction from the exciting, unimportant life of cities to the immensely important, wholly dull business of things growing? ...

Motored round Filey, which is dull, and Whitby, which I like better. Was shown an antique shop made out of part of a castle in which King Richard III slept. Believed that a little, and was then shown some antiques ...

Went up to the castle and on the way there saw a little notice let into the wall. It read: 'Behind this wall lies the grave of Anne Brontë.' I looked over, and stayed looking for a full five minutes. The lettering on the headstone was still perfectly clear. A sheep was kneeling on the grave, cropping the grass. Two more were having a bit of a fight a few yards away. Lovely view over the bay, and I was not depressed.

It is 34 years since I was in Scarborough, where I spent a week's holiday during my first year of business. The entertainment then offered the D'Oyly Carte Co. in Gilbert and Sullivan – it was my first hearing of *The Yeoman* – and Arthur Roberts. To-night they offer an actress I don't know in a play I have never heard of, or more probably forgotten – *The Way Things Happen* – and Greta Garbo in *The Rise of Helga.** ...

Car went all right all day, low petrol consumption, but not quite enough power on the hills. Excellent for 9 h.p. though, and not a shadow of a complaint.

James Agate, Journals, 4 June 1932

* *Edited and renamed to appease British censors,* The Rise of Helga *was a version of* Susan Lenox (Her Fall and Rise), *a risqué 1931 American film starring Greta Garbo and Clark Gable. It had been made before the introduction of Hollywood's Hays Code, which sought to restrict what could and could not be seen on screen – especially pertaining to sex and sexual innuendo.*

CRUMBLING COUNTRY

Read paper over supper. Ramsay MacDonald at Lausanne [Conference] says civilisation is crumbling and end in sight. Isn't he confusing civilisation with capitalism? Saw some slums in Nottingham recently that suggested the sooner something crumbles the better.

James Agate, Journals, 16 June 1932

⁕

PUBS CHANGING WITH THE TIMES

Motored out to Beaconsfield in the evening. Found one of the local pubs has become a road-house. Dancing floor, wireless-gramophone with loud-speaker, twenty tables, licence, and not one single customer.

James Agate, Journals, 1 July 1932

⁕

AEROPLANES OVER LOVERS' HEADS

Yesterday my dear told me she must have a blood test, as she suspects herself of TB. It will be on Thursday. Meanwhile, we wait. Last night we sat up late, talking of Dicky; and comforting ourselves with love after. Aeroplanes were flying over the house. The last went over with a fierce metallic clang, like a dragon.

Sylvia Townsend Warner, Diaries, 19 July 1932

⁕

VISIT TO A SNACK BAR

London. Visited several shops – Selfridges, where we had lunch at an exciting new snack bar with high red leather and chromium-plated stools. We ate huge toast sandwiches and drank iced coffee. We had tea at D. H. Evans;

I bought some scarlet rouge and lipstick and some scent – also a brown, spotted silk scarf.

Barbara Pym, *A Very Private Eye*, 17 July 1933

SHOWERS ON SHAKESPEARE

Longest drought for thirty-odd years ended to-day, and – appropriately enough – Sydney Carroll produced *The Tempest* in the open air at Regent's Park.*

James Agate, Journals, 13 September 1933

* *Performances of Shakespeare in Regent's Park were inaugurated by Sydney Carroll and Robert Atkins in June 1932.*

THE 'SOLDIER SPIRIT'

A little incident typical of the soldier-spirit. We had broken down and Wright was tinkering with the engine. A wounded ex-soldier – he had no legs – passed us on his hand-propelled tricycle. As he went by, he said with a broad grin: 'Want a tow, mate?'

James Agate, Journals, 30 September 1933

WEST FEATHERED

Aunt Nellie and I went into town at about 11. I wore my fur coat, navy blue skirt and fez, and looked rather Turkish-Parisienne. We went to the Carlton and saw Mae West in *I'm No Angel*. She is said to be the rage of everywhere. Fat and not attractive – at least, I didn't think so – a purely physical appeal and crude technique. Her clothes were too fluffy and feathery on the whole.*

Barbara Pym, *A Very Private Eye*, 11 December 1933

* Trading on her ample curves and overtly sexually suggestive wit, Mae West was to fall foul of the censors in the wake of the introduction of the Hays Code in 1934. West's revealing outfits had to be toned down and her dialogue, more often than not self-penned and laden with double entendre, was butchered, and her films waned in popularity as a result.

❦

DEPRESSED WORLD

Beveridge here for the night, back from the USA He is in the depths of gloom, admits that the state of mind and state of things in the USA is far worse than he had thought possible. And as he loathes Soviet Communism he is depressed and hopeless. The callousness of public opinion about the Nazi persecution of the Jewish race, the unwillingness to save them from starvation, is also distressing him.

Beatrice Webb, Diaries, 16 December 1933

❦

PRESS BARON AND BLACKSHIRTS

Lord Rothermere came out in support of Tom Mosley and in favour of British Fascism both in the *Mail* and in the *News*.*

Robert Bruce Lockhart, Diaries, 15 January 1934

* Most famously, the Daily Mail *on 19 January 1934 carried a front-page headline, 'Hurrah for the Blackshirts'. The* Daily Mirror, *traditionally a Labour paper, which Rothermere also owned, went with 'Give the Blackshirts a helping hand' just three days later. The Blackshirts were members of the British Union of Fascists, wearing black uniforms in imitation of Mussolini's Fascist party's uniform.*

❦

STUDENTS JOIN THE STRUGGLE

Up early helping to feed the Hunger Marchers at the Corn Exchange. We piled up blankets – took round tea and porridge – cut bread – buttered it – made and packed meat and jam sandwiches. There was a lot to do, and I did enjoy it. Hilary Sumner-Boyd was there in green velvet trousers – he is pleasant to talk to and looks so exactly like a girl – somehow one doesn't associate him with Communism. At about 9.45 we left together with the Hunger Marchers – the idea of me marching behind the October Club banner (which I did) was ludicrous – also shouting, under the direction of a kind of cheer-leader, '1-2-3-4 – who are *We* for? *We* are *For* the *Working Classes* – *Down* with the *Ruling Classes*. Students join the Workers' struggle' etc. Still, I wish them luck even if I do disapprove of much that Communism stands for.*

Barbara Pym, *A Very Private Eye*, 21 February 1934

* *During the Great Depression, unemployment in Britain reached 3 million. The National Union of Mine Workers organized several hunger marches to draw attention to the plight of those left unwaged. The Hunger March in 1934 was intended as a protest against the often brutal means tests the Unemployed Assistance Board had deployed to assess all new claims for aid.*

FACING UP TO FASCISTS

We dined with Sir Bernard and Lady Partridge. He said, 'Mussolini has a very powerful face, but I can see nothing in Hitler.'

Rev. W. R. Inge, *Diary of a Dean*, 28 July 1934

GOOD GOLF, BAD FILM

Three days of good golf at Littlehampton. Leo described the *Man of Aran* film as the last word in tedium. Must they live there? Can't they go somewhere else? All this on the shingle at midnight watching an ebbing tide that Leo was mortally afraid might turn capricious, flow and engulf him.*

James Agate, Journals, 25 August 1934

*Man of Aran *was Robert Flaherty's documentary portrait of a family's 'hardscrabble island life off the west coast of Ireland'. Acclaimed in its day for its authenticity, it has subsequently been criticized for its staged romantic-fictional liberties.*

⌒⁂⌒

READING UP ON THE REICH

I devour books about Germany: one wants to understand how it is that that gifted race has drifted into disaster.*

Beatrice Webb, Diaries, 7 September 1934

After the death of German President Paul von Hindenburg, the nation's chancellor, Adolf Hitler, called a referendum on 19 August 1934 asking for permission to rule as the Führer, or 'Leader', with absolute dictatorial power. The motion was approved by 90 per cent of the German public.

⌒⁂⌒

REPUTATIONS MADE AND UNMADE

The main events of the past three weeks have been (a) a flight to Australia in two and half days by two men called Scott and Black, and (b) Lloyd George's denunciation of Haig over the matter of Passchendaele. This should put an end to any matter of a statue.*

James Agate, Journals, 30 October 1934

* *Lloyd George once described Field Marshal Sir Douglas Haig, who commanded the British Expeditionary Force on the Western Front during World War I, as 'brilliant to the top of his Army boots'. However, in 1917 he had expressed grave doubts about the offensive Haig masterminded in Flanders that ultimately resulted in heavy casualties at Passchendaele. After Haig's death in 1928, both Lloyd George and Winston Churchill would publish books critical of Haig, and their histories led to Haig being personally blamed, fairly or not, for much of the slaughter at the Somme and Ypres.*

LORD'S DAY BROADCAST

Finished off a busy morning with a glance through the papers and find that G. B. S. [George Bernard Shaw] has been getting into trouble with the Lord's Day Observance Society. Broadcasting on Sunday, the old man said that there was nothing improper about sex, which is entitled to a good share of interest in plays and films. At this, the Lord's Day Observance Society got on its hind-legs and asked the BBC why they allowed the Sabbath to be desecrated with G. B. S.'s nonsense. When interviewed, Shaw said he had gone into the matter years ago and in his own mind settled it once and for all, and that people had better do just what he told them and leave the reasons to him! The old man is perfectly right. If anyone were to ask me who is the best observer of the Lord's Day, I should say George Bernard Shaw, on the principle that all days are the Lord's and G. B. S. observes them all.

James Agate, Journals, 22 January 1935

TOO FLAT-FOOTED TO FIGHT

Today's big news is that Germany has decided to re-arm, and has ordered conscription. This means the end of the Treaty of Versailles. I think France, as usual, is to blame. I think I am personally safe – war won't come for some years and perhaps I shall then be too old and feeble. In any case, my feet are far too flat. Now people are prattling of war again – every few years we have these scares.

Sir Henry 'Chips' Channon, Diaries, 16 March 1935

⌀

A PRO-NAZI PRINCE?

Much gossip about the Prince of Wales's alleged Nazi leanings; he is alleged to have been influenced by Emerald [Cunard] (who is rather *éprise* with Herr Ribbentrop*) through Mrs Simpson … He has just made an extraordinary speech to the British Legion advocating friendship with Germany; it is only a gesture, but a gesture that may be taken seriously in Germany and elsewhere.

Sir Henry 'Chips' Channon, Diaries, 9 June 1935

* *Joachim von Ribbentrop was then Hitler's roving Reich Minister Ambassador-Plenipotentiary at Large. He would be named the German ambassador in London in 1936, and from 1938 and until 1945 served as Reich Minister for Foreign Affairs.*

⌀

MODERN, INSIDE AND OUT

Margaret very pleasant, and the ultra-modern house is charming *inside*. Outside, hideous to my thinking. And especially squatting in the middle of an ancient garden.

Mrs Henry Dudeney, A Lewes Diary, 21 June 1935

⌀

FEVERISHLY COMMITTED

Someone took me to a Group Theatre show in London and I was struck by the freshness and wit of a kind of revue. We arrived late and it was not till the end I discovered it was Auden's *Dance of Death* with Britten's music. They are rehearsing a new Auden show for their Westminster season, *The Dog Beneath the Skin*. I can't understand half the allusions. The Group Theatre and its adherents are mainly very young with a sprinkling of my contemporaries and a few earnest older women whom Rupert forces to attend his strenuous dance and exercise classes as a method of breaking down their psychological 'adhesions'. The atmosphere is feverishly progressive. Revolution in politics, revolution in art; revolution in one's way of life. Few actual party members but it is taken for granted that one sympathises with communism. The poets are all becoming propagandists and pamphleteers. I begin to feel guilty about not being 'politically awakened' and not throwing myself into the movement. 'Writers must come out of their ivory towers,' insists Rupert (with Spender, Isherwood, MacNeice, Auden etc. behind him). 'They must become socially conscious, working for the collective good. They must break down their old bourgeois pride and prejudice and individualism.' To staunch my conscience, I type out manifestos on Revolution in the Theatre and spend my mornings addressing envelopes to possible supporters.

Antonia White, Diaries, 10 August 1935

ANTI-FASCIST ARTISTS

To-day I received particulars of an anti-fascist exhibition to be held in London this autumn; it is to be not so much propaganda as a gesture of solidarity on the part of serious artists of all schools. [Duncan] Grant, [Eric] Gill, [Paul] Nash and [Henry] Moore are to be among the exhibitors, and I thought I deserved an invitation to the show; now I have one. I shall suggest Tommy [Carr] & Geoff [Tibble] as well.

William Townsend, Journals, 3 September 1935

MUSSOLINI THREATENS ABYSSINIA

Jock entirely refuses to take the war danger seriously.* His comment on the alarmist newspaper placard 'Italians in Abyssinia' is: 'Sounds like an opera by Rossini.'

James Agate, Journals, 2 October 1935

* *Mussolini had sent troops into Ethiopia without declaring war; Ethiopia responded to the incursion by declaring war on Italy. The League of Nations determined that Italy was the aggressor and imposed sanctions, but they proved to be toothless.*

⁓

MOUNTING THE PAVEMENT

This morning I had another driving lesson and got on very well except for a few lapses, notably when I went on the pavement at the Sun Corner. However, I'm getting better at it. I had a nice Austin 2-seater to drive.

Barbara Pym, *A Very Private Eye*, 19 November 1935

⁓

SOUND OF MODERN EFFICIENCY

Up early & to Soho Square at 9.45. Some bother over parts for orchestra, but I eventually got down to Blackheath at 11.00 for big TPO recording.

A large orchestra for me – Fl., Ob., Trpt., Harp (Maria Kotchinka – very good), Vln. Vlc. CB, Percussion and wind machine – a splendid team. The music I wrote really comes off well – &, for what is wanted, creates quite alot [*sic*] of sensation! The whole trouble, & what takes so much time, is that over the music has to be spoken a verse – kind of patter – written by Auden – in strict rhythm with the music. To represent the train noises. There is too much to be spoken in a single breath by the one voice (it is essential to keep the same voice & to have no breaks), so we have to record separately – me having to conduct both from an improvised visual metronome – flashes on the screen – a very difficult job! Legg speaks the stuff splendidly tho'.*

Benjamin Britten, *Journeying Boy*, 15 January 1936

* *With a poetic narration by W. H. Auden and music by Britten,* Night Mail *charts the nocturnal operation of a Royal Mail delivery train.*

DEATH OF KING GEORGE V

Every flag was at half-mast yesterday except Buckingham Palace, where there was no flag at all, there being no sovereign. The town like Sunday; all theatres and cinemas closed and all public functions abandoned. Dined quietly with Moray McLaren and Rose-Troup, and at 9.30 went across to Broadcasting House to hear the Prime Minister. Very good and well delivered. Moray said the speech was for all Europe as well as England – 'Hitler and the boys will be listening.' When Baldwin spoke of the Prince of Wales and his tremendous responsibilities there came into his voice, or I thought so, just a hint of the Lord Chief Justice of *Henry IV*, Part 2, Act V, Sc. 2.

James Agate, Journals, 22 January 1936

THE TRAMP TALKS

The Chaplin film. Until last week there were four absolute silences – Outer Space, the grave, the Sphinx, and Charlie Chaplin's. To-day, Tuesday, February 11, 1936, the number of those silences was reduced to three, since in *Modern Times* Chaplin's voice was heard for the first time. It would not be true to say that Charlie spoke, because he didn't. He sang, and his singing was enough to destroy something the world had cherished. The point is not whether Chaplin sang well or ill; he destroyed a mystery. This song of Chaplin's is unforgivable only if it is unique, and if never again under any pretext whatever he utters spoken or singing word.

James Agate, Journals, 11 February 1936

TRIPE IN THE CELLARS

The squalor of this house is beginning to get on my nerves. Nothing is ever cleaned or dusted, the rooms not done out till 5 in the afternoon, and the cloth never even removed from the table. At supper you see the crumbs from breakfast. The most revolting feature is Mrs F. being always in bed on the kitchen sofa. She has a terrible habit of tearing off strips of newspaper, wiping her mouth with them and then throwing them on the floor. Unemptied chamberpot under the table at breakfast this morning. The food is dreadful, too. We are given those little twopenny ready-made steak and kidney pies out of stock. I hear horrible stories, too, about the cellars where the tripe is kept and which are said to swarm with black beetles. Apparently, they only get in fresh supplies of tripe at long intervals. Mrs F. dates events by this. 'Let me see, now. I've had in three lots of froze (frozen tripe) since then,' etc. I judge they get in a consignment of 'froze' about once in a fortnight. Also, it is very tiring being unable to stretch my legs straight out at night.*

George Orwell, Diaries, 22 February 1936

* *This diary entry would form the working notes for a scene in the opening chapter of Orwell's* The Road to Wigan Pier, *his investigation into the life of the urban poor published by Victor Gollancz's new Left Book Club in March 1937.*

WAR IN SPAIN INTENSIFIES

News from Spain still bad, tho' government seems to be gaining ground abit [*sic*] – it varies with what paper one reads. One thing is certain that Fascists are executing hundreds (literally) of Popular Front or Communist members – including many boys of 14–16. Marvellous to have opinions of that strength at that age. I can't help feeling that not until that 'political consciousness' is more general that the world will get out of this mess.*

Benjamin Britten, *Journeying Boy*, 24 July 1936

* *Reeling from the economic after-effects of the Wall Street Crash and the Great Depression, Spain had become sharply politically divided. On the one side there were the Nationalists, a right-wing party backed by landowners, monarchists, the Catholic Church and employers (soon headed by General Franco). Against them were the Republicans, a left-wing party supported by socialists and trade union members. An attempted coup by the army in 1936 plunged the country into a bloody civil war. With Fascists ruling in Germany and Italy, the fate of Spain had global implications, with France, in particular, anxious not to see another continental neighbour fall to a military dictatorship. However, both France and Britain were unwilling to wholeheartedly support the Republicans, who received backing from Soviet Russia, for fear that it might give succour to left-wing agitators in their own countries. But the Republicans' cause was taken up by thousands of young men and women from across Europe and the United States, who joined so-called International Brigades to fight against the right-wing menace to Western democracy in Spain.*

PUBLIC TRANSPORT HIT BY MARCH

Lil came this morning. She brought me jelly, wine, apples, took me to Pritchard's to luncheon and brought me a half pound of chocolates. I *am* getting fat. It *does* grieve me. Sometimes I feel inclined to commit suicide when I see my enormous hulk. I weight 10 stone 9 lbs. Came home to spend the evening in peace and quiet. The Jarrow marchers held up our bus this morning.*

Gladys Langford, Diaries, 31 October 1936

* *Following the closure of the Palmer's shipyard, the north-eastern town of Jarrow had been afflicted by an unemployment rate of 70 per cent. To draw attention to their plight, some 200 men, accompanied by their local MP, Ellen 'Red Ellen' Wilkinson, marched to London to deliver a petition to Parliament. However, Stanley Baldwin, the Conservative prime minister, claimed to be too busy to receive a direct deputation from the men.*

*ᴄ*ᴍ

THE UNWELCOME EFFECT OF FOREIGN TRAVEL

To Wellings' last night. Clowser was there. He's gone 'Anti-Semitic' since his visit to Germany. Very dull weather and school consequently wearisome.

Gladys Langford, Diaries, 2 November 1936

*ᴄ*ᴍ

TOLLS IN SPAIN

Fall of Madrid imminent. Jock was so much upset before lunch that he could hardly work. The cause was the destruction of Goya's frescoes and the danger threatening the Velázquezes at the Prado. My pretended concern is for the 300,000 killed, including 30,000 executed, which I understand to be the latest figures. But this, on my part, is cant. What I mean is that if I had time for the Spanish Civil War, this is what I should first be concerned about. But I am too busy to give a thought to it, and they must fight it out without me.

James Agate, Journals, 6 November 1936

*ᴄ*ᴍ

GREAT FIRE

A bad night, a bad headache and a bad temper in consequence. Feel bilious too – very unusual for me. Crystal Palace* burnt down last night. Duke of Kent among the onlookers – trying on helmets of firemen and getting drenched by hose-pipes. What a nuisance he must have been to the firemen, or did he think he was a reincarnation of Charles II at the Great Fire?

Gladys Langford, Diaries, 1 December 1936

Designed by Sir Joseph Paxton for the Great Exhibition in 1851, the Crystal Palace – in its day one of the most innovative structures ever built and fashioned entirely in cast-iron and plate-glass – had been moved from Hyde Park to Sydenham in 1854. It stood there until fire destroyed it in a few hours on the night of 30 November 1936.

THE ABDICATION CRISIS

We talk, up and down the High Street, in and out of the house, of nothing but the King. Some say he has made over the Duchy of Cornwall to that Simpson fiend. Others say he can't. Some say she is a spy from Russia.

Mrs Henry Dudeney, *A Lewes Diary*, 5 December 1936

It is a quarter past seven, and I have been sitting with the wireless half on all afternoon. There was to be a Cabinet Meeting at half past five o'clock, at which presumably the King's decision was to be made known. So far – nothing. If ever there was an occasion for a 'solemn musick' this was it.

8.56. The wireless news hints much, says little. The PM will not see the King to-night. To-morrow's Cabinet meeting has been cancelled, and the PM will make a statement in the House to-morrow. I thought I detected a defensive note in the plea that Ministers had neither threatened the King nor attempted unduly to hurry him, and that at no time had there been open or formal disagreement.

James Agate, Journals, 6 December 1936

So far as I am concerned, the King abdicated when the news was announced over the wireless at six o'clock last night. The ceremony, for such it was, was moving. Baldwin came out of it very well. It entirely cleared my mind of any possible doubts as to the way in which this thing ought to be looked at.

History will record that Edward VIII found the Kingship of Britain to be insufficient beauty.*

James Agate, Journals, 11 December 1936

---

* *The relationship between Edward VIII and Mrs Wallis Simpson, a twice-married divorcee, was initially a titillating affair to the popular press and public alike. In November 1936, the King proposed entering into a morganatic marriage with Simpson after her latest divorce was agreed. Under such an arrangement she would be accepted as consort rather than queen. But this idea was rejected by Stanley Baldwin's Cabinet and representatives from the dominions, who presented Edward with three options: either finish with Mrs Simpson, marry her against the advice of his ministers (who would then out of necessity resign) or abdicate.*

THE MAD PASSIONS OF THE MIDDLE AGED

At Midday Bay phoned, then my beloved Leonard saying he would meet me this afternoon. He came at 3 p.m. and we indulged in a wild orgy of love-making. No one would realise that the almost cruelly fond bed-mate is the sober, satirical, middle-aged man of office-hours. After all these years, his lightest touch sets all my pulses a'throb, yet I'm glad now that we never married. He is too much engulfed by his family. Yet it gratifies me to know that I, at 46 2/3, can still rouse him to a demonstration of mad passion.

Gladys Langford, Diaries, 28 December 1936

*

VOLUNTEER FOR SPAIN

Hurriedly do some more parts ('Sinfonietta', this time for further reproduction) before meeting Wystan [W. H.] Auden at Tottenham Ct Road. He goes off to Spain (to drive an ambulance) to-morrow. It is terribly sad & I feel ghastly about it, tho' I feel it is perhaps the logical thing for him to do – being such a direct person. Anyhow, it's phenomenally brave. Spend a glorious morning with him (at Lyons Corner House, coffee-drinking). Talk over everything, & he gives me two grand poems – a lullaby, & a big, simple, folky Farewell – that is overwhelmingly tragic and moving.

Benjamin Britten, *Journeying Boy*, 8 January 1937

*

SHELLING OUT FOR THE CORONATION

Streets are packed with people, largely provincials, all agape to see the decorations, which are very similar to those up at the Jubilee and the Royal Weddings. I am weary of the Royal pictures in the cinema programmes, Coronation items in daily papers and weekly magazines. In an animal dealer's, I actually saw tortoises with Union Jacks painted on their backs!

Gladys Langford, Diaries, 8 May 1937

c的

ART FOR SPAIN

We went on together to the Albert Hall. It was the most impressive meeting I have ever been to, and three and half hours later when we had to leave to catch the midnight train it was not over and we were sorry to go. Neither Picasso nor Heinrich Mann appeared, but Picasso offered the good reason that he is painting a canvas of the destruction of Guernica for the Spanish pavilion at the Paris exhibition. But the speeches we heard were good, all of them, and the enthusiasm of the audience was terrific …

Paul Robeson* was the great man of the evening. As there had been some doubt as to whether his broadcast would be sanctioned, as soon as he heard he had flown back from Russia to be here tonight and was properly honoured for it; he dominated the occasion; his personality eclipsed all others as his speech overwhelmed theirs. It was a brave and truly noble speech; the battlefront is everywhere, he said, and every artist must take his stand one side or the other, and, 'I have taken my stand. I stand unalterably in support of the Spanish government.' That a negro artist could say that in an international gathering and that those words should evoke rapturous applause which went on and on is of impressive significance. Robeson speaks for his whole race as possibly no other intentional figure does, and he bestrode this meeting so that the negroes and the Spaniards seemed the same thing; and he sang and so easily filled the air, and it seemed everything at that moment that he was singing was not for two oppressed peoples but for the oppressed everywhere and all the generous aspirations of the unoppressed as well.

William Townsend, Journals, 24 June 1937

* *The black American actor, singer, athlete, civil rights campaigner and political activist Paul Robeson first came to Britain in 1928 as a member of the cast of a West End production of the musical* Show Boat. *While in London he met a group of unemployed Welsh miners who had walked to the capital to draw attention to the hardship they and their families were enduring. He was moved by their stories to arrange a visit to the valleys to see for himself the conditions they were living in.*

cᴍᴄ

WHAT MAKES FASCISM?

The other night, Norman [Cameron] was saying he felt there really was a devil and it was incarnate in the Germans. He felt it would be justifiable to stamp them out. Basil believed they should be given everything they wanted in order to restore their self-respect. The argument became very heated. Basil said, 'You have the mentality that makes fascists.' Norman became angry: he first of all hectored Basil in a school prefect way (Basil had certainly been very provoking in tone all the evening and had put his case arrogantly and badly) and then threw a glass of soda water in his face.

Antonia White, Diaries, 28 June 1937

cᴍᴄ

BLACKSHIRTS IN KENT

Canterbury had its dose of fascism today. [Oswald] Mosley at the Forrester's Hall. The Keables and all our Peacemaker group except David, with a few reinforcements from Wye College and from Sandwich, went down as an opposition body; but three quarters of the audience was [in] opposition. This led to a few scuffles with the gangster stewards, grimacing at every interrupter as if they were all dictators already, to a couple of ejections and a blow on the head from a baton for one young fellow.

Mosley's speech was a very clever one indeed; in fact, beautifully twisted, but when he had got his agricultural policy put across he was clearly out to provoke bad feeling and make excuses for abuse and shouting and whipping up his own followers' enthusiasm. He never hesitated to call an interrupter a bone-head, a village idiot, a puppet who was preventing 'this large and intelligent audience' from listening to him. Two-thirds must have been bone-heads, as they clearly did not like him.

Trickiness is Mosley's greatest virtue; he is not a magnetic personality – even striding down Canterbury's peaceful high street with his bodyguards.

William Townsend, Journals, 5 July 1937

SCUFFLE ON ARMISTICE DAY

The usual feeble dissertation for Armistice Day at school. All a farce! Great War, Boer War or Crimean War are all alike to these children. Many of their fathers are even too young to have fought in it [the Great War]. 'An incident' at the Cenotaph. An alleged lunatic burst through police and military guards and shouted, 'All this hypocrisy! You are arming for a new War!' Wireless listeners heard the scuffle as ten or so policemen lay on him and stifled him. The newspapers say he was picked up unconscious. Poor wretch! Apparently, he was the only sane one there! A woman cried out, 'Lynch him' – oh, the gentle sex.

Gladys Langford, Diaries, 11 November 1937

✒

HITLER'S APPEARANCE

I had a long conversation with Lord Halifax about Germany and his recent visit. He described Hitler's appearance, his khaki shirt, black breeches and patent leather evening shoes. He told me he liked all the Nazi leaders, even Goebbels, and he was much impressed, interested and amused by the visit. He thinks the regime absolutely fantastic, perhaps even too fantastic to be taken seriously. But he is very glad he went, and thinks good will come of it. I was riveted by all he said, and reluctant to let him go.

Sir Henry 'Chips' Channon, Diaries, 5 December 1937

✒

THE KING'S SPEECH

Xmas Day. Surely the quietest I have ever spent. A heavy fog, like that described by Dickens in *Bleak House*, closes in like a pall. My latest complaint is a violent attack of diarrhoea and an awful feeling of sickness.

Listened to the King's speech – very slow in delivery and even more slight in substance. There was one painful pause due to his stammer.*

Gladys Langford, Diaries, 25 December 1937

---

* *Afflicted by a stammer that left him unable to pronounce the letter 'k', Prince Albert had never expected to be king and assumed the Crown reluctantly after his brother abdicated. He underwent speech therapy at the hands of Lionel Logue, an ex-actor from Australia, to improve his public speaking for the radio broadcasts now expected from the monarch.*

MICKEY MOUSE FOR ART HISTORIANS

On the centre page of *The Times*, opposite its special article on the Church Commission, it is announced that after 3 years' work by 600 persons at a cost of £300,000 Mr Walter Disney has finished his fairy-tale film of *Snow White and the Seven Dwarfs*. The universal success of the creator of Mickey Mouse will not escape the art-historian of the future. It is the symptom of the same tendency as much of modern poetry – infantile regression, with a spice of sadism.

As Cicero might have groaned – '*O tempera, o mures!*'*

F. L. Lucas, *Journal Under Terror*, 16 January 1938

* *This translates to: 'Oh what times! Oh what customs!'* Snow White and the Seven Dwarfs *was the first full-length animated feature film in colour and with sound.*

~

WAR IN APRIL

I hear from a source which ought to be reliable about war in April. It appears that the Navy cannot guarantee to defend Hong Kong and the Suez Canal and look after the North Sea. Any two, they say, but not three. As against an alliance between Japan, Italy and Germany, that age-old cocotte France will not say what she will do, we do not know what use Russia would be, and America is indifferent. All the staff at the Foreign Office had their gas-masks tried on last week, and spent some time in a gas-filled chamber. Our Air Force is said to be pretty good, though reprisals seem to me to be mere baby-talk. If Germany is as ruthless as I believe, she will sacrifice Berlin for London in the way the chess-player with the stronger position will force an exchange of queens.

James Agate, *Journals*, 26 January 1938

~

REFUGEES FROM SPAIN

Four thousand Basque children are brought to England to save them from the [Spanish] Civil War.

France has taken 18,000 children to our 4,000, not to speak of hosts of adult refugees; even Belgium has welcomed 4,000. But the rich of the richest country in Europe wish to visit on these infants the crime of their parents in supporting a Government far from Communist but still guilty of the one sin against the Holy Spirit – touching the money of the rich.

F. L. Lucas, *Journal Under Terror*, 6 February 1938

❦

SEASIDE HIT BY SNOW AND STORMS

Snow! Not very thick, but enough to make me a quarter of an hour late. The high seas of the week-end badly damaged Margate Jetty and prom[enade]. Beach huts and rowing boats smashed up.

L. Hughes, Diaries, 14 February 1938

❦

THE MAYFAIR MEN TRIAL

The Old Bailey. This is the fourth and last day of the Hyde Park Hotel jewel robbery case*, in which four young men, educated at the best public schools, receive sentences from eighteen months' hard labour to seven years' penal servitude with 20 strokes of the 'cat'. Crowded court. Celebrities – 'better than any play'. A horrid glamour about the whole affair. I am naturally fascinated by criminals, whose dreadful jauntiness haunts me for days.

James Agate, Journals, 18 February 1938

M. Etienne Bellenger, a Bond Street jeweller, had been beaten and robbed of £13,000 worth of jewels at Hyde Park Hotel. His attackers, Robert Harley, David Wilmer, Peter Jenkins and Christopher Mainwaring Lonsdale, all in their twenties and related to 'prominent families', were found to have lured their victim to a suite in the hotel to commit their crime. Their trial was a sensation, with a spectators gallery stuffed with 'society people', many of whom brought sandwiches with them to avoid losing their seats during the lunch recess.

PLEDGES FOR PEACE

I went to the Pacifist Meeting in the Town Hall. I saw Don Liddell – he and Jock were selling literature and carrying posters. Just before it was about to begin, I saw Jay standing up in the front. I felt rather excited, although I had resolved to put him and all such diversions from me – but I managed to attend well to the meeting. The speakers were George Lansbury, Mary Gamble and J. Middleton Murry. After the meeting, I talked to the Liddells and John Barnicot. We walked along the Corn. Just by Marks and Spencer's, Jay walked past us. I caught him up and asked him if he was going to sign the Peace Pledge. He took my hand and held it very fast. Walking along with him all my unhappiness vanished. We went into the Randolph and, as it was only five to ten, we were able to buy a bottle of Niersteiner to take back with us. In my rooms we drank wine and talked and loved, and I made a half-hearted effort to convert him to Pacifism, though I wasn't entirely converted myself. But he said he thought there were worse things than war, and that if he thought all Beauty was going out of his life he would simply shoot himself.

Barbara Pym, *A Very Private Eye*, 3 March 1938

BIASED BOXING MATCH

Last night came news of the German invasion of Austria. Yet this morning's placards are equally excited about the fight between Farr and Baer. We fiddle, while Vienna burns.*

F. L. Lucas, *Journal Under Terror*, 12 March 1938

* Max Baer's much anticipated second bout against the Welshman Tommy Farr, who was the British and Empire heavyweight champion, took place at Madison Square Garden, in New York City, on 11 March 1938.

⤜

MARCH FOR SPAIN

After a dinner of mussels at the Cervantes with Rob, I went up to Mornington Crescent to join a demonstration marching to the Spanish Embassy with a resolution of support for the Spanish people …

At the meeting at the end of the march it was amusing to notice from faces and remarks around that it irked the communists to forgo the singing of *The Internationale*. No doubt they were justified in feeling it was their show; there would have been nothing at all if they had not organised it, I suppose. Goodness knows what is happening to the Labour Party.

William Townsend, Journals, 22 March 1938

⤜

SEIZED BY AUSTRIA

Another refugee came to see me. A cousin of the last, and a merchant. After four years in exile for his political beliefs he had returned to Vienna six days before Hitler marched in. He was seized and made to wash cars for the Nazis. They did not yet realise he was a Social-Democrat. But he had a bad heart; and so no escape was possible that involved great physical effort.

Accordingly, he took a train – by brief stages to disarm suspicion – to St Polten, to Linz, to Saltzburg, to Zell-am-See, where he pretended to be going for heart-treatment. Thence, sometimes by local buses, sometimes by local trains, he got to Kitzbühel and Innsbruck; and so finally by buses to Feldkirch, where he went to a doctor for his heart and arranged to undergo a cure at Bregenz. (These medical papers might prove useful bona fides, if he were stopped by the police.) Then between 7.30 and 8.00 that evening, he quietly strolled across into Switzerland. So in the end the fugitive reached this country. Heaven grant that the callous and mean-spirited wretches who disgrace the Home Office do not fling him out again.

Other refugees he described as romantically escaping on skis across the Silvretta Pass. And in Vienna, he said, boys and girls of fifteen had been arrested for *laughing* in the street while Hitler was broadcasting.*

F. L. Lucas, *Journal Under Terror*, 27 April 1938

* *As part of Hitler's expansionist schemes to bring all the German-speaking nations in Europe under Nazi control, German troops had marched into Austria unopposed on 12 March 1938. A month later, a referendum was held with results heavily rigged in the Nazis' favour, which purported to show that Austrians approved of German rule.*

∼

A STRONG GERMANY

At Rome last night, after a banquet, Hitler and Mussolini came out on to a balcony and were cheered by, according to the *Observer*, 500,000 people. Does anybody imagine that, if Germany had won the War, Neville Chamberlain and Daladier would today be allowed to take tea together or address a crowd of even 500 people? One doesn't know what methods Germany would have resorted to – sterilisation, alternate German fatherhood, armies of occupation. My view is that as a beginning they would have razed the Ford, Morris and Austin motor works and made everyone walk. The unthinkable fact is that we have made Germany stronger than ever, not because the Peace Terms were too harsh, but because they were not harsh enough. It's no good saying to a mad dog: We'll allow you to go on being a little mad. The fault is that of misplaced idealism. Free Trade is no use unless everyone adopts it. Ditto disarmament; Ditto the League of Nations. The grand mistake is the idealist one of believing that human nature is better than it is, or is likely to become better in reckonable time. I have never held a brief for Northcliffe, but he was right when he said, and said often: 'You must watch those Germans. They will cheat you yet!' They have cheated us, and with our connivance!

James Agate, Journals, 8 May 1938

cy&n

ANTI-SEMITISM ON THE RISE

Dined with Chaim and Vera. Eva Reading came in after. Terribly depressed by her own first impacts with anti-Semitism. It is terrible for her, brought up as an English girl, and she sees it affecting her children.

Even Jimmy de Rothschild, with all the staff at the Ritz bowing and running to serve him, told me with panic that on the golf course at Hoylake this morning they found a swastika and 'Down with the Jews' painted on a putting-green.

Blanche Dugdale, Diaries, 11 July 1938

cy&n

FATALISM OVER HOPE

The renewed tension over Czechoslovakia goes on increasing. But the human nervous-system gets used to this, like other poisons, in increasing doses. I no longer lie awake over Czechoslovakia; not because of more hope, but out of more fatalism.

Germany is playing with 1½ million men on manoeuvres.*

Bluff or war?

F. L. Lucas, Journal Under Terror, 19 August 1938

* *Created after the First World War, Czechoslovakia was a state composed of a majority of Slavic Czech and Slovak people with a minority German-speaking population of 3 million in the Sudetanland, which had formerly been part of the Austrian Empire. Having already annexed Austria, Hitler's ambitions turned to the Sudetanland. By May 1938 he had moved German troops to the Czech border. In the following two months in discussions with Britain's prime minister, Neville Chamberlain, Hitler promised that if granted control of the Sudetenland, he would not seek to invade Slavic Czechoslovakia too.*

⌒୷⌒

HIGH-SCORING HUTTON

By the close of play England had scored 903 for 7 declared! Australia 28 for 2. Many records have been broken in this match. Hutton, the highlight, scored 364 after batting over 10 hours. Bradman has been hurt, so we stand a very real chance of winning the Fifth Test. Went in for a dip tonight with Bert. Water was warm.

L. Hughes, Diaries, 23 August 1938

⌒୷⌒

A SICKENING NAZI SUPPORTER

Miss Unity Mitford, waiting to cheer Hitler at Breslau, is reported to have given herself sunstroke, followed by pleurisy and pneumonia.

F. L. Lucas, Journal Under Terror, 26 August 1938

⌒୷⌒

EMPEROR IN EAST SUSSEX

At Southease after looking at the frescoes and while we were having tea, the Rector told us that Haile Selassie (a name so suggestive of Harry Lauder's song 'Here's a Lassie') had been to his church. He – the Rector – peaceful in his study, presumably chewing the cud of a sermon, when in rushed an agitated last parishioner: 'Come at once. The Abyssian Emperor is here.' The Rector in agitation asks: 'How am I to behave?' 'You are to make a *very deep* bow and *frequently* say "Your Majesty".' This was done.*

Mrs Henry Dudeney, *A Lewes Diary*, 8 September 1938

* After Mussolini's troops invaded Abyssinia, Haile Selassie and his family fled into exile. They would spend much of the next five years in England, with spells in Bath, London and Great Malvern.

UNEASY FIGHTS

War fever raging as in 1913. Placards, wireless, everything going over and over the question. I feel utterly wretched and unsettled. Add to this a heat-wave that makes existence at school most wretched. Went westwards tonight but a full Disney programme at the Tatler kept me away. Saw a fight in progress in Soho Square so fetched a policeman, then departed myself. Not getting concert tickets or anything else while this uneasiness persists.

Gladys Langford, Diaries, 13 September 1938

PREPARING FOR WAR

Nine days of one crisis after another. This afternoon a middle-aged gentlewoman looking like a character in a Dodie Smith play acted by Muriel Aked, called to measure me for my gas-mask. She expressed herself as quite ready to be killed at her job.

'How can man die better than facing fearful odds? Lord Macaulay, you know I learned that verse when I was a girl. Still quite apt, don't you think?'

James Agate, Journals, 24 September 1938

PLANS FOR EVACUATION

News blacker than ever. Mrs Lucas's son called up – Naval Reservist. Plans for general evacuation in progress. Trench-digging everywhere. Long faces, tearful women in streets. Police vans with loudspeakers in Shaftesbury Avenue directing folk to [the] nearest gas-mask station. To Em's. Bee full of plans for getting the family away. His wireless braying through the news again and again.

Gladys Langford, Diaries, 28 September 1938

<hr>

NORMALITY RESUMES

At 3 o'clock this morning the Powers came to agreement over the Czech problem. The crisis is just about past. It has been a very near thing. It depends, however, how long the peace will last. As I came to work I noticed the hastily built dugouts and imagined what the scene would have been had war come. In the evening as things became normal I went to [the] Rink.

L. Hughes, Diaries, 30 September 1938

<hr>

CONVERSATION IN A CRISIS

A peace agreement is signed and war is averted, at any rate temporarily. Bee brought up tea and paper at 6.30 a.m. so I should have the news. I left Em's at 10 a.m., and as I went along Eastern Avenue a workman stopped me and asked if I thought peace would last long? Everybody talks to everyone else now, as in the days of the Great War. I was so pleased to get home. Went westwards this afternoon and to Rosenbergs tonight. Leslie is an ARP [Air Raid Precautions] warden and so is Mr Samuel. The latter has rigged up a gas-proof room.*

Gladys Langford, Diaries, 30 September 1938

* On 29 and 30 September, Benito Mussolini of Italy, the French Premier Edouard Daladier and British Prime Minister Neville Chamberlain met Hitler in Munich to discuss his intention to claim the Sudetenland for the so-called greater German 'homeland'. Two weeks earlier, Neville Chamberlain, pursuing a policy of appeasement intended to prevent another world war, had in effect already assured Hitler that Britain would not oppose a German invasion of the Sudetenland. Now, in exchange for the promise of maintaining peace in Europe, France, Britain and Italy all acceded to Hitler's demands. Neither the Czechs, nor their ally Russia, were consulted and they were left to accept the deal or fight alone to prevent the German troops seizing the region. Chamberlain flew back to Britain having signed a non-aggression pact with Hitler. Greeted by the press and jubilant crowds at Heston airport, West London, he bandied a copy of this document about, maintaining that it signalled 'peace for our time' between Britain and Germany.

LET DOWN BY THE GERMAN CHANCELLOR

The children are very disappointed. They were looking forward to this wholesale exodus into the country. One little boy when told that now they would not go, said: 'I suppose that bloke Hitler has let us down'!

Mrs Henry Dudeney, *A Lewes Diary*, 6 October 1938

AN INFLAMMATORY PENGUIN PAPERBACK

I bought myself a 6d Penguin book to read. Evelyn Waugh's *Vile Bodies*. Filthy and blasphemous. Shall burn it (but finish reading it first!).

Mrs Henry Dudeney, *A Lewes Diary*, 13 October 1938

DREADED NEWS

Armistice Day! And the news of the pogrom in Germany, as bad or worse than I had dreaded or expected.*

Blanche Dugdale, Diaries, 11 November 1938

* *On the night of 9 November 1938, violence against Jews, carefully orchestrated by the German Propaganda Minister Joseph Goebbels to appear a spontaneous reaction to the assignation of a German official in France, broke out across the German Reich. In the next two days, thousands of Jewish businesses, schools and homes were smashed up and looted, over 200 Jewish synagogues were burned and dozens of Jewish citizens were killed. The pogrom has been known ever since as* Kristallnacht, *or the Night of Broken Glass, in reference to the shattered glass from shop windows that littered the streets in towns and cities across Germany.*

⌇

ALL QUIET IN THE STALLS

To the Court Theatre for a revival of *All Quiet on the Western Front*. Very much impressed. This was followed by a film of the Armistice ceremony. The audience was extraordinarily silent throughout both films.

James Agate, Journals, 13 November 1938

⌇

A REFUGEE'S STORY

Rosa is a Jewish refugee, an ex-secretary speaking and writing six languages. She was driven out of her office by the Nazis with a revolver at her head. Her old parents were in a concentration camp for 18 days, and returned to find every valuable taken and every stick of furniture smashed. Her fiancé, to whom she should have been married in October, is deported – but to Shanghai and it is doubtful if they will ever meet again. She has been since August with a Roman

Catholic colonel who worked her nearly to death, telling her daily how the Jews have only themselves to blame and how she ought to be grateful for finding shelter in England. He seems to have been a positive sadist. Then she went to a couple with a baby who worked her from 6 a.m. till midnight, then work her up for baby-minding. I gave her 2s for an Xmas box.

Glady Langford, Diaries, 23 December 1938

⌒⋰⋱⌒

CHRISTMAS ON THE COAST

A real old-fashioned Christmas. Inches deep in snow in Thanet. Spent day fairly quiet. Aunt Harriet came over.

L. Hughes, Diaries, 25 December 1938

CHAPTER FIVE

THE WORLD AT WAR
AGAIN: 1939-1945

The Munich Agreement might have been trumpeted as offering 'peace for our time', but events across the Continent after *Kristallnacht* soon had war in the air again, with storm clouds breaking out not just in Spain but also in Eastern Europe. The true costs of Chamberlain and Daladier's 'devil's bargain' allowing Germany to annex parts of Czechoslovakia would certainly be reckoned with eighteen months later, when on 10 May 1940 the German army drove new tanks, built in Škoda's state-of-the-art Czechoslovakian plant, into France. However, it's clear from some of these correspondents from history that many in Britain initially clung on to the hope that any war would effectively remain, as Neville Chamberlain put it, 'a quarrel in a faraway country between people of whom we know nothing'. The belief that Germany's actions in the east perhaps posed more of a threat to Communist Russia than to Britain or France remained the line of Lord Beaverbrook's *Daily Express* until well into 1939. But in these diaries, journals and letters, the increasing inevitability of 'not if but when' of the war can be read slowly but surely, first as the latest news from Czechoslovakia and then from Poland was absorbed, and schemes for evacuations were revived and troops mobilized.

The familiar litanies of gas masks, shelters and blackouts, rationing and food shortages, allotments and clothing coupons, and the horrific aerial bombardments of the Blitz are, of course, all present. But so, too, are the problems of feeding pets, the complaints about the prime minister being a warmonger (or his speeches and presumptions criticized as being preposterous) and the speculations on the Lend-Lease agreements, which would be needed to supply the toasted Spam sandwiches relished by the deluge – late in the war – of American GIs.

The Second World War would be a new kind of war, one whose atrocities still chill and appal to this day. But it was also a conflict waged in the media with propaganda disseminated in newspapers, leaflets and posters, on film and through newsreels, and over the airwaves. And it was to the BBC that the nation turned to hear Chamberlain announce that this country was 'at war with Germany'.

REFUGEE OBJECTIONS

There was a collection taken in all cinemas and theatres on Saturday and 10% of receipts were made over to the Refugees Fund. Apparently, this does not meet with general approval and there was a demonstration against it in Piccadilly Circus and Leicester Square on Saturday, trouble with the police and thousands of hand-bills distributed declaring refugees were taking away English people's jobs.

Gladys Langford, Diaries, 16 January 1939

PEACEFUL POLICE

An 'Arms for Spain' Demonstration in Trafalgar Square, called by the Aid Spain Committee, which has suddenly become one of the most active organisations. About 10,000 people there; the International Brigade marched in with their flags from the Embankment in a little splatter of rain: their massed flags made lovely colours in the greyness of the square, not too much but a vivid signature for the meeting.

The police were peculiarly submissive and even allowed themselves to be bullied, but there was something a little sinister in that, for last week a similar demonstration was broken up with a good deal of brutality, leading to questions in Parliament, and I have no doubt there was a decision to avoid another stink of the same kind.

William Townsend, Journals, 12 February 1939

⁓

ANNEXATION ANXIETIES

News in this morning's paper of what amounts to the annexation of Czecho by Germany. Went to Czecho Refugee Committee. People had been in direct communication with Prague. The German troops entering the town – Legations besieged by people seeking asylum, and had shut their doors. Uncertainty about a train loaded with 620 women and children, families of our political refugees, which started for Gdynia from Prague yesterday – no news as to whether it had crossed the Polish frontier. The men here wild with anxiety.*

Blanche Dugdale, Diaries, 15 March 1939

* *Breaching the principles of the Munich Pact, on this day German forces invaded and occupied the rest of Czechoslovakia.*

⁓

DOUBLES BY THE DOZEN

The rumour now is that Hitler is either dead or disposed of but has half a dozen doubles, and that Goebbels is the real villain of the piece. Mr Spokes said he couldn't understand why our Secret Service hadn't 'got rid' of Hitler long ago. 'It is always done.' People said the same of Mrs Simpson, now the (so-called) Duchess of Windsor: 'Why don't they bump her off?'

Mrs Henry Dudeney, A Lewes Diary, 15 March 1939

WAR IN THE AIR

To Rosenbergs tonight. Clarrie and Mr Freeman there. Her repugnance for her elderly husband is apparent in her every movement and gesture. She has aged very much and is no longer beautiful, while he is more like Punch than ever. I spoke heatedly to him with reference to his sneering at my interest in Mass Observation, pointing out to him any one person's choice of interest was as good as another's as long as it hurt no one, and my interest in sociology was every whit as laudable as his mania for card playing. Leslie came in later. He and Mr Samuels as air raid wardens were full of plans in case of enemy attack, for war is in the air again now that Hitler has seized Czecho-Slovakia. We all 'listened in' to Mr Chamberlain's speech, and to me the first half of it sounded like self-defence, the second half like jingoism.

Gladys Langford, Diaries, 17 March 1939

*

BILLS ON BRIDGES

As a practical step towards resisting the German menace, it is proposed to decorate Waterloo Bridge with the largest poster ever made. In favour, I understand, of 'voluntary compulsion', the new cant phrase for conscription.*

James Agate, Journals, 19 March 1939

* *This was to be the first time conscription was introduced during peacetime in Britain.*

*

MEDDLING IN EUROPE

Met in the evening on the road Mrs P. D. and had a most irritating talk with her. 'Why shouldn't we let Hitler have colonies?' she insisted, and added: 'We have no right to meddle in Eastern Europe'; and when I brought forward all the arguments about the rights of smaller nations and the many other obvious points, she merely replied: 'If he is stronger than the smaller nations, we can do nothing to stop him from making Germany larger.' I discontinued the argument.

Rom Landau, *Of No Importance*, 3 June 1939

⟳

BOMBINGS IN LONDON

Coming home, my bus missed by a few yards the IRA bomb at Piccadilly Circus. There have been several thrown tonight. The bus conductor was green with fright and an old man alone in the vehicle was distraught.

Gladys Langford, Diaries, 24 June 1939

⟳

PLANNING FOR EVACUATION

Saw several children with franked postcards in their hands, evidently to announce their arrival to parents when they reach the area to which they are being evacuated. Notices on the walls give details about air-raid warnings and signals of gas-attacks; pavements are whitened but people don't seem too overwhelmed as they did last year. It's the old tale of the boy and the wolf. The German envoy or ambassador – whichever he is – has flown to England with Hitler's peace plan. I believe Welling is right and that there will be no war.

Have been reading Calder-Marshall's *The Changing Scene*. He almost makes me think of joining the Communist Party, only I realise all parties are equally shifty to suit their own purposes ...

Gladys Langford, Diaries, 26 August 1939

PETS CULLED

To Maudsley Hospital Outpatients' Department. Closed. Hospital patients evacuated. Saw the almoner, who phoned Dr Ross for me. I have to see him tonight. Lots of people are carrying cats about in baskets, evidently to be destroyed.*

Gladys Langford, Diaries, 29 August 1939

Many thousands of animals were destroyed at the outbreak of the war, when it was believed food shortages would make it difficult to support pets. An unexpected consequence of this was a rapid increase in the number of mice and rats in some urban areas.

EVACUEES AVOIDED

Thank God Dr Irvine rang up to say he was giving me a medical certificate saying my health makes it impossible for me to billet children.

Mrs Henry Dudeney, *A Lewes Diary*, 30 August 1939

✒

WAITING OVER

War broke out this morning between Germany and Poland. When I emerged from Holborn Tube Station on my way to the Zionist Office about 11 a.m., I saw the posters: 'Danzig proclaims return to the Reich – Germans bomb Polish Town.'

I felt a sort of relief that the waiting is over.

Blanche Dugdale, Diaries, 1 September 1939

✒

BRITAIN DECLARES WAR

The Prime Minister's speech in the House last night was accompanied by tremendous lightning, but hardly any thunder. It was more like stage lighting than the real thing. I watched the storm from the Savage Club. One moment, complete darkness; the next, a sheet of vivid green showing Westminster cut out in cardboard like the scenery in a toy theatre. The flashes lasted so long you could count the buildings.

At ten o clock to-day Hibberd, the chief announcer [on the BBC], told us that the Prime Minister would broadcast at eleven o clock ... At 11.15 precisely ... speaking in an intensely English accent, Chamberlain told us that, since Germany had not replied to the ultimatum, England was now at war. At half-past eleven the first air-raid warning goes. Orderly retreat to dug-out. Nothing happens. 'All clear' after half an hour. We go into the street, and I see a man look at his watch and hear him say, 'They're open!'

Presently, Jock comes round in search of his gas-mask ... this morning's air-raid sirens caught him at breakfast in the Strand Corner House, and drove him into the basement. He adjured me to say that his first and chief emotion took the form of the angry exclamation, 'What a very unattractive crowd of people to have to die with!' ...

James Agate, Journals, 3 September 1939

⌒

GUESTS FROM LAMBETH

First came the announcement that we were at war; then there was the first air-raid warning; and in the afternoon the first evacuees arrived from London.

It was about noon that the first air-raid warning was given. We have no air-raid shelters in our village and have dug no trenches. The ditch by the side of the village road and the woods on the hill opposite will have to serve as our shelter in case of need.

A few hours later, two evacuated mothers with three children were brought to my house. I had been warned about their arrival only this morning, and as I possess no spare beds, blankets or pillows, everything had to be improvised. We cleared out my study and the rooms in the attic and tried to make an honourable show with mattresses.

My guests hail from Lambeth. The eldest of them, one of the fattest women I have ever seen, arrived with a baby of two, which was her own, and one of three, which was her grandchild. When, a few hours after their arrival, I went into the study to see how my guests were faring, I found the carpet littered with bits of food and a larger quantity of miscellaneous dirt than it has probably known during all its preceding years.

I replied meekly, finding a certain comfort that, after all, one ruined carpet was not too high a sacrifice for so great a war.

My elation flopped when I remembered that this is only the very first day of the war.

Rom Landau, Of No Importance, 3 September 1939

RUSH ON RINGS

The Camden Town jeweller from whom I bought a cheap wrist-watch told me that he had sold thirty wedding-rings in two days, as against the normal three or four. A poor woman coming in to buy a modest signet ring and asking to have 'From your Loving Wife' engraved on it was told that no engravers were available ... One of the most depressed men in London to-day was the shoekeeper at Chalk Farm whose line is flares, beacons and material for bonfires.

James Agate, Journals, 5 September 1939

A SLOW START

Down to Canterbury in the afternoon. The train crowded, and the platform at Tonbridge and other stations packed with hop-pickers starting the season. Two young soldiers opposite me; they were perfectly happy but had no idea of what was happening to them; for the last few days they had been moved about from place to place doing nothing, now on their way to Shorncliffe to guard the hospital; possibly going to Egypt. There was a pleasant, friendly feeling among the people in the compartment; we chatted away without any violence of feeling or opinion. Concern for the Poles and hope that something will be done quickly to relieve the pressure on them is the general sentiment at the moment.

People are troubled or bewildered by the slow start on the Western Front ... even papers that had no sympathy for Madrid's defenders are recalling the glorious memory of that city and splashing its slogan 'They shall not pass'. The slogans of the Spanish war are no doubt appropriate enough in Poland but it is curious to find them now so approved by the enemies of the Republic, just as it is curious to think of Ward Price leading the *Daily Mail* against German fascism, when a few days ago his books were boosted by the BUF [British Union of Fascists] in their bookshop, and the *Mail* and *Express* had no use for a peace front against aggression.

William Townsend, Journals, 9 September 1939

DISCONTENTED WHISPERS

More tales of discontented evacuees. Child from a neighbouring village said to have set out for London armed with three pairs of socks and a gas-mask. He was found by the police. Woman with two small children billeted near Bishop Stortford was accorded so chilly a reception by her hostess [that] she went back to London with her husband and will ask the authorities for another allocation.

From teacher friends I hear of *their* trials. The children are unruly, foulmouthed and dirty in some instances. Some have infectious complaints.

Gladys Langford, Diaries, 11 September 1939

BLACKSHIRTS BUSYING THEMSELVES

Evidently, [Oswald] Mosley is getting busy again. Several walls are decorated with his Fascist sign and bear slogans 'Mosley for Peace', 'Why fight in a Jews' war?', 'Britons in Khaki, Jews in ARP'[Air Raid Precautions].

Gladys Langford, Diaries, 28 September 1939

FIGHTING FOR POLAND

This morning came the news about the Russo–German mutual assistance Pact over the wireless. Although I expected this, I felt shattered when I actually heard it. We are living at a time when we see the forces behind events, and the direction which may take years to be revealed, with a blinding clarity. The question does arise: what are we fighting for? Though this is not quite the form the Germans put it to us. We aren't fighting for Poland.

Stephen Spender, Journals, 29 September 1939

ALL CATS ARE GREY IN THE BLACKOUT

The blackout time gets a few minutes earlier each evening, so one notices more than ever the drawing in of the autumn evenings. Actually, the weather has been particularly fine lately. The streets glitter a biscuit-yellow all day. The crowds waiting at the bus stops for the few buses give the town an air of festivity. The sandbags on the pavements, the strips of paper on the windows, the balloons in the air, are sufficiently new in the bright sunlight to be interesting and almost gay.

I had lunch with Eliot … I mentioned that I had sent my name to the Ministry of Information and the War Office, but had no reply. He had done ditto to the Foreign Office and has also no reply.

He said he had designed a cover for his children's book about cats.*

Stephen Spender, Journals, 30 September 1939

*A cat lover with a penchant for giving his own pets such preposterous names as Jellylorum, Pettipaws, Wiscus and George Pushdragon, T. S. Eliot composed nonsense poems about cats to amuse his godchildren. These were published as Old Possum's Book of Practical Cats in 1939 and were adapted in 1981 into the box-office record-breaking stage musical Cats by Andrew Lloyd Webber.

CHOOSING TO FIGHT IN THE BRITISH RANKS

Spent a day in London and saw in the papers that all Polish citizens domiciled in England will have to serve in the Polish Legion in France. This news alarmed me. I applied for British naturalization last year, but my papers have not yet come through. Though the causes of Poland and Britain in this war may be identical, it is not immaterial to me personally whether I serve with British or Polish troops. Britain has become for me a reality of tremendous personal concern; Poland is a memory of a distant childhood. To fight in British ranks will be natural to me; among Poles I shall feel a stranger.

Rom Landau, Of No Importance, 24 October 1939

MORE PANSIES, PLEASE

Murray sent a delightful letter and a box of Hanover wafers. He is 'called up' in February and is indignant, as he disapproves of war but, being a member of no sect, he stands no chance as CO [Conscientious Objector].

He says he can't feel moved to kill a German; if he encounters a good-looking one, he'll feel inclined to get closer to admire him, for he'd hate to destroy anything pleasing to the eye! God, send us more 'pansies', say I. Oscar Wilde a criminal, and Napoleon a hero! I ask you.

And *how* ugly London is now. Cold weather causes women to wear the most hideous garments, hoods round moon-faces, kerchiefs around the hatchet type. Fat females and lean hags in trousers, greasy suede jackets. Oh, Eve! Where are thy charms?

Gladys Langford, Diaries, 3 January 1940

LUMPING IT

Food is now being rationed, at least certain things are, like butter and sugar, not to mention bacon, which Mummy has a passion for. I'm more upset about sugar, as I'm used to having four lumps!

Joan Wyndham, *Love Lessons*, 14 January 1940

CENSORS AT WORK

The way the newspapers and the wireless reports try to make the best of the news is maddening, but I think I'm getting the key. 'The Germans attacked such and such a town, the Allies are counter-attacking vigorously' means the Germans have taken the town. The alternative, meaning the same thing, is 'Allies attacking on the outskirts of such and such at town' …

Laurie Latchford, *The Swansea Wartime Diary Of*, 30 April 1940

A WARTIME PRIME MINSTER

Mammy and Daddy have been talking about Mr Chamberlain resigning. It was on the News at 9 last night that Mr Churchill is the new Prime Minister. Daddy says he is a warmonger.*

Brian Williams, Diaries, 11 May 1940

Neville Chamberlain was forced to resign as prime minister when Clement Attlee, leader of the Labour Party, refused – on the grounds of his earlier policy of appeasement – to serve in any national wartime coalition government that Chamberlain might head. This left two Conservative candidates: Lord Halifax, the Foreign Secretary, and Winston Churchill, the First Lord of the Admiralty. Halifax was Chamberlain's preferred choice, but Churchill – a fierce and consistent opponent of any appeasement of Nazi Germany – won the day.

LINE CROSSED

So much for the Maginot Line, the Germans have gone round the end and broken the allied lines at three points! So much for the Maginot Line, with its huge guns and underground accommodation like small towns. It does not carry the full length of the frontiers facing Germany! 'Impregnable' was the adjective the French used …

The formation of the Home Defence Army has, as I thought, been received with enthusiasm. Volunteers are making police stations busy. The enrolment forms ask if the volunteers are willing to serve away from their homes, that is, in other parts of Great Britain.

Rations are being cut: sugar from 12 oz to 8 oz a week each person, and butter 8 oz to 4 oz a week each person from 3 June.

Now all Austrians and Germans from 16 to 60 years of age are to be interned. This must include all those Austrian Jews and German Jews who have been coming into Great Britain ever since 1938 to escape Hitler's oppressive measures. Those coming through Swansea Port have not been in great numbers, but have increased recently. Mostly, they are middle-aged or elderly professional men.

Laurie Latchford, *The Swansea Wartime Diary of*, 16 May 1940

⁓

THE END OF ENGLAND?

The Germans are getting the Channel ports; the pain in my back is agonising. Paching, who cut my hair, said this war would probably mean the end, not of the British Empire but of England, and that the Royal Family and Government would go to Canada and we should be left to the mercy of the Germans.*

Mrs Henry Dudeney, *A Lewes Diary*, 22 May 1940

* *The Royal Family were to remain in Britain throughout the war, with the King and Queen staying in Buckingham Palace for much of the time. The Princesses Elizabeth and Margaret were removed to Windsor Castle for their safety.*

⁓

THE DUNKIRK EVACUATION

Shortly after 7 o'clock we moved off up the railway track towards Dunkerque and dispersed in the sand dunes near to the Hotel Terminus on the front. Here we stayed for the whole morning, breakfasting very unenthusiastically on [illegible] soused herrings once again! The morning passed fairly uneventfully, our hearts being considerably cheered and our hopes raised by the appearance of a Hurricane Fighter patrol, which appeared to be protecting us for the day, but went away for 5 minutes. In came the Nazi bombers again, but their attention once more was directed against Dunkerque rather than us personally. We were still uncertain when we were likely to get shipped, but during the morning Chadwick contacted a Lieut.-Col. who had some rather uncertain control over transhipment of troops, but he promised that if we moved up towards the shore, we should get an early opportunity to move on to the destroyers which were lying offshore immediately below the Hotel Terminus. Acting on this, we moved further forward to a large crater immediately adjacent to the Hotel; the Hurricanes having disappeared, the Nazis arrived and made several abortive attempts on the destroyers lying offshore, and were chased off by really heavy fire from the ships themselves and more than one was brought down. The Major reported having seen planes out to sea dropping magnetic mines and the naval craft replying by firing low over the water, the shells ricocheting over the waves in what he imagined to be an attempt to detonate the mines.

About 4 o'clock, having taken cover many times during the afternoon, we assembled under the Hotel Terminus verandah in the hopes of securing transport to Dunkerque, but this was completely disorganised and only one load got away. Rain commenced falling heavily and, in answer to our fervent prayers, it increased and continued for the whole of our 4-mile trek along the wide promenade of Malo-les-Bains to the jetty at Dunkerque.

Thanks to the providential rain, and I feel sure that only, we were spared a bombing and machine gun attack along the prom where there was little or no cover. Once, we hastily took cover as a plane zoomed in from the sea at low altitude, came up to the beach, banked steeply, showed its Allied circles under the wings and out to sea again!

The last trek along the jetty was nerve-racking, to say the least, when an enemy plane passed over and opened fire on the destroyer that was going to take us to home and safety and we saw the possibility of a last-minute failure.

However, we safely gained our destroyer HMS *Grenade* – the vessel that figured notably in the Namsos evacuation. It was reputed that we had 1,000 souls aboard in addition to the crew. The Navy's hospitality extended to hot tea, bread, butter, jam and drinks and at 1 o'clock in the morning I fed on Force [breakfast cereal], Demerara sugar and Lyle's Golden Syrup! We sailed at 6.35 p.m. and didn't reach Dover until about 2.00 a.m. the following morning. Although we were down below all the time and could not follow our route at all, doubtless this long journey was due to [illegible] up and down the coast each side and following the safe lane across the straits. We were alarmed shortly after starting up by a loud explosion and subsequent noises, which we thought – or rather, hoped – might be a gun! This was verified later by a naval officer, who made solicitous enquiries soon after concerning our welfare. We asked if it was a gun and he replied, 'Yes – some bloody fool fired it by mistake – it happens in the best regulated ships'!! The only other eventful happening was that the vessel stopped to pick up twenty wounded from a small boat, who had apparently been bombed on embarking from the shore.

Reached Dover two-ish and felt really safe and cheerful at last as we stepped ashore – immediately joined our train with issue of chocolate and [an] apple and shortly started off to an unknown destination and slept until we reached Paddock Wood, where we were issued with bread, cheese, tea and [an] apple. Visions of London and immediate leave disappeared as we continued westwards from Redhill and on towards Basingstoke. We finally turned up at Ludgershall about 10 o'clock and were all transported to Perham Down and the RTC's [Replacement Training Centre] palatial mess, where we were made very welcome and fed with a grand meal of ham, tongue, pork pie and salad etc. etc., and then followed [with] hot baths, shave of 2 days' growth of beard and a general freshening-up.

Henry Bond, Diaries, 28 May 1940

* *Outnumbered by German troops, the British Expeditionary Force was forced into an embarrassing retreat in Northern France, evacuating from the seaport of Dunkirk (Dunkerque). It would remain the largest evacuation of Allied forces of the war.*

NEW ENEMY

Italy came into the war last night. The Germans are 30 miles from Paris. In a few weeks, perhaps, everything one has been accustomed to, cares for, may have been destroyed and one will be a prisoner in an invaded country waiting to be destroyed itself.

Antonia White, Diaries, 12 June 1940

ATTACKS ON SHOPS

E[ileen] and I last night walked through Soho to see whether the damage to Italian shops etc. was as reported. It seemed to have been exaggerated in the newspapers, but we did see, I think, 3 shops which had had their windows smashed. The majority had hurriedly labelled themselves 'British'. Gennari's, the Italian grocer's, was plastered all over with printed placards saying: 'This establishment is entirely British.' The Spaghetti House, a shop specialising in Italian foodstuffs, had renamed itself 'British Food Shop'. Another shop proclaimed itself Swiss, and even a French restaurant had labelled itself British. The interesting thing is that all these placards must evidently have been printed beforehand and kept in readiness ...

Disgusting though these attacks on harmless Italian shopkeepers are, they are an interesting phenomenon, because English people, i.e. people of a kind who would be likely to loot shops, don't as a rule take a spontaneous interest in foreign politics. I don't think there was anything of this kind during the Abyssinian war, and the Spanish war simply did not touch the mass of the people. Nor was there any popular move against the Germans resident in England until the last month or two. The low-down, cold-blooded meanness of Mussolini's declaration of war at that moment must have made an impression even on people who as a rule barely read the newspapers.

· George Orwell, Diaries, 12 June 1940

⁓⁓

THE FALL OF FRANCE

The French Army has capitulated. Radio Paris rings with announcements to *auditeurs Francais* [French listeners] about how happy Paris is to be released from her oppressors, mingled with sub-audit horrors about the collapse of the army, the fall of Verdun ...

Talking again of the inferiority complex underlying fascism, we worked out how an inferiority complex of the simplest nature prepared the ruling classes of Europe to turn fascist. After the last war they emerged, hoping again to be socially what they had been before it: the leaders of society. Instead, they found themselves by-passed through the cultural revival that followed the war. Old Prussia, and Mayfair, and Quartier St Germain, all had their noses snubbed by finding the limelight focussed on the leaders of culture ...

I think I envy the French. Hearing Churchill in a very bad paragraph announce we would fight on etc., I found in myself a sense not only of exasperation at the numbers more who must be killed and maimed in a war that never reached its purpose, but also the frustrated impatience of an experimental scientist. For war – this sort of war – is no way to attack fascism. And I am fretted to think how every day my chances of seeing other methods tried out are diminished. I feel like a scientist who has to wait in a queue to get to the laboratory – while both the laboratory and he are under bombardment.

Sylvia Townsend Warner, Diaries, 17 June 1940

⌇

CHURCHILL'S HOPELESS CAUSE

France has packed it in. Churchill has determined that England shall fight on alone. This attitude, according to the press, is ridiculed in Germany. I should think so, too. Now we must wait and see – if we get the chance.

Last night, the sirens went off at about 11.30. About 12.30 I was awakened by a terrific crash. I called the children down into our bedroom. They got into bed with Jess. Then we heard gunfire. The crash turned out to be a bomb on some houses in Vicarage Terrace, killing nine people and injuring a lot more.

The gunfire was from a Spitfire that went up from Duxford and brought down the machine that dropped the bombs.

Jess and I went and had a look at the damage done this morning. Nine houses were just a pile of rubble. They were digging for the bodies. The houses in the next street were stripped of their chimney pots and damaged so that the people had to get out of them. I heard from my brother Fred that later the parson was there, praying over the rubble.

This is all we've got to look forward to now. I think public opinion is growing against the futility of the war, however, so it might be over sooner than is generally expected. I feel certain that Churchill realises, above all people, the hopelessness of *his* cause.

Jack Overhill, *Cambridge at War*, 19 June 1940

⁓

WARM SHRAPNEL

These air-raids are beginning to interfere with the amenities, which is very wrong of them. Bob Leaver and his wife were to call this morning at nine o'clock to motor me to Bexhill, but we judged it wise to wait for the All Clear at ten. Twenty minutes after leaving Croydon we ran into a second warning and had to shelter. The third happened ten miles from Bexhill but we heard no signal, and it was presumably during this raid that we collected the bit of shrapnel which we afterwards found still warm, on the floor of the car. It must have come in through the roof or windows, all of which were closed when we sheltered.

The fourth raid was at tea-time. Five miles from Croydon we had to put in for a slight repair and I asked the garage-proprietor if he lived near at hand. He said, 'Used to!' and pointed across the road, where all that was left of a little villa was the gatepost and the name, 'Figaro'. Alas, it was Figaro here and Figaro there, a heap of rubble, a bit of wall, and the burnt-out remains of three motor-cars. The fifth alarm sounded soon after we got back to town and there were two more before I finally got to sleep.

James Agate, Journals, 31 August 1940

⁓

SWANSEA IN BATTLE OF BRITAIN

A very hot day. Slept late. In the evening, about 9 o'clock, the siren went, followed immediately by bomb explosions. Very soon the air was full of the throb of aeroplane engines punctuated by bomb explosions. The raid developed into a most savage attack. Wave after wave of planes came in from the west. The heavy throb of engines which marks the German bomber, grew, then died away, then grew again as the next wave came up.

I watched the searchlights meet each wave as it came in, and passed high overhead. The bombers showed no uncertainty. A direct flight to their aiming point, the release of their stick of bombs, and then a south turn over the Bristol Channel. The bombers disregarded the searchlights.

It wasn't long before a building on Kilvey Hill, a school I think, caught fire, lighting up the docks.

The raid now showed a distinct pattern: one wave of bombers dropped high explosives and turned away, then the next wave showered down great numbers of incendiary bombs, the following wave dropped high-explosives, and so on. I could see the white flash of the incendiary bombs as they hit the ground and the casing began to burn. There were hundreds of these intense white, flaring lights. Some suddenly ceased to show, as wardens and others put them out, others burnt themselves out, but with the others, the white light turned to an angry, red glow where a fire had started.

When fires started within the town were well alight, the devils began to power-dive the bigger buildings, the engines screeching to a frightening crescendo. At one point, the roar of bomb explosions became almost continuous ...

As I patrolled under the continuous throb and roar of incoming aircraft, a red glow began to spread across the skies from the direction of Swansea. The bombing seemed to become heavier. I toured my sector, visiting all wardens' patrol posts. All wardens are on duty, although one wasn't going to leave his family and the shelter of his garage under his house, unless there was a local incident. As we talked, a bomb fell with a long, drawn-out whistling whine. We all fell on our faces, with our fingers in our ears. The noise passed overhead and then silence ...

I then went to the village vantage point by the steps. As the view opened up, I stopped in shock and horror. I found my mouth open, and my eyes staring. All Swansea Bay was lit by a deep-red light. From the docks area and Weaver's

Flour Mills, fire extended deep into the town. Flames outlined the black of the adjacent buildings. The dock piers and the hulk in the bay stood out plainly in the red fire-reflecting sea. Above rolled slowly a dense mass of orange-red smoke miles high …

Laurie Latchford, *The Swansea Wartime Diary Of*, 1 September 1940

FRETWORK IN THE FLAMES

The biggest air attack launched on London to date started at 5.30 this afternoon and has been going on ever since, the time of writing being 2 a.m.* From the roof of Café Royal got a fine view of the blaze, the Tower Bridge being cut out like fretwork. In the corner of the foreground a large flag fluttered, making the whole thing look like one of those old posters of *A Royal Divorce*, Napoleon's cavalry against a background of red ruin.

James Agate, Journals, 7 September 1940

* *The term Blitzkrieg, or Lightning War, is the name given to the military tactic of mounting intensely concentrated attacks on often narrow fronts, using tanks, planes and artillery to awe and overwhelm the enemy. The Germans deployed it to devastating effect in Poland in 1939, and in Norway, Belgium and France in the opening months of 1940. In Britain, it became closely associated with the aerial bombing raids on British towns and cities that began at the start of September 1940 and continued almost nightly until May 1941.*

⸎

RADIO DEBUT

Princess Elizabeth made her first broadcast – a clear, unaffected voice. No sirens until 7 p.m. I saw something of the damage done a month ago. It's a mournful sight. Air-craft passed over during the news. Bumps in the distance at 11 p.m., said to be at Falmer. 'All clear' at 6 a.m.

Helen Roust, *Brighton's War*, 13 October 1940

⸎

HEARING HAW-HAW

We've had three quiet nights. Enemy planes have been over and the windows have shaken as a sign of bombs, but we've been able to keep abed.

We're quibbling over the new Soviet states, Lithuania, Latvia and Esthonia [*sic*], refusing to recognise them and a few paltry millions involved in the changeover. Only Russia can stop Germany's march into Asia, so we'd better look out. Heard Lord Haw-Haw broadcasting the other night.* He's Germany's pet announcer, caricatured here a lot, but not so silly as this country would like to believe. He referred to Duff Cooper as 'Dud' Cooper, and our hypocrisy instead of democracy.

Jack Overhill, *Cambridge at War*, 20 October 1940

* *William Joyce, known as Lord Haw-Haw, was an American-Irish fascist who had been a member of Oswald Mosley's British Union of Fascists. During the war, he broadcast Nazi propaganda to Britain from Hamburg, introducing each of his announcements with the braying refrain, 'Germany Calling'.*

✒

THE OPEN AIR

The most – what? – impressive, no, that's not it – sight in London on Friday was the queue, mostly children with suitcases, outside Warren st. tube. This was about 11.30. We thought they were evacuees, waiting for a bus. But there they were, in a much longer line, with women, men, more bags & blankets, sitting still at 3. Lining up for the shelter in the night raids – which came, of course. Thus, if they left the tube at 6 (a bad raid on Thursday) they were back again at 11. So to Tavistock sq. With a sigh of relief saw a heap of ruins. Three houses, I shd. say, gone. Basement all rubble. Only relics an old basket chair (bought in Fitzroy sqre days) & Penmans board To Let. Otherwise, bricks & wood splinters. One glass door in the next house hanging. I cd see a piece of my studio wall standing: otherwise, rubble where I wrote so many books. Open air where we sat so many nights, gave so many parties ...

Virginia Woolf, Diaries, 20 October 1940

✒

MOVING TO SNAKEHIPS

After lunch we wandered round a bit, then went to the *thé dansant* at the Café de Paris with Ken 'Snakehips' Johnson and his band of grey-suited Negroes. I hadn't danced for a year. Gosh, it was fun! I got transported into a kind of ecstasy. So did the band, thudding away at an ever-increasing speed; so did slim, grey, beautiful Snakehips swaying lightly on the balls of his feet, while the band played 'I can't dance – I got ants in my pants'.

I apologised for not knowing how to dance properly, but Yuka said, 'What do you mean, you're a positively choreographic nymphomaniac!'

Joan Wyndham, *Love Lessons*, 8 November 1940

⁓

CASUALTIES IN COVENTRY

Last night there was a lot doing. It was a beautiful moonlight night and Jerry was over all the evening and all the night. The siren didn't sound, but I don't know why, as there were bombs dropped in the distance after we went to bed and enemy planes were oomping about just as they liked all the while. I wasn't surprised to hear in Fred's shop the Midlands had had it bad, and today [at] dinnertime when I called at Langford's, the leather and grindery shop, for some rubbers, to hear that Coventry had had a very bad raid, suffering 1,000 casualties. Landford said he heard the news on the 1 o'clock broadcast, adding that the cathedral was down and that when he heard it he felt bad …*

Jack Overhill, *Cambridge at War*, 15 November 1940

* *This Luftwaffe bombing of Coventry, codenamed Operation Mondscheinsonate, or Moonlight Sonata, was intended to destroy the city's factories and manufacturing plants. It was the most devastating raid of the war up to that date.*

⁓

A BACKSTREET ABORTION DURING THE BLITZ

Rowena rings to say, in a dead sort of voice, 'The worst has happened, Billy Bolitho says I am definitely pregnant. Can you lend me fifteen quid till Saturday?' I said I could give her six, which is all I had, because I know just how she feels, and if she doesn't have an abortion before Saturday it will be too late. I met her in Dean Street and we wandered down to Duran's in the icy cold for a delicious lunch. Christ, their pastries are good! Poor Rowena couldn't eat anything.

She says her only other chance is to put lots of ether soap up her bottom for ten days. Billy Bolitho says it's tough-going but infallible, but R. says, 'How will I keep it from my mum if I go around smelling like an operating theatre?'

Joan Wyndham, *Love Lessons*, 4 December 1940

<hr/>

NO SILVER COIN THIS YEAR

No newspapers and no Blitz. Wonder whether we and Hitler will both start a minute after midnight having another go at one another? Came down to the office to write this and clean up the letters.

Home to lunch, where we had quite the best roasted turkey I have ever eaten in my life.

We had all the usual coloured streamers and mistletoe and a Christmas pudding, but without a silver coin this time. Just after lunch we were joined by Margaret to hear the Empire Broadcast. This began well enough with the bells of Coventry Cathedral, but became more and more dreary, with the exception of the Polish troops singing Christmas Carols and the interlude from Ulster. The commentator, or rather compère, was Howard Marshall, who talked more than ever like a clergyman. The King made an excellent speech, and that was that.

Charles Graves, *Off the Record*, 25 December 1940

<hr/>

'AMERICA FIRST'

Roosevelt's made a big 'fireside' speech, backing up England. I'm not impressed and still think this country will conk out. Its ruling class will sell out when it suits them, as the French ruling class did. They're championing their own interests, whatever they are. What hope is there for the future with so many evil forces at work?*

Jack Overhill, *Cambridge at War*, 30 December 1940

* *On 29 December 1940, when President Franklin Delano Roosevelt gave this 'fireside radio chat' broadcast to the American people, he had only recently been re-elected to an unprecedented third term in office. In the re-election campaign, he had pledged to keep his country out of the war unless his nation was attacked. Yet, in this speech he warned his listeners, many of whom retained little appetite for war, that 'if Great Britain [went] down … all the Americas would be living at the point of a gun'.*

CROWD-PULLING DICTATOR

Went with Edgar to the Charlie Chaplin film *The Great Dictator*, which is still drawing huge crowds. It is good, but not quite my cup of tea. I do not like to see Jewish atrocities, even watered down, but the scenes between the two Dictators are very funny.

Blanche Dugdale, Diaries, 18 January 1941

BANDLEADER KILLED

Last night the raid was bad – it was the night they hit the Café de Paris, where Yuka and I danced.

I felt dreadful about it; the bomb fell on the band, killing them all except the drummer – gentle, magnetic Snakehips Johnson with his thin, elegant face and joyous rhythm – the best swing band in London gone.

They were dancing to 'Oh, Johnny' when the bomb fell. The couples on the floor, killed in the blast, stood for some seconds as if they were still dancing, just leaning a little – then they fell, heaped on top of one another.

Joan Wyndham, *Love Lessons*, 9 March 1941

BRIGHTON BAN

Went down to Brighton. It was grey in London but gloriously warm and sunny on arrival. It seemed at least ten degrees warmer, and our local correspondent told me that it had been like this for a fortnight. It felt like the South of France, despite the barbed wire on the beaches and the fact that the piers are out of bounds ...

There are not so many aliens in Brighton, and the place is full of troops. The banning of Brighton after this week-end as a holiday resort is, however, very serious for the town. No doubt many people will take advantage of the looseness of the Government order and will discover sick relatives and other legitimate reasons for allowing them to go down ...

Charles Graves, *Off the Record*, 19 March 1941

WOMEN CALLED UP

Called up for WAAF* – I go in a week, 7th April. All of a sudden I feel dreadfully depressed. Rowena and I went to the Galeries Lafayette and bought tarty underwear.

Joan Wyndham, *Love Lessons*, 31 March 1941

* *The Women's Auxiliary Air Force was established in 1939 with enlistment on a voluntary basis. Conscription of unmarried women between the ages of twenty and thirty began in December 1941.*

⁓

RAF WELCOME

Lunch with Vintners. A young Frenchman recently come over from France via the Pyrenees was at the table. He told us of the feelings of the French, reassuring us that the one thing they long for is to get rid of the Germans. In answer to our enquiry, he said the French are proud and happy to suffer from attacks of our bombers, whom they welcome. The Germans take everything they can lay their hands on from occupied France. Lorries draw up at a man's house, and furniture and everything is looted.

Rev. Maurice Foxell, Diaries, 2 April 1941

⁓

DEATH OF WOOLF

Opening *The Times* this morning I read with astonishment: 'We regret to announce that the death of Mrs Virginia Woolf, missing since last Friday, must now be presumed.' From the discreet notice that followed, it seems that she is presumed to have drowned herself in the river near Rodmell. An attack of her recurring madness, I suppose; the thought of self-destruction is terrible, dramatic and pathetic, and yet (because it is the product of human will) has an Aristotelian inevitability about it, making it very different from all the other sudden deaths we have to contemplate.*

Frances Partridge, Diaries, 3 April 1941

* *Woolf committed suicide by drowning herself in the River Ouse in Sussex on 28 March 1941. Her body was not found until 18 April 1941. She was fifty-nine at the time of her death.*

⌐∕∕⌐

LORD'S BOMBED

Very heavy raid last night, probably the heaviest in many months, so far as London is concerned ... Bomb in Lord's cricket ground (school-boys having their exercise at the nets as usual this morning, a few yards from the crater) and another in St John's Wood churchyard. This one luckily didn't land among the graves, a thing I have been dreading will happen ... Passed this morning a side-street somewhere in Hampstead with one house in it reduced to a pile of rubbish by a bomb – a sight so usual that one hardly notices it. The street is cordoned off, however, digging squads at work, and a line of ambulances waiting. Underneath that huge pile of bricks there are mangled bodies, some of them perhaps alive.

George Orwell, Diaries, 17 April 1941

⌐∕∕⌐

PET PROTECTION

I saw a small collie dog on Coe Fen today wearing a gas-mask. Have just got a pamphlet telling [us] how to make a gas-proof box for the dogs. I shall have to find out more about dog gas-masks.

Jack Overhill, *Cambridge at War*, 21 April 1941

WARTIME PUKKA DO

The officers' cocktail party, a very pukka do indeed, with tents in the garden in spite of the fact that it's still freezing cold. There was lashings of punch and things on sticks, and canapés, and bags of gorgeous creatures with wings and medals and nicotine-stained fingers stalking the lawn.

Our job was to serve drinks and hand round the canapés, but it's really no fun at all watching your betters getting drunk and wolfing down the caviar. Towards the end of the party, we were spending most of our time in the pantry, good and tight on the dregs of the champagne cup, and ended up prostrate on the grass behind the marquee, our pockets stuffed with sausages and cheese-straws.

Joan Wyndham, *Love Is Blue*, 1 May 1941

HESS PARACHUTES INTO SCOTLAND

In the midnight news bulletin ... it was announced that Rudolf Hess* had arrived in England. We were all absolutely stunned. It seems that on Saturday 10th May it was reported that a Messerschmitt 110 was approaching in the direction of Glasgow. As it was known that a plane of this type could not carry sufficient fuel to return to Germany, the report was at first discounted. Later, however, a similar plane crashed somewhere in Scotland and a German officer was found having landed by parachute.

He was suffering from a broken ankle, and at first stated that his name was Horne. He afterwards said that he was Rudolf Hess and produced photographs which he had brought with him to prove his identity.

What all this portends is an absolute mystery, but naturally people are agog with suppositions. Is it a plot or has he sought sanctuary in this country – of all places – from something threatening him in Germany? It is all very queer.

Grace Farmer, Diaries, 12 May 1941

* *Rudolf Hess was one of Hitler's oldest and most loyal associates, having met in Munich shortly after the First World War. Hess became Hitler's personal secretary in 1920 and was involved with the Nazi Party since its inception. By 1941, he was the party's deputy leader. What exactly prompted his decision to fly to Britain and single-handedly attempt to broker a peace deal remains a matter of intense speculation.*

EASTERN FRONT OPENS

On the 9 p.m. News we heard that Germany had gone to war with Russia. Impossible to imagine yet all the implications of this terrific event. The Prime Minister made a magnificent broadcast, focussing thought on the one fixed point, namely that the Russians are fighting for their native land against the Nazis. We must help, forget for the present all else but that.

Blanche Dugdale, Diaries, 22 June 1941

'GOOD STOCK'

Margaret Hill said that all the Lewes girls were having babies by the French-Canadian soldiers in the town. She cynically added that if they must 'sin' they might just as well have babies, as we should want as many as we could get after the war and these soldiers are 'good stock'.

Mrs Henry Dudeney, *A Lewes Diary*, 23 July 1941

TAKING THE BISCUIT

At office 9–7. Did some shopping in dinner hour and was fortunate in getting a chocolate biscuit at Woolworths. Paid Savings Group subscriptions in [the] afternoon and heard the latest news of the group. It is a small group and we are aiming at raising £135 in eight weeks for a machine gun and rubber dingy. Last week's subscriptions were the biggest so far, over £24 …

Annie Beatrice Holness, Diaries, 1 August 1941

ℳ

PRISONERS OF WAR

Leningrad has not fallen, though every day I go to the wireless I expect to hear news of it. Neither has Kiev nor Odessa, and the Russian winter is supposed to begin in a month from now.

Yesterday, on the way to Biddlesden, we saw Italian prisoners at work on the harvest at the top of Tidecombe Hill. It was a glorious afternoon and from where they were there was a view over half of Wiltshire. We caught a glimpse of handsome, dark and youthful faces, and extravagant rows of white teeth, as they smiled and waved to us. Each had a crimson disc sewn on his back and an armed soldier was marching them.

Frances Partridge, Diaries, 17 September 1941

ℳ

HELP YOURSELF TO LYONS

One of Lyons teashops in the Strand is now a 'help yourself' and it seems to have caught on quite nicely. Customers' time is saved and, of course, a number of girls will have been released for other jobs.

During the course of my lunch today, my neighbour, a Canadian girl, told me quite a lot about herself, which naturally passed the time quite pleasantly. She had been here six years and she is of the opinion that people here do not take the war seriously, saying to themselves, 'England can't lose,' and letting their lives follow the lines of this hope. Heard gun-fire during the evening, warnings too, but it had all finished by 10 o'clock.

Kathleen Tipper, Diaries, 22 October 1941

COMMON LOST TO ARMY HUTS

Jess and I had a walk up Long Common with the dogs this afternoon. Army huts of some sort – they are cylindrical in shape – are being rapidly shoved up by soldiers (not at tradesmen's rates) on Short Common. Goodbye to another bit of 'common' rights (no pun intended), as I don't suppose Short Common will be returned to the people again after the war; unless there's changeovers and the people inherit the land.

Jack Overhill, *Cambridge at War*, 23 October 1941

EASTERN ACTION

What a day. The morning papers report huge concentration of Japanese troops in Indo-China and by the time the evening comes the Japs have bombed several of the American bases in the Pacific. I suppose this really does mean America [is] in the war. Mother is convinced that the war will be decided in the East. I wonder.

Kathleen Tipper, Diaries, 7 December 1941

CIVVY STREET SKILLS PUT TO MILITARY USE

From the evening paper:

The Army's best spotter of enemy planes was a soldier who twiddled the knobs of his AA [anti-aircraft] gun predictor so dextrously that he was taken round from batter to batter to teach recruits. His superior officers were amazed at the speed and sensitiveness of his fingers, until one night he was asked what he did in civilian life. 'I was a safe-breaker,' he replied.

James Agate, Journals, 25 February 1942

BLACK MARKET CLEANS UP

Mr Morrison spoke on the radio last night about his new measures to clean up the black market. I am certain that some very important people are behind this traffic, but I can't imagine that they will ever be brought to justice. Our canteen was burgled last night. When I arrived there this evening, everybody was quite excited about the crime … Actually, whoever was responsible is really a downright crook. I think it is a wretched trick to rob a place like the YMCA, because it is there for the convenience of the troops, and all the workers are doing jobs just out of the goodness of their hearts, [and] certainly not for anything they may get out of it. I find myself looking suspiciously at everyone this evening, quite unjustifiably, I know.

Kathleen Tipper, Diaries, 12 March 1942

VILLAGE CLAIMED BY MILITARY

One shock after another! Not only have the military taken over the South Downs but the village of Stanmer is evacuated: the church dismantled and the inhabitants, some of whom were not only born there but their parents and grandparents before them, turned adrift. I hope that we shall bomb Germany to bits!

Mrs Henry Dudeney, A Lewes Diary, 23 April 1942

AGGRESSIVE AMERICANS

Mr Churchill announced in the Commons today that we made another 1,000-plane raid last night, this time on Essen. We lost 35 planes. This announcement came as a surprise as to most of us, as we had been told that it was unlikely that the RAF could carry out more than one of these big raids in seven or eight days. Went to the New Zealand Forces Club again this evening, served in the bar. Many Americans use the Club and in the process of drawing some of them out I discovered most of them think (or know) that they are disliked here and are resentful of the fact. Several of them told me that they think it is because they are paid much more than our troops, but I don't think this is the real cause, because some of the Dominion troops are paid as well as the Americans. I put it down to the fact that they are disliked by many people here because they are so aggressive.

Katheleen Tipper, Diaries, 2 June 1942

⌒⁂⌒

INDIFFERENT SUCCESS

Went down to the *Melody Maker* and saw the editor, Ray Sonin. He says that there are only 2,000 dance-band musicians not yet called up; that all band instruments will cease to be manufactured after August 1st, except for Ensa, the Services, the BBC, and educational purposes; that public reaction to the Middle East is so sensitive that 'Deep in the Heart of Texas' varies in sales weekly from 3,000 to 12,000.

There seems still to be a stalemate position at El Alamein.* Whether this is good or bad remains to be seen. We continue to ground-strafe the German positions and communications. The Germans are proceeding with their attack over the River Don, but the Russians deny the loss of Vornonezh.

Peggy was in Bond Street this afternoon when an aeroplane flew at roof-top height and looked as though it was going to make a crash-landing in Hyde Park. But she heard no crash.

Played poker with indifferent success.

Charles Graves, *Great Days*, 8 July 1942

---

* *El Alamein, in Egypt, was only sixty miles west of the British naval base in Alexandria. It was here that the British general Claude Auchinleck, commanding British, Indian, South*

African and New Zealand troops, battled Field Marshal Erwin Rommel's Afrika Korps and the Italian army for control of North Africa.

⁓

NEW ROCKETS

The sirens sounded at 1.00 a.m. and the all clear was about 3.25 a.m. Three lots of incendiaries were unpleasantly close – the nearest batch being by the canal bridge (Yardley Road) and Mansfield Road, where there was damage and, we believe, one fatal casualty. There was a fire at Marb-lustre wooden buildings. The incendiaries were of the explosive type and went off with loud reports; some seemed to be much later than the 2 minutes …

The new type [of] incendiaries are pretty terrible and there seems to be a doubt as to how to deal with them. Many people have been killed and injured while tackling them – they are not the easy proposition that the old type were.

The new 'rocket gun' type of anti-air defence was in action for the first time during the week, and by the bursts in the sky is spectacular to look at, but by all accounts a bit dangerous for us, for the tubes come down intact, and there were at least two that came down unexploded at Bourneville. These went 17 feet into the ground …

F. T. Lockwood, Diaries, 30 July 1942

⁓

STYGIAN BATHS

[A] hot day, took Peggy out to Lord's to watch Cheltenham play Haileybury. After an hour and half in the sunshine, went off to have a bathe at the International Sportsmen's Club. The new restrictions about electric light are now producing an effect, and it was quite Stygian along the corridor to the swimming pool.

Charles Graves, *Great Days*, 1 August 1942

BIRTHS TREBLE

Mrs Jackson said she met one of those modern girls who said she meant to have 3 babies before the war is over. I said: 'Do ask her to hurry up and make it triplets.'

Mrs Henry Dudeney, *A Lewes Diary*, 26 August 1942

⁓

BACK FROM THE RHINELAND

Called at 5.30 a.m. to have breakfast with the pilots. They have been to Duisburg. It seems quite uncanny that these fellows I had seen only a few hours before had flown all those hundreds of miles to Germany, dropped their bombs on people they would never see, and had flown straight back to their aerodrome and were once more in the dining-room. I did not like to ask whether they had all come back. Fortunately, on this occasion they had done so.

Charles Graves, *Great Days*, 26 August 1942

⁓

VIEW OF ST PAUL'S

London Bridge station, never a place of beauty, is grimy, partly roofless and generally dingy. Outside to the west is a wide chasm where buildings once stood, now cleared of debris, with Guy's Hospital across the gulf. A large water tank or two at each end of the bridge. There are fire pumps on piles in the river to lift the Thames along the pipe lines laid along the pathway.

I look across to St Paul's across gaps in the riverside buildings. Not a clock face survives to tell the time … On the right I pass the shell of St Swithun's, St Stephen's Walbrook is no more and the ruined buildings cleared away. Along to Mansion House station, from which is the open and grand view of St Paul's as even Wren never saw it, except in imagination …

Rev. Maurice Foxell, Diaries, 14 October 1942

'GOOD LUNCH FOR WARTIME'

To Mansion House at one for the banquet for the newly elected Lord Mayor. A good lunch for wartime – turtle soup, fish au gratin, roast turkey and a sweet! Drank well of nice claret.

The main event was a speech by Winston Churchill to an audience in good spirits at the victorious turn of events in N. Africa with its promise of greater things to come: 'But this is not the beginning of the end, rather it is the end of the beginning.' He was, as ever, restrained; his audience's good spirits seemed ahead of his. He knows more than they. Still, it was good to see him looking well and, of course, in good heart.

Rev. Maurice Foxell, Diaries, 10 November 1942

PLANNING FOR THE FUTURE

A memorable day – maybe our ancestors will be able to say that, if the proposals contained in Sir William Beveridge's Report are ever carried out. Somehow, much of the report seems too practical ever to be carried out.

I think the only hope we have of seeing this Report turned into action is the power of the people to insist that after this war we don't slip back as they did after the last, and this Report is something solid for the people to hang their own ideas to. Sir William Beveridge has shown us the way.

Kathleen Tipper, Diaries, 1 December 1942

TOASTED SPAM FOR UNCLE SAM

Joyce and I are on duty all day at the YM. We were quite busy all day. Nowadays, we get a sprinkling of Americans in who will insist on having 'toasted spam sandwiches', which consists of two slices of toast with spam between them. We have been amused at this peculiar taste as far as our canteen goes, most of the spam sent over on Lease-Lend is going back into the stomachs of Americans.

Kathleen Tipper, Diaries, 13 December 1942

CLOTHES CUE FOR ACTION

To the Regal Cinema to see the Russian film *One Day of War*. Enormously impressed by the dignity of this documentary embodying the courage, devotion, steadfastness, cheerfulness, and self-sacrifice of an entire people. The women come out of it splendidly, particularly the girl who had brought back to safety one hundred and sixty-one men lying wounded in the open, and in every case had retrieved his rifle. A great poem. And then, of course, being English, we must follow up this superb picture with a Government snipped showing an encounter between a business damsel and an ATS [Auxiliary Territorial Service] transport driver seated at the driving-wheel of her truck. Gurgles the business lass: 'Darling, I had no idea the ATS uniform could look so marvellous. I envy you, my sweet!' Whereupon the patriotic driver seized her cue and retorts, 'In that case, angel, why not try wearing one yourself?' From which it would seem to be officially recognised that clothes and not duty are the Englishwoman's cue for action.

The 'musical' was some appalling rubbish entitled *Orchestra Wives*. In no other country would that snippet and this inanity have been bracketed with the Russian film.

James Agate, Journals, 8 February 1943

JOINING THE WRENS

A cold day. I washed very carefully, having also had a bath the night before. For today was my WRNS [Women's Royal Naval Service] medical. I felt very weak at the knees and found it difficult to work – I left at twelve, had lunch at the

Buttery, where I fortified myself with roast pork. By this time it was sunny, so I walked down to the army Recruiting Centre where the medical is held. It was one o'clock by this time. There were several other girls there. We were put into a waiting room decorated with ATS posters and a 'No Smoking' notice. I read my novel and talked a bit to the others – various types and ages. First of all, we filled in a medical form – then went upstairs and undressed, except for shoes, knickers and coat – then produced a 'specimen' into a kind of enamel potty with a long handle like a saucepan – of which I was quite glad. Next came examination of eyes, ears, etc., weighing and measuring by an elderly doctor, then heart, lungs etc., by a woman. All quite quick. After that I dressed again and had an interview with an extremely charming WRNS 1st officer – she had my London forms and correspondence but couldn't really tell me much, except that my application was marked 'urgent' and that they probably had something in mind for me. And I mustn't be too impatient. Oh, but I do hope I get in now. My heart is set on it ...

Barbara Pym, *A Very Private Eye*, 8 April 1943

OVER HERE AND AMOROUS

I made a potato and leek soup for supper – then went firewatching. It was a beautiful evening. On the bridge I saw a girl warden (rather plain) being kissed by a Doughboy (a hide-hoe, a sweet and lo, a come-and-go boy). Lucky pigs, I thought.

Barbara Pym, *A Very Private Eye*, 14 April 1943

FALLING FOUL OF THE CENSOR

The letter I wrote to Margery has been returned by the Censor, as I told her about the Air Raid here. I suppose I'm lucky not to be fined. A lengthy paper enclosed saying things you may not say in a letter. Quite right and necessary and wise; but a prison existence we are leading with the additional inconvenience that you don't even know the length of your sentence!

Mrs Henry Dudeney, *A Lewes Diary*, 25 May 1943

⁂

NOTE OF NO RETURN

Well, it came this morning. And when it does come, it's like Love – make no mistake about it, you know. A long envelope with a railway warrant Bristol to Rochester (Single, this time there is No Return). Also, a list of clothes to be taken. No food or drink (nor the smallest of double gins) to be taken there. I am to go on July 7th. My feelings are mixed but mostly I am excited and glad. Everyone at the office very nice. It was a hot day, hard to work.

Barbara Pym, *A Very Private Eye*, 24 June 1943

⁂

ANTI-TEUTON SONG CHARMS PM

At twelve o clock the Prime Ministerial car fetched me and drove me to Chequers. Found Mrs Churchill alone and played a little croquet with her. The PM was very amiable and charming. I played 'Don't Let's Be Beastly to the Germans' over and over again, and he was mad about it.

After tea I had a long talk with him … about de Gaulle (whom he doesn't like and suspects of being a potential little French Fuehrer).

Noël Coward, Diaries, 4 July 1943

⁂

MUSTERING EXCITEMENT

Today we were kitted. We were taken in lorries to Chatham at 8 a.m. – a great herd of us – I was standing in a mass of suitcases, lurching all over the place as we drove very fast. My hat is lovely, every bit as fetching as I'd hoped, but my suit rather large, though it's easier to alter that way. I have a macintosh and greatcoat, 3 pairs of 'hose' (black), gloves, tie, 4 shirts and 9 stiff collars, and two pairs of shoes which are surprisingly comfortable. After that we got respirators. Service respirators are a good deal more comfortable than civilian – we went in the gas chamber. Then had lunch in the WRNS mess.

It all sounds quite simple written down like this, but it's a long, dreary business and we all looked very tired and fed up as we lay in dejected groups in the WRNS fo'c's'le [living quarters at the front of the ship] – I wished I was out of it all – but suddenly, drinking the dregs of a cup of indifferent coffee, my spirits began to lift and when we got back I was quite excited …

Barbara Pym, A Very Private Eye, 20 July 1943

ITALY SURRENDERS

Heard on 6 o'clock news of the unconditional surrender of Italy, which was followed by the National Anthem. I stood and had such a lump in my throat that I could scarcely raise a cheer. It is a glorious bit of news – thank God, thank God!

Rev. Maurice Foxell, Diaries, 8 September 1943

CHANGING SIDES

Yesterday, Italy declared war on Germany. What a strange-made war. Pity they didn't choose our side three years ago.

Barbara Pym, A Very Private Eye, 14 October 1943

A GRIM NEWSREEL

Spent an enjoyable evening at the cinema. Saw *Now, Voyager* – a sentimental and pretty impossible Bette Davis epic – she turns anything into a first-rate film. I think she is far above any other woman on the screen, and I know many other people share my view. Gladys Cooper gave a fine performance in the film. I wonder what it feels like to take parts like this, middle-aged or elderly parts, when she was once considered the most beautiful woman on the English stage? We saw the film of repatriated prisoners, which is being shown as part of a Red Cross appeal in all cinemas this week. It is most moving, unbearably so some of it, but it does seem a disgrace that these men have to appeal to charity. The Government should provide adequately for every man injured in the service of his country. The newsreel contained some grim pictures of the 14th Army in Burma – the most amazing battle pictures I have ever seen containing shots of men hit by snipers, and some most grim shots of dead Japs. This is surely one of the most ghastly battlefronts in the world?*

Kathleen Tipper, Diaries, 19 January 1944

* *British-ruled Burma had fallen to the Japanese in 1942, leading to the mass evacuation of British and Indian ex-pats, dubbed the 'Dunkirk of the East'. By the following year, however, the Allies – under the command of Admiral Louis Mountbatten and Lieutenant General William Slim, and in particular the newly formed British Fourteenth Army – were engaged in an intensive counter-attack to retake the country.*

DANGERS ON THE HOME FRONT

A WAAF [a Women's Auxiliary Air Force member] has been murdered in Well Hall and the whole district is buzzing with it.* Last night, when I got home from the Club, I found my father dressed ready to come meet me, but I had left earlier than usual, so he hadn't started out. He is naturally worried, and I don't really care for walking about alone in the blackout.

Kathleen Tipper, Diaries, 15 February 1944

* *The partly naked body of Iris Miriam Deeley, a twenty-one-year-old WAAF, was discovered on 14 February. She had been strangled. Ernest James Kemp, a gunner in the Royal Artillery, was found guilty of the murder on 18 April 1944. Sentenced to death, he was hanged by the famous executioner Albert Pierrepoint at Wandsworth prison on 6 June 1944.*

⌀

PLAN FOR GOEBBELS NOT BEVERIDGE

Do not the people of this country realise that every minute spent on making the Beveridge Plan or some variation of it practicable is time thrown away unless we have the next Goebbels Plan. After the last war, this country sat back and messed about with a piece of idealistic imbecility called the League of Nations. It disarmed and watched the Germans start preparing for a new war under the pretence of the Strength through Joy Movement.

If I were an austere Nazi I should be already organising a Strength through Repentance Movement, in the certain knowledge that some of our highbrow papers and all the intellectual reviews would be tumbling over each other to head a campaign for supplying Germany with all the battleships, U-boats, aeroplanes, and raw materials essential to a chance of heart.

I have no doubt whatever that we shall win the second World War. I have equally little doubt that our idealists will hand the Germans the third World War on a silver platter.

James Agate, Journals, 2 March 1944

⌀

SMALL COAL, HIGHER WAGES

Over 90,000 miners are now on strike and the position is very serious. I am afraid the miners haven't many friends now. I have heard bitter comments everywhere, many from people I know who are earning many times the amount a miner earns, doing some sit-down job, which isn't as arduous or as dangerous as the miners'. I feel drawn two ways. I don't approve of strike in wartime, but I feel that people forget the awful deal the miners had between the wars and I also think £5 much too little for the work they do. When I paid out 4s 8d a hundredweight for coal that previously cost 2s 1d, I feel that I wouldn't begrudge it so much if the increase went to the men who did it instead of into the coal-owners' pocket ... My father, too, heard from several ex-miners who work for his firm; they say that the coal-owners are keeping the good seams till after the war, making the miners dig the poor seams, which produces this small coal ...

Kathleen Tipper, Diaries, 9 March 1944

⸙

THE BALD RULE OF MEN

When I picked up the *Daily Telegraph* and saw a photograph of 5 bald-headed gentlemen sitting in conference (Colonial Premiers with Churchill, looking as if they were yawning), I flung it from me in disgust. Muddle-headed politicians for the last 25 years have let us in for this.

Mrs Henry Dudeney, *A Lewes Diary*, 2 May 1944

⸙

D-DAY

A date for ever to be known in future history. It was at 9.45 that Gen. Eisenhower announced the invasion on this so-called 'D. Day'; also broadcast was the call of Gen. de Gaulle to the French. There was an air of excitement in London and at midday queues for the papers. On the 1 o'clock news I heard Churchill's statement on the invasion. All went well on this terrific start with less, much less, loss than had been anticipated. The King broadcast at 9 too, in a solemn call to us and our allies to support with prayer this crusade to liberate Europe. So the long-expected assault has begun – God prosper it.

Rev. Maurice Foxell, Diaries, 6 June 1944

DOODLEBUGS ARRIVE

Air war began a new phase. Siren at 12.35 a.m. Planes, bombs and gunfire and it was obvious that a new Hun weapon was making its debut – namely pilotless explosive aircraft, probably radio-controlled. There would be a heavy-sounding engine passing over, sometimes apparently quite low, then silence as the engine stopped, then the explosion shaking and sometimes rocking the house as it fell to earth – a devilish device of German 'frightfulness' which falls they know not where, nor do they care as long as it kills English people. It is a serious problem for our experts to tackle.

Rev. Maurice Foxell, Diaries, 16 June 1944

* Nicknamed 'doodlebugs', the German Fieseler Fi 103 or V1 rockets – V for Vergeltungswaffen, meaning 'retaliatory weapon' – were essentially flying bombs with a rudimentary engine and wings. They were designed to fall out of the sky when they ran out of fuel, and exploded on impact.

DUNKIRK AS REMOTE AS WATERLOO

A flying bomb this morning narrowly missed the War Memorial Hospital and fell on a putting green nearby, causing only windows to be damaged – a lucky miss. The weather continues foul, as apparently it is in France at this time. The Germans are retreating fast in front of our armies towards Rouen, which makes me wonder whether they will retreat from Holland and Belgium first or wait for us to drive them out. Anyway, this amazing advance brings many possibilities forward and we should be surprised at nothing ... The day of Dunkirk and the great German Air Force seems as remote as Waterloo.

Kathleen Tipper, Diaries, 19 August 1944

PARIS LIBERATED

The liberation of Paris was announced in the one o'clock News. In the words of the announcer: 'Fifty thousand of the armed forces of the interior and several hundred thousand of unarmed patriots …'

Not unarmed, I think, but armed haphazardly!

There is a transcendentality of delirium about BBC matters which baffles me.

Tonight, I listened in to a special programme in honour of France. Incidentally, there was a long speech supposed to convey the views of the Man in the Street. This was uttered in an announcer's voice and contained the words 'garish' and 'pristine'. But let that pass. The point is that tonight of all nights, the BBC chose to fade out in the middle of the 'Marseillaise'!

James Agate, Journals, 23 August 1944

INSIPID FIREWORKS

I forgot it was Guy Fawkes Day yesterday, a day I always remember with horror from my youth. Actually, though we always had a lot of fun at home with fireworks, etc., and although I was pretty scared of loud fizzes and bangs, the roast potatoes, chestnuts, and gorgeous bonfires made up for this fact. To children of today, used to fires of Blitz size and the sounds of 1,000-pound bombs exploding and the sight of rockets exploding in the sky, the fireworks we used to have will seem insipid. Lord Moyne, Resident Minister in the Middle East, has been shot in Cairo, and is severely injured. His chauffeur was killed at the same time. Whatever the reasons for this crime, it is a dreadful thing.

Kathleen Tipper, Diaries, 6 November 1944

OMINOUS NEW YEAR'S PROSPECTS

Roused two or three times by distant rocket explosions, which is all very horrid. One on Saturday night fell at S. Croydon.

Thus ends 1944 with its D-Day June, with its hopes of victory before Christmas, with the failing of those hopes, with V2s* following on V1s, and finally with an ambitious German attack in Belgium and Luxembourg which had serious threats but which, for the present, is held. We set out with fresh hopes for victory in 1945 but it looks as if a very tough time must precede it.

Rev. Maurice Foxell, Diaries, 31 December 1944

* *Powered by a liquid ethanol fuel, the V2 rocket was a technological step beyond the V1. It paved the way for both modern ballistic missiles and the rockets that would eventually take people to the moon.*

BOXING DAY SHORTAGES

Mrs Brough said that the shortage of Toilet Rolls is because the Air Force had collared the lot, 2 rolls to each pilot. Something to do with scattering leaflets.

Mrs Henry Dudeney, *A Lewes Diary*, 26 December 1944

RACING TOWARDS BERLIN

Berlin raided again during the night, the fifth time in three days. The Russians are now only 90 miles from Berlin, and the map of Germany with arrows drawing near the capital is now a regular feature of the daily press.

Quite busy at the club. Talked to a terribly burned boy. His face was quite grotesque, but he was cheerful. His hands worried me more. They were so terribly disfigured, and looked much worse. One never knows quite how to treat these boys, whether to look them in the eye as if they looked like Robert Taylor, or to avoid them …

Kathleen Tipper, Diaries, 29 January 1945

BIG BEN BRIGHT AGAIN

The black-out is to end officially on Monday and on Tuesday Big Ben will be lit up after five years' eclipse. Slowly, life reverts to normal.

Sir Henry 'Chips' Channon, Diaries, 19 April 1945

END OF A DICTATOR

I worked and dined alone in Brook's. At 10.30 a member rushed into the morning room announcing that Hitler's death had just come through on the tape. We all ran to read about it. Somehow, I fancy none of us were very excited. We have waited and suffered too long. Three years ago we would have been out of our minds with jubilation and excitement – and with prognostications of a happy issue out of all our afflictions.

James Lees-Milne, Diaries, 1 May 1945

∽✠∽

UNCONDITIONAL SURRENDER

Unconditional surrender of German armies in West Germany, Holland and Denmark to F. M. Montgomery to take effect at 8 a.m. tomorrow. Listened in to it. 'This is the moment,' was Montgomery's comment, and indeed it was. Nearly a million men thus surrendered. Words fail and comment is useless.

Rev. Maurice Foxell, Diaries, 4 May 1945

∽✠∽

VICTORY IN EUROPE

This is VE DAY at last … At midnight I insisted on our joining the revels. It was a very warm night. Thousands of searchlights swept the sky. Otherwise, there were no illuminations and no street lights at all. Claridge's and the Ritz were lit up. We walked down Bond Street passing small groups singing, not boisterously. Piccadilly, however, was full of swarming people and littered with paper.

We walked arm in arm into the middle of Piccadilly Circus, which was brilliantly illuminated with arc lamps. Here the crowds were yelling, singing and laughing. They were orderly and good-humoured. All the English virtues were on the surface. We watched individuals climb the lamp posts and plant flags on the top amidst tumultuous applause from bystanders. We walked down Piccadilly towards the Ritz. In the Green Park there was a huge bonfire under the trees, and one too near one poor tree caught fire … One extraordinary figure, a bearded, naval titan, organised an absurd nonsense game, by calling out the Navy and making them tear around the bonfire carrying the Union Jack; then the RAF; then the Army; then the Land Army, represented by three girls only; then the Americans; then the civilians. If we had been a little drunker we would have joined in … The scene was more Elizabethan than neo-Georgian, a spontaneous peasant game, a dance around the maypole, almost Brueghelian, infinitely bucolic … I thought if we could have a V-night once a month, and invite the Poles, Germans and even the Russians to do what we were doing now, there might never be another war.

James Lees-Milne, Diaries, 8 May 1945

HAPPY, ORDERLY MOBS

Up to town by 9.34 train thinking that my church might be of use to City people. But the City east of St Paul's was empty save for those going Westwards. Decided to hold a service at 12.30. Advertised it in the pubs of the Parish. When time came only Mr and Mrs Patterson, Tuffill and Mrs Macrin present, with Mac on the organ. Meanwhile, thousands at St Paul's. Went to Westminster, great crowd in Parliament Square – a happy, orderly mob on a warm, summerish day. At 3 p.m. heard Churchill through the loudspeakers announce the end of hostilities, the defeat of Germany – and then the cease-fire sounded. All ends at 1 minute past midnight.

Went to a thanksgiving service in the church [at Woldingham] at 8 p.m. – a full church and really hearty singing. Later, M. and I bicycled out to the Ridge to see what we might see. Below were the lights of Oxted; in the far distance were one or two bonfires and an occasional faraway rocket …

Rev. Maurice Foxell, Diaries, 8 May 1945

LABOUR LANDSLIDE

Death robbed Roosevelt of his triumph, and now the mob has stolen Churchill's glory and trampled it under foot. 'The decision of the British public has been recorded in the votes counted today. I have therefore laid down the charge which was placed upon me in darker times.' Words which should make Englishmen blush for a thousand years.

My next reaction was to phone Edgar Lustgarten and tell him that I was applying for naturalisation as a Patagonian. And then I pulled myself together. There is no question of scurviness towards the greatest Englishman since Queen Elizabeth. The seed of today's affair was contained in something Lady Oxford said at lunch at Gwen Chenhall's a few days after Churchill became Prime Minister: 'Winston is the one man who can lead this country to victory. When he has got it he will cry like a baby. He is a fighter who loves fighting; nothing else really interests him, though he may pretend it does. He is the last man to handle the reins of peace.'

Many electors must have asked themselves this question: Am I to vote for Winston and abandon my principles, or should I stick to my principles at the risk of seeming ungrateful? For once, in a way, Churchill seems to have lacked a sense of the stage. His proposal, turned down by the Socialists at the Blackpool Conference, that the Coalition should continue until the end of the war with Japan, when there should be an election, was a mistake. What he should have said was: 'Leave me in power till we've finished off the Japs, when I will retire and not embarrass the country with any nonsense about gratitude.'

He should not have risked defeat …

James Agate, Journals, 26 July 1945

THE ATOMIC BOMB DROPS

The world has been electrified, thrilled and horrified by the atomic bomb; one has been dropped in Japan today. It devastated a whole town and killed a quarter of a million people. It could mean the end of civilization.

Sir Henry 'Chips' Channon, Diaries, 5 August 1945

VICTORY IN JAPAN

VJ Day. We heard the news that Japan had accepted the Allies' Potsdam surrender terms after America had twice used the Atomic Bomb. Danny Knight came bursting into the hut and set up an uproar. Robinson behaved like a child and ended up tipping Knight out of bed, to which Knight retaliated and did likewise to him. In the morning it was announced the camp would close down till Sunday night.

Roland Wiggins, Diaries, 15 August 1945

GREY PROSPECTS

It seems to me that this post-war universe is more fraught with horrifying and combustile dangers even than that of 1938–9. This then, this grey, joyless prospect seeded with ghastly explosives is what the world has torn itself in pieces to produce. But though such reflections haunt my mind, I am also aware of a very strong inclination to turn away from them and merely survey the inner scene – chimney corner, husband, child, friends, plants, cats and crockery.

Frances Partridge, Diaries, 16 September 1945

RECORD JET

A 'Meteor' jet plane landed on the airfield this morning, which was of special interest as a like plane has broken the world speed record at Herne Bay a few days ago. I was surprised at its low landing speed. It has a tricycle undercarriage.

Roland Wiggins, Diaries, 5 November 1945

NAZI WAR TRIALS

Walking along the Strand in the rain and fog, I said to Hughie that trying the Nazi war criminals at Nuremberg was like trying a man's finger for having pulled the trigger of a gun which murdered someone.*

Malcolm Muggeridge, Diaries, 21 November 1945

* *Pointedly held in the German city where the National Socialist Party had staged their annual rallies, the Nuremberg Trials saw the indictment of leading Nazis for perpetrating crimes against humanity and the newly defined crime of genocide. Undertaken between 1945 and 1949, these trials led to the creation of the Universal Declaration of Human Rights in 1948.*

BRITAIN BANKS ON AMERICA

There's much hullabaloo over the loan America has made us. *The Observer* thinks well of it, but the *Economist* and *New Statesman* can't be dismal enough about it. Apparently, Britain can only pay back in goods and America must encourage an export surplus, which means increasing wages in America to absorb this surplus, something Big Business in Yankeeland has no intention of doing; in fact, is bent on doing just the opposite by reducing wages.*

Jack Overhill, *Cambridge at War*, 16 December 1945

* *The loan was brokered by the economist John Maynard Keynes, who had hoped to secure a grant-in-aid for the rebuilding of Britain in recognition of the enormous financial contributions the country had made throughout the war. The loan was finally paid off in 2006.*

CHAPTER SIX

FROM AUSTERITY TO AFFLUENCE: 1946-1959

In July 1945, Labour swept into government with a landslide, led by Clement Attlee. Their electoral campaign had been fought under the slogan 'Let Us Face the Future' and the promise of building a new, more egalitarian society – a Britain where the evils of joblessness and poverty that had plagued the 1930s would be banished for good. Under Labour's plans, the state, as in wartime, was to assume control of essential industries, with coal, gas, steel, electricity, the railways and the airways all being nationalized. In addition, the safety net of a social welfare system that would carry everyone from the cradle to the grave was to be created. The jewel in the crown of these proposals was the National Health Service (NHS), inaugurated in 1948 by Health Minister Aneurin Bevan. The medical establishment fiercely opposed it but the government pushed forward nonetheless.

The NHS's aim was to ensure that no person, however poor, should lack access to medical care, and that these services should be supplied for free and paid for out of general taxation. Those principles, for the most part, still define it today.

Yet the country Labour inherited was nothing short of a wreck. Its towns and cities had been ravaged by bombing, and building of almost any kind had been on hold for the past six years. Housing, labour and commodities were in short supply, and having borrowed heavily to fund the war, Britain was forced to take out rather punitive loans from America – and later accept what amounted to charity – to keep the country afloat. In these circumstances, imperial dominions like India (which was granted independence in 1947) were expenses that could no longer be justified, financially as much as morally. The crumbling Empire's hardy sons and daughters might be encouraged to come to the Mother Country as workers – but only if they were willing to do so at a cut price.

The measures that Sir Stafford Cripps, the rather ascetic President of the Board of Trade, introduced to curb consumption and restrict wages have become synonymous with the late 1940s. And so not without good reason, first-hand accounts from the period are as studded as cloves in a ham with whinging about fuel shortages, queues, price hikes, taxes, strikes and scarcities; and drab bleak winters were made drabber and bleaker by all the aforementioned. Rationing was to continue for close to ten years after the war's end. Austerity defined the period.

The journey from austerity Britain to the place where people – in the opinion of the Conservative Prime Minister Harold Macmillan, at least – had 'never had it so good', unfolds in the pages to come by way of teenage trainspotters, the Festival of Britain, the Coronation of Queen Elizabeth II, the Suez Crisis, Angry Young Men, the Space Race, coffee bars and skiffle groups. Affluence, hinted at here by the appearance of television sets and visits to the Ideal Home Show, is, however, underscored by growing anxieties about the Cold War, atomic weapons and the general increasing pace of change.

⁓

CRABBY START TO THE NEW YEAR

Made a regrettable and most extraordinary discovery this morning. *Pediculus pubis* [pubic lice], Dr Black's dictionary calls it, or them, in its genteel phraseology. Now, this honestly is not through physical contacts for I have had none. I can suggest only the proverbial lavatory seat, perhaps the one in the train last Friday. Public places and conveyances these days are absolutely filthy.

James Lees-Milne, Diaries, 15 January 1946

UNCHANGED BY THE WAR

Back to Rodrigo's for supper. While we were sitting in the kitchen at our meal, Roland Pym walked in. The calmness with which we fell into a normal conversation on the eternal topics reminded me of the Paris school-man who, after years of imprisonment, returned to his students and began his first lecture, 'As I was just saying.'

The war has been more of a gap to us than anything else and does not seem fundamentally to have changed any of my friends.

William Townsend, Journals, 1 May 1946

LOSING THE PINK BITS

My birthday falls on Friday, on Empire Day, and during the evening we wondered whether there would be any Empire left by then.

Kathleen Tipper, Diaries, 19 May 1946

SHORTAGES WORSE THAN DURING THE WAR

Downtown I met several people I knew, and they and the women who hurried from shop to shop looked so harassed, all speaking of 'more difficult to get things than in the war when U-boats were sinking our ships'.

Nella Last, *The Post-War Diaries of Housewife 49*, 5 June 1946

BIKINI BOMB

Well, the atom bomb experiment was made last night, with apparently disappointing results. I would like it put on record that I think now, and have always thought, that far too much cock has been talked about atomic energy. I have no more faith in men of science being infallible than I have of men of God being infallible, principally on account of them being men. I have heard it stated that atomic energy might disturb the course of the earth through the universe; that it might cause devastating tidal waves; that it might transform climates from hot to cold or vice versa; make a hole in the bed of the ocean so that the sea would drain away and extinguish the fires of the earth; suddenly deflect our planet into the orbit of the sun, in which case we should all shrivel up, etc., etc., etc. I am convinced that all it will really do is destroy human beings in large numbers. I have a feeling that the universe and the laws of nature are beyond its scope.*

Noël Coward, Diaries, 1 July 1946

* *This atomic bomb test was conducted by the Americans on Bikini Atoll in the Pacific.*

CAR CONGESTION

It has been announced that parking is now only going to be allowed on one side of New Street, Corporation Street and Colmore Row etc., as the traffic in town [Birmingham] is getting so congested.

Brian Williams, Diaries, 15 January 1947

FUEL CRISIS

This week is being a veritable nightmare. On Sunday afternoon it started to thaw and the snow mostly went. On Monday it froze again very hard, so the slush is like slippery brick. Since Monday we've had no heating in our office apart from one electric fire. And now this is turned off from 9 till 12 and again from 2 till 4 each day. Wrapped in my fur coat with three pullovers underneath, my snow boots kept on, I am still too perished to work properly. The brain becomes atrophied. People are unanimously blaming the Government for a hideous muddle, yet Mr Shinwell still remains Minister of Fuel. I seldom stay in the office now but walk, dictate letters, and move away. Have twice been to the National Gallery, which is heated, to look at the Spanish Exhibition of Velázquez, Goya and El Greco. A number of poor old people sit on benches for hours at a time, their feet wrapped in brown paper, striving to keep warm. At an Historic Buildings Committee meeting yesterday all sat in fur coats, moaning in misery, for no one could concentrate on the agenda.

Most of the large shops are closed; those that are open have no electricity, and no lights except from the odd candle. The streets are blacked out, as in war time, and millions are unemployed, for industries have come to a standstill. Food is becoming very short and the situation is critical and deadly serious as ever it was during the war. The odd thing is apparently that the Government is no more unpopular with the masses than before this debacle.

James Lees-Milne, Diaries, 13 February 1947

OLD TESTAMENT WEATHER

Stories of spreading floods all over the country. The blizzard has moved North. Ghastly destruction of livestock, especially sheep, is being revealed. This poor country is undergoing afflictions like the Ten Plagues.*

Blanche Dugdale, Diaries, 11 March 1947

* *The winter of 1946–7 was one of the severest on record. Starting from 23 January 1947, there were six weeks of snow, the drifts leaving thousands of people cut off and lacking fuel and food, which were already in short supply after the war.*

SHOOT FOR THE MOON

Lunched at the pub at Aylesbury. Was sitting beside a young man who told me he worked at advanced photography with rocket manufacturers. He said there was an Interplanetary Society of six or seven persons, some women, who expect shortly to travel to the moon. They will not be able to return but they will signal back their discoveries and when the oxygen gives out they will die.

James Lees-Milne, Diaries, 24 May 1947

WORKING MUMS TO BLAME

Mrs Higham and I sat on her lawn in deckchairs. She had been to the Social and Moral Welfare this morning and was a bit downcast. She spoke of two 'wasted' young lives and blamed mothers going out to work and their not having a home life. She is like me and bigoted about the importance of home and mother for young things.

Nella Last, *The Post-War Diaries of Housewife 49*, 26 June 1947

RED TO GREEN DEVILRY

Had a coffee at Forte's. The place was positively full of queens! never seen anything quite like it in my life before – it's positively frightening. How many future tradgedy's [*sic*] were present tonight? – god it's horrible to even think of it! Sang all the way home and jumped on a traffic light bumper for sheer devilment and changed it from red to green!

Kenneth Williams, Diaries, 7 January 1948

NEW LOOK, OLD-FASHIONED

The 'new line'* seems to have ousted points problems, the poor quality of coal and even the weather, when women are talking, and I feel wildly amused when the only one *in* fashion, or not caring, are the dowdy old grannies and maiden aunts. It always amused me to see Aunt Sarah's unswept hair, the latest fashion, but which she uncompromisingly stuck to between the Edwardian and these days.

Nella Last, *The Post-War Diaries of Housewife 49*, 8 January 1948

* *Christian Dior's New Look fashion collection had been shown in Paris in 1947, ushering in a new silhouette, with fitted jackets, nipped-in waists, bold shoulders and full skirts in mid-calf lengths defining the style.*

~

GANDHI ASSASSINATED

I have felt very upset today, as Mahatma Gandhi has been assassinated. The story is on the front page of the *Birmingham Mail* and it made me cry. There is a big photo of him which I am cutting out to stick in my big *Boots Scribbling Diary* which I had for Christmas.

The paper says that Gandhi was shot dead with four revolver bullets fired from close range by a young Hindu. Women tried to shield him with their arms, and there were sobbing crowds at the scene of the tragedy.

Inside, there is an article about his visit to this country in Autumn 1930 when he came to the Round Table Conference, proposing Dominion Status for India. He talked with King George V and Queen Mary, and actually came to Birmingham, where he made a speech at Woodbrooke College, Selly Oak.

It has been the wettest January for five years. We have had 4.35 inches of rain up until 9.00 this morning.

Brian Williams, Diaries, 30 January 1948

Gandhi has been assassinated. In my humble opinion, a bloody good thing but far too late.

Noël Coward, Diaries, 30 January 1948

✒

DOCTOR BOYCOTTS THE NHS

Still in bed. Called in doctor, who made expected diagnosis and gave me some different sleeping pills. Discussed with him National Health Scheme. He said he was not participating and proposed to continue operating on a black market or '*maquis*' basis.*

Malcolm Muggeridge, Diaries, 28 May 1948

When the NHS officially came into being on 5 July 1948, 2,751 of Britain's 3,000 hospitals were nationalized. Henceforth, healthcare in the UK was available freely and 'based on need, rather than ability to pay'.

✒

A TRAINSPOTTER'S DEFENCE

As an engine spotter for more than three years,* I can honestly say I have never yet seen an accident caused by this hobby. The majority of spotters do not, as Steam Jacket says, 'hang about a station for the sole purpose of making a list of numbers' – we learn from experience all about the locomotives themselves.

Many boys are members of the 'Spotters' Club', which binds members not to trespass on railway property, nor hinder railway servants in the execution of their duty, and to stop others from doing so. Members do not usually trespass on railway property, etc., because to do so would jeopardise all privileges. There are competitions, special notepaper, a discount on ABC loco books, pen friends in foreign countries, special club greeting cards and visits arranged to places of interest.

Because a few boys make a nuisance of themselves does not mean that everyone does the same. It may be an unprofitable hobby, but certainly it is not dull.

Yours etc.

SPOTTERS CLUB NO. 8316, Acocks Green

Brian Williams, Letter to the *Birmingham Mail*, 7 June 1948

* With the nationalization of the railways in 1948, the government-run network inherited a plethora of trains and engines that had previously been owned and operated by a range of companies. A somewhat unexpected consequence was that trainspotting, the hobby of collecting the numbers of rare locomotives, enjoyed a boom.

⁓⁂⁓

COLD WAR GETS FROSTY

The situation in Berlin is becoming steadily more critical. Coming to be realized by everyone I think now that a showdown is unavoidable, and a showdown might mean war, though I personally think it would be an entirely different sort of war (all wars are different), very much a continuance in a more acute form of the present state of affairs.

Malcolm Muggeridge, Diaries, 24 June 1948

⁓⁂⁓

A TOWERING TALENT

We had to get up early this morning to catch the 7.15 a.m. train to Blackpool. We arrived at 11.50. It is the first time that we have been here and it was a thrill to see the famous Tower where Reginald Dixon plays the Theatre Organ. We have listened to him on the radio.

We played cricket on the beach in the afternoon. The sea was fairly calm. The weather was cloudy but warm.

Brian Williams, Diaries, 24 July 1948

RACE RELATIONS AND RACIST RELATIONS

Bunny (again, with regard to some case of seduction in the *News of the World*): 'Well, in my opinion any white girl who goes off with a coloured man deserves all she gets.'

I was shocked enough to say, 'I call that a pretty disgraceful opinion.'

'It's not fair on the children,' said Bunny, who had meant nothing of the sort, on the retreat.

'Only because people hold opinions like you.'

Strange that a really quite intelligent woman should hold such views. I doubt really if she holds them at all, but simply repeats, without thinking, the opinions of that frightful husband of hers to whom she was so devoted. Though dead this many a year, he still, alas, lives on.*

J. R. Ackerley, Diaries, 11 November 1948

* *The arrival at Tilbury of the HMS* Windrush *carrying with it 492 passengers (and one or two stowaways) from the Caribbean on 22 June 1948 is widely seen as a pivotal moment in Britain becoming a more multicultural society. The* Windrush *had stopped off in Jamaica to pick up servicemen on leave on a return journey from Hong Kong. The ship was far from full, and adverts were placed in the Kingston newspapers offering passage to Britain for around £28 a throw – the equivalent of over £600 today, and no small sum then. The Labour government had recently passed the British Nationality Act, which gave citizenship to everyone across the Commonwealth, with a right to settle in the 'mother country' itself. Some of the Jamaicans who chose to avail themselves of this chance were ex-servicemen, among them wartime wireless operators hoping to re-join the RAF. Many who settled in the UK were directly recruited by the likes of the NHS and London Transport to fill essential job vacancies, yet they faced a good deal of discrimination.*

❦

FALLACIOUS FUTURES

Finished off George Orwell's *1984*, and continued to think much about this question of the future, whether romanticized into a Golden Age, or presented as something nauseatingly horrible. It seemed to me more clearly than ever that the whole idea was a fallacy, and that this fallacy became evident if you applied Orwell's or Aldous Huxley's technique to the past – imagining, for instance, in the days of the Church's dominance, a society wholly priest-ridden. It didn't happen so. The point is that human character has survived intact through enormous changes, and is likely to survive.

Malcolm Muggeridge, Diaries, 19–20 March 1949

❦

BOOTED BY STANLEY MATTHEWS

This morning I went up town to buy a pair of Stanley Matthews football boots at the Co-op. I bought a good pair, size 6, then waited to see Stan Matthews and Ivor Powell. There were hundreds of people trying to get autographs, so much so that there were police and ambulance men holding back the crowd.

I got Powell's autograph.*

Brian Williams, Diaries, 10 September 1949

* *Known as the 'Wizard of the Dribble', Stanley Matthews was the first professional footballer to be knighted. Ivor Powell played alongside Matthews at Blackpool during the war, and the two men became close friends. In 1949 Powell was captain of Williams' local Birmingham side, Aston Villa.*

⤙⤚

NOT SOLD ON SALESMAN

Went to see *Death of a Salesman*. Hysterical, noisy, American play, extremely well produced and extremely well acted by Paul Muni, but how it evoked the American scene and all the horror of it – that superstitious dread of failure and the love of success, wishful thinking etc.

The more I thought about the play the more clear it seemed to me that it was a wholly sentimental affair – a glorified hard-luck story.*

Malcolm Muggeridge, Diaries, 27 September 1949

* *Partially informed by the experiences of seeing his own father's business fail during the Great Depression,* Death of a Salesman *would, despite Muggeridge's damning assessment, make Arthur Miller's name. He won the Pulitzer Prize in 1949 for the play.*

⤙⤚

ORWELLIAN HOSPITAL WEDDING

Before catching our train we went to see Robert and Janetta at Sussex Place. They were just back from a strange wedding-party: Sonia Brownell had that afternoon married George Orwell in hospital where he lies seriously ill with TB. He is said to have a fifty–fifty chance of recovery, and as he is much in love with her everyone hopes the marriage will give him a new interest in life. After the ceremony, Robert and Janetta, Sonia and David Astor had a bridal lunch at the Savoy, without the bridegroom, of course. The curious halo of emotion which invests weddings still lingered in the room, and the Kees had obviously been much moved by the event.

Frances Partridge, Diaries, 13 October 1949

ↄ഍ↄ

NOTHING NEW IN VIENNA

I saw a good film, *The Third Man*, about Vienna. My God, how long ago Vienna seems – at least a couple of hundred years.

But this movie was, of course, about Vienna 1949, full of international police and the black market – though *that's* nothing new.

Jean Rhys, Letter to Maryvonne Moerman, 24 October 1949

ↄ഍ↄ

THE HUME–SETTY MURDER TRIAL

I have been – in fact, still am, for there will be 2 more days of this week before it finishes – sitting through a murder trial at the Old Bailey. I am there representing the R[oyal] Commission on CP [Capital Punishment]. This is not a thing anybody would do for pleasure, one would have thought, though as a matter of fact any spare accommodation in the Court is packed with what journalists called well-dressed women. The thing I can't get used to is that the whole inside of the Court we're in is like the inside of Harrods – light oak panelling, Edwardian baroque plaster ceilings (extremely clean) and tasteful lighting. It's small, and doesn't hold many people. The acoustics are bad.

The man on trial is [Donald] Hume, 29-year-old, charged with the murder of [Stanley] Setty, a Jewish dealer in second-hand cars. I'm relieved to find that one is far less conscious of the prisoner, and that he – or, at any rate, this particular young man – is so riveted by the to-and-fro of the trial that he seems unconscious of himself. His head turns to and fro, as though he were watching tennis.

I don't know whether you read about the Hume–Setty case? Everything happened early last October. Setty disappeared, and dismembered portions of him were found in the Essex marshes, having been parcelled up and dropped from a plane. Hume – who had been making a living by air-smuggling – admits to having dropped the parcels (to oblige friends who gave him cash down for the job) but swears he had no idea what was in the parcels. The police claim Hume stabbed Setty to death in his (Hume's) Finchley Rd flat, in order to rob him.*

Elizabeth Bowen, Letter to Charles Ritchie, 22 January 1950

* *The jury were unable to reach a verdict on the charge of murder in the case. Hume pleaded guilty to the lesser charge of being an accessory to the fact of murder and was sentenced to twelve years in prison; he served eight. On release, he confessed to the killing in an exclusive he sold to the* Sunday Pictorial *newspaper. Having then moved to Switzerland under a new identity, Hume was arrested and convicted of a second murder in 1959: he had shot and killed a taxi driver while fleeing a botched robbery.*

~

CONSUMERISM ODDLY COMMUNIST

With Kitty to the Ideal Home Exhibition*, crowded with people, somewhat tawdry, I thought, and sad in a way since none of those flowing around would be able to have any of the things displayed. This seems to me singularly typical of the contemporary world, which presents felicity always in terms of graphs and statistics and displays rather than of actual well-being. The whole thing reminded me oddly of Russia.

Malcolm Muggeridge, Diaries, 22 March 1950

* *Devised by the* Daily Mail *and first staged at London's Olympia Convention Centre in 1908, the Ideal Home Exhibition, a showcase for the latest in consumer housing and homewares, recorded its highest number of visitors in 1957: 1.5 million.*

BIG MATCH BROADCAST

Had about ten minutes of the Cup Final on Mrs Davies' television set just to see how it was put over. Commentary very languid, I thought, compared with ordinary BBC transmissions.

Malcolm Muggeridge, Diaries, 29 April 1950

⟡

WAR IN KOREA

The Communists have started a war in Korea in direct contravention of the United Nations. It looks like Czechoslovakia all over again. I suppose Mr Truman will soon be flying to Moscow with an umbrella. I think it is serious and may be the beginning of the crack-up. If the human race is that silly, the sooner it destroys itself the better.*

Noël Coward, Diaries, 26 June 1950

* On 25 June 1950 some 75,000 soldiers from the Soviet-backed communist Democratic People's Republic of Korea crossed the 38th parallel into the southern Republic of Korea. In the subsequent war, American troops were deployed to help expel the invaders, in a conflict that the US viewed as a fight against the forces of international communism.

⟡

BLACK TIE FOR BERNARD SHAW

Old Man G. B. Shaw is now dead, and he was ninety-four – he'd had a very good innings. Already they are saying he'll be buried in Westminster Abbey. I bet he would *hate* that. The last writer to have an Abbey burial was Kipling, who was buried in the Poets' Corner in 1936. Shaw passed away peacefully at one minute to five this morning, November 2nd. I will wear me [*sic*] black tie for a week.

Fred Bason, Diaries, 2 November 1950

WEATHERING THE ENGLISH CLIMATE AND DIET

The weather can actually make interesting news. Last week I had my first snow. It came down in little white fluffs; you felt that a gigantic hand had punched a gigantic cotton wool sack open, letting down flurries of cotton shreds. The camera doesn't lie in this respect. Snow is just as you see it in films and in photographs. It snowed for about two hours. The streets were not covered, but the tops of the naked branches of the trees were white with it – a white that showed more beautiful because the limbs of the trees were in comparison stark black. The earth was carpeted ... The closet thing I have seen to it in Trinidad is the stuff that gathers in a refrigerator – not when it gets hard, though.

The meals here are quite different from home. Usually, you start with soup. Then you have the main course. A bit of meat or fish, potatoes (I have eaten potatoes every day of my stay in England, twice a day at Oxford) and either cabbage or cauliflower. Then comes a sweet. Apple and custard or some such stuff. Finally, coffee. You would be surprised how you get accustomed to the coffee habit, after lunch and after dinner. No rice, and I don't miss it. No roti, and I don't miss it. You have bread with your soup, or with the main course. My table manners, which just didn't exist when I was in Trinidad, have improved tremendously. Another thing. The family always has dinner together. In Trinidad this would be impossible. I know.

I met a bunch of West Indians the other day. Harrison gave me Chang's address. I rang him up, and he invited me over. Selvon* was there, with his wife, and Gloria Escoffery. Gloria is a girl who, Harrison tells me, will be somebody one day. From the look of her, I doubt it. She passed around a manuscript of a short story she had written about the race problem. She didn't want me to see it. Then she began talking some rubbish about writing being an exploration ...

I said, 'My dear Gloria, why not write a little pamphlet on the colour question, and settle the whole affair.'

V. S. Naipaul, Letter to his family, 11 December 1950

* *This is the author Samuel Selvon, whose book* The Lonely Londoners, *published in 1956, was the first novel to chronicle the experiences of the growing West Indian community in the capital.*

DARNED AND POLISHED

Tremendously busy day – I don't think I ever stopped working! Polished dining-room, washed up, darned all garments that needing darning in the house, wrote and asked Petula Clark for her autograph, knitted and generally had a busy and happy day.

Hazel K. Macaulife, *Leisure Round Bognor in the '50s*, 7 March 1951

THE FESTIVAL OF BRITAIN

The great Festival of Britain* has opened! The King, in a broadcast to the world from the steps of St Paul's Cathedral this morning, officially declared the festival open. The King with the Queen, Princess Elizabeth, The Duke of Edinburgh and Princess Margaret had driven through beflagged, flower-bedecked streets lined with cheering crowds, to attend an inter-denominational service. There was a colourful procession, announced by heralds, into the Cathedral …

To celebrate the festival, special postage stamps have been issued – a 2½d red stamp and a 4d blue with the Festival emblem. In addition, four other stamps have changed their colours but have kept the same design. The ½d issue is now orange, the 1d stamp blue, the 1½d green and the 2d brown.

I came home from school through town and bought the 2½d and 4d stamps together with a packet of special envelopes. I could not get a first-day cover in town because the Post Office refused to date-stamp my envelope. However, the Acocks Green PO were willing to stamp it for me – on condition that I registered it. This I did and I am expecting it back tomorrow morning …

This evening the City Transport Illuminated Bus went on its first outing. It visited Acocks Green at 9.22 p.m. so we went down the village to see it. There were thousands of people lining its route … The words 'Festival of Britain' flashed on and off but no one really had much chance to see the 'bus properly – it went too fast.

Brian Williams, Diaries, 3 May 1951

* *Largely the brainchild of Gerald Barry, the editor of the* News Chronicle, *the Festival of Britain was intended as an international exhibition of trade and industry along the lines of the Great Exhibition of 1851. However, financial constraints resulted in a more modest festival being staged instead. It was touted as a 'Tonic to the Nation' suffering post-war austerity measures, a celebration of the country's history as well as a showcase of the latest in art, design, technology and science. Its main locus was London's South Bank, where the Festival Hall was erected. As a kind of living, shining example of post-war British architecture, the new Lansbury Estate in Poplar, East London, was also erected.*

I get to Waterloo and meet Vita. We then enter the South Bank Exhibition. We are entranced from the first moment … It is the most intelligent exhibition I have ever visited. I have never seen people so cheered up or so amused, in spite of a fine drizzle of rain and a Scotch mist.

Harold Nicolson, Diaries, 4 May 1951

CAMBRIDGE SPIES VANISH

The watchers failed to pick up Maclean since his departure for the country on Friday and we now learn from the Foreign Office that he was given a day's leave on Saturday. He has not apparently been seen since ...

(Name Redacted) telephoned me at about 11 a.m. asking whether I had heard about Guy Burgess.* I said that I knew he had been sent home by the Foreign Office on account of three motoring offences for speeding, which had caused the embassy embarrassment.

(Name Redacted) then said that he was not referring to that but to Guy Burgess' mysterious disappearance. He had not been seen since Friday ...

Later, in the evening, I spoke to Anthony Blunt, who had been away all day until about 6 p.m. I asked him what he knew about Guy Burgess' disappearance.

Guy Liddell, Diaries, 29 May 1951

Guy Burgess and Donald Maclean were part of a Soviet spy ring, led by Harold 'Kim' Philby, who had all met at Cambridge University during the 1930s. Serving as diplomats and British agents, Burgess and Maclean were recalled from the British Embassy in Washington after confidential documents had gone missing. Tipped off by Philby that they were under suspicion, they disappeared, only reappearing in Soviet Moscow five years later. Philby himself would defect to Russia in 1963. Another of the spies, Anthony Blunt, served for many years as the keeper of the Queen's art collection. Knighted in 1956, his treasonous duplicity was not made public until 1979.

BLUNT INSTRUMENT BEYOND REPROACH

I told Lascelles that I had known Anthony Blunt for about ten years ... I was convinced that he had never been a communist in the full political sense, even during his days at Cambridge.

Tommy said that he was very glad to hear this, since it was quite possible that the story might get round to the Royal Family; he would then be able to say that he had already heard it and looked into it and was satisfied that there was nothing in in it.

He told me that Blunt had on one occasion intimated to the Queen that he was an atheist – Tommy thinks he may well have said an agnostic – and that the Queen had been a little shaken by his remarks.

He was certain that if he now went up and told her that Anthony was a communist, her immediate reaction would be, 'I always told you so.'

Guy Liddell, Diaries, 13 July 1951

⌒ℳ⌒

UNPICKING POWELL AND PRESSBURGER

Spent most of the morning unpicking an old white jumper … Muz and I went to the Theatre Royal Cinema to see *The Tales of Hoffmann*. The film was marvellously directed, and the dancing was really lovely; I didn't care for the singing, though. Opera is not my cup of tea!

Hazel K. Macaulife, *Leisure Round Bognor in the '50s*, 8 August 1951

⌒ℳ⌒

BLUE RIBBONS

Election day. I have been disgustingly laconic about it – at least, I've made a Tory rosette and worn it.

Hazel K. Macaulife, *Leisure Round Bognor in the '50s*, 25 October 1951

⌒ℳ⌒

BRITTEN TAKES SAIL

I managed to get a ticket to the dress rehearsal of *Billy Budd* … Benjamin Britten conducted. The curtain went up on a cloaked figure, the narrator – Peter Pears.

Britten and Forster build in the first two acts a massive picture of life in the navy in the early nineteenth century, with its barbarism … The music is dense with the heaving and howling of the sea, sound of whistles and foghorns and toiling bells, the feel of the mist, the constant changes of atmosphere.

Stephen Spender, Journals, 30 November 1951

A VISION OF BIRMINGHAM

On Wednesday, Birmingham people were able to get an idea of what our city will be like in 1972, because re-development plans were published. There will probably be a twenty-storey skyscraper at the top of the Bull Ring (in fact, the general trend will be upwards rather than outwards), multi-storey car parks, fly-over crossings, a great new Civic Centre round the Hall of Memory, a new Inner Ring Road, etc., etc. It seems a most ambitious and exciting plan.

Brian Williams, Diaries, 4 January 1952

KING LYING IN STATE

King George VI's Lying in State. 7.30–8.30 a.m. Very cold. The hall very dim, footsteps muffled on the thick carpet. The still figures guarding the catafalque – the nose and chin of the very young officer of the Household Cavalry so pink and smooth – eyes hidden. The faces of the Yeoman of the Guard – carved out of wood, lined and pale, one with a small moustache. The glitter of the diamonds in the crown and the white flowers on the coffin.

Barbara Pym, A Very Private Eye, 1 February 1952

NEW QUEEN RETURNS

I applied my ear to the wireless to make sure that the new Queen is safe back from South Africa, which she is.

Lavinia Mynors, Diaries, 7 February 1952

⤳

THE JAZZ SCENE

This is all very proper and formal, there is a kind of controlled enthusiasm. Unselfconscious. Pepsicola [*sic*] and cups of tea and a grey-haired woman collecting the empty cups. It is as respectable as a church youth club.

Barbara Pym, *A Very Private Eye*, 9 June 1952

⤳

JOB SEEKERS FROM IRELAND

In the White Hart in Acton Town, Mike Ned and I met Peteen Lowery and we got a job from him without any bother. Peteen is very strong now – plenty of lorries, lots of men working for him. He's sending us up to Berkshire and we'll be able to live in a camp there. But he didn't let us go without well wetting our lips and we had a great crack for a time there with him. He is from Cornamona (the same as Mike Ned) and another man from the same area was with him. This was Jimmy Patch Nelly. He had been in England for more than twenty-eight years but to see him standing there at the counter with his old dudeen [a traditional clay pipe] in his mouth and talking away in Irish, you'd never know that he had been away from home at all. But that's always the way, of course; those who have been longest from home are those who have most regard for their native background and traditions.

It's wonderful how Lowery got on since he came here. He was only a navvy like the rest of us until he started up on his own and now he has a contracting business almost as big as Murphy over there in Finsbury Park. We said good-bye to him at last and what do you think – didn't he give us a quid each into our hands before we left. A generous man …

We got shelter for the night in Rowton House in Camden Town. My God, you never saw such a place. It was like a large barracks or prison, the number of small, bare cells that were in it. There was nothing wrong with the beds, however, and I had a great sleep even though I felt a bit nervous about some of the 'residents' that I saw as I was dozing off. A worse-looking crowd you wouldn't find anywhere. Two and threepence we paid for the 'kip' …

Donall MacAmhlaigh, An Irish Navvy, 1 December 1952

SEASONAL ADVERTISING AT THE CINEMA

The *Moveitone News* this week had a Christmas feature. A large number of flustered turkeys were driven towards the camera, and the commentator remarked that the Christmas rush was on, or words to that effect. Next, they were seen crowded about their feeding troughs, making their gobbling turkey fuss, and the commentator observed, with dry humour (again, I do not remember his exact words), that it was no use their holding a protest meeting, for they were for it in the morning. Similar facetious jokes followed them wherever they went, hurrying and tramping about in their silly way; for to make them look as silly as possible was no doubt part of the joke and easy to achieve: turkeys, like hens, like all animals, are beautiful in themselves, and have even a dignity when they are leading their own lives, but fowls, in particular, look foolish when they are being frightened.

These jolly, lip-licking sallies, delivered in the rich, cultivated, self-confident voice of one who has no sort of doubt of his own superiority to the animal kingdom, raised no laugh from the considerable audience, I was pleased to note …

J. R. Ackerley, Diaries, 22 December 1952

STILL 'SMALL NATIONS'

We had a long wait in Bristol and I went around at my leisure looking at the place. A lot of bomb damage occurred here in the war but they're building it up again ... Some of the back streets are very squalid but, then, that's hardly any cause for wondering seeing that Bristol is a very old city.

In the afternoon, I took a train from Temple Meads station to Fishguard. My father was on this very same station in 1915 on his way to France with thousands of others that had enlisted in the 'Munsters' to fight for the freedom of 'small nations'. He came home five years later with more sense and fought for the freedom of another small nation – Ireland. Two old women were with me most of the way into Fishguard and although I got fed up with their company, I couldn't ignore their pleasant matronly ways. At any rate, they seemed nearer to a couple of countrywomen in Ireland than they did to a couple of English countrywomen – we were, of course, only a short distance out of Wales.

Donall MacAmhlaigh, *An Irish Navvy*, 22 December 1952

EAST COAST FLOODS

Cold, damp and gales. The Northern Ireland Car Ferry Steamer sank in rough seas with loss of 133 lives. Mike's temperature is OK today and he got up after dinner. He is not eating a lot. The doctor has not been again. Purged mice in the aviary and killed six this evening.

H. A. Berry, Diaries, 31 January 1953

Shocking wet day. The gaps in the sea walls on the coast have not yet been closed and there is danger of further flooding next week.

H. A. Berry, Diaries, 10 February 1953

Cold, wet snow. Gales and snow all over the country. Flood warnings on the coast. The snow in the north is the worst for many years. 9-foot drifts. 40 main roads are blocked, according to the wireless ... We look with dismay at our diminishing coal supplies.

H. A. Berry, Diaries, 11 February 1953

CORONATION OF ELIZABETH II

It had been raining good and proper. I suppose it was 5.15 or 5.30 when Caroline and I set off. We went to Sloane Square on spec, and as all seemed quiet we took a fairly crowded underground which to my great relief stopped goodly at St James. By craning over people reading *The Times*, we gathered the news from the mountains, which was spreading rapidly round the train.

I suppose we were there by 6.15, which we needn't have been, but there was not a dull moment, what with the Air Force Cadets being drawn up and the Peers arriving, two of them in family coaches, and quite soon it seemed the crescendo of the procession. Meriel and I were hit for six by the Lord Mayor's coach, which we had expected to contain the Queen of Tonga, due next and known to be large. The Queen was glorious, waving her powerful arm; we yelled for her, and goodness how we yelled for Winston. The foreign representatives defeated us, as our flag homework was deficient, so we yelled impartially for them all. We could see well into the carriages and were awestruck by the appearance of the Duchess of Kent. As for the Queen of England we saw her well, and cheered and cried and cheered some more. We settled down for the Service, and for some food, too ... The commentator was admirable and the trumpets my undoing. The guns were more a concussion than a noise, and exploded in my vitals. We sang the hymns loudly. It rained a good deal, and they brought us tea and coffee. I threatened Meriel with these drinks unless she would keep her mackintosh on ...

Lavinia Mynors, Diaries, 2 June 1953

I don't think I shall ever forget today. London had never seen anything like this, perhaps never will again. One woke up with a feeling of excitement, expectancy – this was *the* day.

I turned on the radio just before 9.00 a.m. The announcer said, 'This is the BBC. Today is the Coronation Day of Her Majesty Queen Elizabeth. God save the Queen.' And then there was something in the News which added to the growing tension – Everest had been conquered by a New Zealander. What a magnificent Coronation gift to the Queen! …

Brian Williams, Diaries, 2 June 1953

ARRESTED FOR IMPORTUNING

It appears in the papers that Sir John Gielgud has been arrested on a charge of homosexual importuning. He described himself on the charge sheet as 'a clerk of Cowley Street with an income of £1,000 a year'. Why tell these lies? Of course, this is clearly a case of persecution. Poor fellow.

Kenneth Williams, Diaries, 23 October 1953

UNDER MILK WOOD AIRS

Listened in the evening to the radio play by Dylan Thomas about a day in the life of a small Welsh town (Cf. January 1, 1954). Some of it quite good, and even funny (She Couldn't Say No to a Midget), with flashes of true poetry here and there along with much affection and sentimentality.

Malcolm Muggeridge, Diaries, 25 January 1954

OFF THE RATION

Meat rationing finished today, bringing a complete end to rationing after 14 years, and 9 years since the War ended!

Brian Williams, Diaries, 5 July 1954

⌒⋔⌒

CHURCHILL'S SHAMEFUL SLOGAN

More discussion about West Indian immigrants. A Bill is being drafted – but it's not an easy problem. P.M. thinks 'Keep England White' a good slogan!

Harold Macmillan, Diaries, 20 January 1955

⌒⋔⌒

THE RADIO SOAPS

What a sensation tonight! Grace Archer got bumped off. I don't usually listen to *The Archers* but yesterday there was a fire in the stables. Grace went in to rescue the horses, and was struck by a falling beam. Then there was a scene where Grace and Phil were going to hospital in the ambulance, and listeners heard her say, 'Phil, I love you, Phil.' The programme ended with Phil breaking the news that Grace had died in his arms.

I felt astonishingly depressed. I seemed to see Freda and me instead of Grace and Phil. I was glad I was spending the evening with her.

The Archers may be very true to life. But this latest idea is stupid. No one wants the hero to kick the bucket.*

Brian Williams, Diaries, 22 September 1955

---

* The Archers, *BBC radio's soap opera about life in the fictional rural community of Ambridge, has been running since 1950. The episode Williams describes here aired*

somewhat controversially on the same night that ITV began broadcasting. The suspicion remains that it was deliberately scheduled to clash with the BBC's new commercial rival.

~

JET BOMBERS BETTER THAN MICHELANGELO

I talked at a branch of London University called Queen Mary College in the East End. The discussion that followed afterwards was mainly around one thing: which is more beautiful – a statue of Michelangelo or an aeroplane? Hence, of course – is our civilization more, or less, creative than past civilizations?

I was amazed how many of them seemed to think a jet-bomber quite as beautiful as a cathedral. They were obviously unimpressed by arguments that machinery does not last, is as subject to changes of fashion as women's hats. The argument that modern industrialism produces a hideous environment did not interest them either. Someone advanced the view that what has been done in the past has been done and we should not judge our own achievement or even present state of existence by the past at all.

Stephen Spender, Journals, 12 October 1955

~

THE SUEZ CRISIS

Ralph listens all day to the news, looking sunk in gloom. Eden must be raving mad. We have started bombing 'Military Objectives' from the air. In fact, we are at war again, and no one is on our side. America [and] even our colonies repudiate us. I feel extremely fatalistic about the whole thing – only a sort of contempt for anyone who holds the belief that you can solve problems by killing people. Ralph bought all the papers he could get. Today's had pictures of smug-looking airmen tucking into bacon and eggs after bombing some Egyptians. But nearly all the papers come out against Eden, and corny slogans like 'England and France stand alone' or 'Protecting our life-line' are few and simply sickening.

Burgo arrived in the evening, talking and thinking hard about the crisis, or war, or what Eden prefers to call 'Armed Conflict'. He was in Parliament Square last night, where a huge crowd, mostly young, were shouting 'Eden must Go!' and being charged by mounted police with batons. Military veterans crawl out of holes and talk about 'pockets of resistance' and 'mopping up'.*

Frances Partridge, Diaries, 1 November 1956

* *The Suez Canal, the international shipping route that connects the Mediterranean and the Red Sea was developed by Frenchman Ferdinand de Lesseps and opened in 1869. It was owned and operated by the Suez Canal Company, an Anglo-French concern, until 1956, when Egyptian president Gamal Abdel Nasser nationalized it with the intention of using the profits to fund the creation of a new dam at Aswan. It was, however, also used as an assertion of Egypt's post-colonial autonomy. Regarding this as a threat to Britain's economic interests and prestige, Prime Minister Anthony Eden responded by co-ordinating a secret plan to reclaim the canal with the aid of France and Israel.*

∽

REVOLTING STUDENTS

There has been an uprising in Hungary against the Communist regime, and the students here are in a state of great excitement. Some of the more fiery and romantic ones have even gone out to join in the fighting, and some of our friends have actually been put in prison.

Those who have returned sit in the cafe wearing fur hats and looking smug and heroic, which more or less guarantees them free coffees from admiring waitresses.*

Joan Wyndham, *Anything Once*, 11 November 1956

* *In October 1956, Imre Nagy, a moderate politician and a Westernizer, became prime minister of Hungary. Initially, he was able to reach an agreement with Soviet leader Nikita Khrushchev. But on 3 November, Nagy announced that Hungary would leave*

the Warsaw Pact, the collective defence treaty of the Soviet Union's satellite states. The following day, one thousand Russian tanks rolled into Budapest. Within a few days, at least four thousand Hungarians were dead and János Kádár, a Soviet stooge, had been installed as prime minister.

⌇

SKIFFLE GROUP

Our last night. We had a skiffle group* playing [in] the kitchen, and God knows how anyone got served. We flipped pancakes to 'Yellow Dog Bites', fried chips to 'Careless Love', stirred goulash to 'St James's Infirmary'. We jived to the hatch and back again to the stove, beating out the rhythm as we went on saucepan lids, and by the end of the evening there wasn't a drop of cooking sherry left in the house.

Joan Wyndham, *Anything Once*, 10 January 1957

* *Skiffle, a form of shuffling blues, takes its name from the 'rent parties' that arose in Depression-era America that often involved impromptu musical performances held to rustle up money for the landlords. Thanks to the likes of Lonnie Donegan, who embraced the form's three-chord style in the 1950s, skiffle was a catalyst for a British 'DIY' pop revolution. George Harrison, Hank Marvin and Jimmy Page all cut their musical teeth in skiffle bands.*

⌇

MORE IRISH OUTSIDE IRELAND

We got a bit of breakfast near the station and we went off to Mass in Camden Town afterwards. I met so many of my old comrades coming out of the church that I didn't feel in any way downhearted: Michealeen Connolly, Colin Bartley Colmeen, Peter John and Marcus Joe Barbara. It's amazing how there are as many Irishmen around Camden Town as ever there were.

I hung around until the pubs opened. It's not for the sake of the drink

I went in but in the hope of hearing about some job that might be going. There's nothing much doing here, however, if what the lads say is true ... We had great music at the Bedford – fiddles, concertinas and tin whistles – and there was hardly a jig or a reel they didn't play. Dickie, the bucko with me, was astonished, for he never dreamed that anything like this happened outside of Ireland; but he's wrong. This town is, in many ways, more Irish than a lot of the towns at home. More Irish is spoken here and much more Irish music played here.

We had a meal at Pano's place when we left the pub and then we moved down to Marble Arch to listen to [the] speakers there ...

There was a great gas in the Park as usual – some speakers being quite intelligent but the bulk of them quite gone in the head. There was a good discussion at the Catholic stand – intelligent questions and intelligent answers. Everyone has a right to talk in this place – but what do you think, the character with me wanted to go for some of the speakers for attacking the clergy. It's easy to see that hasn't been long away from home ...

Tomorrow, we have to start looking for a job ... There's plenty of building going on in the West End but ... a great deal has been postponed because of the fuel shortage after Suez.

Donall MacAmhlaigh, An Irish Navvy, 3 March 1957

ENDURING ANGER

With Val to see play *Look Back in Anger* by John Osborne ... Play quite execrable – woman ironing, man yelling and snivelling, highbrow smut, 'daring' remarks (reading from Sunday Paper, Bishop of ... asks all to rally round and make hydrogen bomb). Endured play up to point where hero and heroine pretended to be squirrels.*

Malcolm Muggeridge, Diaries, 14 March 1957

* *Legend maintains that on the opening night for* Look Back in Anger *at the Royal Court on 8 May 1956, audience members gasped at the sight of an ironing board on stage. The work was championed by Kenneth Tynan, who claimed in his review for the* Observer *that the play's lead character, the traditional jazz-loving anti-hero Jimmy Porter, was 'the completest young pup in our literature since Hamlet, Prince of Denmark'. The phrase 'Angry Young Men' was subsequently used to describe not just the playwright Osborne, but the whole group of largely lower middle-class, anti-establishment writers who came to prominence in the late 1950s, including novelists John Wain, John Braine and Alan Sillitoe.*

ST PATRICK'S DAY

I put a bit of shamrock in the laps of my coat and went down to Mass in Camden Town at nine o'clock. The church was full and everyone had their bit of shamrock – even some of the Greeks and Jamaicans, a lot of who live around these parts.

You could hardly walk in the street outside the church after Mass, there were so many Irish meeting there and having a bit of sport.

As soon as I got out on the street, I met the MacAndrews and Jim Cannon and great was the welcome we had for one another. We went down to Pano's place for a bite to eat and chewed over the time we were all together working down in Diss in Norfolk. We were dying for the pubs to open and as soon as they were, we were into the Black Cap like a flash. We laid into the 'stout and mild' with a will and, before long, we all felt nicely enough …

I got the bus down to Camden Town. I pushed my way into the Laurel Tree, where most of the Connemara people go and, I need hardly say, it was chockfull of them this night. Most of them were pretty young and spending money as if they had just picked it off the pavement. I saw one chap carrying a trayful of glasses of whiskey from the counter and he had hardly taken two steps before the whole lot of it was spilt on the floor …

I went up to a dance in the Galway Social Club in Greenland Street where I met Marcus Joe Barbara and Martin Cook as soon as I entered the place. They had some nice young dancers over specially from Ireland and the band was superb.

I felt a bit melancholy in the dance-hall after a while and I went out. I don't rightly know what was wrong with me but I couldn't feel any more desire for sport and companionship at all. Whatever came over me, but I felt that I was outside the sport and pleasure somehow and all of a sudden the whole day palled on me. I walked to King's Cross and got a bus home.

Donall MacAmhlaigh, *An Irish Navvy*, 17 March 1957

◦※◦

CURRENT AFFAIRS ON TV

At Lime Grove old familiar scene of *Panorama* programme – camera moving, Richard Dimbleby pronouncing, all the fatuity of an age in the compass of a single scene.*

Malcolm Muggeridge, Diaries, 1 April 1957

* BBC Television's flagship investigative current affairs programme was first broadcast in 1953.

◦※◦

NEVER HAD IT SO GOOD

I went to Bedford on Saturday – a large crowd in the football ground. The speech was well reported in the Sunday press, and I think helped to steady things a bit. The bus strike began – and now looks like ending. There has been a good deal of ugly feeling, sabotage and violence. The Covent Garden porters are on strike – but the effect seems very small.*

Harold Macmillan, Diaries, 26 July 1957

* Macmillan's assertion in this speech that 'most of our people have never had it so good' was widely reported. Though his remarks were directed to a mostly Conservative-voting audience, in retrospect they seem to have marked the moment when consumer affluence supplanted post-war austerity in the collective national consciousness.

CARRY ON REHEARSALS

Out to Pinewood to go practise drilling with a CSM [Company Sergeant Major] of the Queen's for the film *Carry on Sergeant*.*

Kenneth Williams, Diaries, 2 April 1958

* *This first outing for what became the hugely successful* Carry On *series of films, produced by Peter Rogers and directed by Gerald Thomas, was, along with the Anthony Newley vehicle* Idle on Parade, *a cinematic response to the winding down of national conscription. Since 1947, those aged eighteen or over had been obliged to serve in the armed forces for eighteen months. This policy ended in 1960, and the last conscripts were mustered out in 1963.*

A BRAVE NEW WORLD

It's the age of space travel, bases on the Moon. No doubt who owns the Moon will be the next excuse for another war and people will rocket into the universe, into nothingness, and they will meet God in the end. I am sure each man thinks he will be here to see the end of the world. After all, we are nearly in the Brave New World of Huxley. Smelly films are here – space travel very nearly here. Test Tube Babies, Deep Freeze People, radioactive horrors. Sometimes it frightens me but sometimes I accept it all – but all the beauty, the treasures produced by great men – destroyed!

Oh, the bliss, the glory of nail-varnish! Gold and silver. Liquid lushness smelling of pear drops.

Kate Paul, Journal, 6 January 1959

HONEY NOT TO TASTE

I went to *A Taste of Honey*, a squalid little piece about squalid and unattractive people. It was written by an angry young lady of nineteen and is a great success. Personally, I found it fairly dull.*

Noël Coward, Diaries, 5 May 1959

*A Taste of Honey *was written by Shelagh Delaney from Salford and who Kenneth Tynan, in his review of the play for the* Observer, *maintained was '19 years old: and a portent'.*

TV A FUSSY SQUARE

Visiting Robert's flat we admired his new carpet, chair, and moving Irish gramophone records. Then came to the television set, but ah! there we were unable to follow him. He showed us *Tonight*, said to be one of the best programmes. It certainly riveted one's attention in a horrid, compulsive sort of way, yet I was bored and rather disgusted, and longed to be able to unhook my gaze from this little fussy square of confusion and noise on the other side of the room.

Frances Partridge, Diaries, 13 July 1959

ᴄᴍᴄ

OPENING SALLIES IN THE SPACE RACE

Yesterday went again to Farnborough to see the air show with Claire. The Avro Vulcan is very lovely to see. Watched the moon last night at ca. 2200 and noted nothing extraordinary, although at that time *Lunik II* was crashing into it at about 10,000 fps [feet per second]. The Russians claim that they have 'pennants' bearing their insignia which will outlive this collision.*

Edmund Héafod (Osias Bain), Diaries, 14 September 1959

* *The Vulcan was the world's first delta-winged bomber and developed with the capacity of carrying nuclear weapons. Lunik II was the second rocket launched towards the moon by Russia.*

CHAPTER SEVEN

I CAN'T REMEMBER,
I WAS THERE: 1960-1969

Few single decades have become quite so closely associated with a particular concept in our culture as the 1960s. And that particular concept is largely the semi-mythical idea of the casting-off of everything fuddy-duddy: the old grey, fog-bound way of doing things pre-Clean Air Act of 1956, the black-and-white world of the *Picture Post*, of class deference, respect for authority, and the establishment. In its wake came a new 'youthquake' of liberality, an openness to sex, satire, soft (and, later on, psychedelic) drugs, and the hip – or indeed, the 'hippie' – and all that was fresh, radical and progressive in art, film, pop music, advertising and boutique-vended miniskirts and narrow trousers.

Of course, the lived reality, as we shall see, was as much frozen meals in foil from Woolworths and Mosley's blackshirts (back again) marching through the East End, as PVC macs, peace, love and permissiveness.

At the time, the imminent arrival of the 1960s *was* heralded as something rather unparalleled. In September 1959, *Queen* magazine proclaimed the approaching decade as 'the age of Boom'. Their sly editorial stated:

> *Have you woken up? Do you know you are living in a new world?*
> *You don't use words like ersatz or economy label … You are richer*

*than before. You are spending more than you have ever done. Our
hope is that you enjoy it. We don't want you to miss it. Don't wait
till years after to realise you have lived in a remarkable age.*

Bookended by the *Lady Chatterley* ban and the Moon landing, and seeing the
introduction of the birth control pill and the automatic teller machine, life in the
1960s would certainly live up to expectations.

⁓

VIEWING INJUSTICE

Watched TV, including *Panorama* on Apartheid in South Africa. Note racialism
in this wicked world.*

Hugh Selbourne, *A Doctor's Life*, 18 January 1960

* *The system of racial segregation in South Africa known as apartheid was introduced in
1948 by the ruling National Party. The party had been founded shortly before World War I
to advance the interests of Afrikaners of German, Dutch and French Huguenot descent. Its
white-supremacist policies were not lifted until the 1990s.*

⁓

RAILWAYS EQUAL TO RUINED CASTLES

How right you were in raising the matter of Euston Great Arch when you did.*
The bloody British Transport Commission has now come into the open. I am
doing a little piece in the *Telegraph* on Monday week. But that immediately
gives a political slant, because it appears in that paper, to something that is far
more important than politics. I think that there should be a survey made at the
instigation of Parliament of all railway architecture and preservation orders put on
those stations, viaducts, bridges and tunnel entrances which are worth preserving.
In architectural and historic significance they are obviously equal to ruined castles.

John Betjeman, Letter to Woodrow Wyatt, 28 January 1960

* *The Euston Arch, designed by Philip Hardwick, was erected in 1837 as the portico to the London and Birmingham Railway's new Euston Station, one of the first metropolitan train terminals in Europe. In the late 1950s, however, the British Transport Commission embarked on a government plan to modernize the station and the arch was scheduled for demolition. A popular campaign was mounted to save it, spearheaded by the future poet laureate John Betjeman and the architectural historian Nikolaus Pevsner, but to no avail. The arch was demolished in 1962, the bulk of its stonework later found to have been dumped into the River Lea.*

THE KING MAKES A FLEETING VISIT

Elvis Presley has gone back to America after two years in Germany in the army. He changed aeroplanes in Scotland!*

Gyles Brandreth, *Something Sensational to Read in the Train*, 5 March 1960

* *This was to be Elvis Presley's only visit to Britain.*

A GOOD-LOOKING PAIR OF POETS

We had dinner with T. S. Eliot and his wife Valerie. We arrived a little late and found the other guests were already there. They were the poet Ted Hughes and his wife Sylvia Plath, who is also a poet and short-story writer. They were a good-looking pair, Ted Hughes having a craggy Yorkshire handsomeness combined with a certain elongated refinement, very sensitive drooping hands in contrast to his ruggedness, rather soft-toned voice and not saying much.

His wife, who talked more, was a very pretty, intelligent girl from Boston.

Stephen Spender, Journals, 5 April 1960

PINTER'S WAVELENGTH

The Caretaker at the Arts by Pinter, which I went to with fear and dread … I loathed *Dumb Waiter* and *The Room*, but after seeing this I'd like to see them again because I think I'm on to Pinter's wavelength. He is at least a genuine original. I don't think he could write in any other way if he tried. *The Caretaker*, on the face of it, is everything I hate most in the theatre – squalor, repetition, lack of action etc. – but somehow it seizes hold of you. It was magnificently acted by Peter Woodthorpe and Alan Bates and effectively by Donald Pleasence. *Nothing* happens except that somehow it does. The writing is at moments brilliant and quite unlike anyone else's.

Noël Coward, Diaries, 2 May 1960

~

GAY LETTERS URGED

The Homosexual Law Reform Society. Tonight at a Public Meeting held in Caxton Hall chaired by Kenneth Walker, FRCS, with speakers the Rt. Rev., the Lord Bishop of Exeter, Mrs Anne Allen, JP, W. Lindesay Neustatter, MD, BSc, MRCP, and Kingsley Martin.

An overflowing meeting in a large hall with a very sympathetic response to the wishes expressed re. abolition of treatment of homosexuals as criminals … it was indicated that 4% of the population had predominantly homosexual tendencies … audience members were urged to write to their MPs.*

Edmund Héafod (Osias Bain), *Gimani*, 12 May 1960

---

* *In 1954 a government departmental committee was convened to consider laws against male homosexuality dating back to the Buggery Act of 1533, as well as the Criminal Law Amendment Act 1855, which had made all homosexual acts illegal, even if carried out by consenting adults in private. The committee argued for decriminalization, but its recommendations would not be taken up until the Sexual Offences Act in 1967.*

WISHFUL THINKING ABOUT NUCLEAR WAR

Yesterday to the White City stadium to watch the AAA [Amateur Athletics Association] finals. The track events are epics. Rome must surely recapture historic moments toward the end of the summer.

Linus Pauling tonight on disarmament at the St Pancras Town Hall. He has one effective point and this is that nuclear warfare would be of danger to the human species. Beyond that he has hope. The wish to still maintain independent nations in the framework of a policing United Nations. That is sad wishfulness.

Edmund Héafod (Osias Bain), *Gimani*, 17 July 1960

~

BLANKING OUT OVER *LADY CHATTERLEY*

Another of those blank days when I suddenly decide not to go into college. I need this day for reading, for being on my own. This is my stolen day. C. and I are friendly, in a bored sort of way, and make a constant joke of our spinsterhood.

The D. H. Lawrence case is over and he has won. A few people have at last decided his book is not obscene.*

Kate Paul, Journal, 3 November 1960

In 1960, Penguin – whose founder Allen Lane had started the company on the principle of producing books 'that would sell at the price of 10 cigarettes' – released a cheap, unexpurgated paperback edition of D. H. Lawrence's Lady Chatterley's Lover. *The easy availability of a book concerning an adulterous affair between a working-class gamekeeper and the aristocratic wife of a crippled First World War veteran was deemed a threat to public morality, and Penguin was prosecuted under the Obscene Publications Act 1959. At the trial, chief prosecutor Mervyn Griffiths-Jones asked jurors: 'Is it a book you would wish even your wife or servants to read?'*

~

BAN THE BOMB IN BIRMINGHAM

This morning I went on a Nuclear Warfare Disarmament* protest march through the city. It was organised by a group at the University. The world would disarm sensibly if there was some degree of trust. There were barely fifty people on the march. I handed out leaflets to Teddy boys and young mothers. I felt I was participating in a funeral.

Kate Paul, Journal, 5 November 1960

* *The Campaign for Nuclear Disarmament, established in 1957, campaigned for Britain to unilaterally give up its nuclear weapons and enjoyed enormous public support in the late 1950s and early 1960s.*

SHORT SKIRTS AND BEATNIKS

The weather is still cold. I fear I shall have to conform and wear black stockings this winter – I shall look like a bloody beatnik* or first-year art student. I can remember when it was thought outrageous, when we were students at Yeovil, to wear coloured stockings. We used to buy old ladies' beige lyle ones from Denners and dye them in bowls in the common room. We used to dye everything. Once, we dyed a pair of Derek's brand new Y-fronts bright pink and he got really annoyed. Now, every other bloody typist wears them and the same with short skirts. But last year that witch at the bus station cafe in Taunton threw me out because my skirt was too short!

Kate Paul, Journal, 11 December 1960

* *A portmanteau that combined the Beat generation and the Soviet space age, the term 'beatnik' was coined by columnist Herb Caen in an article for the* San Francisco Chronicle *in 1958.*

SEX ED AFTER THE END OF THE *CHATTERLEY* BAN

Addressed my big bad girls on the facts of life … I made it as dull and difficult and diagrammatical as possible, and showed them the drawings of Leonardo da Vinci.

Lavinia Mynors, Diaries, 23 March 1961

~~~

MAN GOES INTO SPACE

Russia puts first man [Yuri Gagarin] into orbit and returns to Earth: orbit 180–187 miles maximum, 101–109 miles minimum, speed 25,000 miles an hour. Epoch-making day in the History of Mankind.

Hugh Selbourne, *A Doctor's Life*, 12 April 1961

~~~

READY MEALS

Supper last night with Julia and Lawrence in their Percy Street flat, eating a frozen Woolworth meal out of foil dishes (no washing-up, my choice of three sorts); much laughter, altogether delightful.

Frances Partridge, Diaries, 27 April 1961

~~~

WICKED WORLD

National Coal Board, 10 bags of coal, £4 11s. 8d. Read newspapers: corruption in Soviet Union, death penalties introduced; arrest of leading generals and cabinet ministers in Persia, also for corruptions; Cuba going Marxist; Tshombe still incarcerated in the Congo; S. Africa on verge of Racial Riots; Angola and Nyasaland in trouble; Eichmann Trial continues.

The Wickedness of Mankind is manifest in all its works, activities and aspirations.

Hugh Selbourne, *A Doctor's Life*, 14 May 1961

◦◦◦

MOON LANDING PLANNED

President Kennedy had announced that the Americans are going to land a man on the moon before the end of the decade.

Gyles Brandreth, *Something Sensational to Read in the Train*, 27 May 1961

◦◦◦

PANIC IN BERLIN

Berlin crisis. Disputation now pointless. Resolved, in all circumstances, to live and die a free man. No tyranny, however odious, no warfare, however destructive, can prevent this. It is what I will do.

Malcolm Muggeridge, Diaries, 14 August 1961

◦◦◦

WALL GOES UP IN BERLIN

A lot of telephoning, morning and evening, to Alec [Douglas-]Home about the 'Berlin Crisis'. The East German authorities have shut down all movement from East to West Berlin. The flood of refugees had reached such proportions – over 3,000 a day – that they were probably almost compelled to take this course. Partly because the West German elections are going on, and partly because the Americans have got very excited, the situation is tense and may become dangerous.*

Harold Macmillan, Diaries, 19 August 1961

* *In 1948 Germany was divided into two countries, the Federal Republic of Germany (West Germany) and the Democratic Republic of Germany (East Germany), the latter being part of the Soviet Communist bloc. The city of Berlin, geographically marooned inside East Germany, remained divided, with its Western half – which had initially been occupied by the US, France and Britain after the Second World War – belonging to West Germany. On 13 August 1961 East Germany began the construction of the wall that would encircle West Berlin.*

THE THIRD WORLD WAR?

Talk is of war and tomorrow I hope to be at a mass protest in Parliament Square. Last night I met Bernie and TG coming out of the pub and we went back to the flat and talked about the reality of war. But on the surface we still plan for a future and I long to buy a cheap sweater to teach in and a brighter bulb for this dull room and now it's very late and I've stayed up clearing out drawers and lining them with newspaper and thoroughly sorting myself out ...

The war could come tonight. One would think that I'd be sad that no one will read these ramblings. Not at all.

Kate Paul, Journal, 10 September 1961

PRAYING FOR THE CND

It rained all day, till about 3 o'c[lock]. Met John Hussey, and we went to Trafalgar Square – or as near as we could get, which was St Martin's in the Fields ... The Police used filthy methods of removing limp, passive people – a man dragged by one arm with his head on the ground ... a woman thrown bodily against a wall ... a police insp. saying, 'If our lads have any more leave stopped, they'll be getting tougher ...' One saw the fascist and the savagery in them start to emerge. The entire crowd that I was in was anti-Police ... One thing became abundantly clear. They hated the bomb, and they hated the uniformed bullies that enforce an unjust law. Leaders arrested were John Osborne, Shelagh Delaney and Vanessa

Redgrave. All I seem to be able to do is send me [*sic*] miserable donations and pray for them all. Number of arrests today were 800-odd.

Kenneth Williams, Diaries, 17 September 1961

THE HANRATTY TRIAL

Made breakfast for M., and read the *Sunday Times* almost without omissions, except of the adverts. Sundays are helpful; they give me time for contemplation, and for preparation for toil in the week ahead. Hanratty has been sentenced to death by Mr Justice Gorman, the longest murder trial in history. The jury is out for ten hours.*

Watched ... *Face to Face*, John Freeman interviewing Cecil Beaton, who looked to me like a homosexual psychopath, but whose intelligence was a modicum above the average.

Hugh Selbourne, A Doctor's Life, 18 February 1962

---

* *A twenty-five-year-old petty crook, James Hanratty was hanged in April 1962 for killing the scientist Michael Gregsten and raping, shooting and leaving for dead Gregsten's lover, Valerie Storie, in what became known as the A6 Murder. Though identified by Storie, there was no forensic evidence against Hanratty and his conviction was popularly held to be a miscarriage of justice. In 2002 a DNA test established 'beyond doubt' that he was guilty.*

TAXING QUESTION FOR SMOKERS

The doctors have come out with a tremendous report on the dangers of smoking – esp. cigarettes. This puts us rather in a fix. For how are we to get £800m indirect revenue from any other source?

Harold Macmillan, Diaries, 8 March 1962

GOD'S OWN GAME

Heavy traffic home, because of football replay; football has replaced Christ.

Hugh Selbourne, A Doctor's Life, 14 March 1962

⟨✧⟩

SATELLITE BROADCASTING

Panorama direct from USA by *Telstar*; amazingly clear picture of 5th Avenue, NY, and the Rockefeller Center, with Richard Dimbleby and James Mossman in a Drug-Store.*

Hugh Selbourne, A Doctor's Life, 30 July 1962

* Telstar 1, launched into space on a Delta rocket on 10 July 1962, was the world's first active communication satellite, enabling TV programmes to be broadcast across the Atlantic.

⟨✧⟩

SODDEN BANK HOLIDAY

No letters today, coldest and wettest bank holiday this century: rain, cloud, gloom and depression.

All the newspapers full of Marilyn Monroe's death.

Common Market* talks break down over Commonwealth agricultural exports; France proving difficult. National Socialist Rally in Norfolk: Nazi thugs.

Hugh Selbourne, A Doctor's Life, 6 August 1962

* On 25 March 1957, France, West Germany, Italy, the Netherlands, Belgium and Luxembourg signed a treaty in Rome establishing the European Economic Community (EEC), also known as the Common Market. It was the first step in Europe's movement

towards economic and political union, and negotiations were ongoing. Britain tried to join the Common Market in 1963, but French president Charles de Gaulle vetoed its membership. It would be another ten years before the UK entered the EEC.

✍

COPY-CAT SUICIDE ·

The day hangs heavily. Marilyn Monroe killed herself yesterday & today an English actress in sympathy did the same. The pointlessness of our way of life – the awful, cheap regard of human life.

Kenneth Williams, Diaries, 7 August 1962

✍

WEAK WILL OF THE WELFARE STATE

Interrupted by the arrival of washing-machine service mechanic, who appeared after ten days of phone calls; his manner lazy and casual, his appearance unprepossessing. Examples of his kind of British workman are multiplying, indifferent to threats of loss of custom. Imagine the wail of lamentation which would go up from the darling public if a doctor had to be called three times, without avail, in an emergency.

In the train disaster on Boxing Day, the driver had ignored the danger signal, and telephone messages for help were not transmitted! The Welfare State is to blame for this decadence in the will and spirit of the people.

Hugh Selbourne, *A Doctor's Life*, 5 January 1963

✍

THE BEATLES DEBUT

Dear Irene,

Thanks for your letter, the LP comes out in two weeks (approx). It's called *Please Please Me* for obvious reasons.

John Lennon, Letters, 25 April 1963

THE COLOUR BAR

How often have we heard similar excuses in the field of housing, from prejudiced landlords: 'We would, of course, take West Indians in our homes, but our neighbours would object,' or from prejudiced employers, 'The workers object to the hiring of coloured workers,' hence the maintenance of a colour bar in its employment policy, etc.

… Clearly, in the context of British economic life (and political considerations of Commonwealth coloured workers among the British working class today) the question of discrimination of coloured workers must be squarely faced and fought as inimical to the unity of the workers.

The implications of the phrase 'it is easy to talk about [the] "colour bar"' is to dangerously minimise this issue. Assuredly, it is far from 'easy' to talk about [the] colour bar – far more experience this indignity, and most coloured workers would prefer forthright struggle for its elimination rather than to 'talk' about it.*

Claudia Jones, Letter to the *Daily Worker*, 7 May 1963

---

* Tentative steps on the road to outlawing such discrimination were taken with the passing of the Race Relations Act 1965, which forbade discrimination on the 'grounds of colour, race, or ethnic or national origins' in public places. But its remit did not extend to housing or employment, and shops were also exempted.

THE PROFUMO SCANDAL

Dined at the British Embassy with the Ormsby Gores. There was much talk of the Profumo case. Dr Stephen Ward was indicted in London yesterday on the charge of receiving money from the physical exertions of call girls. He is expected to 'sing' freely and it is not a pretty tune. How much this episode will damage Macmillan and the Conservative Party remains to be estimated, but the initial repercussions have been severely adverse. Macmillan is accused of collusion with Profumo in the foisting of a lie on the House of Commons, or else of extreme *naiveté*. I do not believe the former, it would be out of character; but he does appear to have displayed a remarkably credulous lack of sophistication.*

David Bruce, *Ambassador to Sixties London*, 9 June 1963

* *John Profumo, the Secretary of State for War in Harold Macmillan's Conservative government, was introduced to the 'showgirl' Christine Keeler at Cliveden, the stately home of Lord Astor, in 1961 by osteopath Stephen Ward, and began a relationship with her. Scandal ensued when it emerged that Keeler had also been sleeping with Yevgeny Ivanov, the Soviet naval attaché, raising fears that British secrets might have been shared over pillow talk. Initially, Profumo denied the affair, but he eventually admitted the truth and resigned from Parliament. Ward died from an overdose of sleeping pills on 3 August 1963.*

⌒⋎⌒

STORMS WRECK SPORTS

Arose at 7.30 a.m.; better weather after yesterday's rain. Wimbledon singles Finals had to be abandoned yesterday because of torrential downpour; the Test Match at Edgbaston was also abandoned. After breakfast, had run around in car with Hazel and David to the centre of Birmingham; great developments, but it appears from what I am told that Birmingham is a conservative stronghold, with much aggressive ill humour towards coloured people. (That is, shits and fascists.)

Hugh Selbourne, *A Doctor's Life*, 7 July 1963

WHITE HOT WILSON

I am following the Party Conferences with interest. It can't be denied: Harold Wilson (also Pisces) is doing rather well. He is promising a new Britain 'forged in the white heat of the scientific revolution'. Forged is the word!

Gyles Brandreth, *Something Sensational to Read in the Train*, 2 October 1963

HIT OR MISS?

Watched *Juke Box Jury* by mistake; astonishing rubbish.*

Hugh Selbourne, *A Doctor's Life*, 16 November 1963

* *Hosted by disc jockey David Jacobs,* Juke Box Jury *first aired on the BBC in 1959. A panel of four celebrity guests passed judgement on the latest pop releases, voting them either a 'Hit' or a 'Miss'.*

ASSASSINATION OF PRESIDENT KENNEDY

Just as I was leaving home to speak in Acton the phone rang and Hilary answered it and it was one of his friends. When he rang off, he said that Kennedy had been shot and I didn't believe it. But we switched on the television and there was a flash saying that he was critically ill in Dallas. I drove to Acton and heard the 7.30 bulletin, just before going into the meeting, which announced that Kennedy had died. It was the most stunning blow and at the beginning of the meeting we all stood in silence for a moment in tribute.

I dashed home to watch TV and hear the details. George Brown was drunk when he was interviewed but everyone else who spoke was sensitive and touched and it was a most moving evening.

Tony Benn, Diaries, 22 November 1963

The world is in mourning for Kennedy – all the newspapers are full of it and likewise TV and radio. Everyone shocked and shopgirls in a dither, unable to give correct change; small groups in the street discussing the tragedy as though their own brother had been murdered.

Kate Paul, Journal, 24 November 1963

⌁

SCARED OF THE BEATLES

I got a letter from D the other day, which of course makes me feel sick with gloom and starts me singing Brenda Lee songs in an echoing wail on my way to work. I now think I was a fool to give him up, though he would have gone to India whatever. Still, he remains, apart from Christopher and Mummy, my only friend, who I know inside out, who I know what he's thinking, still it's no good. No doubt I was right at the time.

And then, no sex, no flat. I do take things for granted, after all. I do tend to forget the dreary necking sessions on MY bed going on till three in the morning, and sad goodbyes, and horrid nights in other people's rooms, ugh, ugh. And him being ill. And depressed and hopeless …

The people I see most of these days are about the squarest intellectuals I have ever met in the whole of my life, so I expect that makes a difference. I think intellectuals are frightened of The Beatles, they think brains will quite soon count for nothing, it's all plain fright. They can't bear to think that someone who does the shake beautifully could be more admired than Robert Helpmann. This is such a new, vital thing; I mean it really excites me, like abstract art excites the phonies; how they can't receive it with open arms, burning with curiosity and sheer ecstasy, I don't know. How different you can be with a little age difference.

Virginia Ironside, Diaries, 14 January 1964

⌁

MOD VS ROCKERS

Brighton is packed with Rockers and Mods. There were several fights & over 50 arrests. Lovely. I saw a great mass of Mods by the Palace Pier, one boy of about 14 or 15 had a gash & blood pouring all over his face. I was abed by 12 o'c.*

Kenneth Williams, Diaries, 17 May 1964

The clash between the rival youth subcultures of Mods (smartly dressed riders of Italian scooters with a love of black American soul and Jamaican blue-beat music) and rockers (motorbike enthusiasts with a penchant for rock 'n' roll as performed by Gene Vincent and Elvis Presley) kicked up over the Easter Bank Holiday of 1964. Some relatively minor scuffles in Clacton, a seaside town in Essex, sparked headlines – 'Youngsters Beat Up Town', Daily Telegraph – and encouraged similar conflicts in Margate, Brighton and elsewhere throughout the summer.

ADVANCES IN FAST FOOD

Lunched at the Golden Egg. Oh, the horror – the cold stuffiness, claustrophobic placing of tables, garish lights and mass-produced food in steel dishes. And the egg-shaped menus! But perhaps one could get something out it. The setting for a breaking-off, or some terrible news or an unwanted declaration of love.

Barbara Pym, *A Very Private Eye*, 27 November 1964

∞

MY KIND OF GENERATION

Much moved by 'Generation X' – a series of tape-recorded interviews with teenagers. One admires again their honesty, lack of pretension, refusal to be bluffed. One sympathized (a little uneasily, perhaps) with their total rejection of the false and hypocritical values on which society operates. But sentimental self-identification with the young is the worst thing you can offer them.

Keith Vaughan, Journals, 13 December 1964

∞

CHURCHILL'S DEATH

It astonished me how great the reaction to Churchill's death was this week. One thought he had been dead for years. But this universal acclaim, this response which goes beyond all political and national bounds, must mean the world sees him as something very important which they have lost. A man who acts without inhibition or self-doubt. The last of the Pre-Freudians.

Not a great man by my standards because he lacked sensibility and the faculty of judgement. He did not need to understand because he had the power to delude. Outside the simple context of war he was mistrusted and rightly, because he had nothing to contribute to the more sophisticated and unheroic problems of living in peace. But it is interesting to see revealed the extent to which the world still looks for a father figure who will simplify the issues and permit heroic solutions. Churchill enabled everyone to live the childish fantasy of his finest hour. How reluctantly we inhabit our century.

Keith Vaughan, Journals, 29 January 1965

Winston's funeral. All through the week London had been working itself up for the great day. The lying-in-state in Westminster Hall had taken place on Wednesday, Thursday and Friday. I went on all three evenings, taking Molly and our doorman, Arthur, on one night, and Anne and Tommy Balogh the second night, and then on the third night Mr Large, who cuts my hair. Each time one saw, even at one o'clock in the morning, the stream of people pouring down the steps of Westminster Hall toward the catafalque ... As one walked through the streets one felt the hush and one noticed the cars stopping suddenly and the people stepping out into the quietness and walking across to Westminster Hall. We as Members of Parliament could just step into the Hall through our side door.

I really hadn't wanted to go to the funeral. But it was obvious that I couldn't be known to have stayed away ... My chief memory is of the pall-bearers, in particular poor Anthony Eden, literally ashen grey, looking as old as Clement Atlee ... Oh, what a faded, declining establishment surrounded me. Aged marshals, grey, dreary ladies, decadent Marlboroughs and Churchills. It was a dying congregation gathered there ... It felt like the end of an epoch, possibly even the end of a nation.

Richard Crossman, Diaries, 30 January 1965

DENIM AND DYLAN

Hooked up with St Martin's student Fernandez, gathering material for this thesis on the influence of the Polish School on British film-makers. Told him there wasn't any, and attemped to sell him on the Czechs. On the loose and with that 'work completed' feeling bought a pair of exciting, sexy denim hipsters in Shaftesbury Avenue – then brown leather belt in posh leather shop in Piccadilly – discover gum gives one the feeling of casual assurance ... Also Bob Dylan record – 'Times a-Changin'' (EXCELLENT).

Lindsay Anderson, Diaries, 7 May 1965

PIRATE RADIO PROPOSALS

Tony Wedgwood Benn put up an elaborate paper in which he proposed to get a firm commitment that the BBC should finance its expanding programme partly by adverting, while on the other hand we should introduce legislation to ban Radio Caroline, the pirate pop station.* I was decisively against him on Radio Caroline because I didn't see any point in losing the votes of young people before the BBC had any real alternative to it.

Richard Crossman, Diaries, 24 May 1965

* *Launched on Easter Sunday in 1964 as an alternative to the rather staid output of the BBC's Light Programme and Radio Luxembourg, Radio Caroline was a pirate pop music radio station that operated from a ship in international waters off the British coast, which put it outside the jurisdiction of the authorities.*

TEACH-IN FOR VIETNAM

The other thing this week that's in my mind is the developing situation in Vietnam ...

On Friday night there was the first 'teach-in' at the LSE in London on Vietnam.* It was based on the 'teach-ins' that have appeared in the United States and which are an aspect of the non-violent movement. I think they probably will have an influence and I'm told that whenever Harold Wilson's name was mentioned at LSE people booed. It may well be that when the time comes the Labour government will have been held to fail not because it was too radical but because it was not radical enough.

Tony Benn, Diaries, 13 June 1965

After the first Indochina War, Vietnam had been partitioned, with communists governing North Vietnam and French-backed anti-communists governing South Vietnam. After the French withdrew in 1954, North Vietnam attempted to reunify the country, with the US coming to the aid of South Vietnam in defence against the 'domino theory' of communist expansion. The military support did not include active troops, however. In March 1965 President Lyndon B. Johnson, with widespread support from the American people, sent the first US combat forces into battle.

MUZAK IN MANCHESTER

The Piccadilly Hotel appears more and more an image of the affluent, tasteless, expense-account society – with its impersonal 'modern' decor, its air-conditioning that doesn't work, its tapes of continuous musak [Muzak, background music] relayed even into the bathroom. Breakfast, we discover, is 10/- extra on top of the 90/- for a room, with 2/- charge for serving in the room and another 2/- if the orange juice is fresh. Such display is made of everything, of decor, service, etc. … that one is positively incited to rebel.

Lindsay Anderson, Diaries, 8 September 1965

INDEPENDENT RHODESIA

Rhodesia has declared its independence. Harold Wilson's 'mission' has failed and England has had one more kick in the puss.* The Welfare State may be all right for improving the living conditions of the mediocre, but it isn't dazzlingly successful in dealing with foreign affairs and colonial administration. I don't see why it should be really, as few of its leaders have been further than Blackpool.

Noël Coward, Diaries, 12 November 1965

* *Ghana had become independent in 1957, Nigeria in 1960, Sierra Leone in 1961 and Kenya in 1963, but Rhodesia's declaration was quite a different matter: the southern African nation had broken free unilaterally, the first British colony to do so since the US declared its independence in 1776.*

⌒⁄⁄⌒

LONELY IN BRITAIN

I bin in the country six months now and I am fine. The man at the employment office sent me to a job. So I working. Life in Jamaica and England is not one. Things have them ups and douns but the thing that friten me very much in London is the loneliness. You dont know any body in this town. Even the black people them is not talking to no strangr just like the white people. I bin in this building now going four long, long monts and I dont no the naim of al the people in the building. the same thing at me workplace. you talk to an Inglish man Munth after mont but you dont ask him for his naim Him not telling you either. The house them close to one other but you no know the nam of you neybour. You don't know if them like you or them hate you. If i be ten yeers in this country i wont know the proper name of ten Englishmen. Sometime I really want to know what it is that is going on in ther heat …

Unknown West Indian, Unposted letter collected in *Journey to an Illusion* by Donald Hinds, 14 February 1966

⌒⁄⁄⌒

A NEW STAR IS BORN

I went with Gladys to see a film called *Alfie* with Michael Caine. Absolutely brilliant. Everyone in it is first-rate. Vivien Merchant brilliant and Michael Caine superb. A big new star. Hurray! Let's hope he doesn't get swollen-headed and take to the bottle ...

Noël Coward, Diaries, 3 April 1966

THE POST OFFICE TOWER

To the Office and then to the Post Office Tower for the public opening with Billy Butlin. I said that there was a new definition of a Cockney: 'Someone born within sight of the new Post Office Tower.'

Tony Benn, Diaries, 19 May 1966

WEATHERING THE TRENDS

Pop is dead and I am becoming the Ann Leslie of the *Daily Mail*. David came round and was hideously drunk and perverted and put me off sex for a day.

Searching for a flat is ghastly; I found this one a day when it snowed and I had to interview girls in Knightsbridge and find out if their knees were cold in their mini-skirts.

Virginia Ironside, Diaries, 11 July 1966

WORLD CUP FOOTBALL VICTORY FOR THE HOST NATION

England have won! Mayhem! Singing, dancing and general happiness. These boys are immortal now! WORLD CHAMPIONS!

Geoff Otton, Diaries, 30 July 1966

⁓

THE LEFT-WING *SUN*

Alix and I got going on the Labour Party … She admitted she was getting persecution mania over the attacks on Mr Wilson and his policy. I wish I'd asked her if she didn't think criticism should always be allowed of any party. The trouble is she reads only the left-wing *Sun*, which is far more critical than *The Times*.

Frances Partridge, Diaries, 8 October 1966

⁓

DISASTER AT ABERFAN

As well as the escape of George Blake from Wormwood Scrubs on Friday night* there was the disaster at Aberfan, the Welsh Valley, where a huge coal tip broke away and ran over a school, killing hundreds of children. Harold Wilson has gone down there by helicopter and stayed there and Callaghan has gone over by motor-car.

I feel the whole thing has been emotionally exploited by the BBC in the most terrible and extravagant way. But I have no doubt that Harold Wilson was profoundly moved. The tragedy gave a macabre background to the weekend.

Richard Crossman, Diaries, 23 October 1966

* *George Blake was a Dutch-born British spy who was tried as a Soviet double agent and sentenced to forty-two years in prison before being sprung out of Wormwood Scrubs and*

fleeing to Russia. On 21 October 1966, 116 children and 28 adults were killed when a coal tip slid down the mountain above Aberfan, South Wales, and engulfed the local junior school, a farm and several houses.

SAVED BY HIPPIES

John took me to the TWW [Television Wales and West] office party, because his flatmate works there. It was full of fat ladies in gold with paper hats, baggy-trousered lunatics whooping, office girls dressed in silver, and secretaries in pink with ill-fitting cups (always). Thin, suburban girls (always thin) dancing with the worst species of man that exists on the worst of all possible earths.

We skip about a bit, get drink via tickets (of course), win a couple of prizes (for dancing in bare feet, no less; wow, what way-out methods) cut the comments baby, baby, baby, I eat the egg from the Scotch eggs because I feel fat and ugly ...

Enter bearded hipster with gorgeous girl. Bearded hipster though, perhaps Jim Ritchie-ish, has a super face under the growth; and I stare in the usual way, just because he looks good ...

'What are you doing here?' I ask in amazement to see such hippies at such an amazingly square function. 'But that's just what we've been asking ourselves about you,' they reply.

That's nice and, god, makes me feel happy.

Virginia Ironside, Diaries, 16 December 1966

'DIRTY DONOVAN'

Cold, grey morning. Went into town. Bought a single of Donovan singing 'Sunshine Superman'. An obsessive tune. George calls him 'Dirty Donovan'. Because of the drugs scandal.*

Joe Orton, Diaries, 4 January 1967

* The Scottish-born folk-rock singer Donovan Philips Leitch, widely seen as Britain's answer to Bob Dylan, was arrested for possession of cannabis in 1966.

⟋𝓂⟍

MEETING A BEATLE

Arrived in Belgravia at ten minutes to eight having caught a 19 bus which dropped me at Hyde Park Corner. I found Chapel Street easily. I didn't want to get there too early so I walked around for a while and came back through the nearby mews. When I got back to the house it was nearly eight o'clock.

I rang the bell and an old man opened the door. He seemed surprised to see me. 'Is this Brian Epstein's house?' I said. 'Yes, sir,' he said, and led the way into the hall. I suddenly realised that the man was the butler. I've never seen one before. He took my coat and I went to the lavatory. When I came out, he'd gone. There was nobody about. I wandered around a large dining-room which was laid for dinner. And then I got to feel strange. The house appeared to be empty. So I went upstairs to the first floor. I heard music, only I couldn't decide where it came from. So I went further upstairs and found myself in a bedroom. I came down again and found the butler. He took me into a room and said in a loud voice, 'Mr Orton.'

Everybody looked up and stood to their feet. I was introduced to one or two people. And Paul McCartney. He was just as the photographs. Only, he'd grown a moustache. His hair was shorter, too. He was playing the latest Beatles recording, 'Penny Lane'. I liked it very much. Then he played the other side – Strawberry something. I didn't like this as much. We talked intermittently. Before we went out to dinner we'd agreed to throw out the idea of setting the film in the thirties. We went down to dinner. The crusted old retainer – looking too much like a butler to be good casting – busied himself in the corner …

We talked of drugs, of mushrooms which give hallucinations – like LSD. 'The drug, not the money,' I said. We talked of tattoos. And, after one or two veiled references, marijuana. I said I'd smoked it in Morocco. The atmosphere relaxed a little …

After a while, Paul McCartney said, 'Let's go upstairs.' So he and I and Peter Brown went upstairs to a room also fitted with a TV … A French photographer arrived with two beautiful youths and a girl. He'd taken a set of new photographs of The Beatles. They wanted one to use on the record sleeve. Excellent photograph. And the four Beatles look different with their moustaches. Like anarchists in the early years of the century …

Joe Orton, Diaries, 24 January 1967

POLAROIDS FOR PORN

Kenneth went to have his passport photograph taken. He had it done by polaroid camera. It cost 7s. 6d for two. No negatives. I'd like a Polaroid camera. Most useful for taking pornographic pictures, I should say. We went then to the record shop to enquire whether the new Beatles' single is out. It won't be on sale till Friday.

Joe Orton, Diaries, 15 February 1967

FOLLOWING THE FASHION

Have done my usual King's Road stint. Up and down, peering through the trendies into the boutiques, grabbing clothes and trying them in front of the mirror, discarding them, deciding I'm too fat, my thighs are pudgy, the colour doesn't suit me, the skirts are too short, too long.

Virginia Ironside, Diaries, 18 March 1967

PERTURBED BY THE POPS

Top of the Pops. 'A Whiter Shade of Pale'. Sad Bach-like tune, but to see it is a kind of nightmare, the dark, brooding youth playing the organ and sung by a man in full Chinese dress even to the pigtail. Decadent and horrible.

Barbara Pym, *A Very Private Eye*, 7 July 1967

HOMOSEXUALITY DECRIMINALIZED

The Lords have passed Leo Abse's bill, legalising homosexuality in England: it's all right between consenting adults in private, except the services! and in Scotland. So it won't do any good for the queens of Dundee & the like.

Kenneth Williams, Diaries, 13 July 1967

BRILLIANT BEATLES

Weather warm. Got up early. Played Sheila's copy of Sergeant Pepper. It's very good. Some numbers I like more than others. 'With a Little Help from My Friends' and 'When I'm Sixty-Four' and 'A Day in the Life'. Certainly, the most brilliant of the Beatles records. They get better all the time. Did very little all day. Went down to the record shop in Sicilian Avenue and bought a copy of the LP.

Joe Orton, Diaries, 20 July 1967

THE PLAYBOY CLUB

Tonight I took [the actress] Georgina Forbes to the Playboy (Bunny) Club, near the Hilton Hotel, for dinner. We dined about nine o'clock in a large gloomy, candle-lit place called the VIP room. A bunny came up and introduced herself as our waitress. She was not topless, nor were any of the other girls, but each wore on her stern an enormous white ruff, an exaggeration of a rabbit's tail. This most prominent portion of their costume is on constant display, for as the dishes are served they approach tables backwards, and it is quite a contortionary feat to handle plates in this manner. The room was crowded, the food good. On other floors gambling was in full swing, with Bunnies acting as croupiers.

David Bruce, *Ambassador to Sixties London*, 7 September 1967

∞

SHIFTING SEXUAL MORES

First day of film, *Carry on Doctor*. I was home by 5 o'c. Went to see *Bonnie & Clyde* at the Warner. This film is certainly v. daring. A scene showing an unsuccessful attempt at intercourse with Warren B[eatty] rolling off the girl & lying there crestfallen, and then she tries to go down on him for the old fellatio and he looks appalled and stops her. The entire cinema welcome this episode – in the W/End! – and there were cries of approval from the auditorium. It was disgraceful, but I had to laugh; not at the episode, but at the audience reaction – that kind of nervous 'Oh! Hallo! What's going on now!' laughter.

Kenneth Williams, Diaries, 14 September 1967

∞

POUND IN YOUR POCKET

There's a lot in the paper about devaluation. Wilson has said in the Commons that it does not affect money in savings etc., in England,* and the Chancellor has said that it means a lowering of the standard of living.
*Quote: 'It will not affect the pound in your pocket'!!

Kenneth Williams, Diaries, 21 November 1967

∞

US EMBASSY PROTEST

The afternoon, for us, passed tranquilly, and no strangers ventured up to the gates, which were locked. Meanwhile, in Grosvenor Square, the largest disturbance ever witnessed in London took place. Viewing it on television, it looked for a time as if the police would be unable to withstand the onslaught of the demonstrators, who at their starting point in Trafalgar Square were estimated to number 15,000 people, of whom I regret to say almost 1,000 were said to be Americans. Potential troublemakers have flown in from Germany, Holland, France and some from the United States. By the time they had foot-slogged their way to the vicinity of the Embassy, the crowd had somewhat diminished, and probably amounted to no more than 10,000.

David Bruce, *Ambassador to Sixties London,* 17 March 1968

RIVERS OF BLOOD

Ted and I were sitting by the telly listening to the six o'clock news when there suddenly was Enoch Powell, white-faced and tight-lipped, delivering his Wolverhampton speech on immigration. As we listened to his relentless words – 'I see the Tiber running with blood' – intense depression gripped us. I knew he had taken the lid off Pandora's box and that race relations in Britain would never be the same again. This is certainly a historic turning point, but in which direction? I believe he has helped make a race war, not only in Britain but perhaps in the world, inevitable.

Barbara Castle, Diaries, 21 April 1968

* *Enoch Powell was a Conservative MP for Wolverhampton South West. This inflammatory address, commonly known as the 'Rivers of Blood' speech, led to his being sacked from the shadow cabinet.*

DOCKERS FOR POWELL

The press is still full of the repercussions of Enoch Powell's speech just before the weekend. Yesterday, 200 dockers came to the House of Commons and shouted obscene things at Labour MPs and called Ian Mikardo a bloody Chinese Jew. He recognised some of the East End Fascist leaders among these guys.

Tony Benn, Diaries, 24 April 1968

⁓

NO REVOLUTION IN SUTTON COLDFIELD

It's 10.20, and I'm just about to go to bed. I've been watching the ten o'clock news – there seems to be a good deal happening this week. The 'Revolution '68' is taking place in France, and it looks as though De Gaulle's regime has been severely shaken. Student riots and demonstrations fill the news tonight – New York, London, Paris, Belgium, Germany, all are feeling the pressure of the militant young. For the time, racial tensions have given place to age-group tensions. It's a strange business. It's probably part of the same syndrome as the hippy love-cult of last year – namely, the desire of the young to change the values of the materialistic, rat-racey consumer society that they are growing up in. Last year, they tried passivity; this year, it's violence … Of course, it doesn't touch me, here in the dead heart of the Midlands. It's impossible to imagine the young people of Sutton Coldfield getting worked up about anything.

David Pringle, Diaries, 23 May 1968

⁓

ANOTHER ASSASSINATION

History repeats itself with ridiculous exactitude. Early today, Senator Robert Kennedy was shot in the head after a political meeting at Los Angeles. His wife was by his side. The latest reports say that he is still alive but in a critical condition. Ballard is right when he says that these public murders are ritual sacrifices. We raise a totem figure, and we destroy it – the Dying God.

David Pringle, Diaries, 5 June 1968

A CHROMOSOME OF DIFFERENCE

In the evening with Margaret to hear Lionel lecture to a learned and deeply interested gathering about chromosomes. Enthralling. It seems that a man who has two or more, instead of only one X chromosome, is definitely more prone to violence and aggression than normal men, while a woman with two or more X chromosomes is merely stupider than normal.

Frances Partridge, Diaries, 19 June 1968

THE BIAFRAN FAMINE

The Biafra situation has reached a lunatic height. There is someone dying every two seconds, they tell us. Supplies are not getting past the military cordons – and films of the emaciated and the dying are being shown on our TV screens. What we have now is a modern concentration camp. Exactly that. Tens of thousands of people have been crowded into one small area of Nigeria and have been left to suffer and die. It is nothing short of a systematic liquidation. Biafra has become a death camp, and now the name has all the emotive overtones of Auschwitz, Belsen and Buchenwald.

David Pringle, Diaries, 9 August 1968

BLACK POWER IN NORTH KEN

In the evening I went to a North Kensington Labour Party meeting, the first one held there, I think, since the '66 election, and some Black Power people were there. They just laughed at the speaker before me. When I got up they began shouting. So I said, 'Look, I don't want to make a speech. I make about three a week and I would much rather listen to you.' So they came forward and sat in the front, a Black Power man abused me and said I was a lord and the British working movement was bourgeois and so on, and it became interesting after that.

Tony Benn, Diaries, 7 October 1968

FRAGMENTS OF A DOUBLE LP

The Beatles' new double LP, which is simply called *The Beatles*, will be out on Friday.* I have still heard no more than a few snatches of the songs on Leslie's transistor radio – but the general excitement is beginning to mount, and Geoff Hall, for one, avows that it is 'brilliant' from what he has heard.

David Pringle, Diaries, 19 November 1968

The album is more commonly known as The White Album, *after its plain cover designed by the pop artist Richard Hamilton.*

THE LSD EXPERIENCE

I've just watched a young American, Dr Allan Cohen, interviewed on TV about LSD and mysticism. Very interesting. He says he first took LSD in 1963 under Timothy Leary, but he has now given it up and is following a mystical course with an Indian guru. He says that 'true' mystical experience can't be obtained from drugs. I find this difficult to understand, but I'm prepared to believe him, since the LSD way does seem to be a little bit too easy to be likely.

David Pringle, Diaries, 12 December 1968

PROTESTS EVERYWHERE

This week, three Czechoslovakian students have burned themselves alive as a protest against Russian domination. In Moscow today, a youth attempted to assassinate the four cosmonauts during their triumphal parade through the city – he has been caught, and I hate to think of what is going to happen to him now. A 20-year-old Englishman has been given four years in prison for trying to burn down the Imperial War Museum because he believed it was an obscenity.

David Pringle, Diaries, 23 January 1969

HIDEOUS TIMES

It's impossible to look at the *Radio Times*, it's so vulgarly hideous and aimed at those whom past beauty is non-existent and present beauty is sex only.

What has psychoanalysis done for the world, when so much violence has still to be released both in fantasy and action? And can people have been even sexually liberated if they need so many strip-tease joints, which one would imagine could only gratify the bottle-up or immature? Why can dress designers not consider the shape of the female form, and why must they so painstakingly deglamourize it? Why must the young either drown reality in drugs or yell slogans of destruction like children in a nursery?

I have just passed a little group of black-haired men standing opposite the Spanish Embassy, shouting at intervals: 'Asesino! Asesino!' They are to demonstrate this afternoon against Franco declaring a state of emergency in Spain.

Frances Partridge, Diaries, 26 January 1969

cᴍᴄ

NUDES IN NOTTING HILL

Number 17 Powis Terrace is one of those late-Victorian stucco terraces in Notting Hill Gate with a vast columned portico and every sign that gentility has long since fled. The houses were now tatty tenements and I climbed up what can only be described as a squalid staircase-well to be met by David [Hockney]. Original is the only word one could ever apply to him with his bleached blond hair and owl spectacles. But I couldn't help loving him and admiring his quick logic and unique perception. He's rather large and square, getting fat in fact, and somehow terribly conscious of it. The whole time I was there he kept on feeling beneath his shirt as though checking up on the expansion of his wodges ...

I don't think that I'd ever before encountered anyone so overtly homosexual ... All over the floor were scattered magazines with male nudes. David picked one up and complained how it had been seized by the Customs and then returned. On its cover was stamped 'Nudes – semi-erect'.

Sir Roy Strong, Diaries, 29 January 1969

⌇

BORING GEORGE BEST

Met Brian at Eastcote Station. Went by tube to Shepherd's Bush – to go to the football place two hours early! Brian told me you had to, to get a good place. He didn't tell me the match didn't start until three o'clock, or that we would have to stand up all the time. By the time the match finished we'd stood there four hours. There were loads and loads of people – the bloke behind kept swearing, and one man told him to belt up because there was 'a little girl' in front of him. Bloody Cheek!

We walked through Shepherd's Bush Market afterwards. There were police on horses, and more people than I've ever seen in one place. George Best was playing, and I'm glad I saw him in real life, but the match was one of the most boring things that ever happened to me and Brian is not wonderful enough to compensate for that.

Yvonne Coppard, Diaries, 15 February 1969

⌇

POP STARS, SIT-INS AND STRIKES

The Apollo 9 astronauts landed safely yesterday, George Harrison was arrested for possessing cannabis, France is passing through another financial crisis, the British economy is imperilled by the 3-week-old strike at Fords, Parliament has been debating the Biafran question, minor sit-ins have occurred at the LSE, Sussex University and elsewhere. In other words, all is much as usual.

David Pringle, Diaries, 14 March 1969

ASSAULTED BY THE WALL OF SOUND

Geoff, Ian and Roger Lee called for me at quarter to seven. We queued for an hour outside Mothers in Erdington, then paid 12/6 to see the Pink Floyd. It was better value than last time, since we managed to get seats and the bar was not totally inaccessible. The group came on at ten o'clock, and they were remarkable. I have never heard such an amazing din. The Pink Floyd have been described as a 'heavy' pop-group, and I think that's apt. Their music is both science-fictional and mystical, with titles like 'Let There Be More Light' and 'Set the Controls for the Heart of the Sun'. They had two guitars, drums and an organ, and the volume was immense. You could feel the bass in your chest; it was a massive assault of sound. The audience loved it. One character was doing a tribal dance in his seat. When we left, we were exhausted.

David Pringle, Diaries, 29 April 1969

BLIND FAITH IN HYDE PARK

A cloudless day, as was yesterday. On Friday, I went with Delyth John, the Welsh girl at work, to the Wyre Forest to collect mayfly larvae. It was an enjoyable outing. Yesterday, Ian and I went to London and lay on the grass in Hyde Park all day, along with tens of thousands of other people. There was a free concert being given in the sunshine by a new group called Blind Faith (Eric Clapton, Ginger Baker, Steve Winwood and Ric Grech) and a number of other performers. It was a strange day – young people dressed in hair and cloaks, skirts very long and very short, one man in a bright red suit with a bunch of purple ribbons dangling from his wide-brimmed hat. The crowd was gentle.

There was a young couple sitting in front of us – a man with frizzy hair and a girl in a short black dress and long white stockings. They had a year-old baby with them in a push-chair. Their son, come with the grown-ups to listen to the music of Clapton and Baker. Born in 1968; what will he live to see and do?

The accents around me were both middle class and working class, the language cheerfully obscene. I have rarely heard the word 'fuck' used so often, and, believe it or not, so pleasantly.

David Pringle, Diaries, 8 June 1969

✧

JOHN LENNON IN A BAG

That Beatle who is married to an Asiatic lady was on *The Frost Programme*. The man is long-haired & unprepossessing, with tin spectacles and this curious nasal, Liverpudlian delivery: the appearance is either grotesque or quaint & the overall impression is one of great foolishness. He and his wife are often 'interviewed' from inside bags in order to achieve 'objectivity' and they have 'lie-ins' whereby they stay in bed for long periods & allow a certain number of people into the room. I think this man's name is Ringo Starr [John Lennon] or something but he began as a 'singer' and instrumentalist with this group called The Beatles and one searches in vain for any valid reason for his being interviewed at all …

Kenneth Williams, Diaries, 15 June 1969

✧

A MAN ON THE MOON

At about three o'clock this morning I awoke from a fitful sleep on the camp-bed in Robert's bedroom. From somewhere, I could hear a distant lonely 'beep' sound, recurring every 30 seconds or so. It is a sound that always reminds me of Christmas 1968 now, and the Apollo 8 mission. But this time, of course, it was the real thing. The next-door neighbours were tuned in to the moon. I got out of bed and went to the window, hoping to see the moon in the sky, but there was just a bright star over the rooftops. I looked along the street, and saw that the downstairs lights were on in several of the houses – people throughout the town, and no doubt throughout the country, were clustered around their television sets. I went back to bed and listened to the faint beeping. It had a familiarity and comfort about it, like the sound of an engine after you have been travelling for six hours.

At eight o'clock, when I went downstairs for breakfast, I found the *Daily Express* lying on the settee in the living room. The enormous headline said: MAN IS ON THE MOON – and underneath were pictures of Neil Armstrong and Edwin Aldrin, space-suited ...

Soon after nine o'clock this morning, I found myself outside a television shop. There, I saw the first pictures – two small, white figures leaping in slow circles against a blurred grey background. It looked just like a scene from a cheap science-fiction film. But it was genuine; men really are on the moon. It gave me the strangest sense of unreality, standing there in a Hinckley street, with my bag in my hand, staring through a shop window at those pictures on the television screens. I had been reading SF [science fiction] for years, and a dozen old stories were going through my mind.

Ballard is right: it becomes difficult to distinguish the fact from the fiction. Would all this be happening now if Clarke hadn't written *Prelude to Space* in 1947, or if Heinlein hadn't published *The Man Who Sold the Moon* in 1950? To what extent is the Apollo 11 mission an acting-out of those fantasies?

David Pringle, Diaries, 21 July 1969

᪐

SONG FOR A MILLION SINGERS

Another long-forgotten library card arrived the other day – this one for Jeff Nuttall's *Bomb Culture,* which I ordered about nine months ago. Anyway, I strolled down to Erdington Library yesterday afternoon and collected the book. I am halfway through it already. Much of it is fascinating. Nuttall traces the development of youth culture from VJ Day to the summer of 1968 – from the hoods of the padded-shouldered, gangster-movie era, through swing music, the teddy-boys, rock 'n' roll, ton-up boys, Elvis Presley, the

Beatles, , beatniks, rhythm and blues, Tamla-Motown, the hippies, Bob Dylan, the students, happenings and love-ins. He says the 'generation gap' opened for the first time in 1945 and that it has grown wider ever since.

John Lennon and Yoko Ono have a record out at the moment called 'Give Peace a Chance'. It has witty lyrics, in which words like masturbation and flagellation and names like Bob Dylan and Norman Mailer recur. There is a powerful, repeated refrain which goes: 'All we are saying is give peace a chance.' Imagine that sung by a million people in Hyde Park! …

David Pringle, Diaries, 30 July 1969

FAMILY SIDES COME OUT

Yarmouth. Feeling devastated I asked my parents to come into the dining room. 'What's happened now?' asked Mother. After walking round the room I said that the last few months had been hell and my marriage has to end. Father did not want to know more, but after a long silence I told them that I am homosexual. 'Well, you didn't get it from my side of the family,' said Mother.

Rev. Dr Malcolm Johnson, *Diary of a Gay Priest*, 9 August 1969

FESTIVAL ROCKS THE TABLOID PRESS

On the Isle of Wight, 150,000 people gathered to hear Bob Dylan – the gutter press are having their work cut out to track down smut in a gathering which seems to be happy and peaceful. 150,000 people and all the violence that the *Mirror* could rake up was a man getting his head cut on a bottle. It shows how evil papers like the *News of the World* and, I am afraid, the *Daily Mirror* are. They have chosen to pick out isolated incidents – a couple making love in a bath of foam, a girl dancing naked – and make them seem like crimes. They are trying their best to indict a younger generation, who seems to be setting a triumphant example to the older generation – an example of how to enjoy oneself, something which most Englishmen don't seem really capable of, especially the cynical pressmen of the *News of the World*. It's all very sad.

Michael Palin, Diaries, 31 August 1969

⌇

SENSES AND SKINHEADS

Rain battering on the window.

The Sunday papers become more and more of a sensory overload. Some highly sexual adverts for bedwear, a psychology and perception test, letters on atrocities in Vietnam, the story of Mick Jagger in Australia, an Oxfam advert showing a leper child with one hand eaten away to a stump, huge colour photographs of primitive tribesmen in New Guinea, the accounts of the Sharon Tate murderers, a front-page plea from the *Sunday Mirror* to the Labour government to reverse their policy towards the Vietnam war, a policeman clutching a girl's hair at a Springboks demonstration, an article by Peter Laurie on over-population. By the time you've been through all that and more, you feel a faint nausea and pressure on the forehead.

Random thoughts: these working-class skinheads are destroying everything that John Lennon and Bob Dylan fought for. They have no respect for the achievements of the past. They make me feel like a member of an older generation, these fifteen- and sixteen-year-old kids with their boots and braces. I suppose it had to happen: back we go to the teds and the rockers. Maybe the long-haired, intellectual hippy thing was going soft and decadent anyway. Doesn't everything?

David Pringle, Diaries, 7 December 1969

⌇

ARRIVAL OF THE M56

We washed and polished the children to take them visiting at Tormarton, John Grigg's home whither Patsy had invited us to tea. The house stands alone, across the road from the village church, a mile or so from the motorway, which at present peters out on the Altrincham land.

Looking from his library window, John said of the motorway: 'It'll affect the village, yes, it already has. From being far off the beaten track, suddenly we're right on it. In many ways it'll be a good thing. Motorways do less violence to landscapes than the railways, about which everyone's now so sentimental.'*

Peter Nichols, Diaries, 27 December 1969

* *Britain's motorway age had been ushered in just over a decade earlier, with the opening of the eight-and-a-half-mile-long Preston bypass on 5 December 1958.*

CHAPTER EIGHT

CRISIS, WHAT CRISIS?: 1970-1979

Rampant inflation reaching a peak of 28 per cent, man-made fibres, flared trousers, IRA bombs, racist skinhead thugs, spiky-haired punks, petrol shortages, power cuts, strikes, unemployment, an oil crisis (or two) and three-day working weeks: in such a summary, life in the 1970s might not sound much fun. And yet, a report by the New Economics Foundation in 2004 rated 1976 as 'Britain's best year ever' in terms of quality of life. One of its compilers, Professor Tim Jackson of Surrey University, argued that the country was both 'happier' and 'better off in the seventies', as there was 'less crime and lower energy consumption'. The gap between the richest and the poorest was also to reach its narrowest in the decade that gave us disco, David Bowie's finest albums, the Muppets and *Star Wars*, making Britain a more equal society than it has been since.

By then, Britain had its first woman as prime minister and its first IVF baby. Another highlight of the period was the rise of feminism and subsequent improvements to sexual equality, with the passing of the Equal Pay Act (1970) and the Domestic Violence and Matrimonial Proceedings Act (1976), both of which were long overdue modernizations that better reflected – and greatly improved – the status of women in the workplace and family life. And the first International Women's Day was staged in 1977.

At times turbulent – and in some places, no doubt, pretty grim – its years, as these witnesses attest, were spent as happily cooking ratatouille and acquiring a Kenwood mixer, as angrily ferreting under sinks for power cut candles and bemoaning the economy.

⸎

IN LIVING COLOUR

Through the coloured screens, we see Biafra surrender, Dubcek relieved of his post by the Soviets, Australian nickel shares boom and a late member of the Bristol Co-op. arrested for spying in East Germany.*

Peter Nichols, Diaries, 5 February 1970

* *The Wimbledon Tennis Championships, shown on BBC Two in July 1967, marked the beginning of colour television broadcasts in Britain. By December 1967, 80 per cent of BBC Two's programmes were shown in colour, and colour broadcasts began on BBC One on 15 November 1969.*

⸎

KAFKA-ESQUE DEPARTURES

The London Airport departure lounge is its usual impersonal 'self': large, sprawling and flabby like a deflated bladder. Only the lighting is telling. It annoys.

An attractive lounge attendant approaches Sam and myself. But Sam is already moving away towards the duty-free counter. The attendant comes up to me, and says something about my being the fiftieth traveller to enter the lounge, or the hundred-and-fiftieth to do so. I'm not really sure, and, 'Would you mind answering a few questions for an independent Airport survey we're carrying out among the passengers in the lounge?'

Pleasant but crisply firm, she asked my name, country of origin, passport, passport number, flight, destination, favourite type of commercial aircraft, et cetera.

I asked her to tell me a little about the purpose of the survey. She did so. It seemed harmless enough. Yet one's always prone to imagine Kafka hovering in the wings ...

Sam returned with a handsome boxed bottle of whisky and a carton of cigarettes. Looking at me quizzically, he said, 'Press catch you, boy! Wha' you tell her? You's a big Black Power celebrity?' ...

Andrew Salkey, *Georgetown Journal*, 15 February 1970

⌒*⌒*

UNSETTLING ENOCH

Looking round the cabin, at the fairly large number of Black passengers, Sam, still tugging the cuff of his shirt jack, remarked, 'Enoch Powell don' like all this, at all, sah. Look like more Black man than White man returnin' to him country, to settle.'

Andrew Salkey, *Georgetown Journal*, 2 March 1970

⌒*⌒*

CONSERVATIVES WIN

The confounding of opinion polls is some, but not much, consolation for the return of a Conservative government, including four old Etonians, a Scottish laird as Foreign Secretary and a hanging-flogging woman as Education Minister [Margaret Thatcher]. John Grigg, also fooled by the polls, spent much of an evening persuading Iris Murdoch and me that we'd been wrong to vote for Wilson.

He claims you may expect more from Heath, an essentially progressive man pretending to be a reactionary, than from Wilson, the polar opposite. Iris was voting, she said, on principle because any Labour government must represent social justice and fair shares better than one that is, by definition, on the side of the status quo ... Bailey's main concern is to save the party from degenerating into Fascism. Out of office, he said, he feared extremists would take over and force them to the right. But what we feared before the polls did happen and Powelites were put in everywhere ...

Peter Nichols, Diaries, 26 May 1970

~~

FAB FOUR SPLIT UPSET

10.30 p.m. I have just been watching an excerpt from the Beatles' latest film *Let it Be* on *Cinema*. Their music is superbly executed. It is sad that they have so failed their public.*

Brian Williams, Diaries, 25 June 1970

* *The Beatles publicly broke up in April 1970, when Paul McCartney announced that he was leaving the group. On 31 December of that year, McCartney sued to dissolve The Beatles as a legal entity; it took five years for the case to be resolved.*

~~

FAILING DUTCH CAPS

In the evening we went to Frank and Barbara, who talked about Dutch caps the whole time and Barbara went on about how either her Dutch cap* falls out in Sidney Street after going to her gynaecologist, or she can't get it out at all. Barbara's excellent for girl chat, however. Very honest. 'It's so nice being married, isn't it,' she said, 'I wouldn't change it for anything, going round with that awful For Sale sign round one's neck.'

Virginia Ironside, Diaries, 25 June 1970

* *Dutch caps, a barrier method of birth control, had been around for decades. The big development in contraceptives was, of course, the pill, which had been made available on the NHS from 1961, although only to married women until 1967.*

HIPPIES IN A FIELD

After lunch we went to the Bath Festival of Blues and Progressive Music held at the Bath and West Showground, Shepton Mallet. At midnight last night, the news bulletin stated that more than a quarter of a million young people were there. Traffic had come to a complete standstill …

I find it very difficult to record my impressions. The vast number of young people sitting, squatting, lying on the ground, a seething mass of dirty, dishevelled, bleary-eyed, spotty-faced, long-haired teenagers, looking for the most part utterly blank and indifferent. The squalor, the litter, the smell of dirty clothes and unwashed bodies, the primitive and utterly inadequate sanitation, the volume of the music (if such it can be called) which actually pained us as we picked our way through the sprawling bodies … I have often said that the hippies represent only a tiny fraction of our young people, but to see a quarter of a million of them … I have today witnessed the most depressing sight of my whole life. God help us. What are we coming to?

Brian Williams, Diaries, 28 June 1970

PASSING UP ON PEACE PIPES

The party was chiefly memorable, I suppose, for the steady consumption of pot in those chocolate cookies and cakes. I had one or two drags on a hash cigarette, but that passing-around of the fag of peace isn't really my 'scene'.

Lindsay Anderson, Diaries, 4 July 1970

✺

DEATH OF ROCK

Jimi Hendrix died when we were in Andover, which is sad because he was the most flamboyant and nicest on the pop scene. I interviewed him once and he was practically incomprehensible, partly because he mumbled, partly because our backgrounds were totally different, but all the same he was exceptionally polite and kind. I saw him when he was first brought over by Chas Chandler. He used to make love to his guitar on stage, play with his teeth and behind his back and finally burn it on stage.

And Janis Joplin died today with 14 hypodermic pricks in her arm. Interviewed her, too, but she was too terrifying (like Annie and me rolled together, cubed, drunk, on our very worst days).

Virginia Ironside, Diaries, 5 October 1970

✺

SIZING UP GERMAINE GREER

I forced Bertie to buy me a ginger cake, which he'd promised, and he told me of his job at Chiswick Tech until Robin came to go to Germaine Greer's *The Female Eunuch** party at Sonny and Gita's. A real blast from the past with Annie, Anthony and Johnny who was peculiarly difficult to talk to as ever, glaze-eyed and appearing to listen to nothing one said but talking all the same. Germaine Greer was looking rather shorter and more normal than usual; Annie says it's because midi-skirts make everyone look so tall and that's why she looked short, and certainly, pint-sized Annie looked quite lofty in her long dress.

Virginia Ironside, Diaries, 12 October 1970

* Greer's book, a bible to the emerging 'women's liberation' movement, was an instant bestseller. To date, it has never gone out of print.

~~

SQUASHES BY THE MILLION

The Kenwood Mixer arrived when I was in my dressing gown. A splendidly nice suburban housewife demonstrated it, impressing on me the lovely sweets I could make and how 'when the family came along' I'd find it invaluable for pureeing baby food. I could use the slicer and shredder for making my own potato crisps ('and at 7d a packet, you need to make your own these days'), I could peel 3lb of potatoes and keep them for weeks in the fridge, she said. I could make the most delicious cocktail drinks and summer fruit squashes and cakes by the million. Pity, of course, that it doesn't do joints. She had a special Kenwood Mixer Demonstrator language, too. Nothing was whisked or mixed or beaten; everything was 'creamed'. The glass holder on the liquidiser was referred to reverently as 'the goblet'. As Nick V. said, he couldn't imagine whether those terms were invented by straight-faced men in the Kenwood trade or giggling advertising men in Mayfair …

Virginia Ironside, Diaries, 30 October 1970

~~

AGED BY LONG-HAIRED LEARNERS

I visited the Library at LSE. Waiting below at the enquiry desk – the rough students with long hair and strange one-sex clothes make me feel old and vulnerable.

Barbara Pym, A Very Private Eye, 9 November 1970

HAIR-RAISING POWER CUTS

More power cuts and at work 2 secretaries went to have their hair done in the lunch hour and had to come back to work with their hair in rollers! In trouble at home again after waking everyone up as I'd forgotten my key. My angry Mum opened the front door to find me kneeling over the contents of my handbag on the doorstep (no moonlight, pitch black). I must have looked as if I was praying (I think I was), but she wasn't impressed and I may have to stay in and watch every episode of *The Partridge Family* on tele!*

Sally George, *Leaving Home in the 1970s*, 16 November 1970

* *By 1970 the majority of the UK's energy-generating power plants were fired by coal, and industrial action by miners affected the electricity network. To conserve resources, electricity was rationed, with power cut off at certain times of the day or week.*

⌇

PAKISTAN'S PLIGHT PLAYED FOR LAUGHS

Death toll of Pakistan's earthquake and tidal wave may reach a million if the expected epidemics follow. In Hampton's witty play *The Philanthropist*, a cynical novelist says that whenever he receives an appeal leaflet telling him he can save an Indian child for the price of a prawn cocktail, he goes straight out and orders a prawn cocktail. This gets a guilty laugh of recognition. The affluent world sends off its tanner on the collection plate, as it also sent a million sterling to Aberfan. And when this disaster's over, its dead counted and forgotten, the millions on the sub-continent will still be there, amid the horrors of Calcutta, messy relic of the East India Company's greed. *Plus ça change.*

Peter Nichols, Diaries, 22 November 1970

⌇

POWELL INTO POWER?

The papers are doing a lot of anxiety-making on the subject of Enoch Powell these days. People are beginning to say that inflation will bring the downfall of the present Conservative government, and that Enoch Powell will be voted into power as leader of a new National administration. There's some sour talk about the Weimar Republic and Hitler. Incredible!

David Pringle, Diaries, 23 November 1970

STRIKE A TORY

Today is the day of the national strike against the Tory government's proposed anti-trade union legislation. There are no newspapers, and repeated electricity failures. But the strike does not on the whole seem to be very extensive. The university is on strike, too – which means in effect that the artists are on strike, but the scientists are continuing work as normal. I'm supposed to attend a history seminar this afternoon, but I won't go to it.*

David Pringle, Diaries, 8 December 1970

* *Prime Minister Edward Heath's Industrial Relations Act, passed in 1971 under the supervision of Robert Carr, the Secretary of State for Employment, made ballots before strikes compulsory and ended union 'closed shop' agreements.*

UNDER-THE-COUNTER CANDLES

This morning we have wintry sun, and so far no absolute cuts, merely great reductions. The shops operate on few lights, 'patriotically', people compare their sufferings, ladies whisper over the counter, 'Any candles?' as if asking for dildos.

Frances Partridge, Diaries, 9 December 1970

TROUBLED BY THE NATIONAL FRONT

To raise one's eyes from one's own life and narrow field of experience is to feel depressed and impotent.

I raised my eyes this evening to respond to an invitation to appear on the platform of an Anti-Apartheid Society meeting at Central Hall.

The celebrity line-up in the first row included Huddleston (The Rev Trev), David Steel, Bernadette Devlin and Susannah York, the only showbiz representative I could see from my place in the raised seats behind which sat a mixed bag of invitees, black, white, cappuccino. We all faced an audience that filled four-fifths of the hall. While they assembled, I spotted several odd types, contemporary Cockney wide-boys, well dressed, expensive haircuts, thickset, with the sort of figures that come from regular workouts in gyms.

Huddleston was the first to speak, with a mild attack on Heath for supplying arms to South Africa. One or two catcalls came from the gallery, no more than you'd expect.

The chairman said that Miss Devlin would have no trouble controlling 'our friends from the National Front', a rash promise as, in fact, she found it quite impossible even to be heard.* The odds were certainly against her, as none of the three table-mikes worked well enough to raise her voice above the rhythmic chanting of 'Trait-or, trait-or', 'Stand by the whites' and 'Red scum out!' The gymnasium men were obviously a controlling claque and kept moving their hecklers about the hall to outwit the stewards, decent young men who hadn't the authority to evict them, only request them to play the game ...

An officer, a sergeant and a dozen constables appeared at the back but did nothing beyond making a show of strength. Heckling subsided briefly. The NF members had been corralled into one part of the gallery where stewards found it easier to localise each shouter. They were then asked to leave and if [they] didn't, police escorted [them] out ...

Peter Nichols, Diaries, 18 January 1971

* A far-right white nationalist political party, the National Front was founded in 1967 and rose to become Britain's fourth largest party by the mid 1970s. It regularly staged marches through areas like Southall, in West London, which were home to immigrants.

<hr>

HORROR OF SODOMY

I speak in the Tower Hamlets Deanery debate on homosexuality and am opposed by the evangelical vicar of Spitalfields, Eddy Stride, who has the air of a shop steward about him. His speech is dominated by the horror of sodomy, and he talks of 'the racked bodies' it produces, whatever that means. Lesbians must find this talk very odd. After the debate, Eddy's lady worker collared me and said, 'You'll be condoning sex with animals next.'

Rev. Dr Malcolm Johnson, *Diary of a Gay Priest*, 18 January 1971

<hr>

THE SOUL OF SOHO

In my quest for work I went to see Gerry of part-publication *Man and Woman*, a ghastly sex-series. He sits in a steaming room in Soho packed with terrible young men with tiny hips, straggly moustaches and wide 'sexy' belts made of old machine-gun bullet holders, with dead hair and bad teeth – and a selection of blousy girls in stained velvet maxi-skirts unbuttoned to the crutch and caterpillar boots with plunging necklines and purple lipstick. Put a little bit of straw on the ground and it would have been like the prison scene in some bawdy Elizabethan telly play.

Gerry turned out to be the most scruffy of the lot and produced a wad of sheets, all marked up in tiny squares showing the articles – all pencilled titles in his illiterate hand – Three in a Bed, Pre-Menstrual Tension, Can Your Husband be your Lover, Are you Frigid, Two's Company, but is Three a Crowd?, etc. etc. Dragging a dirty nail down these columns he paused, I am glad to say, at Are You A Good Friend?, which I immediately claimed as just my subject (for fear he'd give me Orgasm Over Eighty? instead), and shuffled out feeling distinctly tainted ...

Virginia Ironside, Diaries, 19 January 1971

FEWER LETTERS, MORE ARMS

In the broader world today, we are suffering a postal strike, the Americans seem to be stepping up their activities in Cambodia, there has been a right-wing coup in Uganda, Heath is back from Singapore adamant on selling arms to South Africa, Khrushchev's 'memoirs' are in the news, and Apollo 14 is due to blast off for the moon!

David Pringle, Diaries, 27 January 1971

STRIKES, STRIKES, STRIKES

The state of the world has not depressed and obsessed me so much since the war. And I find hardly anyone agrees with me that under Pigling Bland [Prime Minister Edward Heath] and his catastrophically stupid henchmen we're not heading for total disruption – strikes, strikes, strikes, and he does nothing to stop them but grow a few more double chins, go swimming and boating and burble about the 'British people' ...

Frances Partridge, Diaries, 4 February 1971

DECIMAL DAY

Decimal Day.* Today, not only our old currency but a small portion of our everyday language dies forever and is replaced ... Funnily enough, I find myself resenting the new decimal coinage far less than the postal codes (which I fear will one day replace towns with numbers – and after towns streets, and after streets …?), or the all-figure telephone numbers which dealt one mighty blow to local feeling in London and, in the process, made it practically impossible to remember phone numbers.

(Our own area code changed from GULliver to the soulless 485.)

Michael Palin, Diaries, 15 February 1971

* *The decision to replace Britain's centuries-old imperial currency of pounds, shillings and pence (where there were 12 pennies to the shilling and 20 shillings to the pound) was announced in 1966. In its stead would come a currency based on multiples of 10 or 100, where one pound was worth 100 new pence pieces. The planning for Decimal Day, 15 February 1971, took three years, including a period during which the 50p coin enjoyed life as a substitute for the old 10 shilling note.*

THE STONES SPOILED

Lynn was trying to get tickets for the Stones at the Roundhouse this evening but after initially thinking how much I wanted to go, I decided eventually not to as I don't want to see them spoilt. I don't want to see them being clapped after each number and not mobbed. I want to remember them in Liverpool with the mods in their funny little navy blue suits and short, cropped hair (girls) and the boys with their longish hair and sharp clothes, running towards the stage screaming 'Mick, Mick!' and … the compere screaming 'M.' and the yells of response 'I!' (screams) 'C!' 'K' 'MICK JAGGER!', his words drowned in screams and on to the stage screaming into the mike …

Virginia Ironside, Diaries, 14 March 1971

CUP FINAL IN COLOUR

A friend came with his son and daughter to watch the Cup Final on our new colour TV. We pulled the curtains on the bright afternoon, drank iced Pernod and watched Arsenal win. The boy, a Liverpool supporter, cried with grief.

Peter Nichols, Diaries, 8 May 1971

๛

FIXING BUGGERS

I hate Bernadette Devlin as much as I hate the Rev. Ian Paisley, if anything worse.* Now that she is to have an illegitimate baby and may be disowned by her beastly, pious Irish constituents, I find that I am pleased, and hope that they may chuck her out. Yet on principle I am all for sex freedom. In other words, I, like the rest of the hypocritical world, am ready to seize any stick with which to belabour somebody I dislike. That is why buggers are so vulnerable. The moment they get into a fix their enemies will round on them because they are buggers, and not because of the fix they have got into, which may be something quite venal.

James Lees-Milne, Diaries, 4 July 1971

* *Bernadette Devlin was an Irish Catholic Republican politician who, when elected to Parliament for Mid-Ulster in 1969, was Britain's youngest ever female MP, at the age of twenty-one. Paisley, MP for North Antrim who was then leader of the Democratic Unionist Party and one of the most uncompromising Protestant Unionists, was known for denouncing Catholicism and homosexuality in his sermons.*

๛

THE SOUND OF THE SUPER-SONIC JET

The scream of the jet-engine is nothing to the thud of the sonic boom, probably from Concorde, testing.* I was writing an angry reference to it into my play later, trying to recall its exact effect and had reached the 'p' of explosion when it came again, more than just a bang. You hear it before it arrives. Birds and animals are all disturbed and fly or career about.

Peter Nichols, Diaries, 17 August 1971

* The supersonic passenger jet with a distinctive 'dropping nose', the Anglo-French-produced Concorde aircraft went into commercial service from 1976 to 2003.

CRUSADING AGAINST PORNOGRAPHY

The anti-porn campaigners took Trafalgar Square for a 'Festival of Light' this afternoon. The same faces one saw at Billy Graham's crusades at Harringay Arena fifteen years ago – mostly plain or downright ugly people whom life (due to the insanely high valuation put by capitalism on physical attractiveness) had never invited to its party, but who found themselves bidden by the Rev. Billy to an eternal party in heaven.*

Kenneth Tynan, Diaries, 25 September 1971

* Billy Graham was an American evangelist who staged a series of Christian rallies around the world, holding one in London at the Harringay Arena in March 1954. The Festival of Light movement was a Christian organization that campaigned against what it saw as the excesses of the 'permissive society', and pornography and sexual content in the media in particular. Its most prominent supporters included the pop star Cliff Richard, the journalist Malcolm Muggeridge and Mary Whitehouse, a former teacher who spearheaded the 'Clean Up TV Campaign' in 1963.

'OLD WAR HATRED'

The Emperor of Japan is paying us an official visit. This has led to an outburst of old war hatred, and of people on the radio loudly patting themselves on the back for maintaining this hostility. 'I for one shall never forget, and never talk to a Japanese.' This ghastly racism is to be found now even among many civilised people, whether towards the Irish, Germans, Russians or Japanese. And how on earth can they say such things about the Japanese if they for one second remember what we did to them at Hiroshima? How can they talk smugly about forgiveness?

Frances Partridge, Diaries, 6 October 1971

‹✠›

POST OFFICE TOWER BOMBED

Off to hairdresser's at 10.30. Henry told me of the IRA bomb explosion at the Post Office Tower! This is terrible news. It is one of our finest buildings and a telegraph communications centre. I wish they'd get these filthy Irish thugs and shoot them all.

Kenneth Williams, Diaries, 1 November 1971

‹✠›

COMMON MARKET FOR BUSINESS

A public opinion poll shows that a majority of people think that entry into the Common Market will be good for Britain. Equally, a majority think it will be bad for themselves. Here is the paradox of this country in a nutshell – why cannot the people see that if entry is bad for the majority of them, it is by definition bad for England, since they are England. Instead, they cling to the belief that there is a separate abstract entity called 'the good of the country', in the name of which they are willing to abnegate themselves. So brilliantly they are hoodwinked that they fail to realise that, in this case as in so many others, 'the good of the country' equals 'the good of big business'.

Kenneth Tynan, Diaries, 8 November 1971

COLD WORLD

Read the Sunday papers – poisonous rivers, polluted seas, overpopulation – madness – kidney disease – liver flukes and their diabolical practices – the coming Revolution – incurable unemployment. From a warm room I look out on a cold world and wish for a companion.

[The] *Sunday Times* publishes the first of a series of get-fit exercises. Did half of them but gave up from laziness more than exhaustion.

Keith Vaughan, Journals, 30 January 1972

BLOODY SUNDAY

On Sunday, 13 civilians were shot dead by British troops in Derry. There has been much talk about this being 'Britain's Sharpeville', and Bernadette Devlin scratched the Home Secretary's face to make her protest felt. This afternoon, we Sussex students are to demonstrate outside the Army Recruitment Office in Brighton. Although it's raining, I'll go along to see if anything happens.

David Pringle, Diaries, 1 February 1972

007 NO MATCH FOR MINERS

Eric suggested that we all be very naughty and go to see *Diamonds Are Forever*, the latest of the James Bond films, at the Kensington Odeon. After brief and unconvincing heart-searching, we drive over to Kensington – but, alas, have not been in the cinema for more than 20 minutes when the film runs down. After a few minutes there is much clearing of throat, a small light appears in front of the stage and a manager appears to tell us that we are the victims of a power cut (this being the first day of the cuts following four weeks of government intractability in the face of the miners' claim). For half an hour there is a brief, British moment of solidarity amongst the beleaguered cinemagoers, but as we were shirking work, anyway, it looked like a shaft of reprobation from the Great Writer in the sky.

Michael Palin, Diaries, 10 February 1972

ᴄᴍᴄ

ALL CHANGE AT THE ABC

The ABC cafe in Fleet St, opposite the Law Courts – new but ever old. The new names (The Light Bite), the smart orange and olive green and beige and stripped pine decor, the hanging lamps, the new green crockery – but inside the food is the same, the little woman cooking, the West Indian lady serving tea, the nice, bright, efficient lady at the cash desk. You might quote Cavafy's poem about finding a new city, yet everything being the same, meaning oneself sitting there brooding.

Barbara Pym, A Very Private Eye, 20 March 1972

ᴄᴍᴄ

SAVILE'S TRAVELS

Jimmy Savile is an odd one. I spent the evening with him recording *Savile's Travels* from County Hall. It was like being with the Mad Hatter. He didn't stop talking, but none of it quite made sense. He's weird, but I think he means well.*

Gyles Brandreth, *Something Sensational to Read in the Train*, 27 March 1972

At the time of his death in 2011, the former Radio One disc jockey Jimmy Savile was widely mourned as a popular entertainer, known for his charity work, friendships with Margaret Thatcher and Prince Charles, and trademark tracksuits, heavy jewellery and cigars. A year later, he was exposed as a predatory paedophile who had sexually assaulted hundreds of women and children over the course of half a century.

ᴄᴍᴄ

BIG ON BEANS AT BICKERSHAW

Sunlight coming through the tent door. Goat woke up first and confided to me she'd dreamt of a giant hamburger in a Nazi helmet chasing her down Battersea High Street. Pilgrim, whose vegan diet was big on beans, was waking with a series of mild rippling farts, muffled, luckily, by his sleeping-bag. Easing his pale, spidery legs outside the bag, he yawned, stretched and assumed the yoga posture known as the Standing Crane.

We made ourselves some tea on one of the small Calor gas burners and got ready for the hungry hippies – or freaks, as they like to call themselves now – who are lining up outside with their rallying cry of 'Twenty-pee? It's a rip-off!' My stew is bubbling on, but the beans are rock hard – I'm getting worried.

Joan Wyndham, *Anything Once*, 13 May 1972

⌒∦⌒

MUNICH MASSACRE

Jewish hostages had been taken by Arab terrorists at Munich's Olympic Games. Jack Gold had had a bad morning, as his brother-in-law is the team doctor and he'd spent two hours trying to phone Germany to discover that he wasn't among the dead.*

Peter Nichols, Diaries, 5 September 1972

* *Early on 5 September eight Palestinians from the militant group Black September gained entry to the Olympic Village in Munich, and stormed the apartments occupied by the Israeli team. Two people were killed and the remaining athletes were taken hostage. In exchange for their lives, the terrorists demanded the release of 200 Arabs imprisoned by Israel and safe passage out of Germany for themselves. A rescue mission went badly wrong and all nine of the Israeli Olympians perished at the hands of the terrorists.*

RINGS RETURNED

When you are miserable with someone and miserable without them, what do you do? We agreed tearfully that it could not go on and met for one last time at the bus stop so I could give him back his book, *Lord of the Rings*, which I never did finish, and after 2 years it seemed so final. Just as the bus was about to go, I walked away into Chelsea Girl boutique, then turned to see him. He looked so unhappy.

Sally George, *Leaving Home in the 1970s*, 23 October 1972

∽

AN OUTRAGEOUS WINNER

Dinner with John Berger, who last week outraged the polite literary world by accepting the £5,000 Booker McConnell prize for the best novel of the year (*G*) and announcing that he would use half of it to finance his new book about the migrant workers of Europe and give the other half to the Black Panther movement, because of the exploitation of black labour by Booker McConnell in Guyana.

Kenneth Tynan, Diaries, 7 December 1972

∽

BRITAIN INTO EUROPE

Howard Hughes fled the Nicaraguan earthquake, but let into England without a passport and put up in a penthouse suite on Park Lane. If he exists, he's an insane miser and good example of why capitalism is rotten. At least we could save such people from themselves by the painful but beneficial surgery of cutting off their dividends.

Britain went into Europe. Nixon stepped up the bombing. Distillers company fought hard not to pay compensation to the children crippled by thalidomide. Greenwich Park is open to cars again.

Peter Nichols, Diaries, 1 January 1973

LESS HOSTILE VIETNAM

The news today was of a ceasefire in Vietnam; Kissinger and Le Doc Tho grinning and waving for the cameras. Casualty figures for the whole war are still provisional, as the coming of peace prompted last-minute Vietcong land-grabbing attacks to gain ground before the treaties could draw a line.

Peter Nichols, Diaries, 24 January 1973

⤳

STRIKES HIT HOSPITALS

The end of the latest wage-freeze, that right-wing remedy for every social disorder, has brought a relapse into strikes of all kinds. Hospital porters and orderlies are out, leaving piles of soiled laundry to be destroyed for fear of infection. Maternity, child and geriatric services are worst affected. Patsy asked Thelma if she'd mind doing some bed-linen for Lewisham hospital. My dear wife said staunchly she wouldn't touch it, and not out of fastidiousness. Here were some of the worst-paid groups of people doing filthy work on which the nation's health depends, using their only weapon (withholding labour) to draw attention to themselves. She, a shop-steward's daughter, was being asked to break their strike.

Other trades are out, too – gas workers, teachers and train drivers. Are they to be morally blackmailed because they do essential jobs? The Christian ethic that consoled the oppressed and enabled the oppression to continue has at last been shown the door.

Peter Nichols, Diaries, 8 March 1973

⤳

HOTTEST POP PROPERTY

Went to bed. Could not get to sleep, owing to [the] presence of David Bowie and his acolytes in the hotel. Bowie is currently the hottest touring property in Britain, having recently played to 18,000 in Earls Court. Tonight, Bowie was in Edinburgh – and staying a couple of doors down ... They weren't exactly noisy, there was just so many of them. From 2 a.m. to 3 a.m. and beyond it was like trying to sleep through the invasion of Poland.

Michael Palin, Diaries, 19 May 1973

ഗ⁄ⅉⅇ

AN INDIGESTIBLE NEW NOVEL

I got the Ballard novel [*Crash*] on publication day (last Thursday). The book turned out to be 224 pages long, [and] the exclamation mark has been dropped from the title ... I have just finished reading the novel this evening. It has taken me five days, partly because I have been short on time and partly because it is heavy-going and wearily repetitive in parts. I don't know what to say. I feel rather shattered – not because the book is insipid, it certainly isn't that, nor because I morally disapprove of it, although I can see that a lot of people will. Rather, I am shocked by its narrow, obsessive and repetitive tone. The novel fails to expand outwards as I had hoped it would; it is about the car crash and nothing but the car crash. It contains some powerful writing embedded in more flaccid passages. The LSD scenes towards the end are particularly well described, so I do not think that Ballard has lost his literary gifts. However, he may have made a mistake. I shall say no more about it just now and let the book sink into my mind rather more. It's certainly a hard lump to digest.*

David Pringle, Diaries, 3 July 1973

---

* *Containing characters who were sexually aroused by car crashes, Ballard's bold and transgressive novel was widely condemned on publication.*

HARMLESS ENTERTAINMENTS

The knocking of Longford continues. To my relief. It is obvious that society is not going to try once more and ban pornography ...

As a middle-aged, homosexually orientated pervert, obliged through personal inhibitions and timidity, to content himself with an exclusively imaginary sex life, the availability of porn is the greatest benefit to my well-being and mental health, as well as affording me hours of harmless sexual enjoyment.

Keith Vaughan, Journals, 29 September 1973

DYING ELMS

Drove to meet the 6.30 train at Kemble this evening, to pick up Pat Trevor-Roper. As I turned off the Cirencester road, the sun was setting below a bank of rising mist, throwing upon the twilit sky a pinky primrose light. Against this backcloth a row of elms, their feet in the swirl of mist, their arms drooping against the skies, looked tranquil and serene as though they might endure for ever in this setting, a promise that England would remain as I had best loved it. Whereas, of course, it is a miracle that the row of elms has survived, and doubtless by next year these divine trees will be dead. The disease has not yet exterminated every elm in this part of Gloucestershire, as it already has in Worcestershire.* This morning, Alastair Finlinson showed me what happened to the elm. On Fry's land by Wotton, he tore the bark from a dead elm. It came off like parchment. Underneath, the bole was covered with a film of sticky white foam, like castor sugar. This is the fungus that the beetle brings. The fungus throttles the tree so that it cannot breathe.

James Lees-Milne, Diaries, 27 October 1973

---

* *A fungal illness spread by a bark beetle, Dutch elm disease first appeared in Britain in the 1920s. However, a far more virulent strain arrived from North America in the late 1960s, and by the 1970s millions of elm trees were attacked and many died.*

RANSOM REFUSED

Paul Getty III, grandson of the richest man in the world, was kidnapped last July in Italy. A ransom of £1,000,000 was demanded; Grandpa, who has roughly 1,000 million dollars, has refused to pay a cent. The seventeen-year-old boy's parents, who are divorced, did nothing. Last week, his ear was sent through the post to his mother. We now learn that Grandpa is still holding out, maintaining that to pay up would constitute a precedent. The kidnappers have threatened to send one of the boy's feet next.*

Kenneth Tynan, Diaries, 18 November 1973

Getty was sixteen at the time of his abduction and, having been expelled from his private school, was living a Bohemian existence in Rome. Investigators initially suspected the kidnap was a ruse by the young Getty to squeeze some money out of his notoriously tight-fisted relatives, but the kidnappers turned out to be Calabrian bandits with connections to organized crime. He was released on 15 December 1973 after a ransom of around 3 million dollars was paid.

LOW ON ENERGY

I tried 6 garages but no petrol! Went to work on the bus to conserve what little I have. No heating or lighting at work but we were told to work harder and faster to keep warm! Charming, I'm sure! …

Sally George, *Leaving Home in the 1970s*, 2 December 1973

THE THREE-DAY WEEK

Heard that the government is to introduce a 3-day working week* in order to meet the fuel crisis! Apparently, everyone will lose wages in the process! And it applies to everything! Banks, offices, shops, factories etc. etc. It's all mad 'cos obviously, you can't do it generally – with the obvious example of hospitals, say – and it is going to result in some glaring anomalies. The news becomes more depressing every day as we watch democracy simper itself off the bill.

Kenneth Williams, Diaries, 13 December 1973

In an attempt to control inflation, Prime Minister Edward Heath's government passed a series of measures to restrict wage increases throughout 1973; workers responded by staging a number of strikes over the summer. But with the economy reeling from the Organization of Arab Petroleum Exporting Countries oil crisis and the potential of an all-out national miners' strike, Heath declared a state of emergency and the three-day, fuel-saving week.

✤

NEW YEAR, NEW DAY

It is the first time in my life that this day has been a national holiday. The only papers were the evening ones! It is little short of scandalous.

Kenneth Williams, Diaries, 1 January 1974

✤

TV CURFEW ENDS

We now have a miners' strike (starting today) and a General Election (on 28th of this month)! The TV curfew has been lifted so that the major parties can increase the flow of their propaganda.

David Pringle, Diaries, 10 February 1974

✤

ABBA UNKNOWN

Collier has bought *Waterloo*, which he tells me is number one in the charts by Abba, Eurovision Song Contest winners. Who? Radio Two beckons for me, clearly. Joni Mitchell's *Blue* and fish and chips from the local is what passes the evening at 17, Gillotts Close. The Bloomsbury Set reincarnated in Bingham.

David McVay, *Diary of a Football Nobody*, 9 April 1974

BORROWED FINERY

School dragged today. I think it was the hot weather and the thought that for the first time ever my mum was letting me go out with my sisters ... Marcia is letting me wear her old smock dress with matching hot pants and Debbie is letting me wear her old platforms from Chelsea Cobblers! I think the reason they have lent me their clothes is because they don't want me to show them up by wearing my out-of-date ones.

Millie Murray, Diaries, 14 June 1974

A WORLD CUP DIET

The summer diet that began a fortnight ago has not been going to plan. The crisps and chocolate biscuits have disappeared but the pints of beer have not. Worth a drink tonight, though, because Denis Law played in his first, and probably last, game in the World Cup finals.* Scotland beat Zaire 2–0.

David McVay, *Diary of a Football Nobody*, 14 June 1974

* *Eight years after winning the tournament, the English national side failed to qualify for the 1974 World Cup held in West Germany.*

THE REGGAE GROOVE

Six of us went out to the football dance, held in Forest Gate at the Eagle and Child pub. Marcia stopped moaning after a while and by the time we set off I was really excited. It was packed out with people and for the first hour all I was worried about was that I had enough hairpins holding down my false afro puffs. I kept having terrible thoughts that one would drop off, and the whole world (well, the pub) would see the real state of my hair. Shame! Thank goodness nothing bad like that did happen and I … let myself get into the groove of the reggae beat.

Millie Murray, Diaries, 16 June 1974

*

WATERGATE COMPLEX

One of the most satisfying copies of the *Guardian* that has ever come through my letterbox swished onto the mat at 8.00 this morning, bearing front-page news of Nixon's admission that he knew about the Watergate cover-up and personally directed it within five days of the incident.*

Michael Palin, Diaries, 6 August 1974

* *Watergate has become a byword for political malfeasance. The scandal began with the arrest of burglars inside the offices of the Democratic National Committee in the Watergate complex in Washington DC in 1972. The investigation ultimately uncovered a conspiracy to cover up a plethora of bribes and illegal wire-tapping operations, and led to President Richard Nixon's disgrace and resignation.*

*

LORD LUCAN ON THE RUN

Last week, Lord Lucan, a millionaire gambler, murdered his children's nanny, mistaking her in a darkened house for his estranged wife, and then bashed his wife over the head several times with a length of lead piping. What has happened since then is a perfect illustration of the influence of class on British justice. Firstly, four days passed before the police issued a warrant for Lucan's arrest. (British justice hates to put a nobleman in the dock. And British citizens have a similar reluctance to believe a nobleman capable of violent crime. Kathleen admitted that when she first read about the case she assumed that Lucan must have been insane – a conclusion she would never have jumped to had he been called Ginger Noakes and lived in Streatham.) Thus, Lucan had ample time to leave the country if he chose.

Most significantly of all: newspapers and TV shows are full of interviews with Lucan's aristocratic chums, all testifying what an honourable man he is and how unthinkable it is that he should have committed murder* …

Kenneth Tynan, Diaries, 14 November 1974

*An inquest jury concluded in 1975 that Lucan had murdered Sandra Rivet, but he never faced justice. Over the years he was supposedly sighted in India, Australia, Africa and South America; it was also rumoured that he committed suicide and his remains were fed to tigers at his friend John Aspinall's zoo. He was declared dead in 1999, and a death certificate was issued in 2016, allowing his son to inherit the family title.

BIRMINGHAM PUBS BOMBED

The depressing pattern of grey skies, rain and dark days is matched only by the news. In Tunis, Arab guerrillas select an unarmed businessman from a plane they have hijacked and, merely to hurry up the business of forcing the release of six of their murdering compatriots, stand the man in the doorway of the plane and shoot him in the back. This evening, there are two explosions in Birmingham pubs. Seventeen people are killed. An Irish voice gave an 11-minute warning, but so far the Provisionals have not claimed responsibility.

Michael Palin, Diaries, 22 November 1974

YES OR NO TO EUROPE

The referendum Yes or No to Europe. We're so far in now, saying 'no' would be like ringing a doorbell and running away. For which reason alone it would be worth it to see Shifty Wilson's pipe twitching as he thought out his next trick.

I live near the Dover road and certainly don't want any more Italian container trucks bringing another load of fold-up bicycles that no one will ever ride because the streets are crammed with Italian container trucks bringing another load of ...

If that's the sort of benefit we gain from joining, we're better off being a fifth-rate power.

The vote went 2–1 for staying in.

Peter Nichols, Diaries, 5 January 1975

◈

THATCHER GOOD FOR LABOUR

Elizabeth said to me, 'Have you heard the news? Mrs Thatcher has walked it.' I have had a growing conviction that this would happen: she is so clearly the best man among them, and she will, in my view, have an enormous advantage in being a woman, too. I can't help feel a thrill, even though I believe her election will make things much more difficult for us. I have been saying for a long time this country is ready – even more than ready – for a woman Prime Minister. The 'it's time for change from the male sex' version of the old election slogan. After all, men have been running the show as long as anyone can remember and they don't seem to have made much of a job of it. The excitement of switching to a woman might stir a lot of people out of their lethargy. I think it will be a good thing for the Labour Party, too.

Barbara Castle, Diaries, 11 February 1975

◈

BLITZ SPIRIT OF THE NHS

Am in Brompton Hospital for a week of lung-function tests to see how my emphysema's progressing. (Answer: no deterioration, but, of course, no improvement either.) Sharing a National Health ward with five other victims, I'm overwhelmed once again by the efficient courtesy of the doctor, the patient niceness of the (mainly Filipino, black or Irish) nurses, the sheer indispensability of the NHS; for all its faults, what an advertisement for socialism. Atmosphere in the ward one of uneasy conviviality, each man privately seeking evidence to support his necessary conviction that he is less mortally stricken than any of the others. But the camaraderie is genuine: being in this kind of ward is like being in an air-raid shelter during the Blitz.

Kenneth Tynan, Diaries, 7 March 1975

SYMBOLIC DEMONSTRATIONS

Got up early to hand out leaflets at the Angel about [the] National Front demonstration. The Littlejohns were there, too. I quite enjoyed it and felt a glow of righteousness afterwards. Because we'd got up early, I felt rather sleepy ...

Worked some more until A came home. We had a drink and mushrooms on toast and then Gaby called and we went up to the Town Hall for the demo.

Marguerite was there. As was B – very offhand. We waited ages behind a triple phalanx of police and after the NF had marched past with their Union Jacks, B. A. and I hurried down Upper Street to go to the *Red Rag* meeting.* The whole demonstration was entirely symbolic, because there was the NF further down with a drum shouting, 'We've gotta get rid of the Reds,' while all of us had been left stranded at the Town Hall.

Reached *Red Rag* for the end of the meeting. Not too bad – lots of articles, which should be good. The issue won't be out by May 1, but shouldn't be delayed too long ... Tony came home late with some weedy guy he'd picked up at a disco.

Elizabeth Wilson, Diaries, 25 March 1975

* Set up in 1972 by a Marxist feminist collective, Red Rag *was a monthly magazine whose contributors were exclusively women.*

SCREAMING TEENS IN THE RAIN

Teeming rain for last day of rehearsal at the White City Studios.

At the gates of TV Centre, groups of sad girls like clowns waited for the Bay City Rollers, screaming tentatively at the arrival of every vehicle.

Peter Nichols, Diaries, 26 March 1975

GIVING EUROPE A WHIRL

Cast my vote in the Referendum. I voted 'Yes' because I was not, in the end, convinced that the retention of our full sovereignty and the total freedom to make our own decisions, which was the cornerstone of the Noes' case, was jeopardised seriously enough by entering the Market. And I feel that the grey men of Brussels are no worse than the grey men of Whitehall, anyway. But I didn't decide on my vote until this morning, when I read the words of one of my favourite gurus, Keith Waterhouse ... 'I may be naive in hoping that remaining in Europe makes us more European, but after a thousand years of insularity from which we have evolved the bingo parlour, carbonised beer and *Crossroads*, I am inclined to give it a whirl.'

Michael Palin, Diaries, 5 June 1975

⁓

STEAK SUPPER A SUCCESS

Decided that, as the way to a man's heart is through his stomach, I will cook a few meals for Edward on his last weekend here. I will go to the Library and get some books on easy cooking to impress! Going on my recent track record it might be better to get a takeaway in and pass it off as 'home-cooked'. Anyway, I successfully (and with the confidence not to poison anyone) cooked us steak and chips for tea tonight and then we walked in the warm evening breeze to The Claude. They had no beer or lager due to a brewers' strike.

Sally George, *Leaving Home in the 1970s*, 7 June 1975

⁓

A MARCH IN SUPPORT OF LEGALIZED ABORTIONS

A very fine day. I dressed up for the abortion march, long white skirt and cream shirt and silk shawl tied round my hips and put my hair up. Felt I looked rather fine.

We drove down to Charing Cross in the Dutch women's car. Chaotic crowds – thousands and thousands of people. A. & I marched with the Islington Libertarians, not the CP [Communist Party]. The march was beautiful and absolutely huge, like a festival in the wonderful sunshine ...

Elizabeth Wilson, Diaries, 21 June 1975

BACK TO THE FIFTIES

Graffiti – TORIES WANT WAR. Worrying thing about Thatcher is that she has that blind belief/certainty about her own rectitude that may attract plenty of followers. Certainly, in an age of impossibility of (real) certainty. Back to the golf club image – in effect the 50s.

Jon Savage, Diaries, 4 October 1975

THE WHO A KNOCK-OUT

Day three of working for Keith Altham. We are in a single room in Winchester Walk in Victoria with three telephones that never stop ringing ... Keith has perhaps twenty of the biggest groups of the moment on his books, including The Who.

Tonight they were playing the Empire Pool. Keith asked me to arrange 'the press trip' ...

Gingerly, I picked up the receiver and began dialling, unsure of what Keith expected me to do. Detailed instructions, I am coming to understand, are not his style. Also, this didn't seem quite the right moment to tell him that I hadn't got a clue what a press trip *was*, let alone how to organise one.

I suggested we all meet at Oxford Circus tube station at 6 p.m., figuring that was the quickest way to get to Wembley. It's how I would have gone there myself, ordinarily. I arrived at the appointed hour and so did fifteen of Fleet Street's finest rock journalists. Their expressions, which had ranged from the cooly expectant to already quite put out, darkened considerably, however, when I led them down into the tube station, through the barriers and down the escalator on to the platform. It was rush hour, everyone was crammed in like sardines.

This, evidently, was not the means by which they had grown accustomed to being conveyed to gigs by K. A. Publicity ... By the time we reached Wembley Park tube the atmosphere was souring. I needed to pull something out of the bag and quick. Getting out of the station and heading for the Empire Pool, inspiration struck. I suggested an exclusive backstage interview with The Who. Someone even smiled. Though most of them continued to look pretty pissed off, it must be said ... With the writers trailing despondently behind me and after a few wrong turns, I eventually reached the door of The Who's dressing room. Tentatively, I gave it a knock. The door opened. 'Hello, I am Alan Edwards from Keith Altham's office and I've brought some journalists along to meet ...' Before I could finish my sentence, the words 'Fuck off' were yelled and the door slammed ...

I brazened it out and gave the door another knock, this time with more conviction. As it opened I saw Keith Moon fly halfway across the room after being punched out by another member of the band. Before I could work out who'd delivered this stunning blow, someone again bellowed 'Fuck Off' and the door slammed shut ... As we made our way back into the arena, Judith Simons thanked me for giving them a fight to write about. All good publicity, she assured me ...

Alan Edwards, Diaries, 21 October 1975

NO LONGER OF THIS WORLD

General Franco* died at last after being kept alive for so long and in *The Times* I saw dear [novelist] Elizabeth Taylor died yesterday.

Barbara Pym, *A Very Private Eye*, 20 November 1975

* Appointed generalísimo of Nationalist Spain and head of state after the civil war in 1936, Francisco Franco ruled as a dictator for thirty-six years, until his death aged eighty-two.

A SURPRISE RESIGNATION

Most surprising news at midday that Wilson has resigned ... I watched Wilson on the box saying how wonderful he was and had been, and various experts trying to guess what next.

Lavinia Mynors, Diaries, 16 March 1976

POLITICIANS SHOWING THEIR TEETH

I was looking at the *Guardian* in between appointments this morning. What struck my fancy were two pictures: one of Callaghan and Harold Wilson. Both are smiling and showing their teeth. On the back page is another photograph of Ted Heath and he is showing his teeth, smiling famously, as are the other two. These photographs tell a tale. Modern politicians or statesmen are always photographed now as happy, smiling, teeth-showing individuals.

If one looks at photographs of statesmen forty years ago, the practice of smiling and showing one's teeth was not normal. There is something synthetic in the photographs of the average politician today … Ted Heath, who was regarded as an inflexible person but an interesting and nice one by those who knew him, is not any more interesting because he shows teeth in good order.

Paul Martin, Diaries, 29 April 1976

ℳ

GEORGE DAVIS IS INNOCENT

George Davis has been released from prison by Roy Jenkins. I feel a surge of pure delight at the news, which seems to indicate that there is a point to campaigning and demonstrating in a good cause and that the good chaps do occasionally win.*

Kenneth Tynan, Diaries, 11 May 1976

---

* In 1974 Davis had been sentenced to twenty years in prison for his part in an armed robbery on payroll at the London Electricity Board in Ilford, Essex. Although he had previous convictions for handling stolen goods, Davis always claimed he was innocent. Graffiti announcing 'George Davis is innocent' appeared all over the country, and his supporters disrupted an Ashes England vs Australia match at Headingley in 1975 by vandalizing the wicket. After his evidence was reviewed, Davis was released on the ground that forensics did not prove his presence at the scene of the crime. Only eighteen months after his release, however, he was caught robbing the Bank of Cyprus in Holloway, North London, and sent down for fifteen years.

THE LONG, HOT SUMMER

Heatwave continuing. Whole country parched, and trees dying. Found E. naked but for a pair of long blue shorts, with white skin, smarmed hair (for he had just had a bath), flabby muscles, pendulous breasts, looking like Picasso aged 90. How can aesthetic persons bear to be seen in this condition at seventy-four even by their intimates?

James Lees-Milne, Diaries, 7 July 1976

DRY SPELL FOR WALES

I was in Tesco's, grocery shopping, which was heavy and the day was hot! I went to the hairdresser's on the way home as the water rationing from tomorrow means the water will be cut off from 2 p.m. and not on again until 7 a.m. the next day. I don't know how Vi keeps a hairdressing business going. I did notice she had a few gallon containers full of water in the salon. I never thought I would say this in Cardiff, but I wish it would rain!

Sally George, Leaving Home in the 1970s, 19 August 1976

WEST INDIES TRIUMPH

Two days ago I went to Lord's for what (in my present state of health) I seriously feel may be the last time. A one-day match between the invincibly brilliant West Indies team (Richards destroying our bowlers, Roberts destroying our batsmen) and England. Rain and wind at first, then grey cloud, and at last sun, a typically wayward British summer's day, quite untypical of this steaming summer. How I shall miss Lord's on days like this! The green pitch shaded with porridge-grey cloud; the stick figures in white loping and trotting and diving; the occasional fierce leather crack and the sputter of applause. The patience of the game! I love the way it brings together so many kinds of human knowledge – of the weather and its vagaries, of the behaviour of turf and the earth beneath it, of human temperaments under stress, of human reflexes and their preferences, of time and how to use its passing.

Kenneth Tynan, Diaries, 30 August 1976

LOOKING GOOD AHEAD

I took Charles Williams out to lunch. He said that it was evolution that we were going through not revolution. The next three years were crucial. From 1980 to 1990 would be OK because of North Sea oil but what worried him was post-1990, by which time I would be fifty-five.

The look for men changes: ears show, hair is shorter and straighter, suits are in, so is the well-turned-out look. Velvet is out, velvet bow-ties are out. The look is now precise. I have just bought a new evening suit which is plain, well cut, but with no frills or velvet.

Sir Roy Strong, Diaries, 14 September 1976

ROCK DREAMS

Halfway through listening to *Physical Graffiti* by Led Zeppelin this evening I suddenly thought, 'I'm going to play the electric guitar and be in a rock group.' So I'm going to teach myself to play on Adrian's old little guitar and then we'll see! ...

Debsey Wykes, Diaries. 14 September 1976

THE ANTI-MUSIC

A boy called Richard Smith ... invited us to go on to the ICA to 'an evening of prostitution' with Genesis P. Orridge and Coum Transmissions. I hadn't heard of any of the people that were supposed to be on and was confused and thought it was the rock group Genesis ...

The exhibits were things like used tampaxes and pictures of people with blood coming out of them, Nazi insignia, et cetera. I was only mildly surprised to see the tampaxes because only the week before there had been an exhibition of babies' nappies on at the ICA (used) ...

I suppose they're Cosi Fanni Tutti's tampaxes; this moronic-looking girl who was looking rather embarrassed as she 'played' a guitar with her tits out. They were making the most indescribably cacophonous racket with their instruments, apparently deliberately; they were being anti-music or something.

I talked to this normal-looking boy called Paul Buck, who apparently is a complete maniac. He told me that he was writing lyrics for Coum Transmissions, he said that Orridge had been singing songs about Ian Brady and Myra Hindley earlier. I hadn't realised, the lyrics were incomprehensible ... I asked him what he thought of the Sex Pistols and he said he thought they were getting too good, he said, that now they were learning to play their instruments ...

Mary Killen, Diaries, 18 October 1976

⁓

GLASSES FLY AT CLASH CONCERT

Out of bed with the 'flu to see the Clash again. I know now that that song is called 'White Riot' and that it's 'about' the carnival riot. I understand. They play it two or three times to an abusive audience, a few fans and my tape recorder. At the end, not of a set but a set-to, the singer jumps off stage with a helper, who has been lurching with speed-brimmed eyes just a bit too close, and runs through the dispersing crowd to hurl himself at two long-hairs responsible for the heckling and the flying glasses. The crowd clears and circles. A messy, inconclusive fight starts among the beer-slops on the floor. People watch, hollow eyes: the PA plays the Stooges' vicious, vacant 'No Fun'. Everything fuses together.

Jon Savage, Diaries, 5 November 1976

FLAT-PACKED FURNITURE

The neighbourhood where we live is proving to be quite multicultural. Loud reggae on one side and strong curry smells from the terraced housing on the other.

This weekend, Steve went to Sparkbrook to buy some timber to make a centre unit for the living room instead of the conventional 'three-piece suite'. After much consultation of the [Habitat] House Book, he enthusiastically set to work and I thought I would do the same with my flat-packed rocking chair. I was struggling and thought I would need a saw until it was pointed out to me that I had got the seat on back to front!

Sally George, *Leaving Home in the 1970s*, 30 January 1977

BUZZCOCKS, LOUD AND CLEAR

Four bands into the punkathon, numb-out. All the better that the Buzzcocks are so good. They sing and play because they have something to say. It isn't particularly high-flown, brief jottings of everyday small incidents of boredom, frustration and despair, as the supermarkets and the motorways spread. Their image/music mesh is good too – the flat Mancunian accent and laconic dryness fitting the lyrics and cheap-as-a-siren guitar sound.

Jon Savage, Diaries, 16 February 1977

๛

SILVER JUBILEE

Everything seems utterly bleak to me and all these Jubilee celebrations malapropos; in a time of economic recession, the Queen should have set an example of austerity; thousands of pounds wasted on processions and bonfires, which could have been used for better purposes.

Went into Louie at 10.30 to see the impressive state procession from the palace to St Paul's. It was superbly stage-managed and the crowd ecstatically enthusiastic for the Queen. She did a walkabout afterwards, thro' the City to Guildhall, and her good-humoured composure & painstaking consideration for the spectators was extraordinarily moving. We opened a bottle of champagne & had lunch, watching the glittering spectacle on television.

Kenneth Williams, Diaries, 7 June 1977

๛

UNEMPLOYMENT SOARS

The highest total number of unemployed since 1948, when records were first kept, is given today at 1,336,700. This caused Mrs Thatcher in the House of Commons yesterday to tell the Prime Minister that this was the worst unemployment statistic since the thirties. Jim, nevertheless, said his economic policies were succeeding. He is heartened, I suspect, by reports, which I have heard, that the Liberal members have decided to renew their pact with the government.

Paul Martin, Diaries, 27 July 1977

THE KING IS DEAD

Elvis Presley has died at Graceland, his mansion in Memphis, Tennessee. He was 42. It is not clear whether it was drink, drugs, tranquillisers, or what, but it's a sad end to a life that, in its way, shook the world. Literally.

I imagine Showaddywaddy and the Sex Pistols will now take a back seat to make way for an Elvis revival.*

Gyles Brandreth, *Something Sensational to Read in the Train*, 16 August 1977

An estimated 20 million Elvis records were sold on the day after his death, and his recording of 'Way Down' went to No. 1 in the UK charts.

⤳

MATURE MANAGEMENT OF POWER CUTS

A power cut for about 2½ hours, 6.30–9 p.m. Supper was gin and tonic and boiled eggs and toast done on the fire. The old cope better than the young on these occasions, especially in a village.

Barbara Pym, *A Very Private Eye*, 4 November 1977

⤳

CLASHING CONCERNS

I rang the manager of The Clash, a political punk rock group, because there had been a suggestion from the BBC Television Community Unit that I have a four-minute discussion with the group. I have grave doubts about a Cabinet Minister appearing with a punk rock group, given what the media would make of it, and he agreed that four minutes was not enough for a serious discussion. But what he said was interesting. The Clash are apparently very popular with working-class youngsters who don't find anything in our popular culture that meets their needs or reflects their feelings. He told me the group were not really concerned with being commercial and refused a lot of television because it put them into an artificial setting when they were really a live group. They are popular in Sweden, France and Yugoslavia. He said that to get any attention at all you had to be absolutely bizarre, but to try to understand what The Clash were trying to say you had to work really hard because the lyrics were in pidgin French.

Tony Benn, Diaries, 28 December 1977

⌒✐⌒

HIGH-TECH CALCULATIONS

Had a night out at the cinema to see Woody Allen's film *Annie Hall*. The car has broken down twice and the car battery is permanently on charge in the flat. I was sent on a training morning to learn how to use the Kalle Infotec machine – it has a console and stores things and calculates and has quite a few coloured lights! Lack of money has prevented evenings out so we stayed in and watched TV – *Top of the Pops* and *The Good Life*.

Sally George, *Leaving Home in the 1970s*, 2 February 1978

⌒✐⌒

NO NEWS

Britain is living up to its contemporary reputation – no delivery of any papers today, except the *Daily Express* and *Telegraph*. The others are on strike.

Paul Martin, Diaries, 30 March 1978

⌒✐⌒

ROBOTS WRECK *STAR WARS*

I saw *Star Wars* the other day. Difficult to know what all the fuss is about. I thought it a modest (except technically), mildly entertaining picture – except for those two damned arch robots. They nearly wrecked the whole thing in the first ten minutes.

Lindsay Anderson, Diaries, 24 April 1978

HULK BEATS MR HUDSON

I must admit to being seduced into *The Incredible Hulk*, which has just started screening over here. A fabulous series, I must admit. I'd rather have it on than *Upstairs, Downstairs* any day.

Lindsay Anderson, Diaries, 17 July 1978

HOLY SEE

The big news today is the selection of the Archbishop of Cracow, Cardinal Karol Wojtyla, as Pope. He is the first non-Italian in four hundred and fifty years to become head of the Catholic Church … an imaginative appointment, if ever there was one.

Paul Martin, Diaries, 17 October 1978

BAGGING A SEAT AT MCDONALD'S

Collected Rachel from school at twelve and she and I walked into Kentish Town to have lunch at a new McDonald's there. Instead of seats they have perches – sloping plastic shelves which give you the feeling that they are trying to tip everyone out of the restaurant. Not entirely untrue, either – they're obviously designed to discourage quiet sitting and reflection and increase cash flow.

A thought struck me as I left – the bags in which you are given food at McDonald's are almost identical in texture, shape and size with the vomit bags tucked in the seat pockets of aircraft.*

Michael Palin, Diaries, 8 December 1978

---

* *The first UK branch of McDonald's, the American fast-food chain, opened in Woolwich, southeast London, in 1974.*

INNOCENCE RUINED BY REMAKE

Tonight we watched the remake of *Brief Encounter* 1974 with Richard Burton and Sophia Loren. Somehow, the diesel trains, instead of steam trains, and the streetwise actors, ruined the innocence from the different era.

Sally George, *Leaving Home in the 1970s*, 30 December 1978

⟡

ANOTHER STRIKE LOOMING

Britain's main concern today is the continued lorrymen's strike and the petrol drivers who threaten to cut off oil and gas to British car users, with serious indirect consequences affecting food and industry – all because the lorry drivers want more pay. Mrs Thatcher has called for the declaration of a state of emergency. The government over which she would preside would curb union power.

Paul Martin, Diaries, 8 January 1979

⟡

'CRISIS? THERE IS NO CRISIS'

Saw the news. Callaghan arrived back from Guadeloupe saying, 'There is no chaos,' which is a euphemistic way of talking about the lorry drivers ruining *all production* & work in the entire country, but one admires his phlegm.

Kenneth Williams, Diaries, 10 January 1979

⟡

COUNTRY DISPOSING OF RUBBISH

At the moment, the National Union of Public employees is on and off striking too – hospital porters, ambulance men, school porters, dustmen, mortuary workers, etc. In the streets of London the rubbish is piled here and there, spilling out from its bags all over the place. Leicester Square is one large dump and every restaurant is approached through rubbish ...

Sir Roy Strong, Diaries, 21 February 1979

CULINARY ADVENTURES

I made Moussaka and Ratatouille this week, as I am becoming quite adventurous in the kitchen.

Sally George, *Leaving Home in the 1970s*, 28 March 1979

MRS THATCHER BECOMES PM

The *Telegraph* gives Mrs Thatcher a majority of thirty. I think it will be greater. I have a bet of 10p with someone that she will get a majority of 60. She has conducted an able campaign. So has Jim. Whatever happens, Jim Callaghan is an able political leader. [But] the merit of an argument is not necessarily the determining factor in election results.

I went to bed early, in the hope that I might become so absorbed in sleep as not to be tempted to listen to the election returns. Practice and habit, however, had other plans for me. For several hours after 2 o'clock, I lay in bed learning of Maggie's mounting victory, and of my own good guessing on the range of her majority.

Paul Martin, Diaries, 3 May 1979

JEREMY THORPE ON TRIAL

The trial of Jeremy Thorpe and his three co-defendants ended today with verdicts of Not Guilty on the charges of conspiracy to murder Norman Scott, and in Jeremy's case the additional charge of inciting to murder. The case started at the Old Bailey on the 8th of last month, and there have been few days without some new twist in the drama.

For the charge of murder to stick there would, as the Judge frequently pointed out, need to have been incontrovertible evidence of malign intention. But so many witnesses on both sides were such sleazy, untrustworthy characters that it must have been virtually impossible for the jury to determine who was, and was not, telling the truth. So Not Guilty became, it seems, the only possible verdict.

Naturally, Jeremy Thorpe, is delighted, but he must know that his political career is now ended, and that is a severe punishment for so ambitious a man.*

Trevor Beeson, *A Canon's Diary*, 22 June 1979

---

* *Jeremy Thorpe was the leader of the Liberal Party. His political career ended after his acquittal for allegedly hiring a hit man to kill his lover Norman Scott.*

ON THE ROADSHOW

Tony met me at Rachel's with Rachel, Pest and Clare and we waited for the van to go to Harpole for the *John Peel Roadshow*. Had our soundcheck pretty soon after we arrived, were a bit chronic. Had a drink. We were on second and were very average. I felt very boisterous. Matt and Dan came ... and this photographer called Ray Stevenson. In the end, he took pictures of us with John Peel; we were really stoned and giggled and giggled ...

Debsey Wykes, Diaries, 21 July 1979

MOUNTBATTEN ASSASSINATED

The jollity of this hot Bank Holiday Monday has given way to a deep sense of shock at the news of the assassination of Earl Mountbatten of Burma. Evidently, he was on holiday in the fishing village of Mullaghmore, just south of the border between Northern Ireland and the Irish Republic – something he has done for many years past. Late this morning, he set off on a fishing trip with several members of his family, and shortly after leaving the small harbour the boat was torn apart by an IRA bomb.

According to the latest BBC News, the Earl, his grandson Nicholas (aged fourteen), and a boatman (aged seventeen) were killed instantly. His daughter, Lady Brabourne, her son Timothy, and her mother-in-law, the Dowager Lady Brabourne, were seriously injured and are now in intensive care. The IRA has claimed responsibility for the murders and says that the bomb was detonated from the shore by remote control ... The IRA is now conducting a vicious campaign, and eighteen British soldiers were also killed yesterday by another remote-controlled bomb, again near the border, but in County Down on the eastern side of the island ...

There are, I know, those who believe that he was given to self-aggrandisement and that his merits have been overrated, but we shall not hear much of this over the next few days, and a popular public figure will be widely mourned.

Trevor Beeson, *A Canon's Diary*, 27 August 1979

BAFFLED BY SPY DRAMA

As I am not feeling well at the moment (more fluid), I find myself reflecting on the mystery of life and death and the way we all pass through this world in a kind of procession. The whole business is as inexplicable and mysterious as the John Le Carré TV serial *Tinker, Tailor, Soldier, Spy*, which we are all finding so baffling.

Barbara Pym, *A Very Private Eye*, 1 October 1979

THE ART OF SPYING

We have also had the Blunt Affair. Terrific excitement, as the ex-spy was interviewed on television, and the English having a fine old self-righteous time with horror stories of the Spy in the Palace. In the end, old Blunt seems to have come out of the affair with more dignity than anyone else – certainly made Alec Guinness's performance in *Tinker, Tailor, Soldier, Spy* seem pretty crude.

Lindsay Anderson, Letter to Malcolm McDowell, 30 November 1979

CHAPTER NINE

A KICK UP THE
EIGHTIES: 1980-1989

Culturally, decades are rarely as neat as the numbers of their duration. It has, for example, been suggested that the beginning of the 1980s might more reasonably be placed on 4 May 1979 – the day Margaret Thatcher entered Downing Street. For when it comes to the 1980s, it is impossible not to think of Mrs Thatcher. Like Winston Churchill and the Second World War, she personified the years during which she led her country. Before her, Pitt the Younger was the last prime minister to have held office for a whole decade. In 1989 she took to the platform at the Conservative Party conference to be greeted by chants of 'Ten more years!' As it was, she only outlasted the Berlin Wall by a mere twelve months.

What came to be termed as Thatcherism was arguably more enduring and, love her or loathe her and for better or for worse, we are still living with the consequences of many of the policies she pursued, from the privatization of nationalized industries and the deregulation of financial services to the City of London, offering council tenants the right to buy their homes and the efforts to put trade unions under stricter controls.

Things could, of course, have turned out rather differently, as some of the accounts here might serve to remind us. The Falklands War could have been lost. The miners might have been victorious in their strike. And as the women protestors at Greenham Common underlined, the Cold War might have ended with a nuclear attack rather than the collapse of Communism.

Such an Armageddon was not the only concern of those days. With unemployment reaching over 3 million and the emergence of AIDS, anxiety was as common a facet of the 1980s as brashly flaunted affluence. As voices from former MP Gyles Brandreth to novelist Alex Wheatle reveal, people were divided on their opinion of the decade, even as they lived it.

እ

NORTH SEA OIL STRATEGY

The government's strategy becomes apparent: cuts in public spending leading to lower interest rates, a lower rate of inflation and industrial recovery. Then from 1982, the revenue from North Sea oil will be distributed to the nation in the form of tax cuts. The problem is that, by 1982, large chunks of British industry will be so punch-drunk and the nation so divided that we shall be unable to take advantage of the oil revenue. It will disappear in a flood of imports. And what will happen to the North meanwhile? We hear about new redundancies every day.*

Giles Radice, Diaries, 26 March 1980

* *Within a year, Britain was a net exporter of oil and, by the mid-1980s, North Sea oil provided 10 per cent of the Treasury's annual revenue.*

እ

OUT AND PROUD

For the first time I go on the Gay Pride March wearing a dog collar, and walk in the rain with the GCM [Gay Christian Movement] banner from Bressington Place, Victoria to Malet Street. I was very apprehensive but felt I must show at least one cleric has emerged from the closet.

Rev. Dr Malcolm Johnson, Diary of a Gay Priest, 28 June 1980

UNDER THE SPELL OF VIDEO

A depressing foray to Tottenham Court Road/Oxford Street to buy a new 8 mill film to show at Tom's party. Depressing because of the domination in that corner of London of the awful, blinking, hypnotising spell of video … There is video equipment everywhere – video films, video games – and it's like a giant amusement arcade providing a sort of temporary electronic alternative to listlessness. Lights flash and disembodied voices bark out of electronic chess games and football games. There doesn't seem to be much joy around here.

Michael Palin, Diaries, 8 October 1980

THAT JOKE ISN'T FUNNY ANY MORE

To Birmingham, went to the ATV studios at 3 o'c. We did our bit – a talk on racialism in humour – after seeing a particularly vulgar pub act with blasphemous references and snide remarks about Pakistani people. It was me, Gita Mehta & some northern comedian. I said we'd watched something which was unfunny & tasteless & that we'd seen the half-educated talking to the uneducated and this northern comedian did the 'I think he's good & we've all got to earn a living' act.

Kenneth Williams, Diaries, 12 October 1980

HOME ENTERTAINMENT

On the way home we bought a 5-gallon wine kit. Jilly Cooper, the author, was at Hudson's bookshop, so I met her and had my book signed. I was surprised that she is quite a shy person.

We are looking into buying the latest technology – a video recorder. To rent one would be £18 a month.

Sally George, Leaving Home in the 1970s, 15 October 1980

SHOT FOR SOUNDS

We caught our train to London and got to 'Sounds' at 1 p.m. We sat and waited and this fairly short man in jeans and a jacket trundled in with a cheeky face and scruffy hair and said, 'You waiting for me, ladies?' He was Paul Slattery and he was really nice. We got in his car and drove to the old docks and got up on this wall that had a sheer drop on one side leading to some very turbulent waters. Then we took a short ride to another area of the docklands where there was a small farm, one huge pen with goats, hens, geese, a donkey and a horse. The geese were terrifying and when Hester was trying to pat the horse he was stamping and snorting, I wouldn't have gone near him for the world ... We should be in next week, we're dying to be on the front cover but I shouldn't think that'll happen.

Debsey Wykes, Diaries, 26 November 1980

DOING THE RIGHT THING FOR HUMAN RIGHTS

The Human Rights Day service organized by the British Council of Churches held this evening was a good occasion and it is right that the Abbey should be involved in an event of this kind. Sheila Cassidy spoke movingly about the appalling situation in Chile and reminded us that the denial of human rights in countries of any political persuasion is actually increasing.

The service was not, however, without its problems ... A group of Irish campaigners for the IRA's Maze* prisoners requested permission to make their case during the service. This we refused on the grounds that the granting of such a request would require us to give an equal opportunity to those who might wish to speak on behalf of the victims of IRA violence ...

Trevor Beeson, A Canon's Diary, 10 December 1980

Her Majesty's Prison Maze, originally known as the Long Kesh Detention Centre, Belfast, was used to house both Republican and Loyalist paramilitary prisoners from 1971 to 2000.

'STARTING OVER'

Our 1960s semi-detached house is on the market for sale as we can now afford a newer 1970s link-detached house with a Georgian bow window. A rather old-fashioned couple came to view our house and criticised our secondary double-glazing. I woke up yesterday to a news flash on the radio to hear that John Lennon had been shot dead, which is rather tragic and sad.

Sally George, Leaving Home in the 1970s, 10 December 1980

ROYAL ENGAGEMENT

We saw the TV news, which devoted loads of time to the engagement of the Prince of Wales to Diana Spencer; there was a ludicrous interview with such foolish questions & silly answers you thought, 'What are they going on about?'

INT: 'Are you both in love?'

DIANA: 'Oh, yes, very.'

PRINCE: 'What is being in love? A state of mind? You put your own interpretation on it ...'

INT: 'You're both very happy?'

PRINCE: 'Oh, yes.'

I thought they should have shut up.

Kenneth Williams, Diaries, 24 February 1981

Prince Charles and Lady Diana Spencer announced their engagement today but I couldn't help feeling that Charles was pushed into it.

Sally George, Leaving Home in the 1970s, 25 February 1981

DULL SDP

Watched a programme about the birth today of the Social Democratic Party with David Owen & Roy Jenkins and Shirley Williams ... they're all worthy one feels but terribly dull. If they pick up any support in an election I fancy it will be the Orpington kind of success.*

Kenneth Williams, Diaries, 26 March 1981

* *The Social Democratic Party (SDP) was founded in 1981 by Roy Jenkins, David Owen, Bill Rodgers and Shirley Williams, leading figures in Labour who broke with the party over its stance on nuclear weapons and Europe, and the SDP briefly enjoyed a poll rating of over 50 per cent. Here, Williams is looking back to March 1962, when the Liberals scored*

a surprise victory over the Conservatives in a by-election in Orpington, Kent. The Liberals had imagined this to be a harbinger of a potentially dramatic resurgence of the party's fortunes, but such a resurgence ultimately failed to materialize.

⁓

TUTU AT WESTMINSTER

When I heard that Desmond Tutu was in London this weekend and free this morning, I invited him to take my place in the pulpit at Matins. It isn't often that we get a preacher straight from the front line, and the opportunity to hear at first hand about the situation in South Africa was too good to miss.

Desmond is now a key figure, perhaps the key figure, in the struggle against apartheid …

The sermon was electrifying. Powerful statements delivered in Desmond's high-pitched voice rang throughout the Abbey …

His theme was liberation, and drew heavily on biblical material relating to

God, who is seeking to liberate his people – from the destructive power of structural sin expressed through oppressive regimes. In South Africa, he told us, the white man is as much in need of liberation as the black man, for he is bedevilled by anxiety and fear and is driven to invest resources to protect himself against change that would be better used creatively in other spheres.

Trevor Beeson, *A Canon's Diary*, 29 March 1981

◦✲◦

BRIXTON RIOTS

The sun had set over this balmy evening and the battle for Railton Road was raging. About fifty yards down the road, scores of police were employing dustbin lids as makeshift shields to protect them from missiles that were raining towards them. They were trying to advance in an ordered line. As we hacked down low brick walls that fronted terraced housing for more ammunition, we heard the screams, yells and curses, backdropped by sirens, coming from every direction. The heat and smoke from a nearby burnt-out pub troubled our lungs. Some rioters were preparing Molotov cocktails ready to launch into the massed police ranks. I peered upward, and everything seemed to be orange. The street was a jagged carpet of broken glass, petrol, burning cars and fractured bricks and as I looked around, the determination to 'hold' this black quarter of Brixton was evident on the sweat-encased faces of people around me.

Fuelled with revolutionary reggae songs, thirteen of us marched up Mayall Road, knowing that the rest of our task force were lying low in two terraced houses. All lights were switched off. We saw the police about a hundred yards away and all that lay between us was a number of busted, smoking cars. As soon as they were in range we hurled all and sundry into the air. They immediately charged at us. Feeling great fear and excitement, we turned on our heels and ran for our sweet lives, only too aware of what might lie in wait in a south London police cell …

Returning to Railton Road via Brockwell Park, I noticed that the police had gained relative control of the 'front line'. They were housed in numerous green coaches parked behind each other as far as my eye could see, sipping hot drinks from polystyrene cups. Fear was written over their faces. It was an empowering sight to behold ...

Tumper, the proprietor of a 24-hour West Indian food store on Railton Road (his premises remained untouched by rioters), was gaining a roaring trade selling fried dumplings, cheese and bun sandwiches, carrot cake and fish fritters. Queuing up to buy a snack, I bumped into a friend of mine. 'Babylon tek a raas beating, innit,' he said. 'As Marley sang, the slavemaster's tables are turning.'

'Yeah,' I agreed. 'They've felt the crack of a whip.'

Alex Wheatle, Notebooks, 10 April 1981

RECESSION IN PLAIN SIGHT

One notices the recession much. As you go down the escalator on the Underground, the advertisement boards are empty or carry London Transport advertisements. When we had a drink and talked to the house manager of the National Theatre, she admitted a half-sale of tickets for this booking period ... Sales are an all too familiar feature: pre-Christmas sales, January sales, pre-summer sales, summer sales. Shops also disappear.

Sir Roy Strong, Diaries, June 1981

ALL CREATURE COMFORTS

Back home, and our offer of £31,500 (to include carpets) has been accepted on a house in Glascote Close, Shirley in Solihull.

Today in the lunch hour I went to see James Herriot (Alf White) who was signing books in W. H. Smiths. I bought his latest vet book and wished I lived in Yorkshire.

Sally George, *Leaving Home in the 1970s*, 11 June 1981

TYRANTS ON TV

Watched the *Panorama* programme about Iraq and it was the usual pious rubbish about Saddam Hussein being a tyrant & a torturer. When such a leader is removed, the ensuing chaos is deplored by the same censurers.

Kenneth Williams, Diaries, 27 July 1981

ROYAL WEDDING

Stayed at home all morning watching and listening to the Wedding. A. and I greatly moved. It was the best form of pageantry – the fairy-like beauty of the carriages, the coachman's liveries, their cocked hats with tassels hanging from the corners, the grey horses' manes plaited with silver thread, and the ravishing beauty of Lady Diana's dress, train of 25 feet, gossamer veil, her sidelong glances from those large round, blue eyes. She is adorable.

James Lees-Milne, Diaries, 29 July 1981

FALKLANDS JINGOISM

For the first time since Suez, Parliament met today in emergency sessions, the Argentinian forces having invaded and occupied the Falkland Islands yesterday. I went across this morning to conduct Prayers and found the corridors buzzing with shock and outrage.

The chamber was packed to capacity, with some members sitting on the floor, and many occupying seats in the gallery.

The Prime Minister was surprisingly nervous and seemed unsure of herself. She is, of course, carrying a heavy responsibility and is, I suppose, trapped between the need to assert Britain's intention to retain sovereignty over the Falkland Islands, whatever the cost, and the recognition that this crisis would not have arisen had her Government taken action as soon as the Argentinians made their intentions clear.

Michael Foot, the Leader of the Opposition, made a surprisingly belligerent speech for someone whose outlook had always seemed close to pacifism, and the Opposition is generally supporting vigorous action against Argentina ... There was, in fact, a markedly jingoistic element in many of the speeches and anger was turned not so much on Margaret Thatcher as on the Foreign Secretary John Nott.

John Nott's own speech was very poor indeed and he made a serious mistake when he tried to turn the crisis to Party advantage. This didn't come off ... Enoch Powell referred to Margaret Thatcher's reputation as the 'Iron Lady' and ended in his most ominous tones: 'Now we shall see of what metal this lady is made.'

Trevor Beeson, *A Canon's Diary*, 3 April 1982

LOST AT SEA

The news as we returned from Hilltop yesterday was that we have sunk the Argentinian cruiser *General Belgrano* outside the exclusion zone. Obviously, a bad move because of the big loss of life. Lisanne and I and the girls feel very shocked.

I talk to Alan Clark, the buccaneering right-wing Tory military historian, who is also a Plymouth MP, about the situation. He is very contemptuous of the Argentinians, as he is of most foreigners. Then comes the news that one of our destroyers, HMS *Sheffield*, has been sunk by a French missile called an Exocet. It turns out to have been fired from 30 miles away by a fast French Etendard plane. It seems that our ships have little answer to these missiles – our Sea Harriers don't appear to be a match for the Argentinian planes. We have command of the sea, because of our submarines, but not the air. And our ships are being destroyed by the weapons of our allies.

The House of Commons is in a very subdued mood when Nott makes his statement about the *Sheffield* late on Tuesday night.

Is the war worth it? we all ask each other. The lives lost could soon equal the number of Falkland Islanders.

Giles Radice, Diaries, 3 May 1982

⟡

SEASICKNESS

The Falkland Islands. At the back of everything else, this goes on, like sickness – the seasickness never written about or photographed of the soldiers on their ships.

These operations are an automatic function of the capacity to perform them, just as the war in Vietnam was a function of American power. If we didn't have the ships and weapons and men we would never have set off on this expedition. Given the fact that we do have them, we use them; they demand to be used ...

Stephen Spender, Journals, 15 May 1982

⟡

WAR'S END

The Prime Minister interrupted a debate in the House of Commons this afternoon to announce that a report had just been received indicating that Argentinian forces were flying the white flag over Port Stanley. The war was now ended. The House cheered, there was much waving of order papers, and a general feeling of relief that a war which could and should have been avoided had been brought to a satisfactory conclusion relatively speedily – though not without the loss of over 250 British and, it is said, more than 600 Argentinian lives …

Trevor Beeson, *A Canon's Diary*, 14 June 1982

SOUTH ATLANTIC HORRORS

Kathleen was over here just now ringing up her mother, who had just been rung up by her son Robin, just back from, of all things, the Falkland Islands. The war was over when he went, but not the minesweeping, and he has seen some horrifying things. But he was not allowed to say too much.

Lavinia Mynors, Diaries, 15 July 1982

SUBMERGED FOR 159,685 DAYS

The *Mary Rose* was raised from the sea-bed today. It was an extraordinary experience to witness the Tudor battleship slowly break the surface of the water as she was lifted in a giant cradle. She sank on Sunday July 19th 1545, watched by Henry VIII, suddenly keeling over and taking 700 men to their deaths. The King attempted to have her raised, but it has taken 437 years and the expertise of 20th-century technology and the outlay of £4 million to achieve that aim.

Brian Williams, Diaries, 11 October 1982

HITLER DIARIES FAKE

I have also just had a call from a West German newspaper asking for my views on the so-called 'Hitler Diaries', brought to light this week by the hapless Hugh Trevor-Roper, who rushed in declaring them genuine when perhaps he should have thought twice.

Gyles Brandreth, *Something Sensational to Read in the Train*, 29 April 1983

GREENHAM PEACE CAMP

On the train to Newbury.

Greenham is being evicted. I heard it on the radio while I was out buying a loaf of bread.

Transport always seems so unbearably slow at times like these! It will be all over by the time I get there.

That plunk, then panic on hearing the news, 'The Women's Peace Camp at Greenham is being evicted.* Women are lying in the mud in front of bulldozers being dragged away by police.' And here is me so far away. Are they ok? Who's been arrested this time? I want to be there.

The last two evictions I've had to stay in London, watching it on telly, stuck with work commitments here. Ugh, I feel so out of touch with Greenham. So difficult to juggle two lives, find a balance between my life in London and wanting to be living down there, doing absolutely everything I can.

Where is the most politically active place to be?

I'm worried about today. Bad time for an eviction. Even the *Guardian* is slagging off Greenham at the moment.

Jenny Perringer, Diaries, 12 May 1983

* *The Greenham Common Peace Camp began in 1981, when a group of thirty-six women chained themselves to a fence surrounding the American air base in Berkshire to protest against the decision to site ninety-six Cruise nuclear missiles there. The camp was only wound up in 2000.*

CONSERVATIVE LANDSLIDE

The General Election has given the Conservatives a landslide victory and a majority of 144 – the largest since the famous Labour victory in 1945. I don't think that anyone is in the least surprised, because the Labour Party, under the leadership of Michael Foot, has been in some disarray for some time ... I like

Michael Foot, and he is a great Parliamentarian, but it was a disastrous mistake to make him, rather than Denis Healey, Leader …

The Liberal/Social Democrat challenge came to nothing, and its leaders are naturally complaining that a return of 23 seats for 25% of the total votes is a reflection of the unfairness of the 'first past the post' electoral system. A Government with a majority of 144 is unlikely to share this sense of injustice.

Trevor Beeson, *A Canon's Diary*, 10 June 1983

⁓

THE AIDS EPIDEMIC

The AIDS scare is alarming everyone. Last week an article in *The Times* described the symptoms six months after contraction – lethargy, temperature, then swelling of gland nodules, whatever they may be. Then a year's recovery when the patient believes all is well. Then recurrence of temperature etc. and, from whatever complaint thereafter contracted, certain death, owing to immunity to all drugs and treatment. Terror reigns in the minds of all homosexuals.*

James Lees-Milne, Diaries, 31 July 1983

* *Cases of acquired immune deficiency syndrome were first diagnosed among previously healthy gay men in the US. By 1982, health authorities had recognized that intravenous drug users and anyone having unprotected sex were also at risk.*

⁓

MUSWELL HILL MURDERER

The Nilsen murder case – the Sunday papers are full of the trial of this timid little mass-murderer.* The sick, black humour seems to have a flavour of *Richard III*. Nilsen running out of neckties as the strangulations increased; a head boiling on his stove while he walked his dog Bleep; his preference for Sainsbury's air fresheners; his suggestion to the police that the flesh found in his drains was

Kentucky Fried Chicken; even his remark that having corpses was better than going back to an empty house. The headlines squeal 'Mad or Bad, Monster or Maniac, Sick or Evil?'

I ask Jim whether he believes we all have a Nilsen within us. He says, 'Well, certainly not you. You can't boil an egg, never mind someone's head.'

Antony Sher, *Year of the King*, 6 November 1983

* *Known as the Muswell Hill Murderer, Dennis Nilsen, a necrophiliac, killed at least fifteen young men and boys from 1978 to 1983.*

FREE NELSON MANDELA

In this morning's *Guardian* a full-page advertisement for the Free Nelson Mandela Campaign.* Hundreds of signatures, mine among them.

Antony Sher, *Year of the King*, 10 December 1983

* *Mandela would not be freed from prison until 11 February 1990. The apartheid system he'd fought so heroically against was finally dismantled the following year, and when multi-racial elections were held in 1994, Mandela was elected as South Africa's first black president.*

LOATHING OR LOVING MRS THATCHER

I have just had tea with Ted Heath. The way he cannot control his vitriol against Mrs Thatcher is actually comical. He *loathes* her and assumes others must loathe her too. I tried to steer him onto other territory – e.g. Broadstairs – but he kept coming back to 'that woman'. She is 'ruining the country'. I didn't like to tell him, but most people think she is *making* it.

Gyles Brandreth, *Something Sensational to Read in the Train*, 28 February 1984

MINERS' STRIKE

Meeting at the Baggin (Sherwood Miners' Welfare). It definitely looks like a strike, an indefinite strike. It's a shame, we have only about a week's coal left at home and my delivery is due on 4 March. The feeling of some of the men that I have spoken to is to work but the Union recommends industrial action. Always back your union. Without them you are lost. I will back the Union. At the meeting it was packed out. A very good case was put forward in favour of the Union recommendation. A couple of miners put their hands up and argued for continuing to work and everyone listened to the view expressed. When it came to the vote my hand went in favour of action, probably the second to do so, then many other hands went up. The recommendation was in favour of industrial action. I heard that one Silverwood man had tried to commit suicide due to the overtime ban. He was up to his neck in debt with a new house and may do it proper now.

Bruce Wilson, *Yorkshire's Flying Pickets*, 3 March 1984

FLYING PICKETS

Order for today – Ollerton, Notts. Picked team up and set off through Maltby towards Oldcotes crossroads where we were stopped by the police and – here we go again – our names and addresses taken. Gave them some verbal since we were not allowed to go about our business in a so-called free country. The police just smirked at us and told us that we were not going anywhere fast. Started to drive back 'helped' by a police escort, which accompanied us to the South Yorkshire boundary sign again. Felt like royalty for a while, like a motorway jam sandwich, due to the police escorting us ... Felt a bit guilty as the NUM [National Union of Mineworkers] were giving me petrol money and I only put half in the tank as we were struggling to get through the roadblocks.

Bruce Wilson, *Yorkshire's Flying Pickets*, 17 April 1984

LIBYAN EMBASSY SIEGE

Dickie and I go into the West End to see *Scarface*, the new Al Pacino film. The cinema is next to St James's Square where the Libyan Embassy siege continues. We round the corner into Waterloo Place and there's that huge sheet of blue tarpaulin which has been on the TV news all week. It looks like an avant-garde theatre curtain, and indeed a crowd of holidaymakers stand across the street behind barriers, waiting for the show to start. The mood is festive, hot dogs and ice cream, buskers with performing budgies and dogs.

Suddenly, a group of high-ranking police officers arrive, jumping dramatically out of their cars before they've stopped. They hurry across the road clutching briefcases and raincoats, and disappear through the blue curtain. The crowd stirs. Will the show start now that the leading acts have arrived?

We go into the Plaza and watch a relentless, three-hour succession of slayings, mailings and coke-sniffings. Emerge grumpily on to the street at the end, Dickie remarking that it would have been more fun watching the blue curtain.

Antony Sher, *Year of the King*, 20 April 1984

* On 17 April 1984, WPC Yvonne Fletcher was among officers stewarding a small protest outside the Libyan Embassy against the regime of Colonel Muammar Gaddafi. Shots were fired on the demonstrators from the embassy and Fletcher was hit; she later died of her wounds. Under international law the police were not allowed to enter the embassy to collect evidence or apprehend any suspects. The siege ended on 28 April with no arrests and a termination of diplomatic relations between the two nations. Then the Lockerbie bombing occurred on 21 December 1988, masterminded by Libya. Diplomatic relations would not be restored until 1999.

BATTLE OF ORGREAVE

'Here We Go', this is the big one: Orgreave. We … arrive at 8.05 a.m. The scabs' lorries are on the top road. I've never seen so many of our lads altogether, it brought tears to my eyes, for I knew some of them would get hurt, also some of the police would get hurt. I can't get to the front fast enough … It's 8.45 a.m., the lads start the chant of 'Here We Go' and there is one big push … 9.30 a.m., another push. This time the police go berserk and the Riot Squad charge up the field with the 'cavalry' but they do something I have not seen before, they turn to where we are standing peacefully picketing and start hitting whoever they come across. I'm thinking this is it … We go into the field. I see four policemen holding one of our lads on the ground. He's got a bloody head … When I get about ten yards off the bridge the lads are running up the road shouting, 'Get back, they're coming!' … They were being chased by police on horses and with dogs. I stay on the fence and hope for the best. The 'cavalry' are first as usual, then the riot squad. It was around 11.15 a.m. when this was happening. They pass me without incident, the first of many attacks to come on the afternoon delivery and what a bloody afternoon it was. The police get back to their positions. There was some stone throwing going on …

The 'cavalry' and 'riot squad' come again. It's 11.20 a.m. … I glance again across to where Arthur and the lads are and some of them are running. I see one of the riot squad knock Arthur down from behind. The attacker had his riot shield in a raised position … Word must have got out, as an ambulance reversed up the road and two ambulance men get out wearing riot helmets. They ask Arthur what had happened and he told them that he had been hit with a shield. He said he did not feel good and went with them to the ambulance. At the same time, the police continue taking prisoners ... A lad was seen walking down the road with a policeman on either of his sides, he had blood all over his face ... The battle keeps going on and off until 1 p.m.; also, the lads in the bottom field are having their share of battles as well. I don't know about 'Sunday, Bloody Sunday' but it was like 'Monday, Bloody Monday', the worst day yet. We set off home about 1.30 p.m. We can do without days like this. There were seventy-nine hurt and ninety-three arrests.

Arthur Wakefield, *Diary of Yorkshire Miner*, 18 June 1984

* *The clash between police and miners outside a coking plant in Orgreave, South Yorkshire, on 18 June 1984 was the most violent conflict of the strike. In 1991 £425,000 was paid in compensation to thirty-nine miners who sued for assault, wrongful arrest and malicious prosecution.*

⌒*⌒*

A PLAN FOR COAL

Last week Thatcher and the NCB [National Coal Board] started a major propaganda programme. Bet these talks are all part of this strategy. Might get power cuts in the autumn.

In today's *News of the World* [the NCB's] Plan for Coal is virtually the same as they have been saying for the last four months:

> Run down of pits in two years.
> Heavy investment in new super pits.
> Definition of what 'uneconomic' means.

Can't see [the National Union of Miners] agreeing to these – between the lines it says the same as before.

I've heard that Orgreave might be opening tomorrow.

Bruce Wilson, *Yorkshire's Flying Pickets*, 8 July 1984

HEFTY INDIANA JONES

In the evening we went with Bernard to the cinema to see Spielberg's *Indiana Jones and the Temple of Doom*. Maggie enjoyed the fairground cruelty of the film and the audience. Bernard was repelled: 'rock bottom'.

'No different to the Bond films he enjoys,' she said to me afterwards.

'But more animal.'

'I liked the hefty hero.'

Margaret and Brian Buckley, *A Journal for Maggie*, 19 July 1984

THE BRIGHTON BOMB

Arrive at Ipswich to be met by Ken Weetch with the news from Brighton that the IRA have blown up part of the Grand Hotel, which is the Conservative Conference hotel. Mrs Thatcher has narrowly escaped, Norman Tebbit is badly injured, a Tory MP is dead, and the Chief Whip burnt. Touchingly, Sir Keith wanders around the promenade in his dressing gown. I express my shock, horror and sympathy on the local radio.

Giles Radice, Diaries, 12 October 1984

7 UP, GROWN UP

We watched Michael Apted's documentary *28 Up*, with interviews of people who were first seen on television when they were seven. 'I was amused', said Maggie, 'by the cockneys, horrified by the glazed complacency of the upper-class twits, but only really moved by the man living alone in a caravan in the Scottish Highlands, penniless, in tramp's clothes and convict's hairstyle who talked without pretension about the difficulties of fitting into conventional way of life. He'd been such a happy seven-year-old. Maladjusted now more than the others – but at least any adjustment he achieves will be based on reality, the outcome of genuine thought, not the adoption of a role or drug.'*

Margaret and Brian Buckley, *A Journal for Maggie*, 27 November 1984

* *Seven Up!, the first instalment of the series, aired on Granada TV in 1964.*

BOXING DAY FEAST

I hurried disastrously over a turkey risotto and spilt the rice on the larder floor. There was no more, so macaroni was substituted – never mind, we had another fruit fluff by special request from Jonathan.

Lavinia Mynors, Diaries, 26 December 1984

AIDS IN HEADLINES

Our friend Greg Richard, the prison chaplain, dies from an AIDS-related illness, and his photo is on the front page of most newspapers. His parents, who did not know that he was gay or ill, are flying from Australia. It is a very sad day, and to me ominous.

Rev. Dr Malcolm Johnson, *Diary of a Gay Priest*, 31 January 1985

PAINT JOB FOR A MINER

I've been thinking about this all week, on and off, and now I've made my decision. It's 2.40 p.m., I go outside and into the shed to get some paint and a brush. There is a scab living in the 'Wimpeys'. I lived across the road from him for twenty-five years. I'm going to carry out the tradition of our grandfathers, to brand a scab. It's 2.50 p.m. when I get within twenty yards of his house. I keep down low against the privet hedge, and then whilst in a crouching position start to paint SCAB on the causeway. I just get the letter 'S' done when I hear a rustling sound and then a voice. I raise my head and see a figure brandishing a big stick, so I pick up the tin of paint, which is in a plastic bag, and run away. The man chases me. I get about forty yards and then stop and face him, the bag in my hand. I say to him, 'If you hit me with that you will get this in your face.' ...

Arthur Wakefield, *Diary of Yorkshire Miner*, 16 February 1985

THE BRASS BAND PLAYED ON

I'm going to Sheffield City Hall for the annual concert of massed bands and choirs. We arrive at 2.30 p.m. and get ready for rehearsals which start at 4.00 p.m. Mr Relton, our conductor, makes an announcement, 'Gentlemen, it has been announced on television that the Miners' Strike is over.' Some of the chaps cheered and others were silent. I was silent even though I felt the news coming all week. It was like being hit in the guts with a big iron ball ... I hold my head up all through the concert as I have throughout the strike ...

Arthur Wakefield, *Diary of Yorkshire Miner*, 3 March 1985

BACK TO THE SHAFT

My first day back at work, on the day shift. I get up at 4.45 a.m. and set off for work at 5.15 a.m. I wasn't relishing going back without a settlement. I felt cheated by my own membership and my own county. If Yorkshire had been 100 per cent solid we would have had a settlement ... I get my lamp out and make my way to go down the pit but there is a problem with the shaft. It's a cold and frosty morning and we have to stand about for three hours. When we get to the pit shaft there is a scab there. Some of the lads give him some verbal but there are so many men he can't really identify who are shouting at him ...

A few comments are made about the manager's attitude towards us and no one is enthusiastic about doing a lot of work ... In general, there was mixed feeling about the strike. Most men of my age thought that it had been a wasted twelve months as they had missed out on redundancy ... We were due to ride out of the pit at 1.15 p.m. but it's 1.50 p.m., then we have to go for our shower in the pit-head baths. The water is cold and it's 2.30 p.m. by the time I get home.

Arthur Wakefield, *Diary of Yorkshire Miner*, 11 March 1985

DOTTY DISCUSSIONS AT THE WI

To the WI [Women's Institute]. The company was at its nicest and friendliest and the topics discussed were the dottiest ever. We decided to vote against young persons taking drugs, and against acid rain and in favour of the Third World becoming agriculturally self-supporting, and to my surprise, though I had keenly supported it, against the Government being obliged to bury us all for free.

Lavinia Mynors, Diaries, 13 March 1985

LOST THEATRICAL TALENT

To the Belgrade with Bernard: Willy Russell's *Blood Brothers*: 'Unbelievably bad, not only the basic sentiments but every single sentence – pure crap.'
'Looks like he's lost his talent,' I admitted.
'Down a sewer.'
'Who wrote *Educating Rita*?'
'Rita?'

Margaret and Brian Buckley, *A Journal for Maggie*, 7 June 1985

MURDOCH TAKES ON THE UNIONS

Rupert to dinner … He's in the middle of a high-risk manoeuvre to stop the printing unions from printing *The Times*, *Sunday Times*, *News of the World* and the *Sun*. He wants them to go on strike at a moment which will suit him, not just on a Saturday evening mucking up the *Sunday Times*. He has a new problem in that the unions are sacred and reluctant to strike. If they did, he can sack everyone and print with five hundred and twelve people he has lined up who have already learned to work the presses at Tower Hamlets. That would be instead of the four to five thousand currently employed. I am sure he will win but not without hiccups.

Woodrow Wyatt, Journals, 13 January 1986

VISITOR NUMBERS BOMB

Since the American bombing of Libya in April and the consequent terrorist threat to American citizens, the number of visitors to London has declined sharply throughout the summer, and in spite of the Royal Wedding, there have been noticeably fewer visitors to the Abbey.

Trevor Beeson, *A Canon's Diary*, 17 December 1986

LONDON DERELICT

I accompany the location and production manager to North Kensington to look at locations for the scenes at the beginning of the film. To the thirteenth floor of a tower block that won design awards in the sixties, with several young kids in the lift. We walk around other blocks in the area. They are filthy, derelict places, falling down, graffiti-sprayed, wind-blown, grim and humming with the smell of shit, implacable in the hatred of the humanity they embody. The surrounding shops are barricaded with bars and wire mesh. I was brought up in London. It's my city. I'm no Brit but a Londoner. And it's more filthy and run-down than it's ever been.

Hanif Kureishi, 'With Your Tongue Down My Throat', 10 January 1987

CANVASSING A COUNCIL ESTATE

An election has been called. I do some leafleting for the Labour Party. I cover estates that I walk past every day but haven't been inside since the last election. I wonder if they have really changed since the last time around.

I walk off the main road and across the grass to the entrance of the first block. The door is open: the glass in the door is smashed. A woman in filthy clothes stands in the entrance waving her arms around. She is stoned ...

Someone has a sign on their door: 'Don't burgle me I have nothin.' ... One man comes to the door with a barely controlled Alsatian: 'Come and take back this fucking leaflet,' he screams at me, 'Come and get it, mate.'

It is difficult to explain to the people who live here why they should vote Labour; it is difficult to explain to them why they should vote at all.

Hanif Kureishi, 'With Your Tongue Down My Throat', 21 May 1987

HORROR OF JIFFY BAGS

Thames and Hudson sent me a picture book yesterday. I went at the wrapping with a sharp knife, horrible grey stuff fell out all over the floor, and the book itself still remained inviolate. Some sort of JIFFY bag, the latest horror in OBJECTS.

Richard Cobb, Letter to Hugh Trevor-Roper, 13 August 1987

THE GREAT STORM

A freak storm strikes southern England in the early hours of Friday morning. The wind reaches 100 mph and as the storm crosses southern England it leaves a trail of damaged houses, uprooted trees and even deaths in its wake.

I find my party workers [in Chester-le-Street] not particularly sympathetic towards the South's difficulties. Secretly, they may even feel a certain pleasure that the rich South has at last had to suffer.

Giles Radice, Diaries, 16 October 1987

~

POPPY DAY MASSACRE

I was jumpy this evening: a big bomb went off in Enniskillen and killed a lot of people on a Remembrance Day parade. The pictures on the TV were awful, mostly old people, many injured.

Edwina Currie, Diaries, 8 November 1987

~

DOCKLANDS DEVELOPMENTS

Nigel* took me round the whole Docklands area, puffing on a cigar in the front of his grey Rolls-Royce and purring with pleasure, as well he might, at the resurrection of this vast eight-mile scene of desolation … It is a mixture of restored old warehouses, post-modernist buildings and constructions for businesses, restored yuppie old houses, acres of crumbling decay, eruptions of deadly council housing (over 80% of the population live in this, mainly the real East End working class, left from the days when we had a port) and occasionally a church with a spire.

Canary Wharf has quite a history … The project is to build what can be described as the Docklands 'downtown' area, a huge formal working and retail centre which would act as a focus for the whole, in the same way that London falls into areas like Kensington, Chelsea, the West End and the City. The concept includes a grand series of formal squares and circuses, high-rise buildings constructed with linking design modules.

Sir Roy Strong, Diaries, 11 December 1987

Nigel Broakes founded Trafalgar House, one of the nation's largest contractors, and was head of the London Docklands Development Corporation until 1984.

⟜

PRIVATIZATION HITS THE STREETS

The newly privatized tow-away trucks are now operating in Camden and make regular visits to our street. The crews display fearsome zeal, scrambling to get the slings and chains around the offending car before the owner (just doing five minutes' shopping in the market) returns. They are like a gang of executioners hurrying the victim to his doom before a reprieve arrives …

That the operation is on the dubious boundary between commerce and law enforcement could be deduced from the jaunty demeanour of the policeman in charge, who wears his flat cap titled to the back of his head. 'Distancing', the late Erving Goffmann would have called it, the cap enough to call the whole activity into question.

Alan Bennett, *Writing Home*, 10 January 1988

⟜

TEENAGE TV VIEWING ANGST

Mum and Dad live in the 1950s still. We are not allowed to watch anything except bloody stuff like *Wildlife on One* or some stupid thing like that. We have nothing like a video or a computer. Even if we had one we'd have to use it for educational games.

We have to go to bed at 8.30 to 9.00. We are not allowed to watch soap operas, quiz shows, late-night things (i.e. after 8.30), we don't watch sitcoms, films, ITV.

That rules out anything except *The Food & Drink Programme*, which is about the most interesting thing we are allowed to watch, so I pretend I'm interested in it. My whole bloody life is boring. I get up, go to school, come home, do homework, have food, go to bed.

At weekends it's not much different. We get our enjoyment from reading about Greek heroes and Norse myths. I have to read Jane Eyre. So from now on I am going to be very good and pretend to be terribly interested in all these bloody things.

Rowena Macdonald, Diaries, 26 January 1988

⁓

TURNING JAPANESE, IF I PLEASE?

I saw a futon in Habitat. A futon is a sort of Japanese mattress. It was really nice. I would like one. They are very expensive. I would like a really Japanese-y bedroom. All bare with a very low bed and a futon and all screens. It would be lovely. Though where would you put all your stuff?

Rowena Macdonald, Diaries, 30 March 1988

⁓

LOSING YEARS OF LIFE

John McCarthy was finally released today. I don't remember when he was taken hostage but I do remember when Terry Waite was 'cos I always thought he looked like Uncle Ted. He looked like a really nice man. It must be awful to lose 5 years of your life.*

I bought the album *Viva Hate* by Morrissey, mainly for 'Suedehead'. I always remember walking through Greenfield Gardens in Stourbridge on cold winter mornings just before we moved. The air was icy cold and misty and the trees bare and I hummed that song. It's amazing what little things one remembers.

Rowena Macdonald, Diaries, 8 July 1988

* *The journalist John McCarthy was on assignment in Beirut for United Press International Television News when he was taken hostage by the Islamic Jihad. He was held for some 1,943 days before the United Nations were able to secure his release. His mother died while he was still in captivity.*

⌒✐⌒

A NEW CHANNEL

Rupert rang. We talked for an hour … I asked him how his new Sky channel was going. He said, 'Very well.' He is confident about it. He is going to have about four stations, I gather. One is going to have international news all the time, a proper news service. I said, 'It would be antidote then to the BBC and to a lesser extent to ITN. You will probably be impartial.' 'Oh, yes.' 'And if there is a Falklands War again you might even be on our side.' He laughed and said, 'Yes, absolutely.'

Woodrow Wyatt, Journals, 23 November 1988

⌒✐⌒

FATWA AGAINST *SATANIC VERSES*

Ayatollah Khomeini's call for Salman Rushdie to be killed because of his novel *The Satanic Verses* is blasphemous and makes it even more important that socialists are clear about the issues. Everyone regrets the genuine offence caused to thousands of ordinary Muslims because of what they have been told is in Mr Rushdie's book.

And Muslims in Britain are entitled to resent being lectured on tolerance by a society which has often shown its ethnic minorities cruel intolerance and whose prime minister bans books, programmes and interviews at will.

But censorship is wrong …

Thatcher has made liberalism and tolerance deeply unfashionable. But they are still values worth taking a stand on. Not least, because they afford the only real protection for Britain's religious and ethnic minorities.

Diane Abbott, Letter to the *Guardian*, 16 February 1989

There is only one way out of this rat-like existence for him. By recanting his blasphemies publicly, he can win a reprieve to make amends for the wrong he has done. God *is* oft-forgiving, most merciful.

Inayatullah Zaigham, Letter to the *Independent*, 17 February 1989

⸿

THATCHER VISITS HILLSBOROUGH

Margaret had been to Hillsborough to see the football ground where the disaster was yesterday and to see and talk to survivors.*

She said, 'It must be the end of terraces. We must have seats and tickets only.' 'There is no leadership in the Football Association any more,' I said, 'They spend millions on buying players from each other but not on their grounds.'

Woodrow Wyatt, Journals, 16 April 1989

* On 15 April 1989, the FA Cup semi-final match between Liverpool and Nottingham Forest was set to take place at Sheffield Wednesday's Hillsborough ground. Crowds of Liverpool supporters were ushered into already overcrowded standing pens; ninety-six people were crushed to death and hundreds more were injured. The full facts of the catastrophe, and in particular the defamatory tales spun afterwards by the police and the Sun, were only fully revealed in 2016, when the longest inquest in British history was completed. The jurors concluded that the match police commander was 'responsible for manslaughter by gross negligence'.

HORRIFIED BY THE *SUN*

I have purchased the *Sun* newspaper for several years, but after your edition of Wednesday, 19 April, 1989, I will buy no more.

I have two grandsons who were at Hillsborough, in the section of the ground affected by the tragedy. They are honest, truthful, upright young men, who returned home with horror in their eyes but, at the same time, were full of praise from the compassion shown and the help given by supporters to their fellows. This is far from the stories which were printed in your paper and I, for one, know whose version of events to believe …

Name withheld, Letter to the *Sun*, 20 April 1989

GAY PRIDE WITH PURPOSE

The Pride march is the most joyous day in the calendar. Nothing can compare with the elation as the street becomes 'ours' for a few short hours, the whistle blowing, cheering, waving and songs – She'll be coming with a woman when she comes …

The girls and boys on the march are without doubt the handsomest both in mind and body. They have the moral high ground. And each year in spite of Margaret Thatcher's delinquent government, they are happier and more relaxed. Nothing shall turn the tide back now. Clause 28* is a clarion cry to unity, and has given us new purpose …

Derek Jarman, *Modern Nature*, 24 June 1989

* Part of the Local Government Act passed by the Conservative government in 1988, Clause 28 prohibited local authorities from 'promoting' homosexuality or gay 'pretend family relationships', and banned councils from spending money on educational materials and projects perceived to promote gay lifestyles. In 2009, David Cameron, the first Conservative prime minister to attend a Gay Pride event, made a public apology for the infamous legislative clause.

RAVES IN THE EAST MIDLANDS

SOMETHING ODD AND EXCITING HAPPENED tonight. Me and Dobber were walking in Red Lion Square after what was quite a normal Wednesday night in the pub, and this bloke in a car screeched up behind us and said, 'Do you know where the RAVE is?' We were like, 'Err … no.'

Then another car turned up and asked us exactly the same question, which is amazing because that surely means that there are illegal raves going on in LINCOLNSHIRE!

We have GOT to find one. I've never even seen any real drugs up close. I am sort of chuffed indeed that I look like the sort of person that would be into rave.

Rae Earl, *My Fat, Mad Teenage Diary*, 19 July 1989

THE *MARCHIONESS* DISASTER

Many drowned in the Thames when, in the early hours of Sunday morning, a dredger runs down a pleasure boat. The circumstances are bad enough – the party in full swing, the huge black dredger tipping the boat on its side before running it down, but this doesn't stop the reportage making it worse. 'Revellers', says ITN, 'were tipped into the freezing waters.' 'Left struggling in the icy waters of the Thames' is another report. It was actually one of the hottest nights of the year, and one of the rescued says that the water was warm, only very dirty. One sane girl, whose Italian boyfriend is missing, refuses to give her name to reporters because 'she doesn't want to become a news item'. Undeterred by becoming a news item, Mrs Thatcher, in her capacity as Mother of Her People, circles the spot in a police launch and is filmed bending caringly over a computer screen in the incident room.

Alan Bennett, Diaries, 22 August 1989

⌒*ſ*⌒

ACID AND ANGEL DELIGHT

The weekend was full-on. Me and Amy dragged a crate of beer from the station to our village of tents.

I wore espadrilles. I wish I had DMs.

B. thought the lasers in the sky meant it was World War III. I did acid on the Friday. K. came to watch Inspiral Carpets with me on Saturday.

I made Angel Delight. It got kicked over.

Kirsty Allison, Diaries, 3 September 1989

⌒*ſ*⌒

INCOMPREHENSIBLE NEW MACHINES

I find all the new machines quite incomprehensible, can't operate the new ticket machines in the underground. The old ones were easy. With crowds pushing down on me I give up and, embarrassed, wait nearly three minutes at the counter.

'Do you put money in those Mercury telephones or use a card?' I asked a taxi driver.

'Haven't a clue how to operate them,' he said.

So I'm not the only one. Oh, for the simple re-decimal life, where distance was measured in feet and inches, temperature in Fahrenheit.

Derek Jarman, *Modern Nature*, 10 September 1989

NOTTINGHAM IN FIGHTING FORM

After a quick Indian meal, I took Jo up Waverley Street, from the summit of which we looked down on the sea of coloured lights delineating Goose Fair. Immediately, we crested the hill, the hitherto subdued noise – the chugging machinery, the shrieking girls, the snatches of music – jumped in volume. It grew steadily as we walked downhill and entered the crowd, through which the smell of cigarettes and hotdogs wafted.

Supplementing the usual dodgems and helter-skelters were some traditional shows – a hall of mirrors, the Snake Lady, the Tallest Man in Scotland, and even a boxing booth … In the centre of it stood an ancient, red-nosed Irish MC. Alongside him, their muscular arms folded, was a line of battered-looking boxers …

The only people keen to fight [them] were two small boys, aged no more than about eleven. They kept raising their hands. And the Irishman kept saying, 'Sorry, we've nobody your size.'

Paul Willetts, Diaries, 7 October 1989

FALL OF THE BERLIN WALL

THE BERLIN WALL IS COMING DOWN! THE BERLIN WALL IS COMING DOWN! CAN YOU BELIEVE IT?! THERE ARE PEOPLE ON TOP OF THE BERLN WALL HAMMERING IT DOWN WITH AXES – CHEERING AND SHOUTING – IT'S BRILLIANT!

ALL THOSE YEARS BRICKING MYSELF ABOUT NUCLEAR WAR – ABOUT FOUR-MINUTE WARNINGS – ABOUT MELTING – ABOUT BEING AWAY FROM MY MUM WHEN IT STARTS – HAVE GONE! God … all that stress for nothing.

Kids like my nephew have no idea what a better world they will be growing up in. I bet Sting is pissed off, as his song 'Russians' will seem incredibly stupid. However, Elton John can go and see Nikita now!

But I've just realised something depressing: even bloody Communism has collapsed and I still haven't lost my bloody virginity.

Rae Earl, *My Fat, Mad Teenage Diary*, 10 November 1989

FESTIVE SEND-OFF

The fighting carries on in Romania. After a video of the execution of Ceausescu, the newscaster wished us a peaceful Christmas, without much conviction.

Derek Jarman, *Modern Nature*, 26 December 1989

NON-SKIP DISC

FORGOT TO TELL YOU – got a CD player for Christmas. Unfortunately, I currently only have one CD and that's the Eagles' *Greatest Hits* borrowed off one of my mum's friends. Still, it's brilliant – and no more record jumping when I dance.

Rae Earl, *My Fat, Mad Teenage Diary*, 28 December 1989

CHAPTER TEN

LET'S ALL MEET UP IN THE YEAR 2000: 1990-1999

On 12 March 1989 the British computer scientist Tim Berners-Lee delivered a paper to his colleagues at CERN, the European Organization for Nuclear Research, in Geneva. Entitled, rather drably, 'Information Management: A Proposal', it contained a modest outline for a way that computers might be linked over a network so that information could be accessed and shared from any location in the world. Berners-Lee and his colleague Robert Cailliau beavered away on the idea over the course of the next year, presenting a more substantial scheme to CERN on 12 November 1990. They now had a name for their network: the World Wide Web.

The Web debuted to the public on 6 August 1991. Less than two years later, Ted Leonsis of the Internet dial-up service America Online sent his first instant message to his wife, telling her, 'Don't be scared ... it is me. Love you and miss you.' She replied, 'Wow ... this is so cool!' With the founding of search engine Google in 1996–7, the extraordinary journey from Don't Be Scared to Don't Be Evil began in earnest. Even Tim Berners-Lee couldn't possibly have dreamed of where the Internet would take us.

Of course, one change to our lives wrought by the Internet is especially pertinent to this collection: now people could keep and publish a diary online, potentially sharing their thoughts with an audience of millions around the globe. But, as captured in the entries included here from Dickon Edwards – one of the many diarists to move online – access to the Internet was still patchy. For the bulk of the decade – from the poll tax protests and the resignation of Margaret Thatcher to the election of New Labour and the death of Princess Diana – news and personal information continued to be received and exchanged by landline phone calls, newspapers and radio and television broadcasts, and the only tweets anyone had heard about were those made by birds.

The nation's culinary and cultural horizons were expanding in other ways, however. We see the first samplings of guacamole and visits to a conceptual art show featuring works by Damien Hirst. And for all the tumultuous events and the social, political and technological changes that had occurred, taking us from steam trains to cloned sheep, our century was effectively bookended by the passing of one member of the Royal family at its beginning, and of another at its finale.

But where Queen Victoria's death in 1901 marked the end of an age, perhaps Princess Diana's in 1997 augured something new for the twenty-first century to come. The very public displays of mourning that followed her tragic demise, and the outpouring of genuine grief, saw a brief abandonment of traditional British reserve. In its stead came a scepticism towards authority, a demand for a more informal and emotionally honest society and an obsession with celebrity. The genie has never quite gone back in the bottle since.

⁓

CHECK OUT THE PUDDINGS

Visited the food hall at M&S; it has all the English puddings: gooseberry fool, summer pudding, bread and butter, but no queen's pudding, which HB said would be most popular. Check-out like the check-in at a Gay disco.

Derek Jarman, Modern Nature, 13 January 1990

⁓

RIOTS AGAINST POLL TAX

Last night there were riots in London. All the anarchist scum, class-war, random drop-outs and trouble seekers … There is this strain in most Western countries, but it is particularly prevalent in Britain, where this rabble have – confirming their middle-class social origins – their own press in the *Grauniad* [*sic*] and the *Independent*.

Alan Clark, Diaries, 2 April 1990

* *Introduced in Scotland in 1989 and in England and Wales in 1990, the poll tax, or community charge, was promoted by the Conservative government as a fairer means of paying for local services than domestic rates, since it was a universal, flat-rated levy. However, as it was levied equally on everyone regardless of means, many branded it as a regressive measure.*

A LIBERAL DILEMMA

A. and I see a transvestite striding up the street with a mane of hennaed hair, short skirt and long, skinny legs. It's the legs that give him/her away – scrawny, unfleshed and too nobbly for a girl's. He/she has also attracted the attention of someone in the snooker hall above the pub, and there's a lot of shouting. Later, as we are getting into the car, Gary, a young man crippled with arthritis, calls out to A. from the snooker hall. She knows him and asks if it was him that was doing the shouting. 'Yes,' he says proudly. 'You shouldn't.' 'Why?' he asks. 'Because', I put in weakly, 'it's a free country.' 'No, it isn't.' 'Well, you shouldn't,' A. says again: 'I should think about it' – meaning, I suppose, that if it's all right to shout at transvestites, next on the list will be cripples with arthritis. This is lost on Gary, who starts to shout at us, too. It's a comic encounter, and the liberal dilemma it poses impenetrable. We mustn't abuse sexual deviants, but we must also be tolerant of the handicapped who do.

Alan Bennett, *Writing Home*, 17 May 1990

SORTED FOR ES, IF NOT THE RAVE

The police shut down the rave. We've dropped already, so dance in the car park.

Kirsty Allison, Diaries, 16 July 1990

ANNIVERSARY OF BATTLE OF BRITAIN

WHAT a bore! All this fuss about the bloody RAF, the Battle of Britain etc. etc. this coming weekend. The Boys in Blue, red sports cars, bristling moustaches, all of them probably working in garages before the War. Bloody Biggles! Bloody Bader! Bloody Cheshire! Bloody Hillary!

Richard Cobb, Letter to Hugh Trevor-Roper, 11 September 1990

THE PEOPLE'S MARCH

Fiona and I head out across the grass to distant public toilets, and come back singing: 'Thatcher says we've got to pay – we've not paying anyway.'

Back at the assembly point, the march is lining up. There's a solid body of police as far as I can see, lots of police with fluorescent jackets on, stewards with red and white bibs, and TV crews ... Placard forests, pushchairs, homemade APTU [Anti-Poll Tax Union] banners ...

At the gate to Brockwell Park ... people are coming in five and six abreast and there seems to be no end to them. Just back off the gate is a railway bridge and as each section passes under they re-double the singing, whistling and drum-banging, so it's a deafening roar all the time where we're standing ...

One of the stewards by the bus is telling me we only got permission to use Brockwell Park this Wednesday – three days before the demo! Seems you have to get insurance and not a single insurance company would offer a policy. So insurance companies are now the ones who decide whether or not demonstrations are held! Lambeth councillors finally agreed to let us [have] the park – to avoid trouble if the march had nowhere to go ...

At the Caribbean Food Co-op. Stall advertising 'marchers' specials' me and Hugh get vegeburgers and wander back ...

Said goodbye to Jackie, heading out the park, and back by the bus, marchers are dispersing more rapidly than I'd expected.

It's clearly time to go ...

Three times as much air time for minor clashes – provoked by what you can see, even from these shots – is something like a five to one presence in the police favour. There's nothing you can say about the frustration we feel. So far as the BBC is concerned, there never was a People's March Against the Poll Tax.

Sally Brown, *Diary of a People's Marcher*, 20 October 1990

FATEFUL RESIGNATION

Well, now I'm really fucking depressed. Geoffrey Howe resigned tonight. I think the whole thing is falling apart, over Europe too, which is the right issue – but it could let Labour in by default, perhaps less than a year from now.*

Edwina Currie, Diaries, 1 November 1990

* Howe was the last remaining member of Mrs Thatcher's original 1979 Cabinet. His resignation, over Thatcher's policies towards Europe and her personal opposition to a single European currency, precipitated the end of her premiership. After Howe departed, the pro-European Michael Heseltine felt emboldened to stand against her in a leadership contest. She failed to win this outright and resigned. Eventually, Chancellor John Major secured the leadership and succeeded her as prime minister.

cﬀ

MAGGIE OUT

The news? 'Thatcher's resigned.'

Spent stunned minutes in bewilderment and anger.

Then someone said:

'She resigned at the wrong time, I've fought that bloody woman for eleven years ... she's still out of order ... I'm not happy. She's cheated the gallows ... I wanted to see the knife twist, and her personally humiliated.'

An event from a different world, to the extent that I almost expect it to be a hoax, a mistake, or a dream, or her to rescind on it; on the way home I was starting to think it wasn't actually true, until I saw 'OFFICIAL: THATCHER RESIGNS' at the top of Woodhill ... Strange, particularly because it's so 'out of character', especially after her quick re-entry for the 2nd ballot on Tuesday.

Over, just like that, reported 3rd-hand like a ludicrous dream. Though from '79 to '90, I've wanted 'Maggie out' just like everyone around me, I'm not happy about this: anything that helps their precious Party Unity, and lets her look humorous, dignified, emotional – some chance – is a bad thing. So, no sentiment here. The Thatcher Years, they weren't really that bad – but I reckon she *was*.

Joe Brooker, Diaries, 22 November 1990

⌘

HANDOUTS FOR THE HOMELESS

Richard Briers tells me how he was going up the steps from the National on to Waterloo Bridge when he was accosted, as one invariably is, by someone sitting on the landing, begging. 'No, I thought,' said Richard, 'not *again*, and walked on. Only then I heard this lugubrious voice say, "Oh. My favourite actor." So I turned back and gave him a pound.'

That particular pitch is known to be very profitable, partly because of actors and playgoers being more soft-hearted than the general run. The beggars have got themselves so well-organized as to ration the pitch to half an hour apiece on pain of being beaten up. I find it easiest to think of Waterloo Bridge as a toll bridge, and resign myself to paying at least 50p to get across, thus sidestepping any tiresome questions about need or being taken advantage of.

Alan Bennett, *Writing Home*, 8 December 1990

⌘

THE GULF WAR

DEADLINE FOR IRAQ TO WITHDRAW TROOPS FROM KUWAIT. IRAQ DID NOT WITHDRAW. GULF WAR STARTED. I WAS SO SHOCKED, depressed, heartbroken. Saddam Hussein is a pig. I hate him.

Anita Sethi, Diaries, 15 January 1991

⌘

CONFIDENCE IN THE NEW SET

Today I am 19 on 19.1.1991 AND it's a Saturday! This is my special year. Halfway through Foundation and finished the week by starting my painting of a woman with her legs open. Next, I'll paint a male. Had a chat with Hilary. Said I wanted to paint the male in violent and cold colours. Hilary said I was a hypocrite. Then I talked with Greg from Brighton and he confided he was more feminine than male; one of the new set.

Karen McLeod, Diaries, 19 January 1991

GULF WAR PARANOIA

Gave mad Granny Mary a lift. She believes that the Gulf War is a fiction dreamt up by the media, she also believes that the people in the flat above her are drilling to get in – complete paranoia.

Last Christmas she locked herself into her flat and put mad poems up in the windows – 'Who shot the owl, in Avondale Park? Murder most fowl, who shot the owl …' She'd apparently woken one night, heard an owl hooting and then a shot. When I went to see her it was rather creepy …

Virginia Ironside, Diaries, 17 February 1991

HORRORS, REAL AND IMAGINED

Had a mammogram, which involves your boobs being squeezed electronically between two sheets of metal and photographed. Horrible.

Saw *Silence of the Lambs*, famed horror film which wasn't very horrifying.

Virginia Ironside, Diaries, 20 June 1991

DELICIOUS DISH

Work experience at Granada TV studios: I met Vera Duckworth from *Coronation Street*. I'd never heard of her but she obviously expected me to have. She was very sweet ...

I went into a studio and watched a recording of this utterly naff (even naffer than *Blind Date*) quiz show called *Love at First Sight* ... The contestants were awful people, like throwbacks to some earlier stage of evolution. The audience was 90% pensioners ...

Later, we had dinner in a Mexican restaurant with a rather delicious dish called Guacamole made of avocados.

Rowena Macdonald, Diaries, 5 July 1991

◦乢◦

CRACKING THE DRUG CODE

H still in Isle of Wight. Was extremely alarmed because he received three postcards from friends full of weird druggy references ... 'No sign of Stan who has gone up everyone's nose but look forward to meeting Charlie brother of Stan on our return.' My hair stood on end. I mean, in the book of Drug Terms and what they mean Charlie is cocaine and when I rang Scoda, the Standing Committee on Drug Abuse, they told me that Stanley and Oliver were Ecstasy and Acid. It all sounds utterly ridiculous. Anyway, I rang H in quite a tizz and he was very reassuring ... Turns out he's taken acid once but it wasn't his thing and he has as little idea of what Stan and Charlie means as I do, but also thinks C must mean cocaine and thinks his friend is appalling to have sent cards like that ...

Virginia Ironside, Diaries, 1 September 1991

◦乢◦

MAXWELL'S NON-SMOKING HOUSE

Lots of good Maxwell jokes, of course. Did you hear about Bob – bob – bob – bob – bob.

Turns out Mr Full Fathom Five, as he is known at the *Mirror*, certainly was a crook to beat all crooks. Luckily, I didn't have any money in the pension fund as I'm freelance. When he interviewed me he actually had the gall to ask about my pension and when I said I had made my own arrangements, he said: 'Good, good idea.' He was an absolute monster, pure evil. He even bugged his chief executives' offices. Wonderful headline in the *Mirror* with an enormous picture of the security man who had installed the bugs, announcing: 'THIS IS THE BUGGER!'

Everyone has a Maxwell story. Latest is that he was always roaming the corridors sacking people in front of his entourage to show off. One day, he came across a man in a no-smoking zone, smoking. Furious, he demanded to know his name and then told him he was fired for smoking. 'How long have you worked here?' he shouted. 'Seven years, sir,' mumbled the man. Maxwell then worked out how much redundancy he owed him, took a wad of notes from his wallet, thrust £2,000 on him and said: 'Never let me see you again!' It turned out that this man was not an employee at all but on contract hire from another company to repair the typewriters!*

Virginia Ironside, Diaries, 20 November 1991

* *Robert Maxwell, the flamboyant publisher of the* Daily Mirror, *drowned after falling off his yacht while sailing near the Canary Islands on 5 November 1991. The precise circumstances of his demise remain a mystery, but after his death Maxwell was found to have misappropriated millions of pounds from the Mirror Group's pension fund.*

DOPE AT THE DANCE

Yesterday I went to the School Dance. Thank God it's the last one I'll ever have to go to. It was OK but fairly dire. The best thing that happened was two boys got chucked out by a parent for smoking dope. What I want to know is, how did the parents know it was dope; they must have smoked it themselves at one time – hypocritical or what?

Rowena Macdonald, Diaries, 14 December 1991

OUT IN COURT

HB and Howard arrived at eleven. They brought the papers, the court case of Jason Donovan – Straight as Hell, while the rest of us are Queer as Fuck. If Jason makes any money out of this it can only prove that for years we have laboured against the odds.

The Oscars are on TV and Queer Nation demonstrates. Jodie Foster – also the subject of an outing campaign – receives her Oscar; meanwhile, two young fans of Jason who've seen him in the Technicolour Dreamcoat forty-five times say: 'We don't care if he's gay, we love him.'*

Derek Jarman, Smiling in Slow Motion, 1 April 1992

* *The Australian soap opera star and singer Jason Donovan went to court after The Face magazine printed a piece on the 'outing' of gay entertainers. The article merely pointed out that Donovan was being plagued by people seeking to expose him as gay, even though there was no evidence that he was; however, it had been accompanied by a mocked-up picture of Donovan wearing a T-shirt emblazoned with the words 'Queer as Fuck'. Donovan sued and won.*

AN ELECTION EXPERIENCE

General Election – sick and tired of it. It's got to have been the longest 3 weeks ever.

But it has to be said that the campaign has been extraordinary in the way

Labour have dominated the whole thing. Labour have called the shots from start to finish. The Tories have looked defeated and demoralized, and totally without ideas. While Labour have been supremely confident and look like a team that have had a long spell of successful government.

Got a phone call from Walworth Road [Labour HQ] Friday morning asking me to attend the launch of Labour's Youth Cinema Advert …

The whole thing was a bit patronizing and completely stage-managed – but nonetheless quite an experience.

John Rogers, Diaries, 7 April 1992

~

CITY OF LONDON BOMBED

On the number 10 sailing round Hyde Park Corner, the sun comes up.

There is one and half billion pounds of IRA damage in the City. All is normal.

Derek Jarman, *Smiling in Slow Motion*, 13 April 1992

~

DISSING THE DALAI LAMA

Lunch with this canon from Westminster Abbey today. He said that the Dalai Lama had come to the Abbey once and spoken to the congregation and 'quite honestly what he said was the biggest string of platitudes about peace and love I've ever heard and if I'd said it in an ordinary sermon no one would have given me the time of day afterwards'. His argument against Buddhism (the canon's) is that he doesn't like the way you have to strive for levels of spirituality ambitiously in Buddhism, like being promoted in a job, whereas in the Christian religion you are given grace by God.

Virginia Ironside, Diaries, 31 May 1992

~

OLD PUNKS GONGED

Vivienne Westwood accepts an OBE, dipsy bitch. The silly season's with us: our punk friends accept their little medals of betrayal, sit in their vacuous salons and destroy the creative – like woodworm in my dresser, which I will paint with insecticide tomorrow. I would love to place a man-sized insectocutor, lit with royal-blue, to burn up this clothes moth and her like.

Derek Jarman, *Smiling in Slow Motion*, 20 June 1992

LIFE MODELS ART?

Ill. Ill. Ill. Woke up very late in nervous state. Life-modelled at Chapter Arts. One bloke drew me distorted. Another 'A' level student drew only my boobs on red paper. In the break, I said, 'Fill the rest of me in, will you?' …

Karen McLeod, Diaries, 2 October 1992

WOES OF THE ECONOMY

The whole country is in the lurch, absolutely lost in the monetary storm. Everything is falling apart: the roads, industries, health, education, foreign policy and the blessed £. I have felt that the appeals to recovery are hollow, the slide is permanent. Frightened bankers try to drag the unwilling electorate into the monetary union; all *they* see is Brussels interfering with their potato crisps or ruining cheese. The fate of the invisible money which flies around the world at the press of a button seems remote as the virus. How can one muster enthusiasm for ERMs* and exchange rates? Capital fails to deliver; if the £ goes down the shares go up with the prices and queues of unemployed, 1,000 more of them each day.

Derek Jarman, *Smiling in Slow Motion*, 3 October 1992

* *The British pound sterling joined the EU's Exchange Rate Mechanism (ERM) in 1990 and soon struggled to remain inside its designated floating band, which was intended to ensure stability on the currency markets. On 16 September 1992, a date subsequently known as Black Wednesday, the value of the pound dropped, and despite the Conservative Chancellor Norman Lamont buying billions of pounds to prop it up, the pound fell below the minimum rate required and crashed out of the ERM entirely.*

⟡

CHARLES AND DIANA TO PART

At 3.30 today the PM got to his feet to announce the separation of the Prince and Princess of Wales. John Smith was commendably brief. Paddy Ashdown less so. Ted Heath went way over the top. Then (this was truly bizarre) Bob Cryer was on his feet asking us to remember divorces everywhere and telling us that it's poor housing and unemployment that puts marriages under strain and it's all the Government's fault! Next up popped Dennis Skinner to tell us 'we don't need a monarchy anyroad'.

Gyles Brandreth, *Something Sensational to Read in the Train*, 9 December 1992

⟡

THE LOSS OF THE YOUNG HARDER TO BEAR

More on Rudolf in the papers and a request to do 'HIV and the Arts' for *Newsweek*.* I'm not at all certain that anything other than a sense of continuity across the generations – the chance of a young dancer to see the 'great dancer' sitting on his sofa at the edge of the stage – has been lost. Rudolf leapt his last long before the HIV carried him away. I feel the same about Freddie Mercury – is one less Queen album any loss? The answer has to be no.

How many more journeys did Bruce Chatwin have to make? How many more photographs did Mapplethorpe have to snap? Hadn't all of their work been completed? It's friends like David, a twenty-four-year-old at the Slade, who are the loss.

Derek Jarman, *Smiling in Slow Motion*, 11 January 1993

* *Rudolf Nureyev, the Soviet Russian-born ballet dancer who defected to the West in 1961, was diagnosed with HIV in 1984. He died of a heart condition exacerbated by the disease on 6 January 1993.*

SHAMEFUL HOLLYWOOD ENDING

I did not get to sleep last night until midnight because we went to see *Scent of a Woman*. It was three hours with all the ads and waiting. The cinema was packed because it was a Bank Holiday … Al Pacino really does deserve that Oscar. He was fantastic – a blind depressive who has one last fabulous weekend before he puts the lid on himself. Except he doesn't and the movie has a Hollywood ending. What a shame.

Anna Maconochie, Diaries, 2 May 1993

A RIGHT ROYAL ROASTING

Wrote a barmy piece for the newspaper on Major Ron Ferguson, Fergie's dad, who has been up to more capers. The *Today* newspaper keeps asking me to write these blistering pieces on the royals, which I find great fun because it gives me a chance to stop being caring and serious and be bitchy and funny instead. It is like turning into Glenda Slag of *Private Eye* – like speaking a different language. The pieces don't actually start 'Who d'ya think yer kidding, Charles? Up yours, yer maj!' but pretty nearly.

Virginia Ironside, Diaries, 19 May 1993

A CHANGE IN GENDER

Today I met a most impressive human being. Jay Walmsley is a transsexual who works as a man in a high-up position in a large international company, and she wants me to be her spiritual director, which is a challenge because my knowledge of transsexualism is sketchy. However, like all spiritual direction it will be a two-way process and I shall learn a lot.

As John, she married in 1967 and has two daughters. The wife died five years ago, and John began to face up to the fact that since the age of seven he has felt himself to be a woman but has to do all the male things. No one at work knows the situation, but he attends a church in Caterham as a woman and most of the congregation accept her.

Rev. Dr Malcolm Johnson, *Diary of a Gay Priest*, 11 November 1993

THE COVER OF *COSMO*

It is now April, one of my favourite months. I just love it. Astrologically, Aries is meant to go well with Leo and now is the month for Aries. But I do not take that stuff very seriously. Somehow, *Cosmo* covers always have Claudia Schiffer on the cover for April. This month, her hair is too blonde and her dress is naff. I am not a fan ...

Maybe I should write to *Cosmo* and tell them to cut down on Claudia covers ...

Anna Maconochie, Diaries, 3 April 1994

ODDS AGAINST IT

The first National Lottery is drawn tonight. The tabloids have been full of lottery fever all week. I can't say I share their enthusiasm, but all the same I went to the post office and purchased three tickets. There was a long queue.

The jackpot is said to be £7 million … The odds against winning are about 50 million to one.

Chris Mullin, *A Walk-on Part*, 19 November 1994

~

SCHOOLED IN ABUSE

Need to do some serious saving before the next Take That concert tix go on sale.

Jane told this joke at school today: *Why did the Romans build straight roads? So Pakis couldn't build corner shops.* She knows my grandma has a corner shop and lives above it and she still said it in front of me.

Too tired to do homework. Got Maths test tomorrow. Shite. Robbie will never love me because of my skin colour. Bought some foundation from Superdrug but it's the wrong colour. They haven't got my colour.

Anita Sethi, Diaries, 19 January 1995

~

THE DUNBLANE MASSACRE

A school photograph of the children murdered in Dunblane dominates most of today's newspapers. I wept when I saw it. Fifteen beautiful little people, their faces full of hope and innocence, whose lives have been cut short by an inexplicable act of madness. I think of all the years of love and care invested in the bringing up of one small person, wiped out in a single day.*

Chris Mullin, *A Walk-on Part*, 14 March 1996

* *On 13 March 1996, Thomas Hamilton, a one-time local scoutmaster, went on a shooting spree at a primary school in Dunblane, Scotland, killing sixteen children and their teacher. In the wake of this shocking massacre, the government moved to ban almost all handguns from that October onwards.*

TAKE THAT PILGRIMAGE

We all ran up against the wire fence and then Take That got off the plane and you could see them real clear. They stood for a couple of minutes and waved, it was so sweet of them. I'm sure, and so is Lisa, that Mark glanced at us for a few seconds, I could feel his eyes on me. Then they got back on the coach. It felt so crazy and immense. We drove to Mark's, past Jason's. Some girls were hugging each other and it turned out he'd just driven in, in his Dad's red Micra. Seconds later, the garage opened and he came out with his dad, unloaded his suitcase, smiled, but you could tell he was making a special effort. Mark said, 'What you doin' here on such a lovely sunny day, you should be in the park with your boyfriends.'

Anita Sethi, Diaries, 5 April 1996

DODGY HANDSHAKES

[Tony] Blair is in New York. He was pictured on the news last night shaking hands with Henry Kissinger. Really, this is too much. What has rubbing shoulders with a clapped-out war criminal got to do with getting us elected?

Chris Mullin, *A Walk-on Part*, 11 April 1996

CARNAGE IN MANCHESTER

Manchester has just been ripped apart. I was in the city centre and it was packed with Euro 96 tourists and there was police directing the traffic. It was a boiling hot day. Saw areas cordoned off. The traffic was stuck in a massive queue and I was on the road where Band on the Wall is and suddenly there was a massive bang and the whole city shook like it was an earthquake. The buildings right next to us, the derelict shops, kind of exploded – all the glass shattered and fell out and the alarms went off. It was really scary. There was black smoke filling the air and people were standing in the streets looking dazed. It was like something in a book or film. It was the IRA ... It's just disgusting and pointless – how could anyone do it? If the police hadn't moved everyone it would have been complete carnage – so we were pretty lucky. But over 200 people hurt including a little baby ...

Anita Sethi, Diaries , 15 June 1996

LEGENDARY MADCHESTER NIGHT

I got into the Haçienda for the first time. It was freezing cold and pissing it down as we were queuing up, and in the distance could see the great big archway of the bridge, and through that GMEX and a massive warehouse. Some guy was walking up and down the queue offering people pills. Some lads were taking the piss and one said to me: 'What's a poppadom like you doing dressed up like that? Shouldn't you be at home cooking curry?' Thank God we finally lost sight of the idiot ... Inside, there were yellow and black hazard strips on boulders and the music was so fucking loud, that Underworld song over and over again, and we danced loads and it was so buzzing to be out dancing, I felt so free ...

Anita Sethi, Diaries, 22 February 1997

Built in a former yacht builder's warehouse next to the Rochdale Canal and financed by Factory Records, Manchester's Haçienda nightclub was the centre of the Madchester rave scene. It was closed on 28 June 1997, having been dogged by issues over drugs and gang violence.

CALLING ALL COMMUTERS

Feeling absolutely awful I nevertheless go to London for [the] day. Not a success. Went First Class for once. Full of businessmen glued to telephones, very irritating.

James Lees-Milne, Diaries, 10 April 1997

WHAT'S NEW ABOUT LABOUR?

The Tories have had 18 years; 5 years out of power isn't a prospect to scare them. They're a permanent fixture, not necessarily the eternal party of government but always, at the very least, awaiting their next turn; & it's undeniable that their 18 years have set the terms on which others must (do) campaign & (maybe) govern.

But Labour? 5 defeats in a row? What serious party can stomach that?

From 10/4/92 we assumed that the future was about coalitions, compromises, anti-Tory fronts; that was the new realism, & even that not very realistic. Amid Blair's charge, we've forgotten all that; & maybe he's made enough changes to ensure it'll survive as a party for one more term. But still, defeat means far more to us than it does to them.

Joe Brooker, Diaries, 23 April 1997

EURO-SCEPTICAL

Westcountry Television, the region's ITV channel based in Plymouth, invited me to take part in a live debate on their early-evening magazine show. The topic was 'Doomed to decline – the West Country in the Millennium'.

... The big issue for most of the callers on the phone-in was Europe. Nothing you could politely describe as Euro-sceptical either. This was undiluted xenophobia. A man called Hank, choking with rage and fighting back his tears, stuttered: 'I was born British and I want to die British.'

I left the studio slightly dazed and shocked. Anti-European feeling is running high in these parts, that's for sure.

Kit Chapman, *An Innkeeper's Diary*, 24 April 1997

ALL SMILES FOR NEW LABOUR

I wake up to a different world. I very rarely watch TV over breakfast, but this morning I feel obliged to turn it on and catch the pictures of last night's events – the ones I slept through. I am amazed, stunned by the cheering crowds who lined the streets in the middle of the night. It doesn't resemble an election victory so much as a liberation, and Tony Blair and Cherie Blair greet the crowd like conquering heroes. Whichever way you lean politically, there is no ignoring the strength of feeling which lies behind this. The people have spoken, and they've opted for change.

People are smiling a bit more than usual, I find. But when the newsagent asks one of his regulars what she thinks about the new government, she simply replies, 'I don't like politicians.'

Deborah Bull, *A Covent Garden Diary*, 2 May 1997

GREEN LIGHT FOR THE GREENWICH DOME

Incredibly – and against all expectations … Blair has decided to go ahead with the ludicrous Millennium Dome at Greenwich. Absolute madness. The last thing we need, as we close down hospitals and collapse the voluntary sector is a big black hole in Greenwich into which we pour money.

Chris Mullin, *A Walk-on Part*, 19 June 1997

DEATH OF PRINCESS DIANA

Already the improbable was dawning, & true: DIANA DEAD. Suicide? No, a car crash, in a Paris tunnel, late at night on the way back (where?) from dinner at the Ritz. All that farcical fascination with 'Di & Dodi' ends in this warped metal, with people still looking for narrative, cogency & meaning: paparazzi motorcyclists hounded them into it, it seems.

Joe Brooker, Diaries, 31 August 1997

I can't believe it.

The news is saying that the paparazzi chased her to death – fame is so fucking destructive.

Then later today R. came to visit and went on about how everyone is fussing over Diana and no one gives a fuck about the young French tutor he knew who got run over a few weeks ago, that her death never even made it into the papers.

Anita Sethi, Diaries, 31 August 1997

Hysteria over the death of the Princess continues, people 'from all walks of life' queuing down the Mall, not merely to sign the book but to sit there writing for up to 15 minutes at a time. Others, presumably, just write 'Why?', which suggests a certain cosmic awareness while at least having the merit of brevity.

Alan Bennett, Diaries, 2 September 1997

TOPSY-TURVY AFTER DIANA

The public clamour after Diana's death is increasing. Newspapers have devoted whole issues, the television last Sunday was devoted to her entirely, and Kensington Palace and its surrounding park have become a sea of flowers as never-ending waves of devotees turn it into a shrine in her honour. The lighted candles, photographs, and messages pinned to the trees take me back to Kyoto and its Shinto shrines, but the open emotions are more South Asian and belie the Englishness of Kensington Gardens.

It seems that we live in a topsy-turvy world; a woman who was mocked and belittled in her life is now praised and beatified in her death. Most of the papers, particularly the tabloids, managed to sanitise their Sunday editions before they hit news-stands, but one or two old-style items slipped through the net, reminding us that until a few days ago Diana was a woman in the midst of a headline-grabbing love affair, and not the saintly icon she has now become. Alone amongst the papers, the street-vendored *Big Issue*, run, as it presumably is, on a shoestring, could not afford to scrap its print run and remove a tongue-in-cheek, sniping article, written before Sunday morning's tragedy. Instead, they were obliged to insert an apology slip and cross their fingers in hope that their readers wouldn't take offence. It would be too sadly ironic if a charity devoted to one of her 'causes', the homeless, were to suffer deficits through her death.

Deborah Bull, *A Covent Garden Diary*, 4 September 1997

⸉⸉

A NEW PARLIAMENT FOR SCOTLAND

Lovely relaxed day full of beautiful horses. Opened with news of massive Yes victory for Scottish devolution.

Bernard Donoughue, *Westminster Diary*, 12 September 1997

⸉⸉

THE MODERN DOLE

To the local Jobcentre. Bright and modern. Light years away from the old dole office stereotype. Most of the jobs advertised were in private security and care work at anywhere between two and three pounds an hour. All subsidised by the taxpayer through family income supplement and earnings top-up. Trust the Tories to devise a system where the state is subsidising the worst employers. The national minimum wage should put a stop to this, but it won't be of much benefit to the low paid if it is set so low that it simply replaces the existing subsidies. Someone estimated that it would need to be set at about £3.75 an hour to make a difference to the poorest wage earners.

Chris Mullin, *A Walk-on Part*, 16 September 1997

SENSATION AT THE ROYAL ACADEMY

Went to see the 'Sensation' exhibition today at the RA, which was fun.* Fun more than aesthetically pleasing. Feel like I might have nightmares about some things – such as the 3-ft replica of a dead man, naked, called 'Dead Dad' or Damien Hirst's flies being electrocuted. Must think of positive things which happened today as I am getting in [a] negative frame of mind these days.

Rowena Macdonald, Diaries, 1 October 1997

* *The 'Sensation' exhibition was one of the first public major showings of work by the rising generation of artists known as the Young British Artists – or YBAs – and which included Damien Hirst, Tracy Emin, Sarah Lucas, Jake and Dinos Chapman and Gillian Wearing.*

DETESTABLE FESTIVALS

Here I am taking up this journal months after having started it. July was dominated by the problems in the flat and ended with the eviction of our two flat-mates.

This summer I went to all the festivals – except for Glastonbury, which was a sea of mud – with Cornershop. At 19 I would have died for that.

Now I am quite tired of festivals. They are all organised by the same promoter, the stalls are all the same, the guest area is always the same with the same beer company and cafe with a giant yellow and pink strawberry logo.

Reading 97 will stay as the worst festival for me.

Metallica were headlining it; also appearing was Marilyn Manson, a horrible 'gothic' group with a monster as a singer. The festival site was dirty, as much by the 3 to 4-days-old rubbish as by its crowds: hordes of hard rockers and goths in washed-out and torn T-shirts, with badly applied baby powder on their faces.

There were drunk people everywhere.

Cornershop played at 9.30 p.m. and it was a great gig, at least.

Marie Remy, Diaries, 19 October 1997

FILMING *TFI FRIDAY*

The last month has been mad, mad, mad. On Friday 13th of Feb Cornershop appeared on *TFI Friday*, a really bad programme presented /monopolised by Chris Evans, with bands on. I took the Friday afternoon off to go. The whole experience was nice but I was disgusted by the half-naked women that get put in front of the camera.

As guests of the band we were treated really well. I was surprised by that.

The bands stay in a battered house across the road from the recording studio (Riverside Studios). The bands' dressing rooms are on the second floor; on our way there, we saw Chris Evans naked, wet and ugly out of the shower (with a towel on) talking to his producer on the landing.

There is such excitement right now. 'Brimful of Asha' and its remix are about to be released and it is probably the most played tune on the radio in the UK and it has been for the last month and a half.

The album has gone silver (70,000 copies) beyond anyone's expectations. It is hoped that the single will reach the Top Five. They've been invited on *Top of the Pops* for two appearances and 'Brimful of Asha' is being used for a TV advert, for the beer Caffrey's.

The recording of *TFI Friday* was OK, many of our friends then commented on the fact that Tjinder doesn't smile enough, or not at all.

Afterwards, a flush taxi picked us up to go to a restaurant with Garry. A sign of how much things have changed. Tjinder has been warned that he would now get recognised in the street and he had to get used to it.

Marie Remy, Diaries, 7 March 1998

BATTLE OF BUYERS

The other Tuesday I went to buy my copy of 'Brimful of Asha' at Our Price in Barnet. Cornershop were threatened in the charts by Céline Dion, with the title song of the *Titanic* film. When I was in the queue, two girls were buying Céline Dion so it really felt like I was cancelling it out.

Marie Remy, Diaries, 22 March 1998

GOOD FRIDAY AGREEMENT

A kind of (be careful) heroism, to fly in and patch things up with hours to go, and (here's a thought) to take a line on Ulster, to negotiate with its leaders, despite (surely) knowing so much less about it than his permanent state, the civil servants and time-servers, army intelligence and shady secret services – he's gone over all their heads.*

The paper said the UUP [Ulster Unionist Party] were squeezing out the demands of nationalism, raising the spectre of Sinn Fein refusing to sign (and the tables being turned: Adams the spoiling villain again), but by late morning it seemed an agreed deal was on the way after all ...

BBC at one o'clock was one of the most exciting broadcasts I can remember ...

Blair spoke eloquently outside, a Labour man of sorts, invoking a universal story of humanity and hoping in Joycean fashion that 'the burden of history' had been lifted ...

Joe Brooker, Diaries, 10 April 1998

Tony Blair arrived in Belfast to help negotiate the Good Friday Agreement when talks seemed ready to break down. The agreement ended thirty years of sectarian conflict in Northern Ireland.

cℳ⁓

DEATH OF MUSIC INDUSTRY

It's Summer 1998 and the scent of apocalypse is in the air. Perhaps not just yet in the real world, but this week *NME* announces the beginning of the end for the mainstream UK music industry. It's all over! The Phoenix Festival has been cancelled! Bands are being dropped by major labels left, right and centre! The Rolling Stones have to cancel gigs because they can't afford their tax bills! Ah, calamity!

Apparently, pop music is going to be sold entirely online in a few years' time. I'm already way ahead of them. I buy CDs via mail order from online CD stores like Rough Trade and IMVS, from various indie labels' own websites, or even from band homepages ... But we're now told even physical 'product' will be a thing of the past: new music will be downloaded off the Net ... I remember something similar was predicted in the early 90s, that videos and video games were taking over from music full stop. It didn't happen.

Dickon Edwards, Online Diary, 11 June 1998

MADE IN MOROCCO

Report in today's paper that Marks & Spencer – which has hitherto prided itself on having its clothes made in Britain – is putting pressure on its suppliers to relocate to cheap-labour economies: Indonesia, Morocco and Sri Lanka are mentioned.

Chris Mullin, *A Walk-on Part*, 8 September 1998

CLINTON SCANDAL

For days the word had been that the full video of his Grand Jury deposition would kill Clinton's presidency at last.* But I was tremendously impressed, seeing not the wooden orator but a real man, raising eyebrows and shifting his head, his pink face a 53-year-old boy's. His evasions and denials were understandable before this witch-hunt, but he really moved me when he became direct, attacking his 'wrecking-ball' attackers – and surely this is the truth, it is a war, dogs out for blood, and he should turn and make a noise before they tear into him – and in one fine moment of unrestrained sincerity, intoning as if his interlocutors were idiots, 'Did I want this to come out? NO. Was I embarrassed about it? YES. Did I tell her to lie about it? NO' …

Joe Brooker, Diaries, 21 September 1998

* *After repeatedly denying having a relationship with a young White House intern, Monica Lewinsky, US President Bill Clinton was asked about the matter during a deposition on 17 August 1998. In the wake of the publication of independent counsel Kenneth Starr's wide-ranging, four-year investigation into the president, the video of Clinton's testimony was released to the public. Although Clinton was impeached by the House of Representatives for perjury and obstruction of justice, he was acquitted of the charges by the Senate on 12 February 1999.*

OUT LAW

Ron Davies, former Welsh Secretary, when asked if he was gay: 'I don't want to get into that ... I'm aware of some of the stories and rumours in the newspapers ...'

Which, of course, means 'yes'.

Matthew Parris goes on *Newsnight* and casually outs Peter Mandelson, which is odd because he once wrote a piece on how outing was wrong. Clearly, something has happened to change his views. A landslide election defeat of his old party, perhaps.

It's strange the way sexuality is still a source of great umbrage among some of the famous.

Dickon Edwards, Online Diary, 30 October 1998

⁓

EDINBURGH, SUBTITLED

Saw *The Acid House*. Got annoyed that I couldn't understand one in every three words of the dialogue, so heavy are the Edinburgh accents. And I'm British. It says a lot about my cultural conditioning that I can understand films and TV programmes with heavy American and Australian accents far more. If they try and make it a hit in America, like the previous Irvine Welsh film, *Trainspotting*, I'll be interested to see if they use subtitles, like they do for Oasis interviews on MTV. It didn't have Ewan McGregor in it though, which made a change for a recent British film. There's actually a book out about the last few years of the UK film industry, and it had so much Ewan McGregor in it that in the end they had to sell it as a Ewan McGregor biography instead.

Dickon Edwards, Online Diary, 4 January 1999

⁓

THE LAWRENCE INQUIRY

Spoke in the debate on the Stephen Lawrence Inquiry last week. Doreen and Neville Lawrence were watching in the public gallery. Waited three hours to be called, and just when I was, they popped out to get something to eat …

I went through all the things we're campaigning on: full implementation of the recommendation of the Lawrence Report, a New Race Relations Act, recognition of the fact that 50 per cent of those arrested for racist crime last year were under sixteen, and the need for more effective youth services to deal with them.*

Oona King, *House Music*, 2 March 1999

* *Eighteen-year-old Stephen Lawrence, a promising student who wanted to become an architect, was stabbed to death by a gang of white youths in Eltham, south-east London, on 22 April 1993. The mishandling of the investigation into his murder by the Met Police prompted an official inquiry. In February 1999, Sir William Macpherson delivered a damning assessment of the Force, accusing it of 'institutional racism'. In 2012 two of the original five suspects were convicted of the murder with the aid of DNA technology.*

⚜

KOSOVO OUT OF CONTROL

A good debate on the crisis in the Balkans. Powerful speeches from Ken Livingstone and Patrick Cormack, who favour intervention, and an electrifying one from George Galloway, who is opposed. I find myself being pulled one way and then the other … I have a terrible feeling that we are getting into something that could spin completely out of control.

Oh, for the old black-and-white certainties of the Cold War. Now everything is grey and murky and confusing. I feel so useless.

Chris Mullin, *A Walk-on Part*, 25 March 1999

⚜

FOOLISH TELLY

GMTV runs a story on the world's first male pregnancy. Later, the 'father' pulls up his jumper to reveal a cushion, and the whole team cries 'April Fool!' Gordon Kennedy quickly puts on his 'but seriously, folks' expression, and they cut to Kosovo. The viewer is seemingly left expecting Mr Milosovic to give the camera a knowing comedy wink.

Dickon Edwards, Online Diary, 1 April 1999

✦

NEW TERROR

Bomb went off in a Soho pub (The Admiral Nelson) at 6.30 tonight, not more than a 3-minute walk from where I was teaching … I heard siren after siren whizzing past the school and when I heard the helicopters I remarked to the class, 'That's a bomb' – they thought I was joking.

The White Wolves neo-Nazi group have claimed responsibility …

John Rogers, Diaries, 30 April 1999

✦

E-MAIL ETIQUETTE

I'm getting very good at replying to e-mails at the moment. There was a time when I never got around to answering any at all. Now, every electronic missive I receive personally, and that seems to want a reply, is replied to within a week or so. Junk mail and unsolicited mail which is sent to me in a list of other recipients, seemingly just as an address that someone knows, is rapidly deleted. Top of my bugbear list are those so-called 'virus alert' mails. You know the sort of thing. 'Fwd: Do not open any mails with the subject line "Badgers Know No Fear". Please copy and forward this mail to everyone you don't like very much' …

Dickon Edwards, Online Diary, 29 May 1999

GORDON'S GOOD STORY

Gordon Brown addressed the party meeting. Never has a Labour chancellor had such a good story to tell and Gordon made the most of it. Unemployment at a twenty-year low; inflation down to 1960s levels, oodles of money being pumped into the public sector. And, coming shortly, the Working Families Tax Credit, which will make the lowest-paid families up to £60 a week better off.

These days, Gordon exudes an aura of competence and self-confidence which in opposition he lacked. At last, a Labour chancellor who is not at the mercy of events.

Chris Mullin, *A Walk-on Part*, 14 July 1999

PHANTOM MENACE STRIKES BACK

I have only three observations to make concerning the new *Star Wars* film. My excuse is that they seem to have been overlooked elsewhere. Which is something you couldn't say about the film itself.

One of the Naboo fighter pilots is played by Celia Imrie, best known for her work in many a Victoria Wood sketch.

One of the Jedi Council is called Yarael Poof.

The Battle Droids bear a striking resemblance to Jacob Epstein's 1914 bronze sculpture *Torso In Metal* from 'The Rock Drill'.

Well, it makes a change from saying, 'It's not as good as the first three,' doesn't it?

Dickon Edwards, Online Diary, 3 August 1999

ECLIPSE

We watched standing on a rock on a beach at Portreath.

No sun – total cloud cover but it did go spookily dark and very windy. Like the end of the world and there was a feeling that we were all very small and the sky was rushing over us.

Afterwards, we sat in a cafe and ate Cornish pasties.

Rowena Macdonald, Diaries, 7 September 1999

સૂત્ર

MODERN RAIL DISASTER

Reports of the Paddington rail disaster include surreal accounts of rescue workers deafened by a cacophony of abandoned mobile phones ringing like mad: the inappropriate racket of novelty arpeggio trills and vain personalized 'amusing' melody chimes among the carnage and flames giving the tragedy a gut-wrenchingly modern pathos. A sick new homage to The Unknown Commuter: They Couldn't Get A Good Signal. The real tragedy is, of course, Jilly Cooper escaping unscathed.

Dickon Edwards, Online Diary, 12 October 1999

સૂત્ર

NOUGHT FOR NOTHING

The Millennium Bug has popularity and currency as an idea cos it suggests that this 'event' – this wholly man-made notion, which should pass without mishap – has an independence from us, possibly a power over us. It means that the Millennium's not quite just our invention, that we can mark or forget as we like: that it's a bit more of a given, along the capricious lines of natural forces.

By midnight I reckon everything of significance is not only saved to disk, but saved in superfluous multiple copies. This bug business does kind of concentrate the mind: it's had its use. Will has already altered the date on his machine, but couldn't find a way to do it on this; nonetheless, he reckons it may all come to nought. (Nought-nought.)

Joe Brooker, Diaries, 30 December 1999

* In the early days of computing, when processing power was limited, many programs opted to abbreviate four-digit year dates, say 1999, to two digits, say 99, to save space. With the approach of the year 2000 it was feared that many computers would malfunction since 00 might be read as 1900 instead of 2000, a potentially catastrophic problem christened the Y2K or Millennium bug. Governments and companies around the globe spent billions updating their computer systems.

∿

UNEXPECTED MILLENNIUM CELEBRATION

My whole life I thought I'd be at a wild party at the end of the millennium. Instead, I was queuing outside Stratford tube station. It was the only way to get to the Dome. Our friends Keith Khan and Catherine Ugwu were staging the New Year's Eve show, and they'd worked on it for ten years. We queued for hours. The police and London Underground apologised for any inconvenience caused by the unexpectedly large crowds. How could the crowds be unexpected? It was the millennium. Although the police knew 10,000 people would be travelling to the Dome via Stratford, they only brought one X-ray machine ...

Oona King, *House Music*, 31 December 1999

∿

MIDNIGHT, BANG ON

Mick Hucknall was singing 'Stars': I suddenly realized that this wasn't just someone's poor taste (best album ever, they voted it in 1993!), but live sound, for they were performing down the road outside the Naval College. Trafalgar Road some kind of party, scattered people coming and going on the pavement. I stopped and redid my laces, wondered. The sky felt light (10 o'clock in December!): fireworks or my imagination. Ten o'clock. Everything, once again, was about to happen.

The TV on, and at eleven the Eiffel Tower was fizzing with fire, like a rocket about to take off. No, not a rehearsal, the real thing: they were an hour ahead, and aesthetically ahead of everyone else too. What you expect, Mike and I commented to each other, from the nation that brought us Amoros, Battiston, Bossis.

One overwhelming sense from the coverage of this special New Year: a healthy interest in and respect for what the rest of the world was up to, how they were marking it. And not just in different places, but in their different times; though for us everything hinged on a single second of our own time, 'we' were not just content with, but fascinated by, the different moments at which Sydney, Paris, Berlin, New York, DC and LA made their switch. Global reach, but not homogeneity; instead, a rare thing, a revelling in diversity ...

Suddenly ... people were cheering somewhere, here in fact, fireworks were going off.

I raised my watch: midnight, bang on. Satisfaction. Happy New Year, said a stranger: you too, I replied ...

Joe Brooker, Diaries, 31 December 1999

CONTRIBUTORS

BIBLIOGRAPHY

Abbott, Diane, letter to the *Guardian*, 16 February 1989, republished in *The Rushdie File*, edited by Lisa Appignanesi and Sara Maitland (London: ICA/Fourth Estate, 1989)

Ackerley, J. R., *My Sister and Myself: The Diaries of J. R. Ackerley*, edited by Francis King (London: Hutchinson, 1982)

Agate, James, *Ego*, 8 vols (London: Harrap, 1935–1947)

Allison, Kirsty, previously unpublished private diaries of the writer, DJ and filmmaker

Anderson, Lindsay, *The Diaries*, edited by Paul Sutton (London: Methuen, 2004)

Bailey, John, *Letters and Diaries, Edited by His Wife* (London: John Murray, 1935)

Barbellion, W. N. P., *A Last Diary* (London: Chatto & Windus, 1921)

Barbellion, W. N. P., *The Journal of a Disappointed Man* (London: Chatto & Windus, 1919)

Barrie, J. M., *Letters of J. M. Barrie*, edited by Viola Meynell (London: Peter Davies, 1942)

Bason, Fred, *Fred Bason's Diary*, edited by Nicolas Bentley (London: Wingate, 1950)

Bason, Fred, *Fred Bason's Second Diary*, edited by L. A. G. Strong (London: Wingate, 1952)

Bason, Fred, *The Last Bassoon: From the Diaries of Fred Bason*, edited by Noël Coward (London: Parrish, 1960)

Beeson, Trevor, *Window on Westminster: A Canon's Diary 1976–1987* (London: SCM, 2001)

Benn Tony, *Against the Tide: Diaries 1973–76* (London: Hutchinson, 1989)

Benn, Tony, *Conflicts of Interest: Diaries 1977–80*, edited by Ruth Winstone (London: Hutchinson, 1990)

Benn, Tony, *Office without Power: Diaries 1968–72* (London: Hutchinson, 1988)

Benn, Tony, *Out of the Wilderness: Diaries 1963–67* (London: Hutchinson, 1987)

Benn, Tony, *The End of an Era: Diaries 1980–90*, edited by Ruth Winstone (London: Arrow, 1994)

Bennett, Alan, *Writing Home* (London: Faber and Faber, 1994)

Bennett, Arnold, *The Journals of Arnold Bennett 1896–1910*, vol. 1, edited by Newman Flower (London: Cassell, 1932)

Bennett, Arnold, *The Journals of Arnold Bennett 1911–1921*, vol. 2, edited by Newman Flower (London: Cassell, 1932)

Bennett, Arnold, *The Journals of Arnold Bennett 1921–1928*, vol. 3, edited by Newman Flower (London: Cassell, 1933)

Benson, A. C., *The Diary of Arthur Christopher Benson*, edited by Percy Lubbock (London: Hutchinson, 1931)

Berry, H. A., *The Diary of Another Nobody: Life in 1952* (Minehead: Rare Books and Berry, 2007)

Best, Albert, *The Diaries of Albert Best: A Resident of Teignmouth*, edited by Alan Best (Kingskerwell: A. Best, 2008–09)

Best, Albert, quoted in *The Imperial War Museum Book of the First World War: A Great Conflict Recalled in Previously Unpublished Letters, Diaries, Documents and Memoirs*, edited by Malcolm

Brown (London: Sidgwick & Jackson in association with the Imperial War Museum, 1991)

Betjeman, John, *Letters*, edited by Candida Lycett Green (London: Methuen, 2006)

Blumenfeld, R. D., *R. D. B.'s Diary: 1887–1914* (London: William Heinemann, 1930)

Bond, Henry, 700th General Construction Company, Royal Engineers, 'Dunkerque Diary', contributed by Suze Bond to *BBC WW2 People's War: An Archive of World War Two Memories Written by the Public, Gathered by the BBC*, http://www.bbc.co.uk/history/ww2peopleswar/stories/68/a2325368.shtml

Bowen, Elizabeth, *Love's Civil War: Elizabeth Bowen and Charles Ritchie, Letters and Diaries 1941–1973*, edited by Victoria Glendinning with Judith Robertson (London: Simon & Schuster, 2009)

Brandreth, Gyles, *Breaking the Code: The Westminster Diaries, May 1990–May 1997* (London: Weidenfeld & Nicolson, 1999)

Brandreth, Gyles, *Something Sensational to Read in the Train: The Diary of a Lifetime* (London: John Murray, 2009)

Brittain, Vera, *Chronicle of Youth: Great War Diary 1913–1917*, edited by Alan Bishop (London: Phoenix, 2002)

Britten, Benjamin, *Journeying Boy: The Diaries of the Young Benjamin Britten 1928–1938*, selected and edited by John Evans (London: Faber and Faber, 2009)

Brooker, Joseph, previously unpublished private diaries of the musician and academic, copyright Joseph Brooker

Brown, Sally, *Diary of a People's Marcher* (Liverpool: Anteus Graphics, 1991)

Bruce, David, *Ambassador to Sixties London: The Diaries of David Bruce, 1961–1969*, edited by John W. Young and Raj Roy (Dordrecht: Republic of Letters Publishing, 2009)

Buckley, Margaret and Brian, *A Journal for Maggie: 1980–85* (Kenilworth: Chrysalis, 2008)

Bull, Deborah, *Dancing Away: A Covent Garden Diary* (London: Methuen, 1998)

Butterworth, George, *A Diary and Letters, with a Memoir* (York and London: privately published, 1918)

Carrington, Dora, *Carrington: Letters and Extracts from her Diaries*, edited by David Garnett (London: Cape, 1970)

Castle, Barbara, *The Castle Diaries: 1964–1976* (London: Papermac, 1990)

Chadwick, Charlie, *Rough Stuff: The Pre-War Cycling Diaries of Charlie Chadwick*, edited by David Warner (Brighton: John Pinkerton Memorial Publishing Fund, 2014)

Channon, Sir Henry, *Chips: The Diaries of Sir Henry Channon*, edited by Robert Rhodes James (Harmondsworth: Penguin, 1970)

Chapman, Kit, *An Innkeeper's Diary: September 1996–September 1997* (London: Orion, 1999)

Clark, Alan, *Diaries* (London: Weidenfeld & Nicolson, 1993)

Cobb, Richard, *My Dear Hugh: Letters from Richard Cobb to Hugh Trevor-Roper and Others*, edited by Tim Heald (London: Frances Lincoln, 2011)

Conrad, Joseph, *Life & Letters*, edited by G. Jean-Aubry (London: William Heinemann, 1927)

Coppard, Yvonne, extracts from teenage diaries published in *Between You & Me: Real-life Diaries and Letters by Women Writers*, edited by Charlotte Cole (London: Live Wire for the Women's Press, 1998)

Coward, Noël, *The Letters of Noël Coward*, edited by Barry Day (London:

Bloomsbury, 2008)

Coward, Noël, *The Noël Coward Diaries*, edited by Graham Payn and Sheridan Morley (London: Weidenfeld & Nicolson, 1982)

Crossman, Richard, *The Crossman Diaries: Selections from the Diaries of a Cabinet Minister, 1964–1970*, edited by Anthony Howard (London: Mandarin, 1991)

Currie, Edwina, *Diaries: 1987–1992* (London: Little, Brown, 2002)

Curtis, Lionel, Letter to Thomas Jones in Thomas Jones' *A Diary with Letters, 1931–1950* (London: Oxford University Press, 1954)

Donoughue, Bernard, *Westminster Diary: A Reluctant Minister Under Tony Blair* (London: I.B. Tauris, 2016)

Dudeney, Mrs Henry, *A Lewes Diary: 1916–1944*, edited by Diana Crook (Lewes: Tartarus Press and Sussex Archeological Society, 1998)

Dugdale, Blanche Elizabeth, *Baffy: The Diaries of Blanche Dugdale, 1936–1947* edited by N. A. Rose (London: Vallentine Mitchell, 1973)

Earl, Rae, *My Fat, Mad Teenage Diary* (London: Hodder, 2007)

Edwards, Alan, previously unpublished private diaries of the publicist to rock and pop royalty

Edwards, Dickon, online diary

Farmer, Grace, *Our Stolen Years: Wartime Diary and Letters of a Liverpool Couple*, compiled by Martin Salter-Smith (Huddersfield: Central Publishing, 2003)

Foxell, Rev. Maurice, diary extracts published in *The British Diarist* magazine (Ticehurst: 2003)

George, Sally, *Sally's Diary: Leaving Home in the 1970s – Peterborough, Cardiff, Birmingham* (Great Britain: Sally George, 2014)

Gladstone, Mary, *Mary Gladstone (Mrs Drew): Her Diaries and Letters*, edited by Lucy Masterman (London: Methuen, 1930)

Gower, Lord Ronald Sutherland, *Old Diaries: 1881–1901* (London: John Murray, 1902)

Graves, Charles, *Great Days: A Journal from July 8th 1942 to November 2nd 1943* (London: Hutchinson 1944)

Graves, Charles, *Off the Record: A War Diary*, (London: Hutchinson, 1940)

Hardy, Florence Emily, extract from diaries published in *The Life of Thomas Hardy*, edited by Florence Emily Hardy (London: Macmillan, 1933)

Hardy, Thomas, *The Life of Thomas Hardy*, edited by Florence Emily Hardy (London: Macmillan, 1933)

Héafod, Edmund (pseudonym of Osias Bain), *Gimani: A Diary, 13 May 1959– 1 Sept. 1960* (London: Gaberbocchus, 1961)

Hicks, Edward Lee, *The Life and Letters of Edward Lee Hicks, Bishop of Lincoln 1910– 1919*, edited by J. H. Fowler (London: Christophers, 1922)

Holness, Annie Beatrice, *A Londoner in Lancashire 1941–43: The Diary of Annie Beatrice Holness*, edited by Patricia and Robert Malcolmson (Liverpool: The Record Society of Lancashire and Cheshire, 2016)

Hughes, L., previously unpublished private diaries

Inge, Rev. William Ralph, *Diary of a Dean: St. Paul's 1911–1934* (London: Hutchinson, 1949)

Ironside, Virginia, previously unpublished

private diaries of the writer and agony aunt

Jarman, Derek, *Modern Nature: The Journals of Derek Jarman* (London: Vintage, 1992)

Jarman, Derek, *Smiling in Slow Motion*, edited by Keith Collins (London: Century, 2000)

Johnson, Rev. Dr Malcolm, *Diary of a Gay Priest: The Tightrope Walker* (Alresford, Hants: Christian Alternative, 2013)

Jones, Claudia, letter to the *Daily Worker* https://dianelangford.wordpress. com/2015/03/05/claudia-jones-letter-to-daily-worker-1963

Keeling, Frederic 'Ben', *Keeling Letters & Recollections*, edited by E. Townsend (London: George Allen & Unwin, 1918)

Killen, Mary, previously unpublished private diaries of the writer and journalist, copyright Mary Killen

King, Oona, *House Music: The Oona King Diaries* (London: Bloomsbury, 2008)

Kureishi, Hanif, 'With Your Tongue Down My Throat: A Film Diary', *Granta*, Issue 22, Autumn 1987

Landau, Rom, *Of No Importance: A Diary of Private Life* (London: Nicholson and Watson, 1940)

Langford, Gladys, *A Free-spirited Woman: The London Diaries of Gladys Langford, 1936–1940*, edited by Patricia and Robert Malcolmson (Woodbridge: Boydell Press, 2014)

Last, Nella, *Nella Last's Peace: The Post-War Diaries of Housewife 49*, edited by Patricia and Robert Malcolmson (London: Profile Books, 2008)

Latchford, Laurie, *The Swansea Wartime Diary of Laurie Latchford 1940–41*, edited by Kate Elliott Jones and Wendy Cope

(Newport: South Wales Record Society, 2010)

Lawrence, D. H., *The Letters of D. H. Lawrence*, edited by Aldous Huxley (London: William Heinemann, 1932)

Lees-Milne, James, *Caves of Ice: Diaries, 1946–47* (London: Faber, 1984)

Lees-Milne, James, *Diaries: 1971–1983* (London: John Murray, 2008)

Lees-Milne, James, *Diaries: 1984–1997* (London: John Murray, 2011)

Lennon, John, *The John Lennon Letters*, edited by Hunter Davies (London: Weidenfeld & Nicolson, 2012)

Liddell, Guy, diaries released by the National Archives

Lockhart, Robert Bruce, *The Diaries of Sir Robert Bruce Lockhart*, edited by Kenneth Young (London: Macmillan, 1973)

Lockwood, F. T., extracts from diaries published online, https://aghs.jimdo. com/acocks-green-s-vulnerability/extracts-from-the-wartime-diaries-of-frank-taylor-lockwood/

Lomas, Sgt. Maj. Samuel, extracts from diaries published in *The 1916 Diaries of an Irish Rebel and a British Soldier*, edited by Mick O'Farrell (Cork: Mercier Press, 2014)

Lucas, F. L., *Journal Under Terror: 1938* (London: Cassell, 1939)

Lucy, Sir Henry, *The Diary of a Journalist* (London: John Murray, 1920)

Lucy, Sir Henry, *The Diary of a Journalist: Fresh Extracts* (London: John Murray, 1923)

MacAmhlaigh, Donall, *An Irish Navvy: The Diary of an Exile*, translated by Valentin Iremonger (London: Routledge and Kegan Paul, 1964–6)

Macaulife, Hazel K., *Leisure Round Bognor in the '50s: A Teenager's Diary*, edited by

Hazel K. Bell (Hatfield, Herts: HKB Press, 2014)

MacDonagh, Michael, *In London During the Great War: The Diary of a Journalist* (London: Eyre & Spottiswoode, 1935)

MacDonald, James Ramsay, extract quoted in *Ramsay MacDonald: A Biography* by David Marquand (London: Cape, 1977)

Macdonald, Rowena, previously unpublished private diaries of the novelist

Macfie, Robert Scott, from a letter quoted in *The Imperial War Museum Book of the First World War: A Great Conflict Recalled in Previously Unpublished Letters, Diaries, Documents and Memoirs*, edited by Malcolm Brown (London: Sidgwick & Jackson in association with the Imperial War Museum, 1991)

Macmillan, Harold, *The Macmillan Diaries*, edited by Peter Catterall (London: Pan, 2004–12)

Maconochie, Anna, previously unpublished private diaries of the short-story writer and interesting jewellery wearer

Mansfield, Katherine, *Journal of Katherine Mansfield*, edited by J. Middleton Murry (London: Constable, 1927)

Martin, Paul, *The London Diaries 1975–1979* (Ottawa: University of Ottawa Press, 1988)

McLeod, Karen, previously unpublished private diaries of the novelist and performer

McVay, David, *Steak … Diana Ross: Diary of a Football Nobody* (Manchester: Parrs Wood, 2003)

Meinertzhagen, Richard, *Diary of a Black Sheep* (Edinburgh and London: Oliver & Boyd, 1964)

Miles, Mrs Hallie Eustace, *Untold Tales of War-time: A Personal Diary* (London: Palmer, 1930)

Muggeridge, Malcolm, *Like It Was: The Diaries of Malcolm Muggeridge*, selected and edited by John Bright-Holmes (London: Collins, 1981)

Mullin, Chris, *A Walk-on Part: Diaries 1994–1999*, edited by Ruth Winstone (London: Profile Books, 2011)

Murray, Millie, extracts from teenage diaries published in *Between You & Me: Real-life Diaries and Letters by Women Writers*, edited by Charlotte Cole (London: Live Wire for the Women's Press, 1998)

Mynors, Lavinia, *Wise Woman: A Memoir of Lavinia Mynors from Her Diaries and Letters*, edited by Alethea Hayter (Banham: Erskine Press, 1996)

Naipaul, V. S., *Letters Between A Father and Son* (London: Little, Brown, 1999)

Name witheld, letter to the Editor of the *Sun* about the Hillsborough disaster, http://hillsborough.independent.gov.uk/repository/NGN000000030001.html

Nichols, Peter, *Diaries: 1969–1977* (London: Nick Hern, 2000)

Nicolson, Harold, *Diaries and Letters: 1907–1964*, edited by Nigel Nicolson (London: Weidenfeld & Nicolson, 2004)

Oppenheimer, Florence, diaries published online, https://sarahfairhurstjmm.wordpress.com/2014/01/06/the-diary-of-florence-oppenheimer/

Orton, Joe, *The Orton Diaries: Including the Correspondence of Edna Welthorpe and Others*, edited by John Lahr (London: Methuen, 1986)

Orwell, George, *Diaries*, edited by Peter Davison (London: Harvill Secker, 2009)

Otton, Geoff, extracts from his World Cup diaries published in the *Grimsby Telegraph*, 16 July 2016, http://www.grimsbytelegraph.co.uk/football-fan-relives-magical-memories-of-england-s-world-cup-win-with-old-diary-entries/

story-29517414-detail/story.html

Overhill, Jack, *Cambridge at War: The Diary of Jack Overhill, 1939–1945*, edited by Peter Searby (Cambridge: Cambridgeshire Records Society, 2010)

Palin, Michael, *Diaries 1969–1979: The Python Years* (London: Weidenfeld & Nicolson, 2006)

Partridge, Frances, *Diaries: 1939–1945*, edited by Rebecca Wilson (London: Weidenfeld & Nicolson, 2000)

Partridge, Frances, *Everything to Lose: Diaries 1945–1960* (London: Gollancz, 1985)

Paul, Kate, *Journal* (Hay-on-Wye: Carrington Press, 1997)

Perringer, Jenny, extract from diaries quoted in *Greenham Common: Women at the Wire* by Barbara Harford and Sarah Hopkins (London: Women's Press, 1984)

Powell, Ilene, extracts from diaries published online, http://www.telegraph.co.uk/news/uknews/1478000/Diary-of-a-1920s-Bridget-Jones.html

Pringle, David, previously unpublished private diaries of the writer, editor and science-fiction authority

Pym, Barbara, *A Very Private Eye: The Diaries, Letters and Notebooks of Barbara Pym*, edited Hazel Holt and Hilary Pym (Bath: Chivers Press, 1984)

Radice, Giles, *Diaries 1980–2001: From Political Disaster to Election Triumph* (London: Weidenfeld & Nicolson, 2004)

Remy, Marie, previously unpublished private diaries

Repington, Lieut.-Col. C. à Court, *After the War: A Diary* (London: Constable, 1922)

Rhys, Jean, *Letters: 1931–1966*, edited by Francis Wyndham and Diana Melly (Harmondsworth: Penguin, 1985)

Riddell, Lord, *More Pages from My Diary:*

1908–1914 (London: Country Life, 1934)

Ritchie, Charles, *The Siren Years: Undiplomatic Diaries 1937–1945* (London: Macmillan, 1974)

Rogers, John, previously unpublished private diaries of the author and filmmaker

Roust, Helen, *Brighton's War: As Recorded in the Diaries of Helen Roust, A Local Schoolteacher*, compiled by Teresa Dennis (Seaford: S.B. Publications, 2005)

Rowse, A. L., *The Diaries of A. L. Rowse*, edited by Richard Ollard (London: Allen Lane, 2003)

Salkey, Andrew, *Georgetown Journal: A Caribbean Writer's Journey from London via Port of Spain to Georgetown, Guyana, 1970* (London: New Beacon Books, 1972)

Sandhurst, Viscount William Mansfield, *From Day to Day: 1914–1915* (London: Edward Arnold, 1928)

Sassoon, Siegfried, *Diaries: 1915–1918*, edited by Rupert Hart-Davis (London: Faber, 1983)

Sassoon, Siegfried, *Diaries: 1920–1922*, edited by Rupert Hart-Davis (London: Faber, 1981)

Savage, Jon, extracts from his diaries published in Jon Savage, *England's Dreaming: The Sex Pistols and Punk Rock* (London: Faber, 1991)

Selbourne, Hugh, *A Doctor's Life* (London: Cape, 1989)

Sethi, Anita, previously unpublished private diaries of the author and journalist

Sher, Antony, *Year of the King* (London: Chatto & Windus, 1985)

Singh, Bhawani, *Travel Pictures: The Record of a European Tour* (London: Longmans, Green, 1912)

Slate, Ruth, extracts from diaries published in *Dear Girl: Diaries and Letters of Two Working Women 1897–1917*, edited by

Tierl Thompson (London: Women's Press, 1987)

Slawson, Eva, extracts from diaries published in *Dear Girl: The Diaries and Letters of Two Working Women 1897–1917*, edited by Tierl Thompson (London: Women's Press, 1987)

Spender, Stephen, *Journals: 1939–1983*, edited by John Goldsmith (London: Faber, 1992)

Strong, Roy, *The Roy Strong Diaries: 1967–1987*, (London: Weidenfeld & Nicolson, 1997)

Terry, Ellen, letter to Stephen Coleridge, published in *The Heart of Ellen Terry: Twenty-Six Letters* (London: Mills & Boon, 1928)

Tipper, Kathleen, *A Woman in Wartime London: The Diary of Kathleen Tipper, 1941–1945*, edited by Patricia and Robert Malcolmson (London: London Record Society, 2006)

Tower, Winifred, extract from diaries quoted in *The Imperial War Museum Book of the First World War: A Great Conflict Recalled in Previously Unpublished Letters, Diaries, Documents and Memoirs*, edited by Malcolm Brown (London: Sidgwick & Jackson in association with the Imperial War Museum, 1991)

Townsend, William, *The Townsend Journals: An Artist's Record of His Times, 1928–51*, edited by Andrew Forge (London: Tate Gallery, 1976)

Tynan, Kenneth, *The Diaries of Kenneth Tynan*, edited by John Lahr (London: Bloomsbury, 2001)

Unknown West Indian, unposted letter published in *Journey to an Illusion: The West Indian in Britain* by Donald Hinds (London: Heinemann, 1966)

Vaughan, Keith, *Journals, 1939–1977* (London: Murray, 1989)

Vaughan, Keith, *Drawing to a Close: The Final Journals of Keith Vaughan*, edited by Gerard (Hastings: Pagham Press, 2012)

Victoria, Queen, journals published online, http://www.queenvictoriasjournals.org/home.do

Wakefield, Arthur, *The Miners' Strike Day by Day: The Illustrated 1984-5 Diary of Yorkshire Miner Arthur Wakefield*, edited by Brian Elliot (Barnsley: Wharncliffe, 2002)

Warner, Sylvia Townsend, *The Diaries of Sylvia Townsend Warner*, edited by Claire Harman (London: Chatto & Windus, 1994)

Waugh, Evelyn, *The Diaries of Evelyn Waugh*, edited by Michael Davie (London: Weidenfeld & Nicolson, 1976)

Webb, Beatrice, *The Diaries*, 2 vols (London: Virago 1983)

Wheatle, Alex, previously unpublished extract from notebooks of the novelist

White, Antonia, *Diaries: 1926–1957*, edited by Susan Chitty (London: Virago, 1992)

Wiggins, Roland, previously unpublished private diaries

Willetts, Paul, previously unpublished private diaries

Williams, Brian, diaries of the writer and evangelist published online

Williams, Kenneth, *The Kenneth Williams Diaries*, edited by Russell Davies (London: HarperCollins, 1994)

Wilson, Bruce, *Yorkshire's Flying Pickets in the 1984–85 Miners Strike Based on the Diary of Silverwood Miner Bruce Wilson*, edited by Brian Elliott (Barnsley: Wharncliffe Books, 2004)

Wilson, Elizabeth, previously unpublished private diaries

Windsor, King George V of the House of,
extracts from diaries quoted in *King George
the Fifth: His Life and Reign* by Harold
Nicolson (London: Constable, 1952)

Wollaston, A. F. R., *Letters and Diaries
of A. F. R. Wollaston*, edited by Mary
Wollaston (Cambridge: CUP, 1933)

Woolf, Virginia, *The Diary of Virginia
Woolf*, edited by Anne Olivier Bell,
5 vols (London: The Hogarth Press,
1977–84)

Worpole, Doris Emily, previously
unpublished private diaries

Wyatt, Woodrow, *The Journals of Woodrow
Wyatt*, 2 vols, edited by Sarah Curtis
(London: Macmillan 1998–9)

Wykes, Debsey, previously unpublished
private diaries of the musician

Wyndham, Joan, *Anything Once* (London:
Sinclair-Stevenson, 1992)

Wyndham, Joan, *Love Is Blue: A Wartime
Diary* (London: Heinemann, 1986)

Wyndham, Joan, *Love Lessons: A Wartime
Diary* (London: Mandarin, 1995)

Zaigham, Inayatullah, letter to the
Independent, 17 February 1989,
republished in *The Rushdie File*, edited
by Lisa Appignanesi and Sara Maitland
(London: ICA/Fourth Estate, 1989)

ACKNOWLEDGEMENTS

There are a number of people who I'd like to thank for their time, help and efforts in putting *Our History of the Twentieth Century* together.

Firstly I'd like to thank Gabriella Nemeth and Fiona Slater for approaching me with the idea for the book in the first place. For Fiona, that then involved suffering the long and arduous task of having to oversee my turning that idea into an actual book. One whose original draft – unbelievable as it may seem – was nearly twice the size of the already hefty volume you currently hold in your hands. Invaluable in helping nip and tuck that manuscript into a more publishable shape was Robin Dennis, who wielded the red pen with great skill, good humour and grace. Nick Rennison, my former partner in crime on previous diary anthologies, was also there to cast a critical eye over the work in progress; and George Maudsley and Becca Wright, who helped get the thing over the finishing line.

Thanks to Lesley O'Mara and everyone at Michael O Mara Books, and to Ruth Killick for publicity.

A glass should also be raised to all the staff and librarians at the London Metropolitan Archives in Clerkenwell, the local history units at both Southwark and Finsbury libraries, Stoke Newington Library and Hackney Library services, the British Library in St Pancras, the London Library in St James's and the Mass Observation Archive at the University of Sussex, Brighton, all of whom helped supply the various books and diaries that were duly plundered.

Thanks to Richard Boon and Malcolm Garrett for allowing us to use the cover of Buzzcocks' *Spiral Scratch* and Alan Denney for his wonderful photographs.

Cheers to family and friends who have endured me during the period of this book's compilation, and most of all my thanks to my brilliant and beautiful wife, Emily Bick.

A number of diarists, publishers, societies and archivists have been enormously generous with their time, material and expertise during the creation of *Our History*. I'd like to thank the following people for granting permission, or assisting with permissions, for some of the extracts that appear in these pages.

My special thanks, then, to: Kirsty Allison; Gyles Brandreth; David Warner and Andrew Milward and the committee of the Veteran Cycle Club for Charlie Chadwick; Sinéad Tully at I.B. Tauris & Co. Ltd for Bernard Donougue; Ray Russell of the Tartarus Press and Diana Crook for Mrs Henry Dudeney; Alan Edwards; Dickon Edwards; Peter Cotgreave and Dorothy Clayton and the Council of the Record Society of Lancashire and Cheshire for Annie Beatrice Holness; Virginia Ironside; Mary Flatt and John Hunt Publishing for the Rev. Dr Malcolm Johnson; Mary Killen; Rachel Reeder of the Boydell Press, and David Lewis and the London Record Society for both Gladys Langford and Kathleen Tipper; Jeff Child and the South Wales Record Society for Laurie Latchford; Dr S. O. Lucas for F. L. Lucas; Rowena Macdonald; Anna Maconochie; The Curtis Brown Agency for Mass Observation; Karen McLeod; Chris Mullin; Cris de Boos of the Erskine Press for Lavinia Mynors; Nick Hern for Peter Nichols; Miriam Phelan and the Jewish Museum for Florence Oppenheimer; Dr Sarah Bendall and the Cambridgeshire Records Society for Jack Overhill; David Pringle; Laura Morris for Barbara Pym; Marie Remy; John Rogers; Jason Salkey for Andrew Salkey; Jon Savage; Anita Sethi; Alex Wheatle and his agent Laura Susijn; Dan Thompson for Roland Wiggins and L. Hughes; Paul Willetts; Brian Williams and his website editor, Jim Nagel; Elizabeth Wilson; Ken Worpole for Doris Emily Worpole; Debsey Wykes.

Acknowledgements

Bernard Donoughue, *Westminster Diaries: A Reluctant Minister Under Tony Blair*. Reproduced by permission of I. B. Tauris.

Mrs Henry Dudeney, *A Lewes Diary: 1916–1944*. Reproduced with the permission of Ray Russell of the Tartarus Press and Diana Cook.

Blanche Dudgale, *Baffy: The Diaries of Blanche Dugdale, 1936–1947*. Reproduced by permission of Vallentine Mitchell Publishers.

Rae Earl, *My Fat, Mad Teenage Diary*. Reproduced with the permission of Hodder & Stoughton.

Alan Edwards, previously unpublished private diaries © Alan Edwards.

Dickon Edwards, www.dickonedwards.co.uk. Works reproduced with the kind permission of the author.

Charles Graves, *Great Days: A Journal from July 8th 1942 to November 2nd 1943* and *Off the Record: A War Diary* © Penguin Random House.

Annie Beatrice Holness, *A Londoner in Lancashire 1941–43: The Diary of Annie Beatrice Holness*. Reproduced with the permission of Curtis Brown Group Ltd, London on behalf of The Trustees of the Mass Observation Archive © The Mass Observation Archive.

Virginia Ironside, previously unpublished diary reproduced with the kind permission of the author.

Derek Jarman, *Modern Nature: The Journals of Derek Jarman* and *Smiling in Slow Motion* © Penguin Random House.

Rev. Dr Malcolm Johnson, *Diary of a Gay Priest: The Tightrope Walker*. Reproduced with the permission of John Hunt Publishing.

Mary Killen, previously unpublished diary reproduced with the kind permission of the author.

Oona King, *House Music: The Oona King Diaries* © Oona King, 2008, Bloomsbury Publishing Plc.

Hanif Kurieshi, 'With Your Tongue Down My Throat', *Granta* © The Wylie Agency.

Gladys Langford, *A Free-Spirited Woman: The London Diaries of Gladys Langford, 1936–1940* (ed. Patricia and Robert Malcolmson). Reproduced with the permission of the London Record Society.

Nella Last, *Nella Last's Peace: The Post-War Diaries of Housewife 49*. Reproduced by permission of Profile Books.

Laurie Latchford, *The Swansea Wartime Diary of Laurie Latchford 1940–41* (ed. Kate Elliot Jones and Wendy Cope). Reproduced with the permission of the South Wales Record Society.

James Lees-Milne, *Prophesying Peace: Diaries 1944–1945*, *Caves of Ice: Diaries 1946–47*, *Diaries 1971–1983* and *Diaries 1984–1997*. Reproduced by permission of David Higham Associates.

John Lennon, *The John Lennon Letters* (ed. Hunter Davies) © Orion Publishing Group, London.

Guy Liddell, 'Diary of Guy Liddell, Deputy Director General of the Security Service, 1951, Includes Minutes of the Director General's Meetings', National Archives: http://discovery. nationalarchives.gov.uk/details/r/C13200351. http://www.nationalarchives.gov.uk/doc/open-government-licence/version/3/. Open Government Licence under Crown copyright.

Robert Bruce Lockhart, *The Diaries of Sir Robert Bruce Lockhart* (ed. Kenneth Young) © Pan Macmillan.

F. T. Lockwood, https://aghs.jimdo.com/acocks-green-s-vulnerability/extracts-from-the-wartime-diaries-of-frank-taylor-lockwood. Reproduced with the permission of the Lockwood family and Acocks Green History Society.

F. L. Lucas, *Journal Under Terror: 1938*. Permission and thanks go to Dr S. O. Lucas.

Rowena MacDonald, previously unpublished diary reproduced with the kind permission of the author.

Karen McLeod, previously unpublished diary reproduced with the kind permission of the author.

Harold Macmillan, *The Macmillan Diaries* (ed. Peter Catterall) © Pan Macmillan.

Anna Maconochie, previously unpublished diary reproduced with the kind permission of the author.

Paul Martin, *The London Diaries 1975–1979* © University of Ottawa Press.

Chris Mullin, *A Walk-on Part: Diaries 1994–1999* (ed. Ruth Winstone). Reproduced with the permission of Profile Books.

Lavinia Mynors, *Wise Woman: A Memoir of Lavinia Mynors from Her Diaries and Letters* (ed. Alethea Hayter). Reproduced with the permission of Cris de Boos of Erskine Press.

V. S. Naipaul, *Letters Between A Father and Son*. Reproduced with the permission of the Wylie Agency.

Peter Nichols, *Diaries, 1969–1977*. Reproduced by permission of Nick Hern Books.

Harold Nicolson, *Diaries and Letters 1907–1964* (ed. Nigel Nicolson) © Orion Publishing Group, London.

Florence Oppenheimer, https://sarahfairhurstjmm.wordpress.com/2014/01/06/the-diary-of-florence-oppenheimer/. Reproduced with the permission of the Jewish Museum, London.

Joe Orton, *The Orton Diaries: Including the Correspondence of Edna Welthorpe and Others* (ed. John Lahr). Reproduced by permission of Methuen Drama, an imprint of Bloomsbury Publishing.

George Orwell, *Diaries* (ed. Peter Davison) © Penguin Random House.

Geoff Otton, extracts from his world cup diary published in the *Grimsby Telegraph*, 16 July 2016. © *Grimsby Telegraph*.

Jack Overhill, *Cambridge at War: The Diary of Jack Overhill, 1939–1945*. Reproduced with the permission of the Cambridgeshire Records Society.

Michael Palin, *Diaries 1969–1979: The Python Years* © Orion Publishing Group, London.

Frances Partridge, *Diaries: 1939–1945* by Frances Partridge. Published by Weidenfeld and Nicolson, 2001 and *Everything to Lose: 1945–1960* by Frances Partridge. Published by Gollancz, 1999. Both works copyright © Frances Partridge. Reproduced by permission of the author's estate c/o Rogers, Coleridge & White Ltd., 20 Powis Mews, London W11 1JN.

David Pringle, previously unpublished diaries reproduced with the kind permission of the author.

Barbara Pym, *A Very Private Eye: The Diaries, Letters and Notebooks of Barbara Pym* (ed. Hazel Holt and Hillary Pym). Reproduced with the permission of Laura Morris Literary Agency.

Giles Radice, *Diaries 1980–2001: From Political Disaster to Election Triumph* © Orion Publishing Group, London.

Marie Remy, previously unpublished private diaries reproduced with the kind permission of the author.

Jean Rhys, *Letters 1931–1966* (ed. Francis Wyndham and Diana Melly) © Penguin Random House.

John Rogers, previously unpublished private diary reproduced with the kind permission of the author.

A. L. Rowse, *The Diaries of A. L. Rowse* (ed. by Richard Ollard). Reproduced with the permission of Johnson and Alcock.

Andrew Salkey, *Georgetown Journal: A Caribbean Writer's Journal from London via Port of Spain to Georgetown, Guyana*. Reproduced with thanks to Jason Salkey.

Siegfried Sassoon, *Diaries 1915–1918* and *Diaries 1920–1922*. Copyright © Siegfried Sassoon by kind permission of the Estate of George Sassoon.

Jon Savage, *England's Dreaming: Sex Pistols and Punk Rock* © Faber and Faber.

Acknowledgements

Hugh Selbourne, *A Doctor's Life* © Faber and Faber.

Anita Sethi, previously unpublished diary reproduced with the kind permission of the author.

Antony Sher, *The Year of the King*. Reproduced by permission of Nick Hern Books.

Stephen Spender, *Journals, 1939-83* by Stephen Spender © 1992. Reprinted by kind permission of the Stephen Spender Estate.

Sir Roy Strong, *The Roy Strong Diaries 1967–1987* © Orion Publishing Group, London.

Kathleen Tipper, *A Woman in Wartime London: The Diary of Kathleen Tipper 1941–1945*. Reproduced with permission of Curtis Brown Group Ltd, London on behalf of The Trustees of the Mass Observation Archive © The Mass Observation Archive.

William Townsend, *The Townsend Journals: An Artist's Record of His Times, 1928–51* (ed. Andrew Forge) © Tate Publications.

Kenneth Tynan, *The Diaries of Kenneth Tynan* © Kenneth Tynan, 2001, Bloomsbury Publishing Plc.

Keith Vaughan, *Journals, 1939–1977* © Faber and Faber.

Arthur Wakefield, *The Miners' Strike Day by Day*, edited by Brian Elliott and published by Pen and Sword Books.

Evelyn Waugh, *The Diaries of Evelyn Waugh* (ed. Michael Davie) © The Wylie Agency

Beatrice Webb, *The Diaries*, 2 vols, (London: Virago 1983) and British Library of Political and Economic Science, LSE, Passfield Papers. With thanks to Anna Towlson and the LSE.

Alex Wheatle, Notebooks by Alex Wheatle, author of the Crongton Series, Brixton Rock, East of Acre Lane, Island Songs and The Dirty South, amongst others.

Antonia White, *Diaries: 1926–1957*. Reproduced by permission of Little, Brown.

Roland Wiggins, previously unpublished diary reproduced with the kind permission of Dan Thompson of Arlington House, Margate.

Paul Willetts, previously unpublished diary reproduced with the kind permission of the author.

Brian Williams, reproduced with the permission of the author and Jim Nagel.

Kenneth Williams, *The Kenneth Williams Diaries* (ed. Russell Davies) © HarperCollins.

Bruce Wilson, *Yorkshire's Flying Pickets: In the 1984–85 Miners' Strike – Based on the Diary of Silverwood Miner Bruce Wilson*, edited by Brian Elliott and published by Pen and Sword Books.

Elizabeth Wilson, previously unpublished diary reproduced with the kind permission of the author.

Virginia Woolf, *The Diary of Virginia Woolf* © Penguin Random House.

Doris Emily Worpole, previously unpublished private diary reproduced with the permission of Ken Worpole.

Woodrow Wyatt, *The Journals of Woodrow Wyatt* (ed. Sarah Curtis) © Pan Macmillan.

Debsey Wykes, previously unpublished private diary reproduced with the kind permission of the author.

Joan Wyndham, *Anything Once, Love Lessons: A Wartime Diary* and *Love is Blue: A Wartime Diary* © Penguin Random House and United Agents.

Permission has been sought for a number of extracts that are not cited above. Every reasonable effort has been made to secure these permissions before this book went to print. Anyone we have not been able to reach is invited to contact the publisher so that a full acknowledgement may be given in subsequent editions.

ILLUSTRATIONS

INDEX

Index